Praise for Richard Wood's *So Far and No Further!*

"Once in a lifetime comes a book which must force a total shift in the thinking person's perception of an epoch, and of all the prominent characters that featured in it."
—**Michael Hartnack**, *Spectator*

"It is not going to be possible for anyone, ever again, to write anything about the country, or any of the key personalities in the crisis, without detailed reference to it."
—*Eastern Province Herald*

"… by the esteemed historian and biographer, Dr J. R. T Wood."
—**BSAP** *Outpost*

"… a magnificent attempt, by the indefatigable historian, to fill the gap …"
— **James Mitchell**, *The Star*

"His duty as a historian was to tell us what actually happened. He has done so."
—**Michael Hartnack**, *Spectator*

Counter-Strike from the Sky

The Rhodesian All-Arms Fireforce in the War in the Bush 1974-1980

J. R. T. Wood

Also by J. R. T. Wood:

The Public Career of John, Second Earl of Stair, to 1720

The Welensky Papers: A History of the Federation of Rhodesia and Nyasaland, 1953–1963 (1983)

The War Diaries of André Dennison (1989)

So Far and No Further! Rhodesia's bid for independence during the retreat from Empire 1959-1965 (2005)

A Matter of Weeks Rather than Months: Sanctions and Abortive Settlements: 1965–1969 (2008)

Published in 2009 by 30° South Publishers (Pty) Ltd.
28, Ninth Street, Newlands
Johannesburg 2092, South Africa
www.30degreessouth.co.za
info@30degreessouth.co.za

Copyright © J. R. T. Wood, 2009
DVD copyright © 30° South Publishers (Pty) Ltd.

Jacket image by Craig Bone
Design and origination by 30° South Publishers (Pty) Ltd.
Printed and bound by Pinetown Printers, Durban
DVD production by 30° South Publishers (Pty) Ltd.

Photographic credits: The publishers have made every effort to establish copyright ownership of the photographs, however, in a few cases, the trail has gone cold and this has not always been possible. Where a credit is incorrect or a photo unacknowledged, the publishers apologise unreservedly and will endeavour to attend to any oversights in subsequent printings.

ISBN 9781920143336

All rights reserved. No part of this publication may be reproduced, stored in a retrieval system or transmitted in any form by any means; electronic, mechanical, photocopying, recording or otherwise, except brief extracts for the purpose of media review,s without the written permission of the publisher and copyright owners.

*To Carole and Andy
my unflinching support team*

Dr Richard Wood, BA (Hons) (Rhodes), PhD (Edinburgh), FRHistS, was born in Bulawayo, Zimbabwe (then Southern Rhodesia). He was educated at St George's College in Harare (then Salisbury), Rhodes University in Grahamstown, South Africa, and Edinburgh University, Scotland. He was a Commonwealth scholar and is a Fellow of the Royal Historical Society. He was the Ernest Oppenheimer Memorial Research Fellow at the University of Rhodesia and a Professor of History at the University of Durban-Westville, South Africa. He is undoubtedly the foremost historian and researcher on the history of Rhodesia in the decades following World War II and, with exclusive access to the hitherto closed papers of Ian Smith, has written three definitive publications and is currently working on the final volume in the series that will cover the period 1970–1980. He is a renowned military historian, having served as a territorial soldier in the 1st and 8th Battalions, the Rhodesia Regiment, and in the Mapping and Research Unit of the Rhodesian Intelligence Corps. He has also published numerous articles, conference papers and chapters in books, including in a chapter in the recently published Daniel Marston and Cart Malkasian, *Counterinsurgency in Modern Warfare* (Osprey Publishing, Oxford, 2008). Richard has a lifelong interest in matters military, rugby and fly-fishing. He lives in Durban, South Africa with his wife Carole.

Contents

List of Colour Plates — 8

Acknowledgments — 9

Glossary — 11

Foreword *by Charles D. Melson, USMC* — 13

Introduction — 16

Prologue — 19

Chapter 1: The Armed Struggle: The African Nationalist Bid for Power — 22

Chapter 2: The Rhodesian Security Forces prior to 1965 — 25

Chapter 3: The Counter-Insurgency Campaign: 1966–1980 — 35

Chapter 4: Meeting the Challenge of the Insurgency — 50

Chapter 5: The Basic Tool of Fireforce: The Alouette Helicopter — 55

Chapter 6: The Arming of the Helicopter — 61

Chapter 7: The Support Weapons — 67

Chapter 8: The Precursor of Fireforce at the 'Battle of Sinoia': 28 April 1966 — 75

Chapter 9: Exploiting the Agility of the Helicopter — 81

Chapter 10: The Birth of Fireforce — 90

Chapter 11: The Development of Fireforce — 93

Chapter 12: Fireforce Tactics — 96

Chapter 13: Commanding the Fireforce — 99

Chapter 14: A Day in the Life of an RAR Soldier — 119

Chapter 15: Fireforce Writ Large: Operation *Dingo*: Airborne Assault in Mozambique: 23–27 November 1977 — 123

Chapter 16: Fireforce in Action at the Height of the War — 203

Selected Bibliography — 227

Index — 230

List of Colour Plates

I   Alouette G-Car: a painting by Craig Bone
II   'The Battle of Sinoia', 29 April 1966
III   Rhodesian Security Forces: Operational Boundaries
IV   ZANLA and ZPRA: Operational Boundaries
V   K-Car / Matra MG 151 20mm cannon / G-Car
VI   A Fireforce Action of the Phase One: 1974–1976
VII   A Fireforce Action of the Phase Two: 1977–1979
VIII   A Fireforce Action of the Phase Three: Jumbo Fireforce of 1979
IX   Operation *Dingo*, Zulu 1: The Attack on the ZANLA Camp at New Farm, Chimoio: Wednesday, 23 November 1977 (*Salisbury–Beira road overview*)
X   Operation *Dingo*, Zulu 1: The Attack on the ZANLA Camp at New Farm, Chimoio: Wednesday, 23 November (*Chimoio town overview*)
XI   New Farm: ZANLA Complex of Camps (*Dingo*, Zulu 1)
XII   Operation *Dingo*, Zulu 1: Deception at Chimoio at H–4 minutes
XIII   Operation *Dingo*, Zulu 1: Air strike on New Farm, Chmoio at H-Hour
XIV   Operation *Dingo*, Zulu 1: Air strike at New Farm at H+30 seconds
XV   Operation *Dingo*, Zulu 1: Paradrop at New Farm from H+2 minutes
XVI   Operation *Dingo*, Zulu 1: Helicopter action at New Farm at H+5 minutes
XVII   Operation *Dingo*, Zulu 2: The Attack on the ZANLA Camp at Tembué: Saturday, 26 November 1977 (*Tete Province overview*)
XVIII   Operation *Dingo*, Zulu 2: Saturday, 26 November 1977
XIX   Pookie mine-detection vehicle
XX   Lt Rod Smith, 11 Troop, 3 Commando: a painting by Craig Bone

Acknowledgments

The original script of this account was written in the early 1990s and eventually found its way onto my website, www.jrtwood.com, together with my drawings. Several people suggested that I publish it as a book. Among them were my son, Andrew, and Jeremy Hall, once Lance-Corporal Hall, J., 6 Troop, 2 Commando, 1RLI. Then earlier this year, without any prompting, my publisher, Chris Cocks (also a onetime lance-corporal), offered to publish a history of Fireforce, an offer I could not refuse.

Fireforce is an example among many of Rhodesian ingenuity. There was no textbook on which to base strategy and tactics; the Rhodesians wrote that as they went along. The young men who manned the Fireforces are examples of raw courage. Few soldiers have been asked to face jumps into the unknown every day of a deployment. My only direct experience of Fireforce was when, as an 8RR lance-corporal manning an OP, I talked a K-Car onto a line of running men. After 1976 in the company of Dr Graham Child, David Lee, Donovan Slatter, Bill Lacey and 'Winkie' Prentice, all of the Research Section of the Rhodesian Intelligence Corps, I studied Fireforce contacts reports and produced research reports on our findings.

The long time span of the genesis of this book means that it is difficult to recall every assistance given. My family, Carole and Andrew, have had to live with the constant rebuke "I have a book to write". Major Chuck Melson, the Chief Historian of the US Marine Corps has been a valued friend, collaborator and a constant source of research material. Brigadier David Heppenstall, Colonel John Redfern and lieutenant-colonels Garth Barrett and Ron Reid-Daly allowed me sight of the research material on which this book is based. Alex Binda generously passed on photocopies of contact reports. Group Captain Peter Petter-Bowyer and Wing Commander Harold Griffiths allowed me sight of their logbooks. Squadron Leader 'Prop'

Geldenhuys has not only answered numerous questions, supplied copies of his books but went to the trouble to obtain Mozambican maps for me. Paul Naish and Craig Fourie are always ready to help and have supplied me with research material, the latter also kindly making available a plethora of photographs.

Jonathan Harvey, Dennis Croukamp, Fraser Brown, Theo Nel, Jerry Strong, Johan Joubert, Max T, Jon Caffin, Peter Petter-Bowyer, Tom Argyle, Jimmy Swan, Nigel Henson, the late Pete McDonald and Beryl Salt, Claude Botha, Harry Whitehead, Ross Parker, Jeremy Hall, Tony Coom and Dave Heppenstall of the RAR Regimental Association (UK) were also generous with their photos. Craig Bone kindly supplied the cover painting and two of the colour plates.

Among the people with whom I discussed this subject either directly or on the telephone or by email were: Air Marshal Norman Walsh, Lieutenant-General John Hickman, Major-General Leon Jacobs, brigadiers Tom Davidson, Peter Hosking, David Heppenstall and the late John McVey, colonels Mike Pelham and John Redfern, lieutenant-colonels Charlie Aust, Mick McKenna, Ron Reid-Daly, Brian Robinson and Grahame Wilson, Commandant Neal Ellis, Group Captain Peter Petter-Bowyer, Wing Commander Harold Griffiths, majors John Cronin, Peter Hean, Nigel Henson and David Padbury, squadron leaders Prop Geldenhuys, Victor Wightman and Alf Wild, Captain Jacques Dubois, flight lieutenants Michael Borlace, Michael Ronne and the late Flight Victor Cook, Lieutenant Paul Rich, Sergeant Ron Flint, Beaver Shaw, Lance-Corporal Jeremy Hall and my cousin, the late David Arnold. I thank them all and pray for forgiveness from anyone else whom I have forgotten.

Richard Wood
Durban, South Africa
March 2009

Glossary

ANFO	ammonium nitrate and fuel oil explosive mixture
BSAP	British South Africa Police
CIO	Central Intelligence Organization
ComOps	Combined Operations Headquarters
CT	Communist terrorist
FAF	forward airfield
FN	*Fabrique Nationale*, Belgian arms manufacturer
FPLM	*Forças Populares para o Libertação de Moçambique*
Frantan	frangible tank napalm bomb
FRELIMO	*Frente de Libertaçao de Moçambique*
G-Car	Alouette III helicopter troop-carrier
Golf bomb	460kg Rhodesian-made pressure bomb
gomo	hill (Shona)
JOC	Joint Operational Centre
K-Car	Alouette III helicopter gunship
MAG	*Mitrailleuse d'Appui General*, 7.62 x 51mm general-purpose machine gun
MID	Military Intelligence Directorate
Mini-Golf	small version of the Golf bomb
NCO	non-commissioned officer
PATU	Police Anti-Terrorist Unit
QNH	above mean sea level, nautical height
ter/terr	terrorist (slang)
RAF	Royal Air Force
RAR	Rhodesian African Rifles
RhAF	Rhodesian Air Force
RIC	Rhodesian Intelligence Corps

RLI	Rhodesian Light Infantry
RR	Rhodesia Regiment
RRAF	Royal Rhodesian Air Force
RRR	Royal Rhodesia Regiment
SAS	Special Air Service
SB	Special Branch
TTL	Tribal Trust Land
UANC	United African National Council
ZANLA	Zimbabwe African National Liberation Army
ZANU	Zimbabwe African National Union
ZAPU	Zimbabwe African People's Union
ZIPRA	Zimbabwe People's Liberation Army

Foreword

by Charles D. Melson, USMC

Almost a half-century after these 1965-to-1980 events took place, there is still an active interest in the details of the Rhodesian War, the last of the British Empire and Commonwealth's independence struggles in Africa. Recently, this has even seen the reprint of previous accounts but without substantial update.[1] Yet original records and study exist and this narrative is a first-rate example of what the last decades of research work have accomplished.

I feel privileged to be asked to write this foreword as I have neither the academic qualifications of its author, Richard Wood, nor the combat experience of its editor, Chris Cocks. Wood had produced one of the classic company commander's accounts of the Rhodesian War, *The War Diaries of André Dennison*,[2] while Cocks wrote the defining personal memoir of frontline fighting in *Fireforce: One Man's War in the Rhodesian Light Infantry*.[3] Both authors have also been active in continued work and publication of material on the conflict that continues with this current project. I am glad to see my own research has been of use in this effort.[4]

My interest in the conflict in Rhodesia began in 1971 while in Southeast Asia. As a junior leader I was pondering how to do a better job in my small patch of the Vietnam War. Direct exposure to British experience in Malaya and reading about Rhodesia's 'thin white line' seemed to offer other solutions to tactics, techniques and procedures. A number of Americans, including U.S. Marines, served in the Rhodesian security forces during the war, bringing back first-hand experience and recollections. The U.S. Marine Corps maintained a low level of continued curiosity in pseudo techniques, mine- and ambushed-proofed vehicles, and the conduct of operations through the 1980s and 1990s. The Global War on Terrorism witnessed a renewed (or belated) focus on irregular warfare and low-intensity conflict that conventional campaigns in Kuwait and Iraq had failed to quell. At the Marine Corps University, Operation *Dingo* was used as a planning exercise and I have lectured on Rhodesian special operations. Tracking, pseudo operations, mine and ambush countermeasures, and helicopter-borne reaction forces are now essential elements of counter-insurgency campaigns as shown in the current U.S. Army and Marine Corps Counterinsurgency Field Manual (FM 3-44, MCWP 3-33.5).

How does the Rhodesian experience apply to Iraq and Afghanistan is the question asked by Marine and Allied officers and non-commissioned officers? This text provides some of the needed answers. References like this book should be found on professional reading lists and as command and staff course texts. If not, the true professional will buy it 'on their own dime'. Professor Wood uses 16 chapters to describe the development of just one of the tactical innovations coming out of the Rhodesian conflict. This was the successful use of air–ground task forces to eliminate guerrilla bands with the direct application of aerial firepower and maneuver. With the example of similar British, French, American and Portuguese experience, the Rhodesians developed a unique brand of aviation technology, command and control, and effective troop units to meet the situation they faced on the ground. I would argue this was the result of necessity rather than innovation, as the problem was how to cover MMBA ('miles and miles of bloody Africa') with limited manpower. This was the same problem the nationalist insurgents dealt with by flooding the country with large numbers of ill-trained and -equipped terrorists and guerrillas to dominate areas populated by rural black Rhodesians. Fireforce was a concept and application that depended upon killing the insurgent to the detriment of occupying the territory thus cleared by police, militia, auxiliaries and other 'protective' forces with an acute lack of political and material support. The Fireforce 'killing machine' was not a 'hearts and mind' effort. Despite this, it allowed the Rhodesian security forces to fight guerrilla incursions to a stand-still to allow time for political solutions to be negotiated.

Wood covers this from Sinoia to Chimoio by describing the evolution of Fireforce as well as providing context in the form of background on the 'armed struggle' by the nationalists, the security forces' response, and the overall development of the counter-insurgency campaign. From border control and support to the civil power, to the joint operations command, and the implementation of combined operations the evolving civil–military response to the insurgent threat is covered. The place of the internal Fireforces is described, as well as an example of Fireforce 'writ large' with the November 1977 raid on Chimoio, Operation *Dingo*. This shows how a predominantly internal technique worked for external operations. As the road less taken, the use of the concept outside Rhodesia's geographic borders was soon countered by the guerrillas expanding the area covered by their camps and staging points and no longer providing a concentrated target that could be confined successfully. There came a point when Combined Operations Commander Lieutenant-General George P. 'Peter' Walls realized more insurgents could be killed by external rather than internal operations. Fireforce remained the backbone of the internal effort while flying column and Special Forces led the attacks in external operations. The Rhodesian defensive effort focused on holding 'vital asset ground', at the expense of good tactical terrain and other ground. With this, Fireforce soldiered on with almost daily actions and casualties as covered by Wood's final chapter. On 28 December 1979, a last call-out occurred from Grand Reef as a brokered ceasefire went in to effect. Wood's prose, graphics, illustrations, and Cocks' audio-visual presentation successfully bring the reader and viewer into the intense world of Fireforce operations. This is a fully documented work written and edited from the insights of participants. I highly recommend it as the lessons of the past have a relevance to the needs of the present.

Charles D. Melson
Chief Historian, History Division
U. S. Marine Corps

---

[1] Paul Moorcraft and Peter McLaughlin republished their 1982 book *Chimurenga: The War in Rhodesia, 1965–1980* without change or revision.
[2] Ashanti Publishing, 1989.
[3] 30° South Publishers, 2006, first published in 1988 by Galago.
[4] See Charles D. Melson, 'Top Secret War: Rhodesian Special Operations', *Small Wars and Insurgencies*, March 2005, pp. 57–82; and a manuscript draft on Fireforce, 'The Killing Machine', a chapter from a larger unpublished work examining the Rhodesian War.

Introduction

Faced with an insurgency in sparsely inhabited African bush in a country the size of the State of Montana, limited by their inability to field more than 1,500 fighting men on any one day in the years 1966–1980, inhibited by international economic sanctions after Rhodesia declared unilateral independence from Britain in 1965, the Rhodesian security forces sought to maximize their slender air and ground assets in the form of a dozen helicopters and a sparse number of frontline soldiers.

Their solution was to use their aircraft to tackle and extinguish multiple threats over a wide area. What they could not do thereafter was to occupy the ground. It meant that, in the end, they could only fight their enemy into a stalemate.

They possessed the light helicopter, the Aérospatiale Alouette III, capable of carrying four men and their equipment. They had hardy, tough, well-trained regular troops of the Rhodesian Light Infantry and the Rhodesian African Rifles, many of whom had served in the counter-insurgency effort in Malaya as part of Rhodesia's contribution to the defence of the British Commonwealth.

They began by using the helicopter to bolster and support the traditional counter-insurgency tactics of cross-graining patrols, cordon-and-search and tracking. The agile helicopter could leapfrog the trackers along a track, shortening the pursuit of guerrillas before their tracks were lost and they melded into the local population or crossed an international frontier. The helicopter could also place men in stop positions ahead of the trackers.

When pursuing insurgents across the border into the vast uninhabited wastes of the Tete Province of Mozambique, the C Squadron (Rhodesia) of the Special Air Service (SAS) experimented with boxing in insurgent groups by dropping paratroops along four sides of a square. Although the men of the RLI and the RAR were not yet paratroopers, it was clear that helicopter-borne troops could be used to seal an area.

There was a need, however, to drive the pursued to ground, to contain them in the area while their escape routes were being blocked. This was because most times they escaped by using their standard tactic of 'bombshelling' or breaking ranks and fleeing in all directions. The guerrilla fails if he stands and fights. His purpose is to survive and wear down his enemy by forcing him to overextend his forces.

The breakthrough for the Rhodesian forces came in early 1974 when they acquired the French Matra MG151 20mm cannon which gave them the firepower to discourage the 'bombshell' and to suppress and discourage enemy fire which the hitherto-used MAG machine gun could not accomplish.

As experience taught that air and ground commanders needed to co-ordinate their efforts and that the troops, in particular, could be best directed from the air, logic dictated that the two commanders be in the same aircraft. This led the cannon-armed command gunship to be given the radio call sign 'K-Car' (command). The troop-carrying Alouettes were already called 'G-Cars' or general-duties aircraft.

The Fireforce, however, could only be deployed once an insurgent group had been found and finding them posed major difficulties. Here intelligence-gathering was crucial and required imaginative police and other investigative work. The need to discover the insurgents' whereabouts led to the development of the pseudo-gang concept tried elsewhere in Kenya and Malaya. The Selous Scout Regiment was raised to identify the target to which the Fireforce could react.

Tactical innovations and matériel acquisitions enhanced the concept. In 1976 the clandestine purchase of light strike aircraft reinforced the K-Car effort to contain the quarry and give fire support to the troops. After 1977 parachute training meant that the helicopter-borne troops could be reinforced quickly and significantly. Improvements in aircraft weapons also enhanced the potency of air strikes.

This led to the Fireforce concept being adopted for external attacks on major insurgent camps in neighbouring Mozambique and Zambia. Included in this book is the first full account of the audacious Operation *Dingo* in which, in late November 1977, Fireforce tactics writ large were used. They were employed to corral 11,000 trained men and recruits of Robert Mugabe's Zimbabwe National Liberation Army in their sprawling camp complex at Chimoio, deep in Mozambique. In the face of a well-aimed sustained fire from dug-in heavy machine guns, 128 paratroops of the SAS and RLI were dropped to form two sides of a 'box' while the third was lined by 40 helicopter-borne RLI troopers and the fourth was closed by K-Car fire. The intention was to deliver a crushing blow to the insurgent effort by a sustained air and ground attack on its safe haven. The Rhodesians had one pilot and an SAS trooper killed and six RLI–SAS wounded in a two-day effort that killed uncounted thousands of their enemy. A day later, the same force struck again, using the same tactics, hundreds of kilometres into Mozambique, attacking another large training camp at Tembué, in the northeast of the Tete Province towards the Malawian border. *Dingo* created the template for a score or more of such deadly attacks.

The Rhodesian forces would achieve only a stalemate in their war; their fate lay in political hands, but they gained the enviable acknowledgement of being the best counter-insurgency forces of their day.

Prologue

On 22 December 1976, an Aérospatiale Alouette [Lark] III helicopter (configured as a troop-carrying 'G-Car') was rocked by a volley of 7.62mm Soviet-made rifle rounds at 800 feet above ground as it flew down towards the tree savannah of central Rhodesia. Flown by 33-year-old Flight Lieutenant Victor Bernard Cook, the helicopter was carrying a Rhodesian Army medic on a mercy mission. They were en route to treat an African civilian who had been wounded in crossfire in a contact that morning between a Rhodesian Army patrol and the Zimbabwe African National Liberation Army (ZANLA) which supported Robert Mugabe, the future President of Zimbabwe.

The bullets, flashing up from a clearing in the trees, were fired by 27 ZANLA insurgents whose base camp Cook was about to fly over as he descended from a safe height of 9,000 feet above the ground. The bullets severed the Alouette's tail-rotor shaft and wounded Cook in the arms and right foot. Two slammed into the body armour of his technician, Finch Bellringer, leaving him semi-conscious. The medic escaped injury but was in a state of shock.

Vic Cook told Deon du Plessis of *The Star* of Johannesburg that he felt the rounds hit his aircraft and, unable to see where the fire was coming from, took evasive action, plunging down to tree level.

> I levelled off but I was still under heavy fire. I was almost on top of them. A lot more rounds hit us. It was fierce. I felt the controls going, there was vibration. I realized I had to force-land. The fire got fiercer. I picked a place to land. Then I lost tail-rotor control. The chopper swung violently. It would have started cartwheeling. I pulled it up on its tail to knock off forward speed. The speed came down but we continued to yaw. Still I was quite pleased with what

was happening as I had a semblance of control. I touched the power but could not hold it down on to its tail. I managed to pull the nose up a little. All the time they were still shooting. Then I saw them. I thought: "There are about as many as a rugby team."

Sinking rapidly towards a forced landing, Cook saw a group of about five terrorists standing ahead of him shooting. Cook made his decision: "I aimed the aircraft at them deliberately. We thumped down nose first and I lost sight of them."

As the Alouette hit the ground a piece of the control column came off in Cook's hand. The jar of the landing jerked Cook forward. His jaw struck the stub of the control stick, stunning him and cutting his chin deeply. In the heat of the moment, however, he had not yet felt pain from his severely wounded foot. "The engine was still running and I left it idling, hoping this would make them think we were all right."

Cook recalled: "I knew the buggers were coming back. I needed a weapon." He drew his Uzi submachine gun from under his seat but it had been rendered useless by a bullet strike. He reached for the medic's FN rifle but saw the force of the collision with the earth had bent the barrel.

> Then I saw this terr lying beyond the chopper. He may have been hit by the rotor when we came down. I don't know. But he had an AK and all I knew was that he was between me and that weapon. I grabbed his AK and shot him with it. He was shouting in Shona when I shot him. I don't know what he was doing. I don't remember if we even struggled. I shouted to the medic and Bellringer: "Run for the high ground." I ran, but then saw they were not following me. I shouted again: "Let's move!" But Bellringer said: "I can't move."

Cook and the dazed medic dragged Bellringer to the higher ground. Cook then saw the terrorists moving in the bush 100 metres away. With his adrenalin pumping, making him still oblivious to his wounds, he ran forward and fired a magazine from the AK at them.

"I saw other movement and I bolted to another position and ripped off another burst." Cook positioned himself between the enemy and his crew. "Then I went out further and did a few circuits of the chopper. The movement disappeared and I moved from tree to tree and rock to rock. I was in a good strong position."

Cook was "bloody angry" at being forced down, and wanted to pursue the terrorists. He kept tripping, however, and only then did he see the deep gash in his foot. He could see the bone. "After that I didn't feel so aggressive," he said. He helped the medic erect a drip stand for the wounded technician. Of the medical orderly, Cook said: "He was a star. At no stage did he abandon his patient."

The Rhodesian soldiers who had called Cook from Rutenga, in southeastern Rhodesia, were close enough to hear the Alouette crash and the subsequent firing. They radioed for help. Fifty minutes later a Reims-Cessna FTB 337G 'Lynx', twin-engined light aircraft, arrived overhead, heralding the arrival the helicopter-borne infantry of the Fireforce. Cook and his crew were evacuated by helicopter and a follow-up on the tracks on his attackers began.

Cook recalled: "There were four brown jobs [Rhodesian Light Infantry]. They were a beautiful sight."

For his gallantry Victor Cook was awarded the Silver Cross of Rhodesia but said he did not deserve it: "Not when you see what the browns do. Those RLI guys, they are all Silver Cross material."[1]

---

[1] *The Star*, 15 April 1977.

Chapter 1

The Armed Struggle:
The African Nationalist Bid for Power

Vic Cook's action on the morning of 22 December 1967 was only part of a well-worn response to the African nationalist decision of 1962 to adopt the Marxist dialectical prescription that power could only be achieved through the 'Armed Struggle' and not through political evolution. Rhodesia in 1962 was still Southern Rhodesia and senior partner in the Federation of Rhodesia and Nyasaland. By the mid-1950s, African nationalist pressure in the three Federal territories was turning violent. That violence would prod Britain to accelerate the process of decolonization that would lead to her granting independence to Nyasaland (Malawi) and Northern Rhodesia (Zambia) prematurely and thereby dismembering the Federation in December 1963. The refusal of the British to grant Southern Rhodesia independence even though she had been self-governing since 1923 led directly to Ian Smith, then Rhodesian Prime Minister, declaring Rhodesia independent on 11 November 1965.

Smith's declaration had, however, been preceded by the start of the 'Armed Struggle' or 'Second Chimurenga' (the first was the Mashona Rebellion of 1896), founded on the emergence of the militant Youth League in 1957 which gave the African bid for power a new edge. In February 1959, the Southern Rhodesian government responded with a state of emergency, designed to crush resistance quickly so that Federal troops could be released to deal with an uprising led by Dr Hastings Banda in Nyasaland. (Defence was a Federal responsibility.) By then, the British Prime Minister, Harold Macmillan, had decided to speed up the decolonization process dramatically and seek Britain's future in Europe. Nyasaland and Northern Rhodesia were moved rapidly towards independence while in 1961 Southern Rhodesia was given a new constitution, designed to give Africans an enhanced political role and

The Armed Struggle: The African Nationalist Bid for Power

eventual domination. The Southern Rhodesian Prime Minister, Sir Edgar Whitehead, had in fact been seeking quasi-dominion status but the British government was in no mood to give the whites—less than five per cent of the population—perpetual political domination. If Southern Rhodesia wanted to become an independent sovereign nation, she had to accept rule by the majority. While the whites rejected this, it inspired the African nationalists. Their National Democratic Party demanded power and persuaded its leader, Joshua Nkomo, to reverse his acceptance of the 1961 constitution.

Whitehead attempted to meet African aspirations with a number of reforms of racial legislation. When, however, he threatened to tackle the fundamental African grievance over the unequal racial allocation of land, the white electorate ousted him in the general election of 1962. He was succeeded by the Rhodesian Front led by Winston Field who promised not to tamper with land tenure and to secure independence at the demise of the Federation in the next year. Field ignored the land issue and failed to secure independence. His party replaced him in 1963 with Ian Smith, who would take it unilaterally.

Before then, in 1962, mostly urban African agitation had led Whitehead to strengthen his police force, the British South Africa Police. He introduced security legislation and banned the National Democratic Party, only to see it replaced instantly by the Zimbabwe African People's Union (ZAPU). The African nationalists countered with a defiant campaign of intimidation, riots, strikes and sabotage. The favoured weapon was the petrol bomb, aimed mostly at Africans deemed to be collaborating with the whites. It was then that the African nationalists decided on an armed struggle. They flirted with the Eastern Bloc, obtained weapons and sent young men for training in Ghana, Tanganyika and at guerrilla warfare schools in the Soviet Union and its satellite countries. Shortly, the police began to uncover arms caches. Over a thousand arrests of African nationalists followed and Whitehead banned ZAPU. African nationalists set fire to forests at Chipinga on the eastern border and C Squadron, SAS, parachuted in to deal with them.

Thus the war of liberation, the 'Chimurenga', began in late 1962. The pattern of urban violence continued for a year or more and then fizzled out because of good police work and the effectiveness of the law. The African nationalists split into two factions—ZAPU led by Nkomo, and the Zimbabwe African National Union (ZANU) led by the Reverend Ndabaningi Sithole (later to be ousted by Robert Mugabe)—and established themselves in sympathetic Zambia across the Zambezi River. From there, they sent agents into Rhodesia to sabotage railways and the like and to foster rebellion in the urban and rural areas. The urban populations remained unco-operative but the rural people began to harbour the insurgents in 1972 when the success of the rebels of the *Frente de Libertaçao de Moçambique* (FRELIMO) in Mozambique provided the Rhodesian African nationalists with safe havens and supplies close to the border.

Chapter 2

The Rhodesian Security Forces prior to 1965

Internal security, and therefore the counter-insurgency effort, was at first the prime responsibility of the police in the three Federal territories with the assistance firstly of the Federal Army and the Royal Rhodesian Air Force. Once the Federation had gone, the new Rhodesian Army and the RRAF provided the assistance.

Despite the loss of experienced personnel through 'golden handshakes' termination of employment offers at the demise of the Federation, Rhodesia retained enough expertise to contain the small threat posed by ZAPU and ZANU. Good police work, based on intelligence from an informer network, had already stamped out any urban threat. The insurgency was therefore confined to the rural areas where both ZANU and ZAPU sought secure peasant support and recruits.

The British South Africa Police (BSAP) had its roots in the force recruited in 1890 to protect the Pioneer Column sent by Cecil Rhodes's British South Africa Company to exploit the charter it had received from Queen Victoria in the previous year. Responsible for the maintenance of law and order under the Police Act, the BSAP comprised, by the mid-1960s, 7,000 regular white and African policemen, including the small paramilitary Support Unit. A volunteer Police Reserve of 30,000 men and women of all races and the Police Reserve Air Wing reinforced it when necessary. Regulars and volunteers were to be found in the Police Anti-Terrorist Unit when it was formed in the late 1960s. The intelligence effort was co-ordinated by the Central Intelligence Organization (CIO) which incorporated the Special Branch (SB). Winston Field founded the CIO in 1964 to replace the defunct Federal Intelligence and Security Bureau.

The history of the Rhodesian Air Force was intertwined with that of the

Rhodesian Army. The birth of the air force, however, was unintentional. In the mid-1930s, when the re-emergence of a German threat to peace caused nations to re-examine their defences, the members of the Southern Rhodesian Legislative Assembly did likewise. In a gesture of loyalty, they offered Britain £10,000 for the Royal Navy to strengthen imperial defence. They were not expecting the British government to respond with the suggestion that Southern Rhodesia should use the money to establish an air-training unit. This illustrated the unique position of Southern Rhodesia in the British Empire because, despite Britain retaining sovereignty over her, not only was she self-governing but she had the right to defend herself. As external threats hardly existed, defence was left to the only regular force in the colony, the BSAP, reinforced by the part-time white territorials of the Rhodesia Regiment and district rifle platoons, trained by a small Permanent Staff Corps.

The air-training unit was placed under command of the Rhodesia Regiment and, in November 1935, enrolled its first six recruits in the local flying school run by the de Havilland Company at Belvedere Airport, Salisbury (now Harare). There they trained on Wednesday afternoons and weekends in Gipsy Moths and Tiger Moths. In 1937–1939 the Air Unit then acquired six Hawker Hart bombers, six Hawker Audaxes two-seat army co-operation aircraft and three Gloster Gauntlet single-seat fighters stationed at the new military airfield at Cranborne in the southern outskirts of Salisbury.

The imminence of war led to the mobilization of the Air Unit and, on 28 August 1939, Southern Rhodesia was the first country in the British Empire to send her servicemen abroad. Two flights of Harts and Audaxes took off for Kenya to replace No. 233 Squadron of the Royal Air Force which had departed for the Sudan. Again, Southern Rhodesia had demonstrated her loyalty to Britain and would remind Britain of this when relations soured 20 years later.

On 19 September 1939 the Air Unit was renamed the Southern Rhodesian Air Force with its three flights in Kenya becoming No. 1 Squadron. Southern Rhodesia also formed the Rhodesian Air Training Group to train British aircrew under the Empire Training Scheme, building training establishments

The Rhodesian Security Forces prior to 1965

outside Salisbury, Bulawayo and Gwelo (now Gweru), which graduated 2,000 pilots and 300 navigators for the Royal Air Force.

In 1939, the 69,000 whites in Southern Rhodesia were able to spare 10,000 men and women for war. To avoid devastating casualties, major Rhodesian units, with the exception of the soon-to-be raised Rhodesian African Rifles (RAR), were not sent abroad. Instead, Rhodesian servicemen and -women were seconded to the South African and British forces. On 22 April 1940, No. 1 Squadron of the Southern Rhodesian Air Force was absorbed by the Royal Air Force as No. 237 (Rhodesia) Squadron. Two other RAF squadrons, No. 266 and No. 44 had 'Rhodesia' added to their titles. The RAF had 977 Rhodesian officers and 1,432 airmen. Five hundred and seventy-nine were casualties and of those 498 died. Rhodesian airmen won 256 medals. One member of No. 237 (Rhodesia) Squadron was Ian Douglas Smith, later the prime minister.

The end of the war and demobilization left Southern Rhodesia with only two regular defence units, the RAR and the Permanent Staff Corps instructing the territorials of the Rhodesia Regiment. All fit white males between the ages of 18–23 were compelled to attend weekend parades and a short annual camp. Within the Staff Corps there were airmen fresh from war, and their enthusiasm led to the revival in 1947 of the Southern Rhodesian Air Force (SRAF) with a strength of 69 officers and men, flying North American Harvard advanced trainers acquired from the South African Air Force and the Royal Air Force. In 1948, Field Marshal Smuts, the Prime Minister of South Africa, donated a Douglas C-47 Dakota. In 1951, 22 Supermarine Spitfire Mk XXIIs were acquired and flown by short-service regular officers and part-time pilots. The wooden propellers of the Spitfire soon proved a problem, drying and shrinking in the long dry season.

Again, the money for their replacement came from a loyal gesture. The Imperial defence authorities had informed the Southern Rhodesian government that, without jet aircraft, the SRAF was useless for defence of the Empire and should be disbanded. Southern Rhodesia, however, was short of money. The long-serving Southern Rhodesian Prime Minister, Sir Godfrey Huggins, therefore turned for help to his future partner in the coming Federation of Rhodesia and Nyasaland, Roy Welensky, the leader of the unofficial members in the Northern Rhodesian Legislative Council. Not wanting to lose the SRAF and knowing that re-equipment was inevitable once the Federation was in being, Welensky persuaded the Northern Rhodesian government to meet the bill of £200,000 which allowed SRAF to enter the jet age. In 1952–1953, it re-equipped with 16 Percival Provost T52 piston-engined basic trainers, 16 de Havilland Vampire FB9 fighter-bombers and 16 Vampire T11 jet-trainers.[2]

The British sanction of the formation of the Federation of Rhodesia and Nyasaland—an unlikely marriage of a self-governing colony with two protectorates—was the product of a sustained campaign by Roy Welensky and Godfrey Huggins, both of whom hoped to create a great British dominion north of the Limpopo River. Although the Federation did not gain sovereign status, it inherited Southern Rhodesia's right of defence and took over the SRAF and the army units of the three territories. The Queen granted the title 'Royal Rhodesian Air Force' (RRAF) and the RRAF promptly exchanged its khaki uniforms and rank structures for British-style air force blues and ranks.

The new Federal army had four white-officered African battalions, namely the first and second battalions of the King's African Rifles from Nyasaland, the Northern Rhodesia Regiment and the Rhodesian African Rifles (RAR) backed by the Royal Rhodesia Regiment which would expand into ten active territorial and reserve battalions. The RRR was served by its Depot at Llewellin Barracks, Heany, where young non-African males underwent compulsory four and a half months' basic training before serving three years of compulsory territorial service before being transferred to the reserve. For reasons of expense, however, the Southern Rhodesian Armoured Car Regiment, the Southern Rhodesian corps of Engineers and Signals and the Southern Rhodesian Field Artillery Regiment, all territorial units, were disbanded. The support companies of the three active RRR battalions, 1, 2 and 3, received the Staghound Mk II armoured cars and in 1956 the 25-pounder field guns found a home in the new Governor-General's Saluting Troop.

---

[2] J. R. T. Wood, *The Welensky Papers: A History of the Federation of Rhodesia and Nyasaland*, Graham Publishing, Durban, 1983, p. 357.

The Rhodesian Security Forces prior to 1965

Before Federation Rhodesian forces had seen service in defence of the British Empire. In 1950–1953 a 100-man Rhodesian SAS squadron commanded by Major, later Lieutenant-General, Peter Walls fought the Communist insurgency in Malaya. In 1952 the RAR reinforced the British Army in the Suez Canal Zone. Thereafter the Federal Army's regular African battalions in rotation assisted the British counter-insurgency effort in Malaya.

By 1956 the RRAF comprised No. 1 and No. 2 Vampire squadrons, No. 3 transport squadron, with eight C-47 Dakotas and two Percival Pembroke light transports, and No. 4 training squadron, with Provosts. The air station at Thornhill, Gwelo, had been acquired from the departing Royal Air Force Empire Training Scheme and was modernized. To meet a Federal commitment to Commonwealth defence by reinforcing British Middle East Command with an infantry brigade and aircraft, in 1959 the RRAF acquired four Canadair C-4 transports[3] and 15 English Electric Canberra B2 light bombers. In 1958 the Vampire squadrons assisted the Royal Air Force effort against dissidents in the Aden Protectorate. In 1961 Rhodesian transport aircraft supported British forces in the Kuwait crisis and dropped food in a flood-relief operation in Kenya. In 1959–1963 the Canberra squadrons regularly reinforced the Royal Air Force in Cyprus. In 1963 the front-line strength was enhanced when No. 1 Squadron re-equipped with twelve Hawker Hunter FGA9 ground-attack fighters. The RRAF remained small but justly proud of its efficiency. While the Royal Air Force needed a ratio of 300 men per jet aircraft, the Rhodesians could achieve a better rate of serviceability with only 30 men per aircraft.[4]

The role of the RRAF by then was not an entirely external one. From 1956 onwards the Federal forces began to concentrate on internal security operations. In response to awakening African rejection of white rule and the British and French retreat from empire, the RRAF formed No. 6 Squadron, equipped with Provosts, for an internal security role.

---

[3] The C-4 was a general-purpose aircraft, which embodied features of the Douglas DC-4 and DC-6 aircraft and was called the 'Argonaut' by its civilian operators.

[4] Dudley Cowderoy & Roy Nesbit, *War in the Air: Rhodesian Air Force 1935–1980*, Galago, Alberton, 1987, pp. 26–27.

The growing African nationalist unrest led to the call-out of Federal troops to assist the three territorial police forces in combating it. In February 1959 No. 3 Squadron, RRAF, transported Federal troops from Southern Rhodesia to quell the unrest in Nyasaland inspired by Dr Hastings Banda. RRAF Provosts supported the police and troops, dispersing crowds with air-delivered tear-gas canisters, dropping leaflets and undertaking reconnaissance. Vampires and the new Canberra bombers 'showed the flag'. Belgium's sudden decision in 1960 to withdraw from the Congo, creating Zaire, brought mutinies, insurrection and the Katanga crisis. The Federal Army was deployed to the northern border of Northern Rhodesia while the RRAF protected Federal airspace and flew out of the Congo over 2,000 whites fleeing the violence.

Experience in Nyasaland highlighted the need for a means to reinforce troops rapidly. The feasibility of the use of paratroops was examined in March 1960 when the RRAF adapted Dakota aircraft for tests.[5] The acquisition of helicopters was considered but the contemporary helicopters were useless in the Federation's 'hot and high' conditions. The Alouette III helicopter was not yet available.

Then, on 9 May 1960, in a review of Imperial defence, the Chief of Imperial General Staff, Lord Louis Mountbatten, suggested to Welensky (then the Federal Prime Minister) that the Federal contribution to Commonwealth defence should be reduced from an infantry brigade to a re-formed SAS squadron which would provide the Federal Army with paratroops. The mutinies of black soldiers in the Congo in the next month encouraged the Federal government to establish, as insurance, white professional army units, namely: the C Squadron of the SAS, the First Battalion, The Rhodesian Light Infantry (1RLI) and an armoured car squadron.[6] The Territorial Army was expanded and the BSAP recruited a police reserve of 30,000 whites and Africans. The RRAF formed a parachute school to train the SAS and created the RRAF Volunteer Reserve to tap the skills of the civilian population. The SAS squadron promptly served in Aden.

---

[5] Cowderoy & Nesbit, p. 29.

[6] Wood, *Welensky Papers*, p. 801.

The Rhodesian Security Forces prior to 1965

The RRAF then ordered the French-made Aérospatiale SA316B Alouette III helicopter and formed No. 7 Squadron to fly it. It had acquired the essential tool of the later Fireforce. It chose the Alouette not only because it could fly in Rhodesia's 'hot and high' conditions, but also because its price suited the Federal Treasury. The Alouette III was also chosen by the South African and Portuguese air forces which meant that training facilities and expertise could be shared. The Portuguese would later be the first to arm the Alouette with the French-made MG151 20mm cannons. The Alouette III allowed the Federal forces to insert personnel into situations quickly and precisely and to rescue the stranded and the injured. Three Alouettes arrived in April 1962, two in July and three in August 1963. As soon as the first two pilots, trained in France and South Africa, were on strength, they were sent to fly over the African townships, dropping leaflets and tear-gas grenades on rioting crowds, 'sky shouting', acting as airborne and command posts, and generally assisting the police. Given that pilots only have time to listen to snappy transmissions, the BSAP and army were forced to revise their ponderous radio voice procedures.

In the division of assets at the break-up of the Federation in December 1963, the RRAF was returned to Southern Rhodesia with all its aircraft except for three transport aircraft given to Zambia. By then, the RRAF had 1,200 regulars including a General Service Unit of African soldiers for guard and transport duties. Some adjustments were made. The loss of the Rhodesian commitment to Commonwealth defence due to newly independent African countries refusing overflying rights prompted the new commander, Air Vice-Marshal A. M. Bentley, to dispose of some aircraft. He sold the four C4 Canadair Argonaut transport aircraft, six Canberras, three de Havilland Vampire FB9s fighter-bombers and seven Vampire T11 trainers. In addition, he disbanded No. 6 Squadron (then a Canberra squadron) and stored its aircraft. These aircraft would be sorely missed within the decade.[7]

An attempt at the same time to replace the ageing Provost basic trainer received a brusque rebuff. The RRAF approached the United States Consul-

---

[7] J. R. T. Wood, *So Far and No Further! Rhodesia's bid for independence during the retreat from Empire: 1959–1965*, 30° South Publishers, Johannesburg, 2005, p. 177.

General in Salisbury with a purchase order for a number of North American T-28 'Trojan' single-engine training aircraft. The T-28 was the first post-Second World War primary trainer for the US Army and Navy. It also made an ideal, slow, support aircraft capable of carrying a heavy load of ordnance in the form of rockets, machine guns and bombs. It had played this role in the recent anarchy in the Congo and was beginning to be used in South Vietnam. What the RRAF did not know was that the US State Department was applying an unofficial arms embargo, matching a British one, designed to coax the Rhodesian government towards accepting majority rule in the near future. Clifford Dupont, then the Minister of Defence and later the first president of the Republic of Rhodesia, promptly issued a stiff aide mémoire of protest claiming this unilateral action was an unwarranted interference in Rhodesia's internal affairs. The US government, in the person of 'Soapy' Mennen-Williams, Assistant Secretary of State for Africa, took deep offence at this. Mennon-Wiliams was offended because technically Britain was responsible for Rhodesia's external relations and therefore Dupont was not entitled to protest. Unable, in practice, to rein in self-governing Rhodesia, there was little the British government could do. Rhodesia, however, did not receive the T-28 but the discovery of the Anglo-American arms bans was just one more pressure which led to Smith declaring Rhodesia independent a few months later.[8]

The RRAF was concentrated at two bases—New Sarum near Salisbury and Thornhill near Gwelo. New Sarum housed the administration, the photographic and the air movements sections, the aircrew selection centre, the apprentice training school and the parachute training section. Its air units were: No. 3 Squadron (transports), No. 5 Squadron (Canberras) and No. 7 Squadron (Alouettes). Thornhill had No. 1 Squadron (Hawker Hunter Mk IX fighters), No. 2 Squadron (Vampire FB9s) and No. 4 Squadron (Provosts and Vampire T11s) responsible for flying tuition. The trainees first flew Provosts and then Vampire T11s before flying the Vampire FB9s on armament training. Thereafter all pilots rotated through the squadrons, learning to fly

---

[8] Wood, *So Far*, pp. 298, 303 & 313.

The Rhodesian Security Forces prior to 1965

a variety of the aircraft on strength. This gave the RRAF pilots considerable versatility. They would serve tours on helicopters, ground-attack aircraft, fighters, or transports before becoming instructors.[9] The types they flew depended on the pilot's nature. The more sedate pilots would fly transports and Canberra bombers while the more aggressive would be posted to the fighters. Pilots would serve two tours with the squadrons before they were posted on their instructor's courses, flying Provosts on basic flying training for a year or two before going on to jet instruction or taking up instructors' posts with the squadrons.[10]

The Rhodesian Army had 5,000 regulars, the bulk of them in the RAR and the RLI, and the remainder in C Squadron, SAS, and the re-formed Engineer, Signals and Service corps. The loss of its Northern Rhodesian battalions, the 3rd and 7th, had reduced the Royal Rhodesia Regiment to the training of national servicemen at its depot at Llewellin Barracks at Heany Junction outside Bulawayo and eight battalions of territorials and reservists based in the major cities and towns. There was a territorial field artillery regiment and territorials were to be found in the corps of Engineers, Signals and Service. The ranks of the army included veterans of the Malayan and Aden campaigns. In the former, the Rhodesian SAS troopers had pioneered 'tree-jumping' (parachuting into unprepared landing zones). They and the RAR had been blooded in the fleeting contacts in the undergrowth and had learned the techniques of jungle warfare including small-unit tactics, cross-graining, tracking, ambushing and inter-service co-operation. The officer corps had participated in the Malayan civil–military counter-insurgency structure.[11]

In 1964, in preparation for combating the insurgency, Ian Smith took the

---

[9] David Arnold, draft typescript for Bruce Hoffman, Jennifer M. Taw, David Arnold, *Lessons for Contemporary Counterinsurgencies: The Rhodesian Experience*, RAND Corporation, Santa Monica, 1991, p. 229.

[10] Written comments on the author's script by Wing Commander Harold Griffiths, 8–9 April 1992.

[11] Telephone conversations with brigadiers Peter Hosking and Tom Davidson and lieutenant-colonels Mick McKenna, Brian Robinson and Ron Reid-Daly, February 2007.

chair of the new Security Council on which sat the service commanders and heads of relevant ministries. The council was advised by the Counter-Insurgency Committee, also chaired by Smith, and served by the commanders, the Director, CIO, and appropriate officials. It had two sub-committees: the Operations Co-ordinating Committee (OCC) and the Counter-Insurgency Civil Committee. The latter, manned by the heads of appropriate ministries, planned and co-ordinated the civil aspects of the campaign such as the construction of roads, airfields and protected villages. It also advised on the psychological aspects. The service commanders and the Director, CIO, who constituted the OCC, directed operations and, with the assistance of the Joint Planning Staff, evolved a common doctrine and modus operandi. After 1966 when the first incursions were made, they set up Joint Operations Centres (JOCs), served by army, air force, BSAP and SB senior officers, to command the all-arms effort in the field. The JOC would meet daily to review and plan operations and to issue a situation report or sitrep. When operational needs dictated it, the JOC would establish sub-JOCs to deal with specific areas.

Even though the services remained answerable to their individual headquarters, this command-by-consensus worked. The implementation of a JOC's plans by its disparate subordinates was not, however, always satisfactory and the different approaches to problems produced some indecision. A major disadvantage was the dominance of immediate tactical requirements over the need to devise a national strategy. The discontent would lead to the creation of a Combined Operations Headquarters (ComOps) in March 1977 but it could never be quite the Malayan model because Malaya had an executive governor while Rhodesia had an elected prime minister and cabinet government. It meant that the Commander, Combined Operations, Lieutenant-General Peter Walls, remained answerable to the Prime Minister and his Cabinet and never had the free hand which Field Marshal Templer, as executive Governor and Commander-in-Chief, had enjoyed in Malaya.

Chapter 3

The Counter-Insurgency Campaign:
1966-1980

The counter-insurgency campaign went through five phases dictated by the political situation until the ceasefire in 1980 and the election of Mugabe.

Phase 1: 1966–1972
Realizing that, with the willing help of the South Africans, Portuguese and others, Rhodesia could survive the sanctions, the British Prime Minister, Harold Wilson, sought to negotiate a settlement. Several attempts, including meeting on the warships, *Tiger* and *Fearless* failed, however, and in 1969 Ian Smith declared Rhodesia to be a republic and enacted a new constitution which aimed at racial parity of representation. This was rejected by the British and, to secure the vital international legitimacy, Smith settled with the new Conservative government of Edward Heath in 1972 only to see the settlement terms rejected by the British Pearce Commission based on a six per cent sample of African opinion, obtained amidst an uproar generated by the African nationalists.

In 1962–1965 its paucity of trained manpower had restricted ZAPU's Zimbabwe People's Liberation Army (ZIPRA) to a pinpricking sabotage programme directed mostly at railway lines and soft targets. It was ZANU's armed wing, ZANLA, which mounted the first incursion from Zambia into Rhodesia in April 1966 on the unsophisticated assumption that the African people would rise. ZIPRA followed suit in July, sending in a small team. Another 30 small-scale and fruitless incursions would follow but at least both movements were formulating their strategies in contrast to the reactive one of the Rhodesians. ZIPRA, advised by Soviet instructors, aimed to mount a conventional threat. ZANLA adopted the Maoist concept of revolution but never progressed very far through its phases and was never capable of positional warfare.

Chapter 3

The threat was easily contained after an initial hiccup when the Police Commissioner, Frank Barfoot, felt compelled by his duty to preserve law and order to call up his Police Reserve to deal with the first ZANLA incursion rather than involve the army. The somewhat inept but successful 'Battle of Chinhoyi' (previously 'Sinoia') on 27 April 1966 (now celebrated as a national holiday) led the OCC to insist on implementing the JOC system. What aided the success thereafter was the timely notice of incursions given by informers in the ranks of ZANU and ZAPU. This was supplemented by information volunteered by the rural Africans and by a steady stream of press-ganged ZANLA and ZIPRA deserters. Schisms within the African nationalist ranks were exploited by the CIO with disinformation and even assassination. ZIPRA and its ally, the African National Congress of South Africa, also made the mistake twice, in 1967 and 1968, of establishing bases in uninhabited areas where the absence of other human spoor betrayed them. The involvement of the ANC was also a mistake as it supplied the excuse for direct South African intervention. South Africa deployed police reinforcements and supplied military hardware.

While the completeness of their defeats depressed both ZIPRA and ZANLA, the Rhodesian security forces enjoyed a solid grounding in joint-service counter-insurgency actions which allowed them to hone their small-unit tactics. The four-man 'stick' (half-section) emerged as the basic formation, equipped with a Belgian *Fabrique Nationale* (FN) *Mitrailleuse d'Appui General* (MAG) 7.62x51mm machine gun (the general-purpose weapon designed by Ernest Vervier in the 1950s and adopted by NATO in 1958 and by the Rhodesian Army in 1966), a high-frequency radio and three riflemen armed with the FN FAL 7.62mm rifle. Understanding the psychological importance of not harming, and therefore antagonizing, the innocent, emphasis was laid on the accuracy of the riflemen, teaching them to attempt the single aimed round rather than the traditional 'double-tap'. The Rhodesians developed tracking and other skills, setting up the Tracker Combat School at Kariba in 1970 and evolving the five-man tracker-combat concept now being taught to the US Marines.

The mistake was to leave the intelligence requirements to the SB personnel who, untrained in military intelligence, did not assist the military-planning cycle. A myth has arisen, however, that the Rhodesian security forces did not expect ZANLA to take advantage of the southward advance into Mozambique's Tete Province of the insurgents of *Frente de Libertaçao de Moçambique* (FRELIMO) to penetrate Rhodesia's northeastern border. In fact, the Rhodesians mounted Operation *Tripper* to assist the Portuguese with tracking FRELIMO and to stop ZANLA crossing the Zambezi River. The Rhodesians knew that ZANLA, albeit in small numbers, had begun to subvert the people who lived along this vulnerable border but the lack of manpower meant the African district assistants of the Internal Affairs Department could not be protected and intelligence on ZANLA's whereabouts began to dry up.

Another mistake was to fail to heed the warnings from the Rhodesian Army that, despite the presence of two 100-man companies of South African Police, its regular component was over-stretched when merely assisting the BSAP with border control. The former Federal Prime Minister, Sir Roy Welensky, suggested raising ten RAR battalions but, because the immediate threat seemed so minor and funds were short, the Treasury and the Department of Defence were fatally deaf to all pleas.

These were nevertheless good years for Rhodesians. They were winning all the battles and countering the sanctions. This was assisted by ZANU's and ZAPU's proclaimed adherence to Marxism which gave credibility to the Rhodesian government's anti-Communist stance which struck a chord in the United States and elsewhere, particularly among the conservative Arab states and Iran.

Phase 2: 1972–1974

In 1972, the rejection of the Home–Smith settlement and the success of FRELIMO against the Portuguese in Mozambique emboldened the African nationalists. ZANLA's attack on the white-owned Altena Farm in the northeastern Centenary district on 23 December 1972 opened a new phase of the war.

Having acquired sufficient finance, aid, weapons and a growing number

Chapter 3

of young men, Herbert Chitepo, the external ZANU leader, at last adopted a telling strategy. He aimed to stretch the security forces and thereby dent white morale by forcing the mobilization of large numbers of territorials and reservists, seriously affecting industry, commerce and agriculture. Chitepo, however, was assassinated by the CIO, sowing discord in ZANU's ranks. True to the Maoist template, ZANLA divided Rhodesia into provinces and sectors and sought to politicize the rural people, establishing local committees, security procedures and infiltration routes. They recruited contact men, feeders, porters, co-opted the local spirit mediums and cached arms and ammunition. Communications were by courier and letter (a system which the Rhodesians exploited). They also planted anti-tank landmines in the roads in the attempt to paralyze large areas.

The Rhodesians responded vigorously, setting up Operation *Hurricane* with its JOC at Centenary (Operation *Hurricane* would endure until the ceasefire in 1980) and hunting down the insurgents. Filling tyres with water and sandbagging truck beds reduced the lethality of the landmines. The threat prompted a rapid development of mine-protected vehicles with the aid of South Africa's Council for Scientific and Industrial Research (CSIR). The fruits of this research are deployed in Iraq today. Recalling their Malayan experience, the Rhodesians moved rural Africans in the northeast into protected villages. This move was not entirely a success. The reason was that, unlike the Malayan insurgents who were largely Chinese and the villagers mostly Malays, the ZANLA personnel were sons of the people being moved. Furthermore, the Rhodesians deployed inadequate numbers of ill-armed Internal Affairs administrators to protect the villages instead of arming a local militia. The reason for this was the fear that unsupervised militias would be subverted.

The Rhodesians understood the importance of psychological warfare but were always hampered by never achieving more than the Africans' passive acceptance of the status quo. It meant the Rhodesians could not yet evolve a counter-insurgency strategy, leaving them to concentrate on containment.

The vastness of the operational area and the small number of troops available demanded fast, mobile reaction. Instead of wasting effort on mostly fruitless cross-graining patrols,[12] the Rhodesian response was to develop an airborne rapid-reaction force, called Fireforce, to intercept, trap and destroy the elusive enemy once his whereabouts had been established. Despite the small number of troops involved, the Fireforce units would achieve kill rates of over 80:1. Securing Fireforce targets was achieved by observation, intelligence, patrolling, finding spoor, aerial visual- and photo-reconnaissance. The SAS penetrated the neighbouring countries to identify incoming groups, their routes and supplies. Intelligence was gleaned from villagers and captured insurgents but much was lost through poor interrogation techniques and the use of force because the handful of effective SB interrogators was not always available. The most successful move was the use of pseudo-gangs suggested by the ecologist, Allan Savory, in 1966, and advised by Ian Henderson, the Kenyan exponent of pseudo-warfare, and promoted by Brigadier John Hickman in 1973.[13] The role of the pseudo-terrorist was given to the new Selous Scouts Regiment which deployed captured-and-turned insurgents to impersonate ZANLA and ZIPRA sections to uncover the contact men, the sources of food and comfort, and to pinpoint the insurgent groups for Fireforce.[14] To remedy the inadequacies of entirely relying on policemen to collect and interpret intelligence, the Military Intelligence Directorate (MID) was set up in 1973. To inhibit rather than prevent cross-border movement, because Rhodesia lacked the manpower to keep it under surveillance, a mined barrier was laid along the northern and eastern border to harass infiltrators and would kill some 8,000 ZANLA by 1980.[15]

The success of all these measures led to the number of insurgents within the country being reduced to 60 in 1974 and all of them confined to the northeast. The insurgency was being contained but, of course, everything depended on a political settlement.

---

[12] Alexandre Binda, *The Saints: The Rhodesian Light Infantry*, 30° South Publishers, Johannesburg, 2007, p. 158.

[13] Ken Flower, *Serving Secretly, Rhodesia's CIO Chief on Record*, Galago, Alberton, 1987, p. 114.

[14] See Lieutenant-Colonel Ron Reid-Daly, *Top Secret War*, Galago, Alberton, 1982.

[15] Information given to Colonel Mike Pelham, Commander of the Rhodesian Corps of Engineers, by ZANLA commanders in 1984, interview with Colonel Pelham, 7 December 1995.

Phase 3: 1974–1977

The military coup in Portugal in April 1974 robbed Rhodesia of one of her two allies and exposed her long eastern and southeastern border to infiltration by ZANLA. At the same time, ZIPRA intensified its forays from Zambia through Botswana and across the Zambezi. Rhodesia's only secure border was that with South Africa. South Africa's Prime Minister, B. J. Vorster, however, preferred to have a compliant African government as a northern neighbour. Accordingly, he withdrew his police and interrupted Rhodesian ammunition and supplies to force Smith to settle. The upshot was a failed ceasefire in 1974, fruitless negotiations with ZANU and ZAPU in 1975 and the intensification of the war in 1976.

ZANLA concentrated on politicizing the rural folk, by fair means or foul, while ZIPRA preferred to wait. Both forces built up their strength with a growing supply of willing recruits. The intensification of the war, combined with other factors, induced white emigration and forced recognition of political realities. Even so, the most vulnerable of whites, the farmers, remained on the land. Six thousand of them would be still there in 1980.

The intensification provoked Rhodesian cross-border raids, limited to camp attacks because the Rhodesian government was fearful of world reaction and would not allow the destruction of the strategic infrastructure of the neighbouring territories. It allowed, however, 'hot pursuit' operations because the Paris Pact of 1928 deemed these legal. The first major raid was in October 1974 by the SAS against a ZIPRA camp and munitions dump in southern Zambia. There followed an attack in early 1976 against ZANLA staging posts in Mozambique's Gaza Province at the Sabi–Lundi junction and Pafuri on the Limpopo. Then, in August 1976, a Selous Scouts vehicle column killed 1,200 inmates of the main ZANLA camp at Nyadzonya in the Manica Province of Mozambique. This provoked the dreaded world outcry and gave the South African Prime Minister, B. J. Vorster, the excuse to pull out his helicopter pilots and enlist Kissinger (eager to help after the Angolan débâcle of 1975 which led to Soviet–Cuban intrusion into southern Africa) to put pressure on Smith to concede majority rule.

The constant deployment produced battle-hardened, resourceful and

The Counter-Insurgency Campaign: 1966-1980

daring troops. Only able to deploy 1,400 men in the field on the average day in the 1970s, the Rhodesian forces often could not muster the classic 3:1 ratio in attack. As will be seen, on Operation *Dingo*, in November 1977, 165 SAS and RLI paratroops jumped into a camp complex at Chimoio, Mozambique, holding 9,000–11,000 insurgents and killed 5,000, and then after a day's resupply, jumped into the Tembué camp deep in Mozambique's Tete Province, killing hundreds more.

Psychological warfare, however, that vital ingredient of successful counter-insurgency campaigns, remained impossible until the support of the people had been won by political reform.

Aside from raiding, the Rhodesians refined their techniques further. Fireforces were strengthened with Dakotas, carrying 16–20 RLI or RAR paratroopers, and fixed-wing support, usually the Lynx (the Cessna 337G) and sometimes Hunter fighters or Canberra bombers. These aircraft were given a new range of locally produced weapons in 1977.[16]

The need to detect the landmines produced the purely Rhodesian-invented 'Pookie', the world's first mine-detection vehicle, capable of finding a mine when travelling at 50 mph. From 1972–1980 there were 2,504 detonations by vehicles of landmines (mainly Soviet TM series), killing 632 people and injuring 4,410. The mining of roads increased as the war intensified. In 1978, 894 mines were detonated or recovered at the rate of 2.44 mines a day. In 1979, 2,089 mines were dealt with at the rate of 5.72 mines a day. Between 1976 and 1980, built at a cost of less than repairing a mine-damaged vehicle, the 68 Pookies detected over 550 landmines, saving hundreds of lives and, riding on under-inflated racing slicks, never detonated one. Twelve Pookies were damaged in ambushes by command-detonated landmines or rockets. An RPG rocket through the armoured windscreen killed the only driver to die. When ZANLA realized that the Pookie was blunting their landmine offensive, ambushes became more frequent. These were countered by arming the Pookie with the 'Spider' 24-barrel 12-gauge shotgun, simultaneously covering a 270° arc with buckshot. The insurgents held the Spider in such

---

[16] Cowderoy & Nesbit, pp. 119–124; Interview with Group Captain Peter Petter-Bowyer, 24 March 1992.

awe that they began to let the Pookies through the ambushes and attacked the convoys instead.

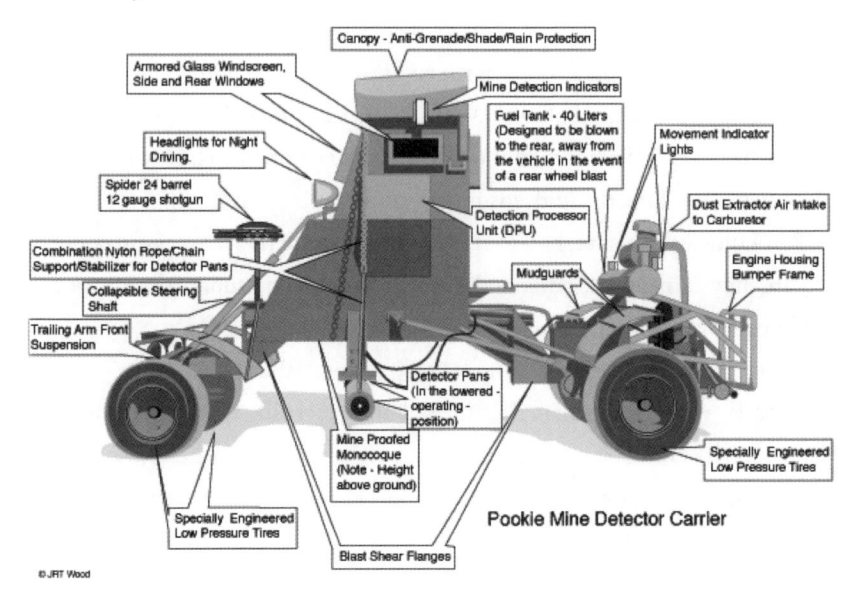

Pookie Mine Detector Carrier

Labels: Canopy - Anti-Grenade/Shade/Rain Protection; Armored Glass Windscreen, Side and Rear Windows; Mine Detection Indicators; Fuel Tank - 40 Liters (Designed to be blown to the rear, away from the vehicle in the event of a rear wheel blast); Movement Indicator Lights; Headlights for Night Driving; Spider 24 barrel 12 gauge shotgun; Detection Processor Unit (DPU); Dust Extractor Air Intake to Carburetor; Combination Nylon Rope/Chain Support/Stabilizer for Detector Pans; Mudguards; Engine Housing Bumper Frame; Collapsible Steering Shaft; Trailing Arm Front Suspension; Detector Pans (In the lowered - operating - position); Mine Proofed Monocoque (Note - Height above ground); Specially Engineered Low Pressure Tires; Specially Engineered Low Pressure Tires; Blast Shear Flanges.

© JRT Wood

New units were formed. The Psychological Warfare Unit attempted to fill a glaring need. The Grey's Scouts Regiment exploited the capabilities of the hardy Boer pony in bush warfare.[17] The Guard Force defended the spreading protected villages and other assets. The Rhodesian Intelligence Corps (RIC) gave the army a field intelligence unit.

The SB, however, retained its briefing role and continued to inhibit the planning cycle. Because of the successful marriage of army and SB personnel in the Selous Scouts, it was suggested that the Selous Scouts take over the intelligence function to provide the vital military ingredient. The Police Commissioner, however, vetoed such an intrusion into the SB's prerogative.[18]

In the event, assisted by 8 Signal Squadron which monitored radio traffic in neighbouring countries, processing some 10,000 FRELIMO–Zambian

---

[17] Interview with Lieutenant-Colonel Mick McKenna, former commander, Grey's Scouts, 7 December 1995.

[18] J. K. Cilliers, *Counter-Insurgency in Rhodesia*, Croom Helm, London, 1985, p. 226; Interview with the late Captain A. R. Eastwood, c. 1982.

signals a month, the MID gradually took responsibility for supporting the increasing external operations. What the MID neglected was counter-intelligence and failed to discover why raiding forces found some camps empty. Later at least one SB member frustrated assassination attempts on Mugabe and would be decorated by him for doing so. Elements of the SB also became involved in the use of biological and chemical warfare but, although the extent was minor, it has given rise to some conjecture and some wild extrapolations.[19] Excluded from such machinations, the RIC, for its part, at least gave a military dimension to the coverage of intelligence and supplied the security forces with updated maps and research findings on a variety of military problems.

What altered the course of the campaign was a decision by Vorster to force Smith to change course, to compel him to accept majority rule, something which Vorster himself could not stomach for South Africa. What assisted Vorster were the cumulative effects of the UN economic sanctions, the oil crisis of the mid-1970s, the Rhodesian insurgency being sustained by Zambia, Mozambique and Botswana providing safe havens and the aid that the Rhodesian insurgents received from the Eastern Bloc and sympathetic countries in the West.

In September 1976, anxious for change, Vorster accepted an offer of assistance of Dr Henry Kissinger, President Gerald Ford's Secretary of State, to convince Smith to accept the inevitability of majority rule. Vorster did so by cutting off fuel and ammunition supplies. Smith had no choice but to agree on 23 September to introduce majority rule within two years. The result was a failed conference at Geneva in November–December 1976 with all the African nationalists, including the externally based movements of Robert Mugabe's ZANU and its rival organization, Joshua Nkomo's Zimbabwe African People's Union (ZAPU).

In late 1976 pressure grew to copy the Malayan precedent and, as has been said, have a 'Director of Operations' instead of command by consensus. After initial hesitation, Smith formed, in March 1977, the Ministry of

---

[19] Jim Parker, *Assignment Selous Scouts: Inside story of a Rhodesian SB Officer*, Galago, Alberton, 2006, p. 155.

Combined Operations and appointed Lieutenant-General Peter Walls as Commander, Combined Operations (ComOps). This, coupled with the increasing declaration of martial law in affected districts, produced a more co-ordinated effort. Walls, however, did not outrank the army commander, Lieutenant-General John Hickman, and, in reality, was simply the chairman of the National JOC (NatJOC), a looser organization which replaced the OCC. He lacked the power to enforce his will on the NatJOC which was further weakened by the Police Commissioner and the Director, CIO, sending deputies to it. The district administration and the BSAP continued to formulate and execute their own plans. While ComOps prepared operational orders, its intelligence staff had no evaluating role and did not become the focus of the intelligence community to improve the strategic planning cycle. Walls sought clarification of his role but was ignored. The over-abundance of anomalies led to friction between the commanders.

The Rhodesian war effort remained reactive and lacking in a coherent strategy. Walls, nevertheless, understood that the military could still only strive to contain the war.

Phase 4: 1977–1979

After fruitless negotiations with the African nationalists on a plan devised by the British Labour government and the Carter Administration, in late 1977, in the midst of Operation *Dingo* and fulfilling his promise to Vorster and Kissinger, Smith announced he would negotiate with African nationalists other than the factions led by Nkomo and Mugabe and accept majority rule. The upshot was the political settlement of March 1978 and the formation of the interim government of Smith, Bishop Abel Muzorewa, the Reverend Ndabaningi Sithole (who had been ousted from the leadership of ZANU by Mugabe) and Chief Jeremiah Chirau to devise the new, fully democratic constitution and prepare for a general election.

ZANU and ZAPU responded by forming a political coalition called the Patriotic Front. In reality, however, their forces fought each other whenever they met. ZANLA also intensified the war at great cost with Fireforce taking a fearful toll. ZANLA also had severe logistical problems and lacked the morale, the discipline and the training for positional warfare. ZIPRA had conventional forces but lacked a bridgehead across the Zambezi River and air support.

The increased fighting and prospect of being ruled by an African prime minister shook the Rhodesian whites. Casualties remained light but whites began to emigrate at the rate of 2,000 a month. Despite an infinite supply of eager African recruits, budgetary constraints and the shortage of training staff meant that the security forces could not expand fast enough to match the growth of ZANLA and ZIPRA and were soon outnumbered except at times of total mobilization.

Even so, the Rhodesian war effort improved and, with the prospect of success in the political field at last, ComOps produced a strategy in 1978 with coherent goals which broke the reactive mould. This involved:

1. Protecting 'Vital Asset Ground' (mines, factories, key farming areas, bridges, railways, fuel dumps, and the like).
2. Denying the insurgents the 'Ground of Tactical Importance' (the African rural areas) as a base from which to mount attacks on crucial assets by:
    i. Inserting large numbers of armed auxiliaries (loyal to Muzorewa and Sithole) into these areas to assist in the re-establishment of the civil administration and to destroy the links between the insurgents and their supporters.
    ii. Using Fireforce and high-density troop operations against insurgent-infested areas.
3. Preventing incursions through border control.
4. Raiding neighbouring countries to disrupt the systems of command and control of ZANLA and ZIPRA, to destroy base facilities, ammunition and food supplies, to harass the reinforcements, and to hamper movement by aerial bombardment, mining and ambushing of routes.

An addendum to this plan was the sponsoring by the CIO of the anti-FRELIMO resistance movement, the *Resistência Nacional Moçambicana* (RNM, also known as MNR, or Renamo) which began to weaken FRELIMO and allow the Rhodesians greater freedom of action against ZANLA in Mozambique.

Although many in the Rhodesian security establishment did not grasp the potential of the auxiliary forces, the 10,000 auxiliaries, deployed among the rural Africans, began to deny the insurgents the countryside. For the first time there were forces to occupy the ground which the Fireforce won. Information began to flow again from the people and Fireforce became more deadly. The operational demands, however, were excessive. Fireforces deployed two, three times a day. Many external air and ground attacks were mounted, even on the outskirts of Lusaka in Zambia, but economic targets remained inviolate. MID became more effective in the analysis of intelligence and the army was strengthened by the formation of the Rhodesia Defence Regiment to supplement the Guard Force in guarding vital points.

Phase 5: April 1979–March 1980

The election of Muzorewa in April 1979 offered the only chance for the counter-insurgency war to be won because, voting in a 62 per cent poll, the African population dealt ZANLA and ZIPRA a stunning defeat by defying their orders to abstain. The Rhodesian security forces mobilized 60,000 men to neutralize the threat to the election. Two hundred and thirty insurgents were killed in the three days of the election and 650 overall in April. The others went to ground or surrendered. The ZANLA commanders left the country for orders and for six weeks the war stood still. If Margaret Thatcher had adhered to her election promise to recognize this internationally monitored result, the insurgency could have been defeated. Instead, Thatcher reneged and the murders of Africans increased as the insurgents strove to re-establish themselves. The morale of the security forces and the public sank. At the same time, planning to rob ZANLA of victory at a decisive moment, ZIPRA deployed a 3,000-strong vanguard into Rhodesia to prepare the way for its Soviet-trained motorized conventional army. ZANLA responded with an offensive into Matabeleland, ZIPRA's heartland. Although ZANLA sent 10,000 men into Rhodesia, including some FRELIMO volunteers, it was in dire straits due to constant Fireforce action, the external raids, the unease of

Mozambique, their host country, and the denial of ground by the auxiliaries. The peace achieved at the Lancaster House Conference in London came none too soon for ZANLA.[20] Its real accomplishment was political. Its long campaign of intimidation ensured that Mugabe would win the 1980 election.

Muzorewa could have achieved a stronger bargaining position if he had adopted a total strategy.[21] Instead, while his security forces strove to contain the situation in expectation of a political solution, his political and military aims were not tied in closely enough. He could have exerted economic pressure and threatened a conventional war on Zambia and Mozambique to cease aiding his enemies. He could have stalled to allow time for his auxiliaries and Fireforce to weaken the hold of the insurgents within the country while his forces crippled the supply lines of ZANLA and ZIPRA and the RNM kept FRELIMO at bay. The humiliation of this could have caused the fall of the FRELIMO leader, Samora Machel. The Soviets might have offered some help but Machel had seen what had happened to Angola and would have hesitated to take it. The Cubans could have intervened but this was unlikely as they were already over-extended in Angola. In any case, South Africa would have immediately reacted. There were political dangers but Rhodesia had demonstrated that she could withstand international pressure.

Muzorewa could have enjoyed a number of options. A separate deal with Nkomo's ZAPU would have been possible. The Lancaster House peace talks could have been stalled until the pressure on Zambia and Mozambique began to tell. Limited Western recognition might have been forthcoming to prevent a regional war. Muzorewa could have dictated the peace terms and his apparent strength would have appealed to the electorate because, like Mugabe, he could threaten the resumption of the war.

Muzorewa's external operations did contain the ZIPRA threat from Zambia, by blowing bridges and leaving Zambia totally dependent on a single

---

[20] Interview, Petter-Bowyer, 24 March 1992.

[21] G. K. Burke, 'Insurgency in Rhodesia—The Implications', *RUSI and Brassey's Defence Yearbook 1978–79*, London, 1980, pp. 26–40.

railway line through Rhodesia to South Africa. The raids steadily raised the odds in Mozambique to force FRELIMO to cease supporting ZANU and ZANLA. The Rhodesian forces attacked bridges in the Gaza Province to cut ZANLA's supply lines. They planned to do likewise in the Manica, Sofala and Tete provinces had they not been stopped, perhaps because the British were bent on achieving a settlement embracing all players including Mugabe, and the South Africans wanted to woo Machel to deny a safe haven to the South African ANC. Muzorewa also weakly allowed the British to divide his delegation at Lancaster House while Mugabe and Nkomo delayed signing anything to gain time to build their political support within Rhodesia and recoup their losses.

Enforcing the Lancaster House ceasefire, the Commonwealth Monitoring Force restrained the Rhodesian forces and ostensibly confined the ZANLA and ZIPRA forces to a number of assembly-point camps. The British, however, ignored the presence of mostly recruits in the camps and the absence of the hard-core insurgents who remained outside among the population and ensured that Mugabe won the election. The British, with too few troops to intervene, accepted the result despite the overwhelming evidence of intimidation.

The Rhodesian forces flirted with, but rejected the idea of a coup because only Britain could confer sovereignty. Instead they concentrated on forcing the British to re-schedule the election. Lord Carrington, the British Foreign and Commonwealth Secretary, aided and abetted by Ken Flower, the head of the CIO, and P. K. Allum, the Police Commissioner, ignored the evidence of widespread intimidation supplied not only by the Rhodesian forces but also by the British monitors.[22]

In the end, the leaders of the intelligence establishment had betrayed their own, perhaps for the sake of their pensions. Flower went on to serve Mugabe and his Marxist aspirations, and the CIO would become a feared secret police organization rather than an intelligence agency. The war had cost ZANLA

---

[22] Interview with Colonel John Redfern, Director, Military Intelligence, c. 1982.

and ZIPRA 40,000[23] dead at a cost of 1,735 Rhodesian dead—a ratio of 23:1. A flawed election placed Mugabe in power and, bent on the retention of power, he has ruined a once thriving state. Where once food was exported and the policemen went unarmed, famine and terror stalk the land. All the Rhodesian military had gained out of the failure of the counter-insurgency campaign was an enviable reputation.

---

[23] John Cronin & Robert C. Mackenzie, 'Counter-Insurgency in Southern Africa', a paper delivered to the Center for Strategic and International Studies, Washington DC, 1986.

Chapter 4

Meeting the Challenge of the Insurgency

The first challenge that Ian Smith's unilateral declaration of independence (UDI) on 11 November 1965 posed the RRAF (which in 1970 would drop 'Royal' from its title when Rhodesia became a republic) was not its role in dealing with the insurgency. It was how to subvert the consequent international sanctions designed to prevent it from obtaining spares and aircraft. This was met with ingenuity and subterfuge. Jet engines were a particular challenge as, prior to the UDI, they had been sent to Rolls Royce in Britain for servicing. The UDI prompted the British to seize 14 Avon Series 207 engines being serviced in Britain for the RRAF. This loss forced the RRAF technicians to service and maintain the engines and equipment they had with the help of local industry. Difficulties in procuring starter cartridges led to the discovery that the Canberra engines could be started with compressed air, and a truck's starter motor instead of cartridges would start the Provost. The cost of servicing by Rolls Royce of the starter motors for the Hunters had been £14,000 per motor. The RRAF technicians taught themselves to strip starter motors and service them at a cost of 76 pence per unit! That nine of the twelve Hunters were still flying 16 years later was a measure of their success. By dint of subterfuge, Rhodesia also bought from Belgium 42 Avon 207 jet engines in 1966 and ten years later would acquire more from Oman where they had been buried in sand. Spares and weapons were secured through clandestine purchasing and by local manufacture and ingenuity.

The international embargo against Rhodesia meant that jet fighters and bombers could not be purchased from abroad but it was possible to acquire light aircraft and spares. In August 1967, given seven Provosts, No. 6 Squadron was revived to take over No. 4 Squadron's role of basic flying training. No. 4 Squadron was entrusted with the counter-insurgency role using Provosts,

Cessna 185s and ten new Aermacchi AL60-B2Ls. The Provost, however, was the only one which could be used safely to deliver light 17-gallon frantan (der. frangible tank, i.e. napalm) bombs because it sported two .303in Browning Mk II machine guns, each capable of firing 1,200 rounds a minute, with which to suppress fire from the ground during a bombing run.

Assembling them from kits, the Rhodesians called the AL60-B2Ls, 'Trojans', to confuse the outside world. In fact, despite the earlier-mentioned American refusal in 1965 to sell North American T-28 'Trojans', 28 French-refurbished T-28s[24] had been bought from France in 1966–1967 but the ship carrying them had turned back within sight of Cape Town when the US government threatened to revoke all the manufacturing licences held by the French. Needing something more than a reconnaissance–passenger-carrying light aircraft, the Rhodesians armed the new aircraft with SNEB 37mm air-to-ground rockets to give them an offensive ground-support role. The Trojan did not, however, entirely replace the ageing Provost as a dive-bomber because it could not be fitted with machine guns.[25]

Although the dwindling Provost fleet had received reinforcement in the form of eleven former RAF machines, brought into Rhodesia by subterfuge in 1973–1974, something new and reliable was required.[26] In January 1976, 21 Reims Cessna FTB 337G Lynxes, twin-boom, twin piston-engined light attack aircraft, replaced the Trojans and Provosts. The Lynxes were purchased from the Free French Air Force ace, Pierre Clostermann, and clandestinely flown from France by Rhodesian and French pilots. The Lynx was not the military version of the 337 and had to be adapted by the Rhodesian Air Force. Four hard points were fitted under the wings to carry 37mm SNEB rocket

---

[24] The French Air Force evaluated the T-28 and consequently Sud Aviation modified a considerable number of ex-USAF T-28s. These aircraft, called 'Fennecs' were given 1,425hp Wright R-1820-56S radial air-cooled engines, two 12.5mm machine guns in a pod under each wing and four mountings for 300lb bombs. Bill Gunston, editor, *The Encyclopaedia of World Air Power*, Hamlyn-Aerospace, London, 1981, p. 286.

[25] P. J. H. Petter-Bowyer, *Winds of Destruction: The autobiography of a Rhodesian combat pilot*, 30° South Publishers, Johannesburg, 2005, p. 182.

[26] Winston, Brent, *Rhodesian Air Force: The Sanctions Busters*, Freeworld Publications, Nelspruit, 2001, pp. 51–52.

Chapter 4

pods and frantan bombs. The frantan, however, presented a problem because it had to be delivered as low as 300 feet above ground. Almost immediately, a Lynx pilot, Russell Broadbent, complained that his bombing run on 11 April 1976 without covering fire had verged on the suicidal. Broadbent suggested the firing of SNEB rockets during the run. This was seen as ill-advised because not only would the pilot be distracted by having to fiddle with the armament-selection switch while concentrating on the target in a dive but, due to the delivery height of the frantan, would be vulnerable to shrapnel from the bursting rockets. The answer was to fit a pair of .303in machine guns but it was found that, if mounted under the wing along with other ordnance, they created unacceptable drag. Fixing streamlined machine gun pods to the cabin roof proved to be the answer and all Lynxes were duly armed with twin .303in Brownings. [27]

Also in 1976, six Britten-Norman BN-A Islanders were obtained for No. 3 Squadron to join additional Dakotas, a Cessna 421A and a Beech 95 C-55 Baron. In 1977, 31 SIAI Marchetti SF260 Genets were bought to replace the Provost trainers of No. 6 Squadron and to provide more light attack aircraft after being fitted with underwing gun pods. In 1978, a new squadron, No. 8, was created to fly eleven second-hand and smuggled-in Agusta Bell 205A Cheetah (Huey) helicopters.

Time caught up with the Canberras and the Vampires and they became dangerous to fly. A Canberra B2 was rebuilt from spare parts and the South Africans sold the Rhodesians surplus Vampire FB52s and T11s. In the mid-1970s, when the T11s were beyond repair, South Africa set up a flying school in Durban where young Rhodesians flew Impala jet trainers. The South African Air Force also allowed the Rhodesians to man, fly and maintain a Mirage III squadron to equip them to fly advanced aircraft. When needed, furthermore, the South African Canberra B12s would reinforce the Rhodesian Canberra force.

In terms of a secret agreement between the three Rhodesian, South African and Portuguese governments for the defence of southern Africa

---

[27] Petter-Bowyer, p. 263.

(known secretly as Operation *Alcora*), the South Africans also built two advanced airfields, capable of handling jet aircraft, at Wankie, just south of Victoria Falls, and at Fylde, near Hartley, west of Salisbury. The Rhodesian contribution to Operation *Alcora* was photo-reconnaissance of Africa south of the Congo River using high-flying Canberras. On one mission, a Canberra photographed the port at Dar es Salaam.[28] The Portuguese contribution was to pay for the processing of the film by the South Africans. This collaboration ended after the coup in Portugal in 1974.

More important was the contribution of South African helicopters and crews. These were sent into Rhodesia to support the South African Police Field Force units after African National Congress of South Africa infiltrators were encountered during Operation *Nickel* in northwestern Rhodesia in 1967. After the South African Police withdrew in 1974–1975, the aircrews were seconded to the Rhodesian Air Force as Alpha Flight of No. 7 Squadron or were allowed to 'join' the Rhodesian Air Force for three-year tours of duty without affecting their South African pay and conditions. When major cross-border operations were being mounted, such was the co-operation with the South African Air Force that the Rhodesians could field 50 helicopters.

The South African helicopter force was, however, a double-edged sword on occasions. The South African Prime Minister, B. J. Vorster, used it to apply political pressure on the Rhodesian government. In 1976, for example, when he was seeking to coerce Ian Smith into accepting majority rule, Vorster withdrew 27 pilots on the pretext of protesting at the escalation of the Rhodesian war, represented by the raid by the Rhodesian Selous Scouts on the ZANLA camp at Nyadzonya in Mozambique on 8 August. Vorster also interrupted Rhodesia's supplies of ammunition and fuel, forcing Ian Smith to accept the settlement proposals offered to him in September by the US Secretary of State, Henry Kissinger. Once Smith's acceptance of majority rule had produced the first African-dominated government, that of Bishop Muzorewa, the South African support was liberally renewed with, among other aid, two South African-manned Fireforces established in late 1979

---

[28] Michael Hamence & Winston Brent, *Canberra in Southern Africa Service*, Freeworld Publications, Nelspruit, 1998, pp. 23–25

in the south of Matabeleland, with four South African Aérospatiale Pumas transporting South African Parabats (paratroopers) with Rhodesian pilots and army personnel assisting.

When the Rhodesian Air Force required long-range transports for cross-border operations, it borrowed them from the commercial airline, Air Trans Africa, whose owner, Jack Malloch, was an officer in the Volunteer Reserve and a former member of Ian Smith's wartime Spitfire squadron. Malloch, who ran a sustained exercise in the evasion of sanctions, brought in many vital spares. Other members of the Volunteer Reserve were used to staff forward airfields (FAFs) in the operational areas, established once the insurgency became a fact of life, to provide air support for the ground forces. Eventually there were nine such bases: FAF1 (Wankie); FAF2 (Kariba); FAF3 (Centenary); FAF4 (Mount Darwin); FAF5 (Mtoko); FAF6 (Chipinga); FAF7 (Buffalo Range); FAF8 (Grand Reef); and FAF9 (Rutenga). In addition, impromptu FAFs would be created anywhere there was a 1,000-metre runway.

It was from the FAFs that the helicopters and aircraft assigned to Fireforce operated. Thornhill and New Sarum provided facilities for major maintenance and repair but the helicopter units of four to six aircraft were mostly self-sufficient because each helicopter crew comprised a pilot and a qualified technician who maintained the aircraft as well as manning its machine guns or cannons. The jet squadrons based at Thornhill and New Sarum, being in the centre of Rhodesia, were able to provide quick response anywhere when a target serious enough required their attention.

The Rhodesian Air Force, however, remained the smallest of the Rhodesian security forces. Its greatest strength in the 1970s was only ever 2,300 personnel (150 of them pilots) and including the General Service Unit which became the Rhodesian Air Force Regiment and was deployed to guard its installations.

Chapter 5

The Basic Tool of Fireforce:
The Alouette Helicopter

As has been said, once the Rhodesians adopted the helicopter in 1962, they fully exploited its agility, its ability to hover, to land and take off in almost impossible terrain. The helicopter has unique features to offer the military. Under anything but truly abnormal conditions, helicopters can ascend or descend at steep angles, allowing them to operate from confined and unimproved areas such as forest clearings and narrow valleys.

There was nothing new in the military use of helicopters. As soon as helicopters were available, the air forces and armies of the world gave them a multitude of tasks. The first workable machines appeared in the Second World War in the form of the American Sikorsky R-6A and the German Flettner F1 282 Kolibri. Thereafter, developing rapidly in capability, helicopters were engaged in casualty evacuation in Korea and moving troops and equipment to combat insurgents in Malaya, French Indo-China and in Kenya. In Algeria, the French created the first 'gunships', Alouette IIs armed with machine guns, to support parachute troops and helicopter-borne infantry carried in American-made Vertol H-21 twin-rotor helicopters.

There was a clear need for helicopters in Rhodesia but almost all of the terrain is over 2,000 feet above sea level and the climate is hot. As height and heat drastically reduced the efficiency of existing helicopter piston engines, a special helicopter was required. Such a helicopter was provided by the French who had taken the lead early in the race to design light turboshaft engines capable of flying at most required altitudes.

The man of vision in France was Joseph Szydlowski, who founded the *Société Turboméca* in 1938 and worked on small gas turbines throughout the Second World War despite the Nazi occupation of his factory. By 1949, he had manufactured the Artouste Mk II gas turbine, producing 400-shaft horsepower and, at 253lbs, weighing less than half of any equivalent piston engine. The American Boeing Company was also working on gas turbines and one powered the first gas-turbine helicopter in the world, the United States Navy's Kaman K-225 twin-rotor 'egg-beater' which flew on 10 December 1951. Boeing, however, soon lost interest in light jet engines and left the field to the French.

In 1953, the Artouste Mark II replaced the radial piston engine of the Sud-Aviation (later Aérospatiale) SE3120 Alouette, a small crop-spraying helicopter. This gave the Alouette II such a unique performance that the *Société Turboméca* became the leading supplier of small turbine helicopter engines in the western world. The Alouette II had an open girder frame, an exposed engine, a skid landing gear and a bubble canopy. Aside from the pilot, it could carry four passengers, or two stretchers and two sitting wounded, or a 1,100lb load either in a sling under the fuselage or in the form of mounted guns, missiles or homing torpedoes. In June 1955 this little aircraft set a new world height record for helicopters by climbing to 26,932 feet and quickly found a ready market in 33 countries.

Turboméca's next jet engine, the Astazou (de-rated from 530 to 350 shaft horsepower) gave constant power under any conditions of height and hot climate. It doubled the load-carrying capacity of the Alouette II and led to even wider sales. The Indian version, the HAL Cheetah, proved able to take off and land at heights above 24,600 feet in the Himalayas. In June 1958 the Alouette II set a height record for helicopters at 36,037 feet.

The arrival of the even more powerful Artouste engine (de-rated from 870 to 570 shaft horsepower) resulted in the bigger Alouette III. It first flew on 28 February 1959 and was soon performing spectacularly. Eschewing a throttle, its engine was governed to achieve a constant output of 33,500 revolutions per minute and its tail rotor spinning at precisely 2,001 rpm. Control of its speed was achieved by its rotor controls. In June 1960 it landed and took off carrying seven people at an altitude of 15,780 feet on Mont Blanc in the French Alps. In November 1960, carrying two crew members and a 550lbs load, it landed and took off at an altitude of 19,698 feet. This was unprecedented in the world of helicopters.

The Basic Tool of Fireforce: The Alouette Helicopter

The Alouette III SA316B could accommodate the pilot and six fully equipped troops. Its passenger seats were easily removed, allowing the carriage of a variety of different loads. Experience in combat led the Rhodesians to remove the doors and to reverse the front passenger seats to widen the available floor space to make it easier to exit the helicopter quickly, to increase the cargo capacity and thereby gain flexibility.[29] The new arrangement allowed the Alouette III to carry two stretcher cases and two seated wounded. A hoist could be fitted with a 380lb (175kg) capacity to allow casualties and other loads to be winched up. There was provision for an under-floor external sling for cargoes weighing up to 1,650lbs (750kgs). In emergencies, men could be 'hot' extracted from tight corners by trailing a trapeze bar underneath the aircraft onto which four men could clip themselves if they were wearing specially designed Pegasus harnesses. Those forced to use this method were not just buffeted by the slipstream and the downdraught but were often dragged through treetops as the pilots sought to evade ground fire. It was not an experience to be happily repeated.

Produced after first flying on 27 June 1968 and exported after 1970, the SA319B Alouette III was powered by the Astazou XIV (de-rated from 870 to 600 shaft horsepower) which was even more effective in 'hot and high' conditions and more economical. The SA319B had strengthened main- and tail-rotor transmissions. It weighed slightly more but could carry a heavier payload. It enjoyed a maximum speed of 124 mph at sea level and a cruising speed of 115 mph. Its service ceiling was 13,100 feet and its hovering ceiling in ground effect was 9,450 feet. Out of ground effect, the hovering ceiling was 5,000 feet. Its range at optimum altitude was 335 miles, slightly longer than its predecessor. In practice, however, it was considerably shorter. Under Rhodesian conditions, when loaded with troops, the Alouette would fly at 65 knots (or 75 mph) and at 84 knots (or 97 mph) with a light load. At 84 knots, its range was 242 miles (210 nautical miles). The Alouette III SA316B 'K-Car' gunship, armed with a 20mm cannon and ammunition, and a crew of three, had an endurance of an hour and a quarter to an hour and a half

---

[29] Interview, Petter-Bowyer, 24 March 1992.

when loaded with 600lbs of fuel. The troop-carrying SA316B 'G-Car' with 400lbs of fuel, a crew of two and four fully equipped troops had an average endurance of 45 minutes.

The Rhodesians adopted the names, 'G-Car' and 'K-Car', for a number of reasons. 'G' stood for 'General Duties' in military parlance. 'K' was adopted for the cannon-armed Alouette III. There were also phonetic reasons given the often-poor radio reception. The addition of 'Car' was, perhaps, because the BSAP had called their patrol cars 'B-Cars'. As the well-known BBC television police series, 'Z-Cars', was being screened in Rhodesia in the late 1960s and, as the international vehicle number plate for South Africa was 'ZA', the title 'Z-Car' was given to South African Police Alouettes.[30]

Both the Alouette III SA316B and SA319B were bought by Rhodesia while finding favour in 68 other countries.[31] How many of each type Rhodesia possessed has not been revealed. Given international sanctions as a consequence of the unilateral declaration of independence by Ian Smith on 11 November 1965, clarity of records cannot be expected. As has been said: three were acquired in April 1962 (one damaged beyond repair on 17 January 1972), two in July 1962 and three (with hoists) in August 1963. After the UDI and despite the imposition of sanctions, four were acquired in August 1968 (two of them damaged beyond repair on 1 July 1970 and 20 November 1973 respectively), one in April 1972 (damaged beyond repair on 17 March 1977), five in December 1972, two in January 1974, one in July 1974, two in January 1975, two in March 1975, four in June 1975 (one of them shot down on 18 May 1977), one in February 1977; five were acquired at an unknown date, three in June 1979 and finally twelve at a further unknown date. How many on this list were actually owned by Rhodesia and how many were on loan from South Africa is not clear.[32] At one stage, 27 South African

---

[30] Interview, Petter-Bowyer, 24 March 1992.

[31] Bill Gunston & John Batchelor, *Phoebus History of the World Wars, Special, Helicopters 1900–1960*, Phoebus Publishing, London, 1977, p. 45; Gunston, *The Encyclopaedia of World Air Power*, pp. 65–66.

[32] W. A. Brent, *Rhodesian Air Force: A Brief History 1947–1980*, Freeworld Publications, Kwambonambi, 1987, pp. 13–14.

The Basic Tool of Fireforce: The Alouette Helicopter

helicopters were deployed in Rhodesia. Within No. 7 (Helicopter) Squadron, the South African Alouettes were designated Alpha Flight. In 1980, when Rhodesia had become Zimbabwe, the Air Force of Zimbabwe was left with eight Alouettes which gives some indication of what it really owned. There were many more helicopters brought down by fire from the ground than listed and some were rebuilt. In fact, all Alouettes are rebuilt totally in the course of their preventive-maintenance cycle. The engine would be changed after 1,200 flying hours and the airframe after 3,600.[33] In the difficult times after 1965, many helicopters were built entirely from spares.[34]

By deft evasion of the international sanctions and the consequent arms embargo, eleven Italian Agusta-Bell 205A helicopters (the Rhodesians called them 'Cheetahs') were imported in August 1978. Two of the later model, the AB214 (which had a more powerful engine), were acquired shortly thereafter. The AB205A was the celebrated American 'Huey' of Vietnam fame built under licence in Italy. It had a range of 400 kilometres and a maximum speed of 126 miles per hour. It was designed to carry eleven passengers but because these particular AB205As were elderly, and after armour and twin .303in machine guns had been fitted, they could transport eight troops. Thus, they had a greater range and double the carrying capacity of the Alouettes. In 1979, the use of the AB205A Cheetahs on external operations into neighbouring countries meant that the Fireforces engaged in internal operations were not constantly robbed of their Alouette IIIs. This allowed the creation of large 'Jumbo' Fireforces which contributed to the increased casualties inflicted on the insurgent forces.

The purchase and immediate fate of the Rhodesian AB205As before they arrived in Rhodesia is not clear. They came to Rhodesia via the Comoro Islands, a common route for embargoed items. It is believed that a customer in Kuwait ordered 13 AB205As from Agusta in Italy. They were delivered by ship in Beirut, were unloaded and moved to Kaslik, a Maronite suburb

---

[33] Telephone conversation with Squadron Leader W. E. Brown, 25 March 1992.

[34] The airframe was tubular and filled with nitrogen. To detect cracks, soap would be spread over the airframe before the pressure of the gas was tested. The technician would look for telltale bubbles. Interview, Petter-Bowyer, 24 March 1992.

of Beirut. Then they were bartered for arms from Israel for Major Haddad's Christian militia in southern Lebanon. The Rhodesians were led to believe that they had purchased new aircraft but the AB205As they received were beyond their safe flying life. With vital parts corroded, the Rhodesians had a major task in restoring the aircraft to a flying condition. Early in their operational life, one AB205A was lost when its tail rotor sheared on 12 February 1979 but otherwise they were to make a significant contribution to the counter-insurgency operations.

The importance of helicopters to Rhodesia was such that, when its counter-insurgency war was at its height, No. 7 Squadron was the largest squadron in the world with 40 Rhodesian pilots and some 20 seconded South African Air Force pilots, flying 45 aircraft. Pilots served three-year tours on the different aircraft types of the Rhodesian Air Force. When, because of political pressures, South African pilots were withdrawn, the loss was made up by seconding senior qualified personnel from headquarters (after a five-hour re-familiarization course) and by calling up former pilots who had returned to civilian life.

Chapter 6

The Arming of the Helicopter

A key to the use of the helicopter was the arming of it, giving it both an offensive and defensive capability.

At first, however, although the RRAF Alouettes helicopters were armed on occasions with single MAG 7.62mm machine guns, they were expressly forbidden to engage insurgents in an offensive 'gunship' role. The reason was that international sanctions made it difficult to secure new helicopters to replace any which were shot down.[35] The air force's attitude would change in late 1973 when it became possible to create a viable gunship.

The feasibility of arming the Alouette III had been examined in September–October 1965. As a result, the RRAF had decided to mount the available weapon, the Belgian MAG 7.62mm machine gun (with a cyclic rate of fire of 650 rounds a minute) at the port rear doorway of the Alouette. Modifications to the standard MAG were minimal. The bipod and the wooden butt were removed. The rear buffer-spring housing was padded and a short wooden handle projecting to the left of the weapon was added. Because the normal aperture gunsight was retained, the first evaluation of the weapon in flight early in November 1965 did not produce spectacular results and further modifications were obviously necessary to achieve offset shooting. After the first use of the MAG near Sinoia on 27 April 1966, Squadron Leader John Rogers of No. 7 Squadron and Flight Lieutenant Peter Petter-Bowyer, a veteran of the incident, took a direct interest in the modifications. These progressed from a wire-ring-and-bead gunsight to the GM2 Reflector Gunsight and, finally the Collimateur lightweight reflector gunsight which greatly improved accuracy. By August 1966 the weapon's mounting progressed from an A frame or a simple post to a stand made in the RRAF

---

[35] Arnold, p. 232.

machine shops which had two safety features. It collected and retained spent cartridge cases and ammunition belts, preventing them being blown out into the slipstream and into the tail rotor. It also limited the weapon's travel to prevent an over-enthusiastic gunner from hitting the main rotor blades. In addition, a padded chest plate and twin handgrips were added to the weapon to improve the gunner's handling of the weapon and steadiness of his aim.

Because of initial difficulty in firing the MAG accurately from a moving helicopter on 27 April 1966, No. 7 Squadron added air gunnery training to the education of its technicians. This included a written examination on the weapon's characteristics, handling and operational requirements. Those who passed earned an Air Gunner's Brevet.[36] In August 1967 a squadron air-weapons camp was held and, a month later, the station commander at New Sarum, Group Captain Dickie Bradshaw awarded all its 13 students with their brevets.

Thereafter a modified lightweight MAG mount provided extra rigidity to the gunsight and improved accuracy. In 1972 a modified ammunition box and a feed chute were fitted to minimize the twisting effect of airflow on the ammunition belts which slowed the rate of fire and often jammed the gun.[37]

In this early period the helicopters were treated as such precious objects that the Rhodesian Army liked to believe that the Rhodesian Air Force would only allow their men on board with clean boots. Certainly all weapons had to be cleared and all magazines removed. The pressure of war would bring relaxation of such rules to such an extent that a black RAR soldier boarded a helicopter at Marymount Mission in the northeast with a 42Z rifle grenade still mounted on the muzzle of his rifle and accidentally discharged it through the roof of the Alouette.[38]

The use of the MAG endured to 1976 when it was replaced in the Alouette G-Car with the more potent fit of twin faster-firing .303in Browning Mk

---

[36] British Empire and Commonwealth Museum, Rhodesian Army Association Papers (BECM, RAAP): Scrapbook: No. 7 Squadron, Rhodesian Air Force.

[37] BECM, RAAP, No. 7 Squadron, Rhodesian Air Force, diary, 1972.

[38] Interview with Major Nigel Henson, 3 November 1991.

II machine guns. With its cyclic firing rate of 1,200 rounds a minute, the Browning Mk II had served as the British turret and wing gun of the Second World War and as the wing guns of the Rhodesian Air Force's Provost aircraft and to the South African Alouette G-Cars. The Rhodesian G-Cars carried 500 rounds per gun.[39] When the South African Puma helicopters were deployed, they were armed with twin side-firing .5in or .303in Brownings.[40]

Before then, in late 1973, the Rhodesians were able to convert an Alouette III into a viable gunship. The reason was they had acquired the potent French Matra MG151 20mm cannon and its floor fitting which catered for its weight and recoil. Derived from the German MGFF and MG151 20mm cannons mounted in the Messerschmitt 109 and Focke-Wulf 190 fighters, the Matra MG151 cannon fired a shell with a short cartridge which contained less-than-normal propellant. This reduced the recoil of the gun and the low muzzle velocity and slow rate of fire made it suitable for the Alouette. To allow deflection shooting the gun was equipped with a Collimateur reflector gunsight which was calibrated for the cannon to be fired at 90 degrees to the fore and aft axis of an Alouette travelling at 65 knots at an altitude 800 feet above ground. The guns were initially obtained from the Portuguese and, for a long time, so were the high-explosive incendiary (HEI) shells which were loaded in trays holding 200 or 400 on them. As they cost $Rh35 each, the shells were expensive and difficult to obtain and, as the weight of the ammunition affected the range of the helicopter, the Rhodesians adjusted the cyclic rate of fire downwards to 350 rounds per minute. In addition, the gunners limited themselves to bursts of three rounds or less and would regard themselves as off form if more than five were expended per enemy killed. A good gunner would be able to fire accurately at lower than 800 feet and indeed some preferred 600 feet.

The HEI rounds were highly effective except when fired on soft ground which negated their explosive effect because the shells would bury themselves in it before detonating. This was because the shell had to decelerate sharply

---

[39] Telephone conversation with Beaver Shaw, 13 November 1991.

[40] Interview with Commandant Neal Ellis, 2 November 1991.

for their inertial fuses to be activated. Consequently, the gunners would look for rocks or hard ground to fire at to ensure the shells exploded on contact and to maximize the effect of the shrapnel. In Fireforce actions a high proportion of the enemy were killed and wounded as a result of 20mm fire. As the 20mm HEI shells were prone to explode prematurely on contact with tree branches, the gunners took to inserting one solid after every five HEI rounds in the ammunition trays. The gunners ceased early on to load tracer rounds with which to correct their aim because, fired at a range of 800 feet, the explosion of the shell was sufficiently bright.

To solve the problem of the shells burying themselves in soft ground or exploding prematurely on trees, other weapons were tried. Twin Browning .5in heavy machine guns were fitted in 1976 but were abandoned because of their weight and, since the .5in bullet was solid, not explosive, a direct hit had to be scored to kill or wound. This could be achieved with the smaller .303in round. Twin-.5in Brownings were used on 18 August 1976 in a contact in the eastern border area by a second K-Car, flying with Fireforce Alpha. The 20mm cannon and sweep line of 3 Commando, 1RLI, killed eleven ZANLA cadres. The Brownings fired 214 .50in rounds but were dismissed as "ineffectual as [the] ground [was] hard and [they had] no shrapnel effect". The same complaint was levelled at the .303in Browning machine gun on 6 October 1978 by Major Don Price, the commander of Fireforce Delta (manned by his 1 (Independent) Company RAR). He had been forced to switch to a G-Car because the K-Car had crashed on the previous day and the twin-.303in Brownings of his and the other G-Cars had failed to knock down any of their fast running, scattering enemy.[41]

Later, in 1979, some K-Cars were equipped with four Mk II .303in Browning machine guns slaved to a remote hand-operated sighting and hydraulic driver system code-named 'Katoog' (Cat's eye). A product of this project would be a highly successful helmet sight. Peter Petter-Bowyer, as Staff Officer (Planning), was involved in this development, called the Dalmatian Project, at the Council for Scientific and Industrial Research (CSIR) in South Africa.

---

[41] BECM, RAAP, Contact Reports, Contact, 6 October 1978.

After the initial successes of the mid to late '60s against ZAPU and ZANU infiltrations from across the Zambezi River, the Rhodesian security forces found it increasingly difficult to make contact with the enemy, who was quickly changing his tactics and evaporating into the local populace. Here, Rhodesian troops are involved in a follow-up operation in the mid '60s on the Zambezi escarpment. *Photo Craig Fourie collection*

Above: The Rhodesian Air Force was forced to rely on an aging fleet. Here a Canberra, two Hawker Hunters and a Vampire (rear) are pictured over Kyle Dam. This photo is pre-1970 as the markings are RRAF, the Royal Rhodesian Air Force. *Photo Peter Petter-Bowyer / Winds of Destruction*

Left: An Alouette III uplifts ZANU dead in the Zambezi Valley during 1968's Operation *Cauldron*. *Photo Tony Coom*

Group Captain Peter Petter-Bowyer in his younger days, after his first solo flight on a Vampire T11. 'PB', as he was affectionately known, was a visionary air force officer and one of the first proponents of the Fireforce concept. *Photo Peter Petter-Bowyer / Winds of Destruction*

Typical terrain in which the guerrillas operated. *Photo Peter Petter-Bowyer / Winds of Destruction*

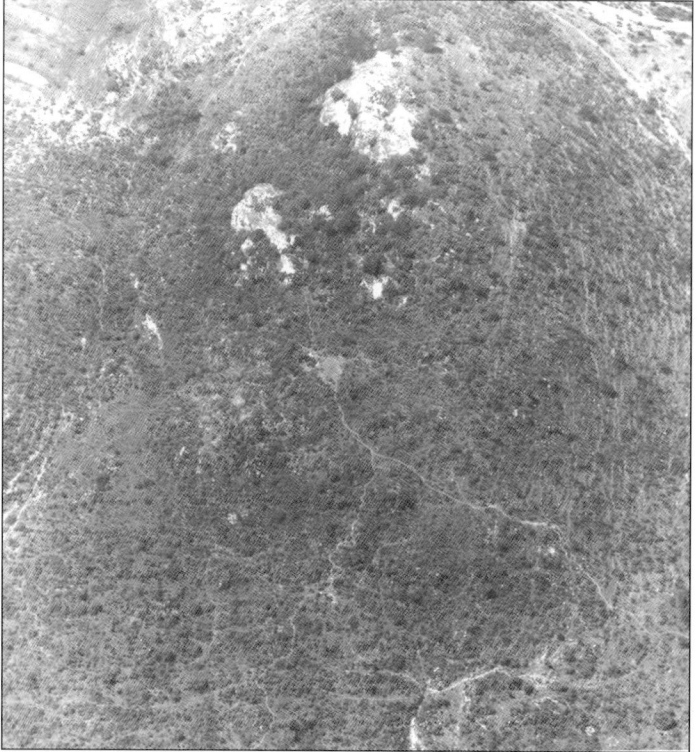

Petter-Bowyer was one of the first to appreciate the value of aerial tracking and recce. Of this photo he says: "Note the profusion of pathways. Sweeping around the hill from top to right are typical cattle tramlines. Others are normal human routing paths. The squiggly pathway centre bottom leading to the regular path rising from right to centre is the telltale indication leading to the terrorist base among large trees within the rocky outcrops at photo centre." *Photo Peter Petter-Bowyer / Winds of Destruction*

A flight of four Canberras and six Hawker Hunters. *Photo Peter Petter-Bowyer / Winds of Destruction*

An Alouette G-Car troop-carrier. In 1975 many of the G-Cars were still armed with the 7.62 MAG machine guns, as in this photo, but soon gave way to mounted twin .303 Browning machine guns. *Photo RLI scrapbooks*

By 1976 most G-Cars were fitted with twin .303 Brownings. *Photo Tom Argyle*

Top: The South African-designed Dalmation Alpha Fit—four Brownings mounted in the K-Car. It was prone to stoppages and was replaced by the more effective 20mm cannon. *Photo Beryl Salt / A Pride of Eagles*

Above: The Dalmation Alpha Fit from another perspective. *Photo Johan Joubert*

Major, later Lieutenant-Colonel, Ron Reid-Daly, founder of the Selous Scout Regiment. The Scouts, through their clandestine pseudo methods and effective OPs, revolutionized counter-insurgency warfare in southern Africa by successfully finding the elusive enemy. In no small part was this unit responsible for the success of Fireforce. *Photo Craig Fourie collection*

Lieutenant-General Peter Walls, Commander Combined Operations (ComOps), a fine officer and a former CO 1RLI, who had seen action with the SAS in Malaya. His task, to co-ordinate the war effort between the rival services and the politicians, was an unenviable one. *Photo RAR Regimental Association (UK)*

Below: Prime Minister Ian Smith is taught the intricacies of a 42Z rifle grenade by an RAR warrant officer. *Photo RAR Regimental Association (UK)*

A 1975 photo of an Alouette G-Car gunner-tech on his 7.62 MAG, with Collimateur gun sight. *Photo RLI scrapbooks*

Top right: RLI troopers deplane on Fireforce operations, 1975. *Photo RLI scrapbooks*

Centre: K-Car with mounted 20mm cannon, the biggest killer of the war. *Photo Max T*

Left: An RLI stick is uplifted on a Fireforce operation in the Operation *Hurricane* area, 1975. *Photo RLI scrapbooks*

20mm cannon—the gunner-tech's view. *Photo Max T*

This Hunter DFGA 9 armament layout excludes air-to-air missiles and Rhodesian-made frantan (napalm). *Back row from left*: 130lb white practice bomb (local), 1,000lb GP bomb (imported), 50gal frantan (imported), 450kg Golf bomb (local), 4 x 30mm Aden cannon gun-pack. *Middle row from left*: 250lb GP bomb (imported), 68mm Matra rocket pod (imported), flechette dispenser (local). *Front row*: 30mm cannon shells and 68mm Matra rockets. *Photo Peter Petter-Bowyer / Winds of Destruction*

Above left: A pair of Alouette G-Cars hurrying to a Fireforce action. *Photo Peter Petter-Bowyer / Winds of Destruction*

Above right: A three-ship Dakota DC-3 formation over typical Rhodesian countryside.

Left: Hawker Hunter. *Photo Craig Fourie collection*

A still-armed Hunter touches down. *Photo Craig Fourie collection*

Right: The flechette—another of Petter-Bowyer's nasty little designs—was used with devastating effect during Operation *Dingo*. Even the slowest projectile, such as this one pictured here, suffering from excessive retardation, was capable of lethal results. *Photo Peter Petter-Bowyer / Winds of Destruction*

Left: An Alouette G-Car 'dusts off' during a Fireforce action. *Photo Claude Botha*

Below: Alouette G-Car. *Photo Max T*

An armed Lynx taxiies out to a Fireforce action. This versatile aircraft was a key component in Fireforce, in either a ground-attack, aerial recce or Telstar role. *Photo RLI scrapbooks*

The Lynx undercarriage was unusual in that after selection, the main legs would dangle about like broken limbs before the hydraulics caught up. *Photo Beryl Salt / A Pride of Eagles*

A Lynx airborne. *Photo Beryl Salt / A Pride of Eagles*

Above left: This sequence shows a Hunter dropping frantan (napalm). *Photo Peter Petter-Bowyer / Winds of Destruction*

Above right: An RAR MAG gunner and rifleman warily sweep through thick bush. The RAR acquitted itself with distinction on Fireforce duties. *Photo RAR Regimental Association (UK)*

An RAR stick leader on the radio. *Photo RAR Regimental Association (UK)*

The business end of an RAR gunner's MAG. RAR MAG gunners typically wore several belts of ammunition draped over their shoulders and chests. *Photo RAR Regimental Association (UK)*

RAR soldiers take a bead. *Photo RAR Regimental Association (UK)*

A ZANLA cadre has met his fate, courtesy of an RAR Fireforce action. *Photo RAR Regimental Association (UK)*

Top: An RAR MAG gunner, bipods down, in ambush position. *Photo RAR Regimental Association (UK)*

Above left: Alouette pilots were renowned for their skill and daring. This is Mike Borlace being awarded the Silver Cross of Rhodesia (SCR) for bravery—an extraordinarily talented airman. *Photo Peter Petter-Bowyer / Winds of Destruction*

Above right: Air Lieutenant Kerry Fynn, K-Car pilot, was killed in a mid-air collision with another Alouette during a Fireforce action. His tech, as well as the tech from the other helicopter, was also killed. Mid-air collisions were, in the main, rare but did inevitably occur in the heat of battle. *Photo Craig Fourie collection*

Because of a shortage of helicopters the Rhodesians were forced to adopt other methods of getting troops quickly into Fireforce actions. At the end of 1976, the decision was made to para-train the RLI and RAR. By the end of 1977, both regiments were fully para-trained, no mean feat considering the limited PTS (Parachute Training School) facilities at New Sarum. In 1978, to lighten the PTS load, the South Africans began parachute courses for Rhodesian troops at Tempe Base in Bloemfontein. *Photo Theo Nel*

A brace of dead ZANLA guerrillas, again, courtesy of an RAR Fireforce. Note the ubiquitous Communist Chinese chest webbing. *Photo RAR Regimental Association (UK)*

An aerial shot of a forward airfield, this one FAF 5 at JOC Mtoko in the Operation *Hurricane* area. Mtoko was a permanent Fireforce base as can be seen by the extensive and developed infrastructure. A 'Paradak' is taxiing out of the protected revetments onto the runway. *Photo RAR Regimental Association (UK)*

Top left: RAR paras 'kit up' for a Fireforce operation. *Photo RAR Regimental Association (UK)*

Top right: RAR paras emplane. *Photo RAR Regimental Association (UK)*

Above left: RAR paras ready for final dispatchers' check prior to boarding. *Photo RAR Regimental Association (UK)*

Above right: RAR soldiers constructing a bunker at a temporary Fireforce base. *Photo RAR Regimental Association (UK)*

Top: Chopper techs prepare their Alouettes for a Fireforce call-out.

Centre: At an isolated airfield, RLI stick leaders converge on the K-Car for a briefing during a refuelling stop en route to a Fireforce call-out. In the background soldiers can be seen rolling away empty fuel drums. *Photo Claude Botha*

Left: The 'landtail', pulled over to the side of the Umtali road in the Operation *Thrasher* area, is busy refuelling two G-Cars. *Photo Claude Botha*

Above left: Fireforce gets rolling. *Photo Claude Botha*

Above right: 3 Commando, 1RLI troops prepare for a call-out next to the aircraft revetments. The man crouching is daubing himself with camouflage cream with considerable care. He applies it in streaks to break up the shine, as opposed to smearing it. *Photo Claude Botha*

Above: An RLI second-wave MAG gunner hurries across to the Paradak, just returned from dropping its load of paras, to catch news of a Fireforce operation. *Photo Claude Botha*

Above: 2 Commando, 1RLI paras en route to their Fireforce DZ. The paratrooper, foreground left, is wearing shorts. *Photo Jimmy Swan*

Left: A Support Commando, 1RLI para 'kitted up' and ready to jump. This trooper is 17 years old. *Photo Jon Caffin*

Above: A pair of RLI stick leaders back at Grand Reef after a Fireforce contact. *Photo Bruce Kidd*

An RAR NCO checks his MAG gunner's belt. *Photo RAR Regimental Association (UK)*

Above: RAR soldiers prepare to move out. *Photo RAR Regimental Association (UK)*

Right: The classic portrait of an RAR MAG gunner. *Photo RAR Regimental Association (UK)*

Below: RAR troops cautiously sweep through acacia woodland terrain. *Photo RAR Regimental Association (UK)*

Far left: Joshua Nkomo, nationalist leader and chairman of ZAPU, supported by the Soviets. *Photo Peter Petter-Bowyer / Winds of Destruction*

Left: General Josiah Tongogara, astute commander of ZANLA forces. Mugabe saw him as a threat and had him assassinated in Mozambique in 1980.

Fireforce operations in mopane scrubland terrain in the Zambezi Valley. *Photo Dennis Croukamp*

Above left: Air Marshal Frank Mussell commanded the Rhodesian Air Force from 1977–1980. *Photo Beryl Salt / A Pride of Eagles*

Above right: Captain Grahame Wilson, commanded Stop 6, B Troop, SAS on Operation *Dingo*. *Photo Craig Fourie collection*

The Arming of the Helicopter

He brought it back to Rhodesia to test it in the field in 1978. Ted Lunt flew the Dalmatian-fit helicopter, while Petter-Bowyer, flying a reconnaissance aircraft and using his skills as a recce pilot, found him targets. So successful was this combination that, in the first week of trials, 31 ZANLA insurgents were killed. Petter-Bowyer and Lunt and his technician, Bob Thompson, would attack the target and then call in Fireforce to get troops on the ground to complete the operation. On the first flight, on 23 June 1978, Petter-Bowyer found an occupied insurgent camp and talked Lunt onto it. Bob Thompson expended a mere Rhodesian $Rh172.80 of .303in ammunition, killing six insurgents.[42] The four-gun fit was mostly used thereafter in the role of a second K-Car. The Dalmatian K-Cars achieved devastating results in 1979, flying at treetop height with each gun firing at a cyclic rate of 1,150 rounds a minute. The Dalmatians were used to drive the enemy into the open where they became targets for the 20mm. The innovation was not entirely successful as the .303in bullet, of course, lacked the explosive effect of the 20mm shell. Furthermore, the Browning Mk IIs seemed more prone to jamming than the MG151 cannon.

By February 1974 a dedicated Alouette III gunship, the K-Car, was ready for trials. Its rear seats had been replaced with an armoured seat for the gunner positioned to fire the cannon out of the rear port doorway. The pilot was also given a matching seat which gave him protection from below and behind and partially from the side. Trials on the Inkomo range in March, May and June 1974 not only familiarized the air gunners but also led to further modifications of the aircraft. One made in June was the fitting of a rearward-facing front seat for the army officer in command of the troops carried in the Alouette G-Cars. In September 1974, to deny the Soviet SAM-7 heat-seeking anti-aircraft rocket (the Strela) any infrared reflection on which to lock, the Alouettes were given a matt paint-finish and were fitted with exhaust shrouds on their engines which deflected their jet blast upward. Provided with new rainproof covers for the cockpits and RT60B

---

[42] Prop Geldenhuys, *Rhodesian Air Force Operations*, Just Done Productions, Durban, 2007, p. 259; Interview, Petter-Bowyer, 24 March 1992.

radio rescue beacons, the K-Cars were ready for action.⁴³ The fitting of the new armoured seats to all helicopters began in November and the G-Cars were equipped with rope-descent arms to aid in the depositing of troops on the ground. The Fireforce was also ready.

The Alouette III is a magnificent military machine, capable of being operated well beyond what its designers expected. It uses jet fuel (paraffin) but can operate on diesel and even petrol in a dire emergency but only for a short flight. It is capable of absorbing astonishing quantities of small-arms fire and even hits from anti-tank rockets. One flown by Ted Lunt and carrying Major Pieter Farndell of Support Commando, Rhodesian Light Infantry, was hit in the tail section by an RPG7 rocket and still brought them home safely. On 14 October 1978, Dick Paxton's Alouette III K-Car, with Major Nigel Henson (also of Support Commando) aboard, was riddled by small-arms fire when it flew slowly at a low altitude over a hidden insurgent camp. Paxton had been directed there by an incorrect map reference supplied by the personnel of an observation post (OP) overlooking the target. With all his instruments shattered and a blade punctured, he was still able to climb to his operational height, 800 feet, orbit, and put down suppressive fire, before flying out.⁴⁴ On 19 October 1976, the celebrated pilot and later Selous Scout, Michael Borlace, brought an Alouette III G-Car home to Fort Victoria airfield with tail-rotor control failure and landed it without harm to its crew and its complement of African soldiers. As has been seen, Flight Lieutenant Victor Cook was able to land his Alouette even after its tail-rotor drive shaft had been severed. The command Alouette helicopter flown by Wing Commander Norman Walsh on Operation *Dingo* in Mozambique took a 12.7mm round through the rotor and still made it to safety. The impression must not be given, however, that the Alouette was invulnerable because a hit in the engine or the main rotor gearbox could be fatal.⁴⁵

---

⁴³ BECM, RAAP, Scrapbook: No. 7 Squadron, Rhodesian Air Force.

⁴⁴ Papers in Private Hands (PPH) RLI Papers (RLIP), Support Commando 1RLI, Contact Reports, 6 January, 1977 to 5 December 1978, contact report by Major N. D. Henson, 14 October 1978.

⁴⁵ Interview, Petter-Bowyer, 24 March 1992.

Chapter 7

The Support Weapons

A major blunder was Rhodesia's failure to invest in the production of ammunition even though it possessed an iron and steel industry and associated enterprises. Instead it had to purchase ammunition with some difficulty from abroad, with South Africa being the main supplier. It was a mistake to be utterly dependent on external sources as events in 1976 proved when the South African Prime Minister, B. J. Vorster, twisted Smith's arm by withholding ammunition and fuel.

Although nothing was done to rectify this mistake, the Rhodesians did exploit their possession of a factory making nitrogenous fertilizer which provided a basic ingredient for the common high explosive, ANFO, which is used in the mining industry. The ingredients are ammonium nitrate pellets mixed with diesel which, when detonated, result in a high-velocity explosion. Thus ANFO allowed the local production of a singularly lethal range of bombs designed not only to improve the striking power of the jet aircraft but also those of the light aircraft such as the Cessna 377 Lynxes.

The Mk II or 'Alpha' bomb (as the first in the range of new projects) was designed to replace the Mk I 20lb bomb. The Mk I had been withdrawn from service with the Canberra after several had detonated prematurely on 4 April 1974, destroying Canberra No. 2155, and killing air sub-lieutenants Keith Goddard and Richard Airey, her pilot and navigator. Intended for conventional warfare in the immediate aftermath of the Second World War, the Canberra was designed to carry the 250, 500 and 1,000lb range of bombs to attack hard targets like bridges, bunkers and buildings. To arm the Canberra for the counter-insurgency warfare, and particularly attacks on concentrations of insurgents, the Rhodesians had adopted the locally produced Mk I 20lb wire-bound fragmentation bomb with a proximity fuse which detonated it

Chapter 7

close to the ground. The Rhodesian Air Force's drawing office designed an aluminium bomb box to allow a Canberra to carry 96 Mk Is in its bomb bay to achieve the saturation of a target. There were three problems, however. The first was that accurate delivery required flying at a low altitude but, to avoid damage from its own bombs, the aircraft could not go lower than 1,500 feet above ground, the perfect height for the Strela missiles and within the range of the anti-aircraft guns possessed by the insurgents. The second was that the bomb pattern was a line of small bombs running through a target and not smothering it. The third problem was that the Mk I bombs on release could jostle together in the turbulent air stream within the opened bomb bay and, with armed proximity fuses, explode prematurely. The mid-air explosion on 4 April 1974 had not only killed Goddard and Airey but had robbed No. 5 Squadron of a role because there were few targets for its heavy bombs.

The challenge of returning the Canberra to the front line of the growing counter-insurgency effort was taken up by Group Captain Peter Petter-Bowyer when directing projects in early 1976 in collaboration with Squadron Leader Ron Dyer, the Senior Officer Air Armaments. Because the range of conventional bombs in stock was having a limited effect as too much of the blast and shrapnel was projected harmlessly upwards, Petter-Bowyer proposed saturating a target with small spherical bouncing bombs. He did so after reading of the use of hundreds of steel balls dropped from speeding United States Air Force jet fighters to shred the jungle in Vietnam. He understood that, to be effective and to achieve a concentrated spread, the proposed bombs had to be delivered at a height of less than 500 feet above ground at over 250 knots. An advantage of this was that the aircraft would be too close for a Strela missile to arm while presenting a fleeting target to the opposition's machine guns. In addition, the high air resistance of a round bomb would slow it sufficiently to allow it to explode well behind the bomber. A cluster of round bombs, affected by each other's turbulent, tumbling slipstream, would spread laterally to smother a wide area.

Taking three weeks from concept to acceptance in early 1976, Petter-Bowyer's team included a local engineering firm, Cochrane & Son, and the

The Support Weapons

Rhodesian Air Force's small armament section to produce the prototype of the Alpha bomb, a football-sized, spherical bouncing bomb. The section's technicians were called on to perform tasks, like filling bombs, that no other air force required. The Alpha bomb had a double casing containing 250 hard rubber balls. The optimum bombing height and speed was 300 feet above the ground at 350 knots. This spread the bombs and produced a forward bounce of some 18 metres at a maximum height of four metres before an ingenious three-way detonator and a delayed fuse exploded the descending bomb at three metres above the ground. Forty-five per cent of the casing—against seven and a half per cent of the conventional anti-personnel bomb—would saturate the target. To provide multiple air-bursts over a wide area, 300 bombs would be carried in six specially designed hoppers fitted in a Canberra bomb bay. As each hopper carried 50 bombs, the Canberra's crew had the choice of dropping one or a series of hopper-loads or all at once. Spraying outwards, 300 bombs would devastate an area of 100 metres wide and 1,000 metres long. These bombs were particularly feared by ZANLA and ZIPRA and would wreak fearful damage on insurgent concentrations.[46]

The second ANFO bomb was the 'Golf' (being seventh in the series of projects) which was ready for production by March 1977. Seeking a percussion bomb to clear bush-hiding insurgents, Petter-Bowyer had toyed with the concept of a fuel-air bomb using ethylene oxide. As the latter was unstable, expensive and difficult to procure, he settled on a 450kg double-skinned ANFO percussion bomb. In this case some 71,000 pieces of chopped 10mm steel bar filled the space between the skins. It sported a 984mm-long probe in the nose which contained a pentolite booster charge which meant it would explode the bomb's 123kg of ANFO above ground. A second pentolite charge in the rear of the bomb casing detonated simultaneously, compressing the explosion to ensure maximum sideways effect. The compression of the explosion was such that the tail fin was often found at the impact point. The shock wave travelling at 2,745 metres per second was capable of stunning at 120 metres. The Golf bomb would be released by a Hunter at 4,500 feet above

---

[46] Petter-Bowyer, pp. 272–276.

the ground in a 60° dive at 400 knots. As the safety height was 2,000 feet, the aircraft required a six-G pull-out to avoid shrapnel. The bomb would impact the ground at a 72° angle and clear 90 metres of bush, killing anything within that range with blast and beyond it with shrapnel. The Golf bomb's safety distance for supporting troops was 1,000 metres if they were behind solid cover and 2,000 metres if they were in the open. The early version of the Golf had one bomb in a pair retarded by a vane to separate their points of impact for maximum effect. The vane was soon replaced by a more efficient locally made drogue parachute. The result was a bush-clearing pattern some 90 metres wide and 135 metres long.

The stunning success of this bomb led Petter-Bowyer and his team to provide the Lynx in 1978 with a similar capability to flatten the bush and to kill men in cover by designing the Juliet or Mini-Golf. Again it had a double skin filled with chopped steel bar. It had, however, no tail. Instead it had a large drogue parachute which arrested its fall and ensured it impacted the ground vertically. The nose cone held a steel ball or 'seeker', the outer casing of an Alpha bomb, which contained an electrical contact switch and was attached to a five-metre-long electrical cable. This connected the switch to the bomb's batteries and to the detonator sited in the rear of the ANFO filling to achieve a downward and sideways explosion. The release of the parachute coincided with the dropping of the ball. The optimum height for the release was 300 feet above ground to allow time for the pendulum movement of the seeker to settle down and to strike the ground vertically beneath the bomb. The detonation occurred when the switch struck the ground, producing a five-metre-high, shallow, cone-shaped blast of 30–40 metres radius. This would not only shred the bush but also kill anyone hiding in depressions, behind rocks and the like. Flight Lieutenant Spook Geraty, flying a Lynx, used the first bomb in anger on 18 June 1978. On 20 June, the renowned recce pilot, Flight Lieutenant Cocky Benecke, dropped four Mini-Golfs, killing seven insurgents. The Mini-Golf became a standard Fireforce support weapon. Too many failures to explode, however, led to the replacement of the cable detonator with the metre-long probe of the Golf bomb.

To enhance the capability of the newly acquired Lynx further, Petter-

The Support Weapons

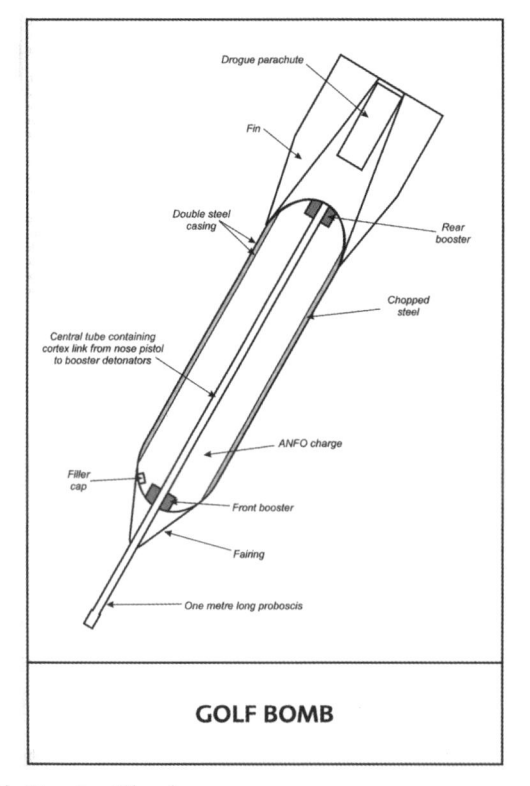

GOLF BOMB

Diagrams by Genevieve Edwards

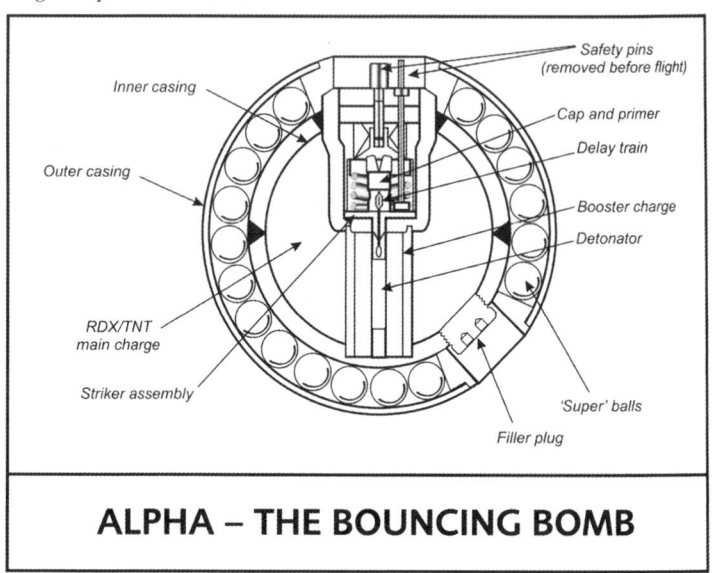

ALPHA – THE BOUNCING BOMB

The Rhodesian All-Arms Fireforce in the War in the Bush 1974–1980

Chapter 7

Bowyer's project team also sought to improve the locally manufactured light frantan/napalm bomb, a metal cylinder with front and rear cones. The name 'Napalm' derives from the original 1943 ingredients aluminium naphthenate and aluminium palmate which were used to thicken petroleum into a gel. This has been superseded by Napalm B, a mixture of benzene, gasoline and polystyrene-thickener which burns at 850° Celsius and three times longer than the original gel. Some Western bombs were simply metal tanks, others metal cylinders with fins to pitch them downwards and away from their parent aircraft. None had stabilizing fins which made accurate delivery impossible but then napalm was intended to be an area weapon and usually dropped in clusters. Counter-insurgency demands accurate weapons to limit damage to unintended targets and thereby to public morale. The Rhodesians required a bomb with a predictable trajectory so that accurate aiming was possible, preferably with a forward fiery splash. The Rhodesian-made 17-gallon napalm bomb gave unsatisfactory results in terms of accuracy, spread and unburned fuel because the bursting charge ruptured the steel container in an unpredictable manner. The Lynx, being a light aircraft, also required the least drag possible when fitted with the bomb. What was required was an accurately delivered low-drag container that decimated on impact and sprayed the napalm droplets evenly. The Rhodesians moulded their new container out of woven glass net reinforced with asbestos fibres and bound with phenolic resin and, to ensure detonation, added two modified Alpha bomb fuses to ignite the flash compound. The resultant 16-gallon 'Frantan', or frangible tank, shattered on impact and spewed forward a cloud of flaming droplets. This gave the Lynx the ability to bomb accurately and predictably. These characteristics led to Hunters being armed on occasions with the new 16-gallon bomb in preference to the imported, and therefore expensive, 50-gallon steel napalm container.

A key requirement of air support in any counter-insurgency effort is an accurate and reliably visible target marker. The RRAF had experience of rockets, having acquired stocks of 60lb air-to-ground rockets, dating from the Second World War, which were fitted to rails under the wings of its jet aircraft. After 1965 it procured by devious means internationally the French-made Matra 68mm rockets and pod dispensers for its Hunters and the SNEB 37mm rockets and pods for its light aircraft, the Provost, the Trojan and the Lynx. The Rhodesian technical team was able to adjust the firing mechanism of the pods to allow the firing of single rockets or ripples of them.

The 37mm rocket, however, disappointed the Rhodesians because the head often buried itself on contact with the earth before detonating, throwing its fragments mostly harmlessly upwards. The problem of the target marker was solved in the early 1970s by inserting a mild steel tube containing 200 grams of white phosphorus between the high-explosive head of the 37mm rocket and its propellant chamber. The marker rocket was not only successful but improved the fragmentation of the head. Petter-Bowyer's team then improved the explosive effect of the standard rocket tenfold by filling the extension tube with 100 grams of TNT, producing the 'Long Tom' rocket. Hundreds of the smoke and explosive extensions were machined, filled and assembled by the air force armourers at Thornhill. The heavier extended 'Long Tom' rocket was slower in flight but just as stable and accurate.[47]

A little-used, cheap weapon invented by Petter-Bowyer to arm the Hunter was nothing more than a six-inch steel nail stuck into the three-finned plastic flight of a playing dart. A local nail manufacturer supplied Petter-Bowyer with the headless nails. To achieve a wide dispersal on release, 4,500 darts were tucked together alternatively forward and backward and packed into a four-panelled, streamlined fibreglass container or dispenser. A pair of dispensers would be fitted to the hard points under a Hunter's wing. Diving at 450 knots, the pilot would line up on his target with his gunsight and release the dispensers. After half a second of flight, explosive charges in the nose cones of the dispensers would split apart their panels, releasing a cloud of darts. The flying nails, pushed wider by their neighbours' slipstream, would fan out to cover a wide area. The contents of a pair of dispensers would riddle an area 70 metres wide by 900 metres long. On 30 October 1977 this happened in a contact in the Sengwe Tribal Trust Land in southeastern Rhodesia with

---

[47] Cowderoy & Nesbit, pp. 119–124; Interview, Petter-Bowyer, 24 March 1992, information supplied by Alf Wild.

eleven insurgents being killed in the area of the flechette strike.[48] On 27 May 1979 flechettes killed 26 top ZANLA commanders after an observation team overlooking the Burma Valley on Rhodesia's eastern border had spotted their meeting. The leader of the group was struck by 26 flechettes.[49] This silent killer was greatly feared by ZANLA. Its use, however, was limited by it being named 'flechette' before it was realized that the 'flechette' rifle round was an internationally banned weapon. The result was that it was decreed that it should only be used internally or in remote external areas.[50]

---

[48] Petter-Bowyer, p. 303.

[49] Petter-Bowyer, p. 353.

[50] Anon. 'The Armament Story', The Zimbabwe Medal Society Journal, No. 61, March 2008, p. 29; Cowderoy & Nesbit, pp. 119–124; Interview, Petter-Bowyer, 24 March 1992.

Chapter 8

The Precursor of Fireforce at the 'Battle of Sinoia': 28 April 1966

Given that Rhodesia could only deploy 1,400 men on any one day in the years 1966–1980, a highly mobile means of tackling and eliminating insurgent groups was offered by the possession of the helicopter despite the limitation of the Alouette III's ability to carry only four soldiers and its short range.

The first use of armed helicopters supporting ground forces, on 28 April 1966, however, reached a level approaching farce but had important consequences. This engagement is now graced with the title of the 'Battle of Sinoia' and its date celebrated in Zimbabwe as a public holiday to mark the beginning of the 'Chimurenga' or War of Liberation.[51]

On 3 April 1966 a well-led and disciplined unit of 20 armed members of ZANU, including Abel Denga, and 18-year-old Master Tresha, veterans of ZANU's Crocodile Gang (the murderers of Petrus Oberholzer on 4 July 1964), had crossed the Zambezi River near Chirundu from Zambia. They were armed with Soviet SKS 7.62mm rifles, French MAT-49 9mm submachine guns, German Luger 9mm pistols, Soviet F1 and RGD5 grenades, seven- and 14-ounce slabs of Soviet TNT, German electrical detonators and connector-capped fuses.[52] Their purpose, ordained by Herbert Chitepo, the external leader of ZANU, was multifold. Firstly, it was to blow up the abandoned oil pipeline which, until the international oil embargo, had supplied oil to Umtali (now called Mutare) from the Mozambican port of Beira. Secondly, it was to impress ZANU's potential paymasters from the Organization of African Unity. Thirdly, it was to inspire young Africans to join the armed struggle and, fourthly, to harass and to frighten the whites into emigrating.

---

[51] Peter Stiff, *Selous Scouts: A Pictorial Account*, Galago, Alberton, 1984, pp. 23–24.

[52] BECM RAAP, Army HQ, Incident at Sinoia: 29 April 1966.

The group moved southward through the bush, eventually marching 185 kilometres down the power line to Salisbury from the Kariba hydro-electric dam. When they reached the small town of Sinoia (now Chinhoyi) they split up. Five men, commanded by Brown Chigwada, left for Umtali to blow up the oil pipeline and to attack white farmers. Comrade Mudukuti and one other departed to destroy bridges on the main road south of Fort Victoria (now Masvingo) over which fuel was being transported from South Africa. Denga, Tresha and four others headed towards the Zwimba Tribal Trust Land, north of Hartley (now Chegutu). The task of the final group of seven was not only to subvert the Midlands but also to topple the electrical pylons en route. The members of the group were steadily killed or captured over the following weeks but not before they had murdered a white farmer, Johannes Viljoen, and his wife Johanna at Gadzema on 16 May 1966. Before then, the group of seven had based themselves near Red Mine on Hunyani Farm just northeast of Sinoia, to sabotage the pylons. Their training was deficient and they often inserted the detonator into the Soviet TNT slabs in the wrong place, missing the primer, and simply blowing the slab to pieces. They also mounted an ineffectual attack on a police station.[53]

These incidents brought Flight Lieutenant Peter Petter-Bowyer, as the standby pilot (fresh from a conversion course to helicopters), to Sinoia in an Alouette III to support the BSAP's efforts to root out the gang. In the process of attempting to uncover their whereabouts, an African SB police officer, posing as a ZANU sympathizer, made contact with them through a local informer. The 'sympathizer' then contacted SB Headquarters, which in turn alerted the BSAP officer in charge at Sinoia, Chief Superintendent John Cannon DFC, a former RAF bomber pilot.

The information was passed to the Operations Co-ordinating Committee (set up in 1964 by Winston Field and comprising the commanders of the Rhodesian Army, the RRAF, the BSAP and Ken Flower of the CIO). The question posed was whether to arrest and try the ZANU 'Armageddon

---

[53] J. R. T. Wood, *A Matter of Weeks rather than Months: The Impasse between Harold Wilson and Ian Smith: Sanctions, Aborted Settlements and War: 1965–1969*, Trafford, Victoria, 2008, pp. 70–71 & 84.

The Precursor of Fireforce at the 'Battle of Sinoia': 28 April 1966

Group', as they were nicknamed, or to allow them to continue their operations in the hope of uncovering their African nationalist contacts. The majority of the OCC preferred the second option but the Police Commissioner, Frank Barfoot, being directly responsible for internal security and, therefore, the maintenance of law and order under the Police Act, decided he could not endanger the public by leaving them at large any longer. He ordered that the group be arrested or eliminated. In doing so, he confined the operation to his policemen, supported by the RRAF. This angered the Rhodesian Army, which, unlike the BSAP, had adopted counter-insurgency as its primary role as far back as 1956 and had focused its training upon it. The BSAP had handled all incursions to date but was not specially trained in counter-insurgency operations in the field. So, instead of using the army's regular soldiers, Barfoot chose to call up the local Police Reserve, barely trained white farmers, to reinforce the regular policemen stationed at Sinoia and elements of the BSAP paramilitary Support Unit. Backing this force were four RRAF Alouette helicopters, one of them armed hastily with an MAG 7.62mm machine gun with standard infantry iron sights which made deflection shooting difficult.

The Armageddon Group, however, was proving elusive despite having been kept under observation from a nearby hill. They were confident enough not to move away, and escaped being cornered by never sleeping in the same place twice. A sighting of three of them buying food within 100 metres of the police station led to a vain search of Sinoia's Old Location African Township. On 28 April, the Armageddon Group chose to send their 'sympathizer', who possessed a Ford Anglia station wagon, to fetch supplies and ammunition from African nationalists in Salisbury. Their plan was to meet him at 11.00 the next day at the junction of the old and new main roads east of Sinoia and just east of the Hunyani River and re-equip themselves for an attack on a nearby white-owned farm.

Briefed by the 'sympathizer' when he reached Salisbury, the BSAP arranged to have his station wagon followed discreetly back to his rendezvous east of Sinoia the next day. This was done both by Detective Inspector 'Dusty' Binns in a vehicle and by Flight Lieutenant Murray Hofmeyr, flying the armed Alouette at 11,000 feet. In advance of the 'sympathizer's' return, John Cannon deployed his 40 armed policemen to cordon off the rendezvous area. All the men deployed were dressed in highly visible blue denim riot uniforms, not exactly suited to fighting in the bush, and the police reservists were armed with vintage bolt-action .303in Lee-Enfield rifles, which put them at a disadvantage when facing the semi-automatic rifles of their quarry.

The unexpected happened. The 'sympathizer' stopped at the designated rendezvous point, but strode off into the bush southward, instead of northward as planned. He reappeared, turned his vehicle round and drove back up the road to tell Binns that the Armageddon Group were some 300 metres south of the junction. Cannon quickly redeployed his cordons with the aid of three of the helicopters. The sight and sound of the helicopters sent the Armageddon Group to ground while the net closed. Once the stop groups were in place, a poorly co-ordinated sweep began from the west, made more farcical by the lack of training of those involved and the incompatibility of the RRAF and BSAP radios, which meant the helicopters had to land to convey instructions. In the southwestern corner, where the two police lines started to converge, Pilot Officer David Becks had to do just this to prevent them shooting each other.

The action began when Petter-Bowyer, commanding the helicopter detachment, spotted what he thought was a policeman standing under a tree. Lacking an internal intercom, Petter-Bowyer, shouting, pointed out the man to his four policemen aboard. He was horrified when the response was one of his policemen firing out of the aircraft's window, his Sterling submachine gun's 9mm bullets passing through the spinning tilted blades. The enraged Petter-Bowyer deposited his passengers on the road before resuming his patrol over the area. Near the Hunyani River an African in a white shirt fired at him. Unarmed, flying Petter-Bowyer called in Hofmeyr to respond with his MAG. Due to inexperience, Petter-Bowyer was orbiting right and did not realize that he was on a collision course with Hofmeyr, who was banking left to bring his gun to bear. Petter-Bowyer was watching the man on the ground running with bullets kicking up dust around him, when Hofmeyr's incoming shadow alerted him to break away. Fireforce aircraft would adhere to the left orbit in future. Petter-Bowyer broke away. Hofmeyr's technician, George-Carmichael, fired 147 rounds in four bursts before bringing down his quarry just south of the power line. Such expenditure, Air Force Headquarters later ruled, was intolerable. In fact, given the lack of proper sights for deflection shooting, the amount of rounds fired was modest. Petter-Bowyer next spotted two figures in the bush off the old road but before he alerted Hofmeyr, they looked up and he saw their white faces. He waved them back to the road. They were detective inspectors Bill Freeman and 'Dusty' Binns who had driven up the road and plunged into the bush ahead of one of the sweep lines, anxious not to miss the fun. The sweep lines were also lucky enough not to hit each other as they converged through the bush firing enthusiastically. One excited group clustered around a dead body, unwittingly exposing themselves to two concealed insurgents. They were saved by Major Billy Conn, second in command the Rhodesian Light Infantry, who shouted a warning and then shot and killed an insurgent in the act of throwing a grenade. The grenade exploded, killing the terrorist's companion. Conn was there by chance. He had been driving through Sinoia with John Moore, his quartermaster-sergeant, en route from Salisbury to visit his troops at Chirundu.[54] Noticing the action and volunteering their services to Cannon, Conn and Moore had joined the sweep line. The line reformed and eliminated the remaining cadres.

The action was over by 13.55, six insurgents had been killed and one mortally wounded. ZANU had lost comrades Simon Chimbodza, Christopher Chatambudza, Nathan Charumuka, Godwin Manyerenyere, Peter (surname unknown), Ephraim Shenjere and David Guzuzu.[55] ZANU

---

[54] Interview with Major-General Leon Jacobs, 8 January 2007.

[55] BECM, RAAP, Army HQ, Incident at Sinoia: 29 April 1966; Lieutenant-Colonel Ron Reid-Daly, 'War in Rhodesia', in Al J. Venter (ed), *Challenge: Southern Africa within the African Revolutionary Context*, Gibraltar, Ashanti, 1989, p. 149; Interviews with: Petter-Bowyer, 24 March 1992 & Jacobs, 8 January 2007; Petter-Bowyer, pp. 127–133; Cowderoy & Nesbitt, pp. 43–48; Flower, pp 104–106; John Lovett, *Contact: Rhodesia at War*, Galaxie Press, Salisbury, 1977, p. 177; Peter Godwin & Ian Hancock, *'Rhodesians Never Die': The Impact of War and Political Change on White Rhodesia, c. 1970–1980*, Oxford University Press, Oxford, 1993, pp. 89–90; David Martin & Phyllis Johnson, *The Struggle for Zimbabwe: The Chimurenga*

promptly and predictably issued wild claims about killing 25 policemen, wounding 30 and shooting down two helicopters, lies which would only feed the myth. Washington Malianga, a ZANU spokesman in Lusaka, was nevertheless correct when he stated on 30 April that the 'battle' of Sinoia was "only the beginning". What ZANU gained immediately was that for the first time it received funds from the OAU. Petter-Bowyer was awarded the Military Forces Commendation for his coolness under fire and for his control of the operation.[56]

This incident had profound effects. The anger of the army at being excluded led to future operations being planned and handled by all arms of the security forces, controlled by Joint Operations Centres (JOCs) on which all services were represented. The gathering and use of intelligence was centralized with the SB reporting to the Central Intelligence Organization. In March 1977, all operations came under a single commander, Lieutenant-General Peter Walls, as Commander, Combined Operations (ComOps).[57]

Dissatisfaction with his own lack of preparation led Petter-Bowyer, when an instructor, to train his men to fly with maximum weight. He also stressed the need for map-reading skills. The Rhodesian Air Force came to demand that its pilots be capable of reading maps so well that they could navigate with a margin of error of 50 metres to find their target.

When the war intensified from December 1972, and white farmhouses were attacked in northeastern Rhodesia, there was a need for a quick-reaction force and helicopters obviously offered the quickest and most effective method of deploying one. It was apparent that a helicopter gunship could drastically aid the rapid elimination of the enemy.

War, Zimbabwe Publishing House, Harare, 1981, pp. vii & 9–12; Paul L. Moorcraft & Peter McLaughlin, *CHIMURENGA! The War in Rhodesia 1965–1980*, Sygma/Collins, Marshalltown, 1982, pp. 17 & 80–81; Barbara Cole, *The Elite: The Story of The Rhodesian Special Air Service*, Three Knights Publishing, Amanzimtoti, 1984, p. 27.

[56] Lovett, p. 177. This was not a medal but a small silver or bronze pick pinned to the ribbon of the General Service Medal. It denoted acts of bravery, distinguished service or continuous devotion to duty.

[57] Reid-Daly, 'War in Rhodesia' p. 149; Cowderoy & Nesbit, pp. 43–48; Flower, p. 106.

Chapter 9

Exploiting the Agility of the Helicopter

The wide speed range and high manoeuvrability at slow speeds enables helicopters to fly safely at low altitudes using hills and trees as cover. In counter-insurgency warfare, where there are no front lines, the choice can be made of the most concealed line of approach to the enemy. The noise of the engines will alert him, but the reflection of the sound of low-flying helicopters can deceive him as to the direction being taken. Helicopters can achieve surprise through 'contour-flying' (flying just above the treetops, following the contours of the land). They can confuse by using 'dummy' deployments of infantry stop groups and can, as the Rhodesians showed, employ a shock effect by putting down lethal fire.

The Alouette III lacked the aerobatic capabilities of more modern helicopters. Nevertheless, a Rhodesian Alouette, configured as the K-Car gunship, flown by Charles Goatley, with Beaver Shaw manning the 20mm cannon, had the distinction of shooting down a Botswana Defence Force Islander on 9 August 1979.[58] This happened when Goatley was covering a recovery by helicopters of troops from an external operation against a ZIPRA base at Francistown.[59]

The French had designed the Alouette II and III as purely clear-weather, daylight machines and therefore had not fitted the necessary night-flying equipment. For example, the principal compass was an E2A when, in other aircraft, it was a standby device. Consequently, the Rhodesian pilots would

---

[58] Conversation, Beaver Shaw, 13 November 1991.

[59] *Keesing's Contemporary Archives*, Keesing's Publications Ltd., London, 8 February 1980, Vol. XXVII, p. 30073

fly at night if they could see the horizon. Their take-offs and landings required only minimum illumination. The ability of the helicopter to fly at high or low altitudes and to decelerate rapidly, combined with the capacity for slow forward speed and vertical landing, allows it to be flown under marginal weather conditions.

The insistence on a minimum horizon was the product of an accident, which killed Air Lieutenant Guy Munton-Jackson and his technician, Flight Sergeant Peter J. Garden, on 17 January 1972. Munton-Jackson was flying one of a pair of Alouette IIIs en route from New Sarum, Salisbury, to Thornhill. The Alouettes were caught in a heavy thunderstorm and an attempt was made to bring them in on a radar approach. One Alouette succeeded but Munton-Jackson crashed. It was not known whether Munton-Jackson became disorientated but the Rhodesian Air Force decreed that its helicopters would only fly when a horizon was visible. The pressure of the war, however, would lead to that ruling often being ignored. In the interests of safety, the officers commanding No. 7 Squadron made every effort to enforce the ruling but precedents had been set and it was difficult to convince the ground forces that a casualty evacuation, for example, was impossible because of the lack of a horizon. Pilots found themselves in difficult and invidious positions but, as the war progressed, they began to transgress the rule less and less. They were so often in danger that they could not be persuaded to take even greater risks.[60]

The lack of direction-finding equipment had led Flight Lieutenant Peter Petter-Bowyer, in 1969, to stray northwest into Zambia, when flying a load of ammunition and weapons before dawn from Thornhill, Gwelo, to Binga, on the Zambezi River. Low on fuel and lost, Petter-Bowyer landed next to a farm near Livingstone to ask where he was. An African enlightened him but did not tell him that he had landed next to ZAPU's base at 'Freedom Farm'. This Petter-Bowyer did not discover until he had landed back in Rhodesia at the Victoria Falls and was told so by Air Vice-Marshal Harold Hawkins, the commander of the air force. The net result was that the Alouettes were fitted

---

[60] Interview, Petter-Bowyer, 24 March 1992; comments by Wing Commander Harold Griffiths, 8–9 April 1992.

with Becker radio direction-finders.[61]

Engine and rotor noise remained a problem because they betrayed the approach of an attacking force. On 5 February 1979, during Operation *Dabchick*, a raid on ZANLA's Mucheneze Camp across Rhodesia's southeastern border in Mozambique, the SAS call sign watching the camp heard the approaching AB205A Cheetahs eight minutes before they arrived. Because the insurgents were used to hearing light aircraft on reconnaissance missions, the Rhodesians often flew a noisy Aermacchi AL60-B2L Trojan, with its propellers set on fine pitch, ahead of the Fireforce to mask the sound of approaching helicopters. Peter Petter-Bowyer did this when leading Fireforce to camps he had discovered by his aerial reconnaissance. Engine noise was also used to confuse. As will be seen later, on Operation *Dingo*, in November 1977, a DC-8 jet airliner was flown over ZANLA camps near Chimoio to startle and then reassure their inhabitants that it was on a commercial flight to Malawi and to mask the approach of attacking Hunters. While the DC-8 rumbled away, the Hunters struck.

Crucial factors with regard to masking noise were terrain and wind direction. An approaching Fireforce would plot its flight to the target with these in mind. In 1979 a Fireforce would fly from Centenary in a southerly half circle, having to refuel on the way, to attack targets in the Sipolilo area in order to exploit an easterly wind to muffle its approach. The warning given by the noise of aircraft led to Fireforce commanders asking the personnel on an OP to warn them when the aircraft could be heard. Often the aircraft would be heard when they were four minutes from the target. Four minutes would give some insurgents time to run a kilometre and a half. Every minute wasted in finding them allowed them to flee a further 500 metres. This meant that the orbit of the searching aircraft had to be widened continuously.

Helicopters can be used to seize objectives which otherwise are out of reach of ground troops due to obstacles or enemy action. Helicopters permit the placement of firepower and troops virtually anywhere. For example, two Alouettes would carry a mortar team, one with the mortar tube and

---

[61] Petter-Bower, p. 107.

ammunition and the other the crew. Once the mortar was in action, the second helicopter pilot provided aerial spotting which produced hits on target often with the third bomb fired. This was practised from 1971 onwards but was not widely used because the 20mm cannon of the K-Car gave the Fireforces such potent and instant firepower. The helicopter crews were also used to observe and correct the fall of shot for the Rhodesian Field Artillery Regiment. Vic Cook did this at night, flying above Leopard Rock Hotel in the Vumba (on the eastern border of Rhodesia) and spotting for the 5.5in medium guns harassing Machipanda in Mozambique. The second shell hit the target.

Helicopters can land troops in tactical formations, ready for immediate action. They offer the battlefield commander the flexibility to deploy troops and their logistical support over a wide area, enabling him to exploit a tactical situation. Although the Alouette III lacked the modern 'mast-mounted' sighting equipment which allows a helicopter to remain in a hull-down position, protected from enemy observation and ground fire, it could still stand-off and wait for the moment to use its firepower to optimum effect.

Helicopters can also quickly retrieve troops, weapons and equipment from threatened positions or for rapid redeployment. With troop ladders, or close-to-the-ground hovering, troops can be landed or recovered while the helicopter remains in flight. Rhodesian Army units on external operations in Mozambique and elsewhere wore special 'Pegasus' harnesses, which afforded them 'hot extraction' literally from the grasp of a pursuing enemy. A hovering Alouette would lower a trapeze bar attached to the cargo sling capable of carrying four troopers. The troopers would hook on and the Alouette would lift them away. Once out of range, the pilot would land as soon as possible to allow the troops to board the aircraft. 'Hot extraction' could be an uncomfortable ride when the pilot, under fire, headed for the treetops and dragged the men on the trapeze bar through them. On occasion, a pair of Hunters would distract the enemy pursuers while the G-Car recovered its human load. The aircrews dreaded 'hot extractions' as they regarded them as the most dangerous of their flying duties because they involved flying deep into hostile territory, sometimes refuelling twice from fuel caches to reach their objective.

The ability to change the nature of the helicopter's load at short notice

Expoliting the Agility of the Helicopter

is a major asset. Cargo can be carried in an external sling and delivered to inaccessible spots. The Alouette in Rhodesia had a daily role of placing radio relay teams on high features, resupplying them and recovering them. Helicopters can bring back damaged and discarded equipment which otherwise would be abandoned or destroyed. The Rhodesian Alouettes and AB205As frequently brought back captured weapons from neighbouring territories.

The ability to extract wounded from any terrain meant that any injured serviceman could be evacuated usually within an hour and flown for treatment. This drastically reduced fatalities and boosted the morale of the ordinary soldier.

The helicopter, of course, has its limitations. It consumes fuel at a high rate, which limits its range and ability to carry loads. The load-carrying capacity decreases with increases in altitude, humidity and temperature. The Rhodesians compensated for this by establishing aviation fuel dumps at district commissioners' camps, rural police stations and the like. They also sent forward fuel in trucks and tankers with the 'land-tail' convoy of reinforcements for a deployed Fireforce so that fuel would be on hand. The 'land-tail' would intend to get to within ten minutes' flying time from the target to be of any assistance. If vehicles could not approach the area in time, Dakota aircraft would fly in fuel to the nearest airstrip or para-drop it close to the Fireforce target area. On external operations the Rhodesians would para-drop fuel into temporary administrative bases set up in remote areas of Zambia and Mozambique along the flight path of helicopters. In the case of the second phase of Operation *Dingo* in October 1977, two administrative bases were needed to allow the helicopters to reach Tembué camp in central Mozambique near the Malawian border. The personnel at these administrative bases had no easy task because the areas were full of trees and rocks among which the drums would land. There would be little time before the attacking helicopters would be returning to refuel and helicopters could not land near drums on pallets to which parachutes were still attached because of the danger of fatal entanglement. On Operation *Mascot*, an attack on the ZANLA camp at Maroro near Tembué in Mozambique in August 1978, the drums landed among a cluster of 'buffalo beans'. A stinging encounter with buffalo beans is never forgotten.[62] Indeed, what scared the bush-wise farmers in the Police Reserve PATU (Police Anti-Terrorist Unit) most were: firstly, buffalo beans; secondly, unpredictable rhino; and then terrorists. Elephants, carnivores, scavengers, buffaloes, crocodiles, snakes, scorpions and centipedes did not perturb them. The two-inch-long beans are readily shaken from their vines entwined in trees, covering anyone in range with fine, stinging hairs which can be best removed by plastering mud over affected areas and peeling it off when dried, taking the hairs with it.[63]

Weight and balance in a helicopter drastically affect the flight control and loads have to be carefully distributed. Helicopter operations are handicapped by poor weather conditions such as hail, heavy rain and winds in excess of 30 knots. Crosswind velocities of ten to 15 knots and downwind velocities above five knots will affect the selection of the direction of landing or take-off.

It is more fatiguing for pilots to fly helicopters than fixed-wing aircraft. The helicopter is unstable by nature and a loss of control for more than a few seconds spells disaster. The need to keep the right hand on the cyclic-pitch control column makes the holding of maps awkward. In the case of Rhodesia, the helicopter crews, unlike other aircrew, faced danger every time they flew their daily tasks. This in itself was wearying.

Helicopters require more maintenance than fixed-wing aircraft and have considerably less range. To reduce crew fatigue when refuelling in the bush, rolling drums and setting up hand pumps, the resourceful Peter Petter-Bowyer in 1968 designed a refuelling system based on a simple suction pipe using the Alouette's engine. This meant that the engine did not have to be switched off, relieving the crew of the problem of restarting. He asked for the device to be patented and the proceeds go to the Air Force Benevolent Fund but it was not and soon appeared in other helicopters elsewhere in the

---

[62] Interview, Petter-Bowyer, 24 March 1992.

[63] Jim Barker, *Paradise Plundered: The Story of a Zimbabwean Farm*, Jim Barker, Harare, 2007, p. 145.

world. Surprisingly, after 1972, the Rhodesian Air Force, however, adopted the South African practice of carrying a small petrol-driven two-stroke pump, despite the danger of carrying highly flammable petrol in action.[64]

While a transport aircraft can deploy 20 or more paratroops in a single drop, the Alouette and the AB205A helicopters can only bring in small groups. Transport aircraft, however, are less able to make a concealed approach, cannot land anywhere and lack the flexibility of the helicopter which allows quick modifications of its role to meet changing situations. The troop-carrying aircraft, of course, has a greater range but once its paratroops have been dropped, their quick recovery is difficult without helicopters to ferry them out. The Rhodesians, possessed of sufficient Douglas C-47 'Paradaks' (Dakotas configured for paratrooping), used them in combination with helicopter-borne troops both on internal and external Fireforce operations.

Other than Fireforce operations, the Rhodesian Alouette had many other roles to play. Its use in police urban operations led to all policemen being trained in correct procedures of boarding and leaving helicopters with full equipment. The Alouette inserted and supported the Special Urban Emergency Units (SWAT teams) of the police, lowering them by winch onto the roofs of buildings. In the rural areas, the helicopter's unique ability to fly at a reasonable speed close to the ground was exploited in tracking insurgents. Trained trackers could follow a track from the air, which meant that the enemy could be quickly contacted. At the instigation of Peter Petter-Bowyer, dogs were trained to follow a scent while its handler followed it in a helicopter. Dogs with radios strapped onto their backs, allowed the helicopter to follow at a discreet distance until contact was made.[65] Dogs, of course, need a scent to follow and scents are based on moisture. In the dry, hot conditions of the Rhodesian veld, scents did not last long after mid-morning, reducing the value of the tracker dog.

Aside from those allocated to the Fireforces, individual or pairs of Alouette III G-Cars were often positioned around the country to reinforce local law

---

[64] Petter-Bowyer, p. 107.

[65] Notes faxed to the author by Group Captain Peter Petter-Bowyer.

and order efforts. They would be sent to Rutenga in the southeast, to Inyanga barracks in the east or elsewhere to support the BSAP and army units. They had routine but vital tasks such as resupplying the radio relay teams positioned on high local features. They also assisted trackers by leapfrogging them along the tracks or stop groups into positions to cut off the quarry.

These pilots had to be remarkably ingenious. Their success rate was never high but the disruptive effect was enormous as the pilot and the troops, often reservists, harried the enemy. Vic Cook recalled the constant use of 'dummy' drops to confuse the enemy as he tried to convince ZANLA gangs that they were surrounded when in reality he was moving four men at a time.

In addition, the gangs that a single helicopter could confront were often large. Cook found himself alone in the air on 26 November 1976 when tackling 85 heavily armed ZANLA cadres on the eastern border. Led by John Barnes, flying a K-Car, and supported by Clive Ward in a Lynx, Cook and Bill McQuaid, an American, had flown two empty G-Cars from Mtoko (now Mutoko) northeast of Salisbury to deal with an incursion from Mozambique. The incursion was discovered when security forces detained African women who had been feeding a ZANLA group in the Inyanga North Tribal Trust. The group's stated intention was to attack Inyanga village and later the Grand Reef Airport, west of Umtali. Lacking available troops at Mtoko, the plan was that Cook and McQuaid would pick up men from a territorial company of the Rhodesia Regiment in the Inyanga area and deploy them. To find the enemy, the women were carried aloft to point out their position but nothing was seen. Eventually, Barnes had his technician, Mike Upton, fire speculative 20mm rounds into a wooded area and provoked a murderous reply from a heavy DshK 12.7mm machine gun and other weapons. The K-Car was hit but Upton continued to fire, killing five insurgents, until his MG151 cannon jammed. McQuaid's G-Car, flying close to the trees, was also hit. It was so severely damaged that he was just able to coax it to safety over a nearby hill before putting it down. The K-Car returned to Mtoko, leaving Cook and Ward in a running fight lasting seven to eight hours. Cook used the terrain to advantage, popping up from behind ridges to fire on the ZANLA insurgents, drawing hot responses. He moved the RR troops, in sticks of four, to cut off the enemy and late in the fight put all the MAG gunners in an ambush position. The Rhodesian effort was rewarded by the harried ZANLA cadres beating a retreat, leaving behind 14 dead (eleven killed by the aircraft) and two captured comrades. In deploying his troops, Cook had made so many hard landings that finally his left undercarriage axle broke. As the upper oleo strut, from which the wheel still hung, was banging against the helicopter's side, he hovered over a tree to allow his technician, Rory Perhat, to break off a branch from a tree and wedge it into the broken end. Cook flew back to Mtoko but obviously could not land without crashing and damaging the aircraft. The ground crew built a cradle of sandbags to support the G-Car and Cook landed gently on it, ending a long day.[66]

---

[66] Geldenhuys, p. 252, interview with the late Victor Cook.

Chapter 10

The Birth of Fireforce

Deployed in January 1974, the Fireforce enjoyed its first action a month later, on 24 February, after being called in by Lieutenant Dale Collett of the new counter-insurgency unit, the Selous Scouts.[67]

Fireforce was the logical development of the increasing practice of moving troops in helicopters in response to incidents and when tracking insurgents. This had happened in the early operations in the Zambezi Valley. In addition, the SAS had experimented in the Tete Province of Mozambique dropping paratroops in an attempt to envelop an insurgent group which had abducted a white civil servant in the Department of Lands, Gerald Hawkesworth, on 11 January 1973. The Rhodesians were also aware of the use of helicopter-borne infantry to surround insurgents by the French in Algeria. They had, in addition, been participating in similar operations in Mozambique with the Portuguese forces. This had led to operations in Rhodesia when an air strike would be followed by the arrival of helicopter-borne troops to sweep through the target. On 15 February 1974 Peter Petter-Bowyer, then commanding No. 4 Squadron and already a noted reconnaissance pilot, found a camp on a ridge near the Ruya River, north of Mount Darwin. Within two hours, flying a Trojan, he led an aerial attack on it with two Provosts, firing rockets and 330 .303in rounds and dropping four frantan bombs. Immediately afterwards five Alouettes landed 20 RLI troopers to assault the camp. The troops killed seven of their enemy. This proved the value of having a dedicated force standing by, waiting for action, instead of scratching around for whatever units were in the vicinity of such a sighting or incident. On 24 February Lieutenant Dale Collett, on one of the first

---

[67] Reid-Daly, *Top Secret War*, pp. 84–85.

Selous Scouts pseudo-terrorist operation, had his men convince the ZANLA contact men in the Kandeya Tribal Trust Land, north of Mount Darwin, that they were a new ZANLA group just arrived from Mozambique. The contact men revealed the presence of a dozen ZANLA cadres in a nearby camp. Collett did a close-in reconnaissance and then directed helicopter-borne RLI troops onto the target. The result was the largest kill, six dead and one wounded, since the start of Operation *Hurricane* 14 months previously.[68] The impersonation of ZANLA cadres by the Selous Scouts would become a major source of information to which the fledgling Fireforce would react. After the Selous Scouts had discovered a considerable ZANLA presence at Bobogrande Kraal in the Chiweshe TTL on 15 April 1974, RAR helicopter-borne troops were used to seal off the area. The commander of the troops, however, chose to be landed on a rocky pinnacle to direct the action, leaving the pilot of his Alouette and the Selous Scout, Mike Hardy, to attempt to assist them. The result was a frustrating ten killed and four captured out of 26 who had been present.[69]

The key ingredient of Fireforce, the K-Car, which doubled as a gunship and an airborne command post, was not yet in action. In March 1974 trials with the Matra 151 20mm cannon were successful but some minor modifications were needed to the gunship.[70] Trials continued in May, familiarizing the pilots with flying at the optimum height. Flak jackets were acquired. In June 1974, as has been said, a seat for an army commander was devised.[71] The frequent use of helicopter-borne reaction troops continued meanwhile.

On 4 June the first K-Cars went into action. Northeast of Mount Darwin, Peter Petter-Bowyer found a camp which an RLI Fireforce attempted to seal off. The three G-Cars landed three stop groups of four men each and left to ferry in more. The paucity of troops on the ground meant they killed only two insurgents while eight escaped. Rob McGregor's K-Car was in action

---

[68] PPH, Citations, 0886, Lieutenant C. D.; Reid Daly, *Top Secret War*, pp. 82-84.

[69] Reid-Daly, *Top Secret War*, pp. 102-103.

[70] BECM, RAAP, No. 7 Squadron, Rhodesian Air Force, diary, March 1974.

[71] BECM, RAAP, No. 7 Squadron, Rhodesian Air Force, diary, June 1974.

twice northeast of Mount Darwin. In his first sortie, his gunner, Henry Jarvie, fired 19 20mm cannon shells at a hut from which insurgent fire had pinned down the Fireforce troops. Two insurgents died, including a sought-after leader. Later in the day, John Annan's K-Car fired 25 20mm shells in an attack on a camp ten miles east of Rushinga in northeastern Rhodesia. The attack was fruitless due to problems experienced by the call sign on the ground in directing the Fireforce in fading light.[72] Six days later, Fireforce deployed again only to find the quarry had left a camp an hour previously.[73]

By 21 June two Fireforces had been established: one at Centenary and the other at Mount Darwin. The Mount Darwin Fireforce, Support Group, 1RLI, was in action immediately, killing 15 insurgents and capturing five wounded men. On 3 July, attempting to contain some 25 ZANLA cadres east of Mount Darwin, George Wrigley's K-Car killed seven and wounded one. The others fled before the stop groups could shut off their escape routes. Such actions would be a weekly pattern and later a daily one as the war intensified.

---

[72] Petter-Bowyer, pp. 234–235.

[73] Prop Geldenhuys, p. 207.

Chapter 11

The Development of Fireforce

Fireforce went through three phases of development: Phase One: 1974–1976, Phase Two: 1977–1979 and Phase Three: 1979–1980.

Phase One: 1974–1976
At first there would be a preliminary briefing before take-off if the Fireforce were not needed immediately. If called out to a sighting, the K-Car would be talked onto the target by personnel manning an OP. The problem of parallax, the difficulty of judging the relation between the position of an aircraft in the sky to that of a target on the ground, often caused delays which afforded the enemy time to escape. To solve the difficulty, the K-Car gunner would drop a smoke grenade over the approximate area of the target to allow the OP unit to use the smoke as a reference point to redirect the K-Car to the target. The K-Car would then pull up to its optimum orbiting height of 800 feet and put down 20mm cannon fire to annihilate the enemy or at least to drive him to ground to be dealt with by the ground troops. The G-Cars would fly in a wider prearranged orbit, waiting for orders from the Fireforce commander to land their four-man stop groups to seal the escape routes. This was a somewhat rigid, slow and cumbersome procedure and was at times fruitless because the enemy had fled. It was soon realized that the aircrew had to look outside the circle constantly as the insurgents covered the ground at an astonishing, adrenaline-fuelled rate of 500 metres a minute.

Phase Two: 1976–1979
In this period, changes drastically improved the success ratio. The Fireforces were given Dakota-loads of paratroops to reinforce the helicopter-borne stop groups. The briefing would normally be held at the refuelling stop en route to the target. This was done to save time and because by then the men of the

OP might have crucial information on further enemy movement or the lack thereof. By 1977 it was realized that the K-Car needed to fly in from behind and over the OP to be able see what the observer was seeing and therefore waste no time in finding and marking the target with a white-smoke generator. The K-Car would pull up and fire on the enemy. To avoid any delay when waiting for orders from the Fireforce commander, the G-Cars were given some autonomy. As the G-Cars arrived, they would fly directly to prescribed stop positions on the escape routes and orbit them. If the G-Car crew spotted the enemy, they could land their stop groups without reference to the Fireforce commander. If the enemy were not spotted, there would be no landing which meant the troops remained airborne for quick deployment elsewhere. There would also be an alternative plan—Plan Alpha. The Fireforce commander would simply state "Plan Alpha" and the G-Cars would deposit their stop groups on the predetermined stop positions which meant minimum delay in bottling up the enemy. Once the escape routes were sealed, the Fireforce commander would order the dropping of his paratroopers to sweep the area, driving the quarry into the open where the 20mm cannon could deal with them or into the ambushes of the stop groups. The achievement of Phase Two was that the quick positioning of stops often trapped the enemy.

Phase Three: 1979–1980

In 1979, not only did the Fireforces expand to as many as six but also 'Jumbo' Fireforce came into being due to the constant availability of G-Cars. They were available because the forces deployed on external operations at last could exploit the longer-range and greater troop-carrying capacity of the AB205A 'Cheetah' helicopters (Hueys). The Jumbo Fireforce comprised two Fireforces, giving it two K-Cars, eight G-Cars, a Dakota and a Lynx, often with the support of No. 1 Squadron's Hunters. When the Fireforce was seven minutes out from the target, the two K-Cars would accelerate towards the target. Once directed onto the target, the K-Cars (being used like tanks on the battlefield) would immediately attack without pulling up, seeking to kill or at least traumatize the enemy. The Fireforce commander might bring in the supporting jet aircraft immediately to use their devastating firepower to lower the enemy's morale further. The effect would be to 'stabilize' the situation. Those insurgents who survived would go to ground. The stops would be in position quickly and the paratroops would follow to sweep the area. Actions that used to take an entire morning or a day thenceforth were often over in an hour. The commander of Support Commando, 1RLI, Major Nigel Henson, recalls tackling and killing 22 insurgents at 06.00. By 07.00 his Fireforce was in action against ten more and, having dealt with them, was in a third contact by mid-morning.

In this last phase, the exclusive role of the RLI was Fireforce, scoring formidable tallies of kills. Their manpower limitations, naturally, meant that other units continued in the role. Fireforce Delta, based in Wankie, for example, continued to be manned by the national servicemen of 1 (Independent) Company, RAR bolstered by the paratroops of 2RAR. In late 1979, in the south of Matabeleland, South African Parabats, under Rhodesian command, served clandestinely in the role, using South African aircraft.

In the period after the election of Muzorewa's government in April 1979 until the ceasefire in December 1979, the Fireforces killed 1,680 insurgents of which, 1 Commando, RLI, killed 450, 2 Commando 350, 3 Commando 410, and Support Commando 470.

Major André Dennison's fine A Company, 2RAR, by contrast, killed 403 insurgents in the period September 1977 to July 1979. Perhaps there is no comparison but, in nine years of campaigning in Malaya, the British SAS killed 108 of their enemy.

Major Henson, who commanded Support Commando for two and a half years (1977–1979), was called out 111 times. Of these call-outs, 77 were in 1979 and 68 of them resulted in contacts. In 1979, only one in six call-outs were unproductive 'lemons' and this he attributes to the full deployment of the Selous Scouts on the OPs and their professionalism as well as to the experienced dedication to their task of the aircrews and his men. There had always been a high rate of unsuccessful call-outs but many of them were the product of the Fireforce not spending time combing the area. In many cases, if nothing appeared, despite the sighting by the OP unit, the Fireforce would depart. Of course, it was often ordered away by the JOC to a new target.

Chapter 12

Fireforce Tactics

An infantry company of the RAR or a commando of the RLI would be designated as a Fireforce at a forward airfield for six weeks or sometimes several months. By 1977 all regular infantry were trained paratroops and would in turn be deployed by helicopter or parachute or brought in as reinforcements from the vehicles of the 'land-tail'.

There were a number of considerations as to where the Fireforce base would be sited in an operational area. As it needed only a 950-metre-long airstrip in the bush capable of taking a Dakota, there were a variety of geographical options for choosing a site for a base. As its role, however, was to react to incidents as they arose and, as intelligence played such a role in Fireforce operations, it was important to base the Fireforce close to the JOC and its major intelligence agencies such as the SB.

For a Fireforce to trap and eliminate ZANLA or ZIPRA insurgents, their whereabouts had to be discovered. This was accomplished by a variety of means.

One method was the use of the 'road runner' or a bugged portable commercial transistor radio. The BSAP SB left 'road runners' lying around in likely areas, or on the shelves of rural stores, so that the insurgents would pick them up and take them back to their unit. The 'road runners' were also supplied to double agents, such as the Reverend Kandoreka (a close colleague of Bishop Muzorewa and supporter of ZANLA), who were providing the insurgent gangs in the field with supplies.[74] The 'road runner' contained a homing device which was activated by the radio being switched off and could be picked up by an aircraft's homing equipment. The sound of an aircraft

---

[74] Interview with Lieutenant-Colonel Ron Reid-Daly, 3 November 1991.

would prompt the insurgents to switch off the radio, ironically, therefore transmitting their position to the aircraft. Once 'road runners' were known to be in an area, the Rhodesian Air Force would send up a helicopter or a Lynx with a Beckerradio direction-finder to detect the signals. A second Lynx, flying on a parallel or opposing course, would secure second co-ordinates. The criss-crossing of the direction-finding by the two aircraft would secure a likely area of a kilometre-square into which a Fireforce would descend. Numerous insurgents were taken by surprise by the unheralded arrival of a Fireforce.[75] The lack of precision in target identification and the absence of an OP to talk the Fireforce on, however, meant that many would escape.[76] There was a more sinister version of the 'road runner', one containing a charge which exploded when the radio was switched on.

Fireforces would react to incidents such as ambushes, farm attacks and sightings. They would be called in when trackers or cross-graining patrols made contact with the enemy. As the Rhodesian Army patrols comprised half-sections of four men called 'sticks' (each stick possessing a VHF radio and an MAG machine gun), it was of great comfort to know that reinforcement in the form of the formidable Fireforce was merely an hour's flying time away.

Intelligence gathered by the SB, and other agencies such as the Selous Scouts, through their pseudo-gang operations, often resulted in Fireforce action. Information would come from a Selous Scout detachment, disguised as ZANLA and 'operating' with them, that there would be a ZANLA meeting at a particular time and location. Fireforce would then arrive at the meeting. While Selous Scouts-generated information produced results, intelligence generally tended to be dated at least and too often produced 'lemons' as the quarry had moved on.

An important method of detecting the insurgents was by aerial reconnaissance. By the early 1970s a number of pilots, flying Provosts, Trojans, Cessna 185s and later Lynxes, became highly skilled. When

---

[75] J. R. T. Wood, *The War Diaries of André Dennison*, Ashanti Publishing, Gibraltar, 1989, p. 185 fn. 7.

[76] Interview with Major Nigel Henson, 3 November 1991.

commanding No. 4 Squadron in the early 1970s, Peter Petter-Bowyer taught himself and his pilots the telltale signs of human habitation in the bush. In particular, he became adept at spotting 'crapping' patterns in the wilder parts which betrayed the presence of hidden camps. He noticed a series of radiating short paths from a dense clump of bush, for example, and discovered that they were made by insurgents going about their daily functions. The level of success of reaction to these sightings and interpretations was satisfactorily high. The most skilled of these was Kevin 'Cocky' Benecke who was possessed of the most phenomenal eyesight and could see men on the ground under the shaded cover of trees when others could not. The air force's medical officer, Doctor Brian Knight, discovered that Benecke had a minor visual defect in the green-brown range which enabled him to distinguish dark objects in shade which people with normal eyesight could not see. This meant that, when Benecke summoned Fireforce to a camp, it was guaranteed to be occupied.[77]

Selous Scouts' pseudo operations were combined with the practice of establishing clandestine OPs overlooking known infiltration routes, villages of sympathizers and sources of food and water. Analysis by the Rhodesian Intelligence Corps (RIC) in early 1979 would show that the highest ratio of success by Fireforces was achieved when the unit manning the OP called them in. The OP personnel would observe the pattern of life and detect anything out of the ordinary. This could be an unusual amount of cooking taking place or lines of women carrying cooked food into groves of trees and other hiding places. The skilled OP operators were the Selous Scouts but all units were given this task with greater or lesser success. The problem of the OP was to remain undetected by the local population and it took considerable skill at concealment. Once he was certain there was an insurgent presence, the commander of the OP would summon Fireforce. Success depended on his skill at map-reading so that he could direct Fireforce with precision to the target.[78]

---

[77] Notes, Peter Petter-Bowyer.

[78] BECM, RAAP, RIC Research Report No. 30 'Examination of Contact Reports Received by RIC by 17 March 1979'.

Chapter 13

Commanding the Fireforce

The pressures upon a Fireforce commander were intense, particularly as his area of responsibility would be vast and his resources few. Furthermore, he was acting in an environment, an aircraft, which was not his. Not being one of theirs, the air force would be eyeing him particularly critically. His troops demanded kills as a measure of success. The personnel on the OPs would evaluate the quality of his reaction to their sightings.

The burden of command was heavy and his position a lonely one. Successful Fireforce commanders had to be men of imagination, precision and high and varying skills.

The Fireforce commander had a multitude of responsibilities. The choice of a site for his base was a first consideration when he assumed command. If satisfied by its strategic position, he would review the base's tactical position in terms of its vulnerability to attack, its defences, alarm system and the protection of the aircraft. The Rhodesians protected their aircraft from ground attack at the forward airfields by housing them in revetments made out of fuel drums filled with sand, topped by fences and roofed by loosely strung heavy diamond-mesh wire netting. The sand in the drums would absorb any bullets or shrapnel. The fences would detonate any incoming rockets, negating the effect of their hollow-charge explosive heads. Finally, trials showed that mortar rounds would not detonate on the netting. In the course of the war, no aircraft were damaged by mortar bombs fired at the aircraft pens.[79] The Fireforce troops needed also to be reasonably and securely housed, close to the aircraft for speedy call-outs.

The Fireforce commander would be concerned with the communication

---

[79] Anon, p. 30.

systems, the radios that were so vital for his operations, and efficacy of the joint operations room. In the last three years of the war, the RIC was able to supply maps on which the up-to-date information he would need for his briefings had been overlaid.

He had to achieve a close rapport with the senior pilot who would fly him in the K-Car and command the supporting aircraft. Indeed, most Fireforce commanders, particularly new ones, had much to learn from the experienced pilots flying them who had seen so much and had worked with so many Fireforce commanders.[80]

Both men required the active support of the forward airfield (FAF) commander, the SB representative, and the technicians and base personnel.

The Fireforce commander had to know what other forces were deployed in his area, their tasks and how many would be available as reinforcements for Fireforce actions. He could never have enough men.

All related equipment had to be checked. Of crucial importance was his aircraft helmet and headset. The helmet was not just worn for protection. It muffled the engine noise, making it easier to hear transmissions. Just as vital were the K-Car's intercom and radios, his means of conversing with the pilot and the troops on the ground. Thus, the pressel (transmitting) switch of the commander's microphone and the headset's connections would be tested. A spare headset would be carried in case his failed (as it sometimes did), forcing the pilot to command the battle. The G-Cars had headsets for all stick leaders so that they could follow all developments while in the air. The troops' VHF sets, particularly the telehand sets, had to be serviceable as more than one operation was hampered by faulty radios transmitting continuous carrier signal which blocked all other transmissions. The K-Car would carry two A63/A76 VHF radios, one a spare for the ground troops and the other for the commander if he had to disembark in the event the K-Car being forced down by ground fire or mechanical malfunction or if it had to depart for refuelling. In the K-Car with him, he would carry the radio codes and, in particular, the daily Shackle code. In action, some Fireforce commanders

---

[80] Binda, p. 181.

would wear gloves to prevent their thumbs from blistering through the repeated use of the pressel switch. All would don flak jackets to protect them from fire from the ground when orbiting above the battle.

The K-Car would also carry a spare FN 7.62mm rifle to replace any of those of the troops which malfunctioned. The pilot, the technician and commander would have with them their personal FN rifles and the pilot a 9mm submachine gun (normally an Uzi) for use if they found themselves forced to land. The technician also would fire his rifle if his MG151 cannon malfunctioned. Aircrew, on occasions, joined in the fight on the ground after being shot down. Air Lieutenant Michael Borlace and his technician, Michael Upton, did just that on 27 March 1976.[81] For that eventuality, the Fireforce commander was fully equipped with rifle and webbing (containing ammunition, grenades, compass, medical kit, and rations), binoculars, a map, a pen and notebook.

The School of Infantry checklists reminded the Fireforce commander that he could not be distracted by airsickness and had to carry the necessary pills if susceptible. Airsick commanders would have short careers because the K-Car pilots would not tolerate them. The checklists ordered him to have with him a talc board and chinagraph pencils. In practice, however, he would write crucial information on the aircraft's Perspex windscreen. He would pack in a briefcase complete with 1:250,000 and 1:50,000 map coverage of the operational area. The maps had to be correctly folded and indexed so that the correct one could be quickly found in the air. He would pencil in numerous sets of co-ordinates to avoid having to unfold the whole map in the gusty cockpit.

The Fireforce commander would ensure the K-Car was carrying small yellow smoke grenades for target marking. After 22 September 1976, the first deployment of paratroops on the Fireforce (24 SAS paratroopers dropped in the *Repulse* area to reinforce helicopter-borne troops in an action which killed nine insurgents[82]), the commander would check that all the helicopters

---

[81] Prop Geldenhuys, p. 101.

[82] Log Book of Parachute Descents with Special Air Service of Lieutenant G. A. Wilson, entry 21, 22 September 1976.

had on board large smoke generators for marking dropping zones for the paratroopers and indicating wind direction. The generators were locally produced and were designed by what Peter Petter-Bowyer describes as 'an American pyromaniac' whom local industry found for him. The generators produced dense white smoke for three minutes.[83] The G-Cars would also carry hoods for captives and plastic body bags for fatalities

Each Fireforce 'stick' of four comprised: a junior officer, NCO or senior trooper, armed with an FN rifle and equipped with a VHF A63/A76 radio; two riflemen, one with first aid training; and a machine gunner carrying a MAG 7.62mm machine gun. The MAG weighed 29lbs and its normal load of ammunition almost as much but its heavy weight of rate of fire often won a fight and it was highly prized. Indeed, when they could, the stick commanders would draw two MAGs for their section. If a night ambush were contemplated, and if weight were not a consideration, the stick would be issued with claymore anti-personnel mines. As they had to move rapidly over the ground, the troops dressed in camouflage T-shirts, shorts and light running shoes or canvas hockey boots. They would carry little else other than ammunition, grenades, water, medical kits and basic rations. Short sharp action meant that they usually returned to base by nightfall for redeployment in the morning. If they expected to set a night ambush after the contact, regulation camouflage denim uniforms or one-piece jumpsuits would be worn and light sleeping bags carried. The white troops blackened their skins to reduce the visibility of their skins.

Because it was crucial to the Fireforce commander to be able to see the positions of his troops on the ground (to avoid sticks firing on each other and more), methods of visual identification would be adopted. Troops would use strobe lights (if available), heliographs, orange 'Day-Glo' or white panels, smoke and white phosphorus grenades, or flares. A marking flare capable of travelling a kilometre was still not available by May 1979 despite requests.[84] Often the troops would simply wave the white back of their maps. One

---

[83] Petter-Bowyer, p. 276.

[84] BECM, RAAP, Contact Reports, Contact, 6 May 1979.

Support Commando stick leader, 'Messus' Moore, was asked to reveal his position by displaying his map. He replied that, as he had forgotten his map, he would hold up his cigarette packet. His Fireforce commander, Major Nigel Henson, surprised to see the upheld packet, transmitted the query: "Stop 1, are they Kingsgate or Madison [two Rhodesian cigarette brands]?"

Most vital was the teamwork within the K-Car. The Fireforce commander would take every opportunity to discuss methods, ideas, latest tactics and lessons learnt with his K-Car pilot. They would find time to practise their roles in the air. As the pilot had the aircraft to fly as well as co-ordinating the movements of all the other aircraft involved, and the air gunner/technician sat well back behind the 20mm cannon, it was the Fireforce commander who could concentrate solely on spotting the enemy. Sitting on the left side front rear-facing seat, he was well positioned to do so. Thus, he could play a crucial role in target identification, for example. This had to be rapid and precise. On spotting the enemy, he would call a course correction—"Hard left!"—while pointing out a feature close to target and ordering the gunner to fire off two rounds. He would then correct the gunner's aim from the strike of the shells.

Fireforce commanders and pilots, of course, had much on their minds and very often keen-eyed, experienced gunners saw the enemy first. Following the course of the action intensely, the gunners would prompt the Fireforce commander on orientation, the whereabouts of stop groups and other details.

The Fireforce commander had also to understand what the aircraft could and could not do—particularly how long it could fly. Such matters were, of course, the responsibility of the pilots but experience taught the commanders to keep an independent eye on the fuel gauge, as they had to base their plans on the aircraft's endurance.[85]

Before any action, there was much initial planning to be done and the Fireforce commander, his second in command, his officers, the senior and other pilots, the FAF commander and the operations and intelligence officers

---

[85] Interview with Major Nigel Henson, 3 November 1991.

would meet to review the current intelligence, discuss activating call-outs, and general modus operandi.

The air force personnel would explain how many aircraft were available. The use of the Dakota would be reviewed including the height and number of para-drops, the drop procedure, the radio channel for drops, emergency drills and the use of 'wanker' sticks (men dropped purely to collect the parachutes as sanctions made their replacement costly and difficult). The 'wanker' sticks, however, often found themselves in action when fleeing insurgents broke through sweep lines. The Lynx and its weapons would be discussed. Command, briefing and spare radio channels would be allocated. The Fireforce commander would select an alternative VHF channel for the ground troops so that the command net did not become cluttered. This channel could be monitored by the accompanying Lynx on its second radio. Aircraft formations to be used en route to targets, the masking of aircraft noise and associated problems would be examined. Colour codes would be selected: for example, 'G-Car 1' might become 'Yellow 1'. The arrangements for refuelling and re-arming would be laid down. Finally, the equipment to be carried by the aircraft would be reviewed—the smoke generator, spare VHF radios, spare rifles, body bags etc.

The Fireforce commander would describe the stop details, namely the call signs, their equipment and the dispersal of medics and trackers among the sticks. He would deal with the accompanying vehicle convoy, the 'land-tail', selecting its commander, escorts, medics, trackers and the 'second wave' reinforcements. There was a tendency for everyone at a Fireforce base to volunteer for the 'land-tail' but essential functions at the base could not be neglected, men had to be fed on their return and much more.

There would be a general briefing of all personnel on call-outs, briefings and methods. This briefing would include: the OP's talk-on; target marking (using the Lynx or the K-Car to deliver smoke or the firing by the OP of Icarus and Very pistol flares, the 37mm SNEB rocket marker (the shoulder-held launcher which Petter-Bowyer had developed} or Miniflares; target correction; the marking of the position of the troops (by orange Day-Glo or white panels or by waving the white back of maps or the use of smoke grenades, flares, instant light, heliograph); smoke signals (blue for casevac, orange for radio failure, white phosphorus for a contact and the white generator for a dropping zone). Details of the casevac procedures would be given along with the proximity of hospitals or mobile resuscitation units. The use of air support, tactics in general and post-contact procedures would be discussed.

The meeting would review the recovery of the helicopter-borne troops, the paratroops, their parachutes, the second-wave sticks and the dead and captured insurgents, their weapons and kit. The information required from an OP for a call-out would be laid down—the map number; the OP's position or 'locstat', call sign, radio channel; the locstat of the enemy, their numbers, weapons, dress and current activity. The Fireforce would want to know: if the OP could still see the enemy or where they were last seen; their escape routes; the nature of the terrain; possible landing and drop zones; the compass bearing from the OP to the target; the proposed method for the OP marking the target; and the locstats of other OPs or nearby troops.

If time allowed, all Fireforce and base personnel including the Rhodesian Air Force would practise the immediate action on call-out, familiarizing themselves with emplaning, deplaning and other drills. The troops would practise fire and movement, movement across open ground, cave and obstacle clearing and other tactics. They would zero their weapons on the range and practise quick-reaction snap-shooting on jungle ranges (bush ranges with targets that sprung up).[86]

Out in the field, hidden in the hills, would be the OPs of the Selous Scouts or of other Rhodesian Army or BSAP units. Once a target was spotted, the OP commander would report to his unit, supplying his locstat, call sign etc. He would stand by, observing the enemy while Fireforce was activated. Everything would be done with a minimum of words for efficiency. The OP commander would be ready to update his report for the incoming Fireforce.

At the call-out, sometimes initiated by the sounding of a klaxon, the troops of the Fireforce would follow the rehearsed procedures. In the early stages,

---

[86] Arnold, pp. 236–237.

the reaction times were as little as four minutes. It was soon learnt that time taken in briefing was more valuable than speed and the Fireforce would take ten minutes to get airborne. It still depended on the nature of the reported incident. The first question asked was always: "How much time have we got?" Often, there was no choice but to get the aircraft airborne and to plan on the way to the target. In addition, a refuelling stop on the way would provide time for a methodical briefing.

The Fireforce commander and the K-Car pilot would make a quick appreciation of the OP's report and devise a plan to preserve the element of surprise and annihilate the enemy. The K-Car pilot would examine the route and consider various options such an initial air strike by the Lynx (some Fireforces preceded attacks with a Mini-Golf bomb) or, if the target warranted it, by Canberras or Hunters, to stun the enemy and drive them to ground. He could make use of noise cover by sending a Trojan or Lynx ahead of the helicopters. Alternatively the entire Fireforce could arrive simultaneously from different directions or the K-Car would accelerate to arrive over the target first to allow the Fireforce commander to orientate himself, confirm the OP's information and to reassess his appreciation before his troops arrived. The Fireforce commander and the K-Car pilot would select the optimum killing zones into which the enemy could be driven. They would identify escape routes, such as thickly bushed riverbeds and ravines (also known as re-entrants) and propose to block them by stop groups. To contain the insurgents they would plan dummy drops of stop groups by the G-Cars and the positioning of their assault troops near enough to the target to be able to exploit the shock of the initial air strike by the K-Car or fixed-wing aircraft. They would select a rendezvous for the aircraft to meet the vehicles of the 'land-tail'. This would be as close as possible to the target area and in a sufficiently open area to allow two or more helicopters to land, refuel and re-arm simultaneously. To avoid casualties and the loss of vehicles, the 'land-tail' would often only approach on tar roads to preclude the danger of landmines. The Fireforce commander and the K-Car pilot would select dropping zones for the paratroopers with a view to bringing them quickly into the action. They would plot the position of other security forces in the area to avoid firing on them and to employ them, perhaps, on the periphery of the battle to intercept any fugitives. They would review their firepower requirements. Teargas to drive insurgents out of difficult places, such as caves, could be carried. Finally, they would consider having a deputy Fireforce commander carried in the Lynx to co-ordinate the resupply by the 'land-tail', using the aircraft's second radio, and to relay any developments to the JOC. The Lynx pilot, himself, might be used for these tasks.

The plan would be presented at the overall briefing. The K-Car pilot would brief the aircrews and operational staff on the aircraft involved, air strikes, routing plans and refuelling, the attack directions, the drop plans, refuelling and recovery arrangements. Of particular importance were the direction of the orbits and the pilots' awareness of each other in the aerial melee over the target area. Collisions were an ever-present danger and happened on occasions. On Tuesday, 2 January 1979, during Fireforce action near Selukwe, the K-Car, flown by Air Lieutenant Ray Bolton, descended to bring its 20mm cannon to bear on insurgents in thick bush and collided with the G-Car of Air Lieutenant Kerry Fynn who, having sighted and engaged the target, was talking him onto it. Both pilots were concentrating on the target and Bolton could not see the G-Car hidden below and behind him. Fynn and his technician, Corporal Anthony Turner, were killed as were the Fireforce commander, Captain Douglas Havnar of Support Company, 10RR, and the K-Car gunner, Sergeant Brian Cutmore. Bolton survived when the K-Car landed upside down, straddling the lips of a ditch, which allowed his head to escape hitting the earth.[87]

The Fireforce commander would brief his stick and the second-wave commanders on the plan and the known details of the target such as the map reference, the estimated numbers of enemy, their dress, weapons and current activity. He would allocate the radio channels and appoint the helicopter-borne stop groups, giving them simple call signs such as 'Stop 1', 'Stop 2' and placing Stop 1 in G-Car 'Yellow 1', Stop 2 in 'Yellow 2' and so forth. Because the aircraft would orbit left, as their weapons were mounted on the

---

[87] Interview with Major Barrie Jones, 14 September 1990, Geldenhuys, p. 157.

left, he would describe the counter-clockwise sequence of the landing of the helicopter-borne troops in the order of their stop numbers so that he could remember where they were and everyone could recall easily who was on their flank. He would point out the dropping zone for the paratroopers and give details of the deployment of the second wave and the equipment and ammunition to be carried by the 'land-tail' vehicles. If he assigned a stick the task of searching for the enemy, the Fireforce commander had to ensure that it contained trackers or that he could reinforce it with trackers.

The Fireforce commander would remind the stick commanders of pro-words to be used such as those for indication of position: "Stop 1. Show map" or "Show Day-Glo", "Throw smoke". Another order would be "Go 2 for uplift". A most important statement was "Terrs visual" because too often a stop group would catch sight of the enemy but, when trying to report the sighting in a normal manner, would be told "Wait, out" by a busy Fireforce commander fielding a multitude of calls.

The stick leader would in turn brief and inspect his men, checking the number and condition of their loaded magazines, machine-gun belts, grenades, field dressings, rations, water bottles, sleeping kit. He would share out: the spare radio batteries, the pangas (machetes) and toggle ropes (for use in difficult country). He would check the medic pack and detail who would carry it. He would show his men where he carried his morphine. If he and his men were whites, they would apply camouflage cream. He had to ensure that all controlled stores, such as compasses and binoculars, and his codes were secure and waterproof. He had to remember that he had a clean white backing to his map, that he had written on his hand his radio call sign for the day, 'Stop 1'. He would detail his men's positions in the G-Car and remind them of the emplaning and deplaning drills. The MAG gunner would take the rear right seat to give the aircraft additional firepower if the pilot requested it, to keep enemy heads down when landing, for example. The riflemen would not fire from the aircraft because, unlike the MAG, the FN ejected the spent cartridge case 45° upwards—into the spinning main rotor blades or out the open doors and rearwards into the tail-rotor. The aircraft guns for this reason ejected into chutes. The riflemen would take the

Commanding the Fireforce

front seats, leaving the stick commander the middle rear seat and the spare headset so that he could follow the progress of the deployment and receive his orders.

The paratroop commander would detail the dropping sequence of the four-man sticks. He would remind his men to watch where the rest of them landed and prescribe where they would regroup.

All stick leaders would remind their men of: tactics, formations, the drills for clearing kraals and caves, for crossing open ground, the use of fire and movement, what to do if the radio failed, arcs of responsibility, hand signals; action on contact with the enemy, the use of smoke, of grenades, target indication. Men would be assigned the searching of bodies and warned against looting. Chains of command within the stick would be established and everyone would be apprised call signs and radio channels.

The stick commander had to remember to answer his radio first time, (in Support Commando failure to answer immediately would draw the response of a cannon shell from the K-Car which would have an electrifying effect—it would also confirm that a radio was not working). He had to remember that he was responsible for the success of his men. If he had 'wankers' or useless members in his stick, he was to report on them to his troop or platoon commander. He was warned: "If you don't brief your stick properly you will have your arse kicked."

Once the Fireforce was airborne, the responsibilities of the K-Car pilot were navigation, communication with OP, including the OP's talk-on to the target, and the co-ordination of helicopters and fixed-wing aircraft. The Fireforce commander and the K-Car pilot would consult the OP for an update on the target, review the plan and brief the stick commanders and the G-Car pilots over the radio on any changes. If the call-out had been rapid, this might be the first briefing or the first briefing might be held at the refuelling stop en route. The Fireforce commander would order the drivers of the vehicles of the 'land tail' to move the second-wave sticks to their rendezvous point to be ready for uplift by the G-Cars. He would remind the sticks how they would be able to recognize the K-Car, by its rotating beacon or by letters or numbers on its belly or by the height, 800 feet, at which it flew. The G-Cars, by contrast, would be hugging the treetops to present as fleeting a target as possible.

The Fireforce commander would establish communications with other ground forces to confirm what call signs were in the area, their position in relation to the target, and who was the senior call sign.

When reviewing his selected dropping zone, the Fireforce commander would ignore a few trees on the dropping zone, but heavily wooded areas could be dangerous, as were rocks, sloping ground, power lines and 15-to-20-knot winds.

On arrival, the OP commander would brief the Fireforce commander on the latest information and talk the K-Car onto the target, indicating it with a tracer bullet or other means.[88] Hearing the K-Car approaching behind him, Ron Flint, a somewhat flustered 5RR reservist sergeant, pointed his pencil flare projector, depressed his radio handset's pressel switch, and barked: "Marking target NOW!" The pencil flare refused to ignite. Coolly observing Flint's agitated efforts, the K-Car pilot laconically commented as he rose above him: "Don't worry; I can see where your finger is pointing." On another occasion, great difficulty was experienced in spotting the smoke of the target-marker (the adapted 37mm SNEB aircraft rocket), because the Selous Scout on the OP, an African sergeant, had marked the target so well that the rocket was embedded in the chest of one of the enemy, dampening the smoke. The Selous Scouts did not, however, always mark targets because they would be acting as pseudo gangs and wanted to appear to the local Africans as the survivors of any contact.[89]

Because his own disorientation was a real possibility as the K-Car orbited, the Fireforce commander would select the most prominent feature to the north of the target as a main reference point and orientate himself with the target area's hills, rivers, roads, maize fields and habitation and the direction in which the terrain and rivers ran. He had to orientate his troops because paratroopers, in particular, usually had difficulty in seeing the target area. All

---

[88] Plasticized OP cards in the author's possession.

[89] Interview, Petter-Bowyer, 24 March 1992.

troops had to know where they were and who was on their flanks.

Pulling up to 800 feet the K-Car pilot would control all aircraft movements and the use of their weapons.

As overall commander, the Fireforce commander bore the responsibility for the success of the engagement and would make his final tactical appreciation, bearing in mind the speed of the enemy's flight in acting to prevent their breakout. He would want to 'stabilize' them to ensure their elimination or capture. The insurgents could be expected to 'bombshell', fleeing in all directions, to make it difficult to track them. Thus, dummy drops would be used to convince them that there was no way out of the trap. The orbiting aircraft would deter them from moving across open ground and a pre-planned fixed-wing air strike or a burst of K-Car cannon fire could stun them into immobility. The Fireforce commander, however, would not deposit his men on the ground until he had a clear idea of the nature of the target.

The Fireforce commander would quickly confirm with the K-Car pilot where the stops should be placed before the K-Car pilot directed the G-Cars to their landing zones. The commander was trained to draw a sketch-map of the contact area and to mark on it the positions of stop groups. When a stop group moved, he would re-mark its position on the sketch-map to avoid contacts between friendly forces. Firm control from the air by the Fireforce commander was crucial so he had to remain over the target area at all times, changing to another aircraft if necessary. He also had to be ready to react speedily to new situations. If the insurgents escaped, he had to deploy his trackers early to establish the direction of the enemy's flight so that he could leapfrog his stops ahead to cut them off.

Once his men were on the ground, the Fireforce commander had to recognize their problems and assist them with them. If a stick's radio failed, and if he could not land to replace it with the spare, he would ensure that the stick did not move and therefore not blunder into a killing ground. As soon as he could, he would combine them with a stick which had communications. He was not to set his sticks impossible tasks nor expect them to take independent action. He had to ensure they remained properly orientated and appreciate their difficulties in crossing terrain and not overestimate the speed at which they could move. It was not advisable merely to give men on the ground the grid reference of their objective. It would be preferable to describe the route or have the K-Car fly towards and over the objective. Anything that could assist the sweep and stop troops would enhance their performance.

It was vital to brief the sticks continuously by radio on what the enemy was doing. This did not mean that the Fireforce commander had to provide a running commentary because the stick leaders would be monitoring to the radio transmissions. The Fireforce commander was, of course, in a superb position to guide his men as he orbited the target at 600–800 feet.

In quiet moments the Fireforce commander would have the K-Car orbit the sticks to confirm their positions and to reassure them. The sight of the supporting fixed-wing aircraft striking the target was always good for morale as was the rapid evacuation of any casualties by the stand-by G-Car. Prompt congratulations from the K-Car for any success also boosted morale and preserved the vital intimate trust between the commander in the air and the men on the ground.

There were fundamental rules with regard to tactics which could not be broken. The first was never to sweep uphill, always downhill. The second was never to advance into the sun, and the third was always to sweep from cover into open ground, never from open ground into cover. Major Henson recalls that, whenever he broke these rules, he lost men, five in all. In addition, he would only break the rules because time was pressing, the sun was setting and there was no time to get his men round to the top of a hill to start a downward sweep.

It was imperative that the Fireforce commander appeared and sounded calm and confident. Any displays of impatience, excitement or anger would only rattle inexperienced sticks and prompt a mutinous reaction from experienced ones slogging through thick bush in the heat. Calm tones and clear, crisp explanations had a sobering effect on jittery ground forces. This was particularly important when dealing with African forces whose command of English was often imperfect and who might not understand brisk, terse commands, and mistake 'affirmative' for 'negative', for example. The Fireforce commander would allow time for aircraft noise to diminish before

Commanding the Fireforce

speaking to a stick and would arrange that aircraft orbits were sufficiently high and distant to avoid deafening the stick leaders. An important duty was to control radio transmissions to prevent the channels becoming cluttered with unnecessary 'waffle'.

The Dakota bearing the paratroops would have flown to an IP (intermediate point) four minutes away, out of earshot, to await developments. The Fireforce commander would use his helicopter-borne stops and his firepower to stabilize the situation by immobilizing the enemy. Once he had stopped their flight and driven them to ground, he would bring in his paratroops to sweep the area, driving the enemy into the open (the favoured killing ground of the aircraft) or into the waiting stop groups.

Before ordering the dropping of his paratroops, the Fireforce commander would ask his K-Car pilot or the first available G-Car one to confirm that the landing zone was suitable, bearing in mind the vulnerabilities of the paratroopers—exposure to enemy fire in the air, cross-winds and rough landing zones. Because the Dakotas lacked radio altimeters, the G-Car might establish, by landing, the precise altitude of the LZ and transmit the QNH setting for the Dakota's altimeter, using as a datum the standard pressure setting of 1013.2 millibars which would allow the Dakota crew to achieve the correct dropping height. The K-Car or G-Car would mark the centre of the dropping zone with smoke and talk the Dakota in.

Where possible, the troops would be dropped facing the contact area, in the direction of their sweep. It took considerable skill by the pilots to ensure that the paratroopers landed on the often small dropping zones. It required positioning the Dakota precisely, flying at 90 knots with its flaps set half down, the speed required to create sufficient slipstream to open the canopies. For mutual defence and for efficiency it was essential that the paratroops landed close to each other. To expose the paratroops to ground fire for the shortest time, the prescribed height for a drop was 500 feet above ground and never lower than 450 feet. The parachute used, however, was the D-10 American parachute which required 250 feet to open fully which meant drops were often made from 300 feet so that none of the paratroops drifted off the dropping zone. The Fireforce paratrooper carried little more than his weapon, ammunition, grenades, and water and thus was not as heavily burdened as usual in military jumps. Nevertheless, the advice of 'rather too high than too low' was sound. On 17 February 1978, paratroops from A Company, 2RAR, were dropped at 300 feet due to an error of 150 feet in the setting of their Dakota's altimeters. Their commander, Major André Dennison, estimated that the canopies were open for only nine seconds before the men struck the ground mercifully unharmed.[90] John Hopkins, late of the RAR, maintains that in fact the RAR probably held the record as 16 paratroopers commanded by Lieutenant 'Blackie' Swart jumped on 9 October 1978 at something less than 300 feet, through a pilot error. They hit the ground only as their parachutes filled fully. None were killed in the fall but eight were injured, four of them seriously. Four days later, an MAG gunner died from a fatty embolism being released into his bloodstream.[91] The RLI, however, would dispute the record as in 1979 a Support Commando drop near Rushinga left 14 of 22 men injured when their Dakota maintained a constant height over rising ground. The first men went out at 250 feet and the last at two hundred.[92]

On landing, the paratroops would marry up using a separate radio channel and once in formation, report 'ready' to the Fireforce commander. They would lay out an identification panel and face the contact area. The Fireforce commander would attempt to observe the landing so that further indications were not necessary and await the radio call from the senior paratrooper that everything was ready. The parachutes would be picked up after the contact by the closest troops or a 'wanker' stick would be dropped to collect and guard them.

The Fireforce commander also had to brief all fresh troops on their way to the contact. While doing all this, he would keep the JOC informed so that it could plan its wider reaction. He would bring in his reinforcements as soon as possible as there could never be enough troops on the ground

---

[90] Wood, *The War Diaries of André Dennison*, p. 191.

[91] Hopkins MSS, John Fairey to the author.

[92] Interview, Henson, 3 November 1991.

and he might need a reserve on hand for decisive action or for unforeseen eventualities. When the reinforcements arrived the K-Car would lead their helicopters through the pattern of landing zones, ordering each G-Car to deploy its troops when the particular landing zone was flown over, to maintain the order of the deployment.

The enemy had to be attacked immediately and never left alive and unattended. Sweep lines were to disarm and to frisk the captured or dead immediately to ensure no one escaped by feigning death. It was essential that the first captured insurgent was flown out immediately for proper and prompt interrogation to learn precisely how many enemy were in the area, what their intentions were, where they intended to rendezvous, their destination, last base and name of their leader. The Fireforce commander would take care not to compromise the identity of captives because in many cases they would be 'turned' and recruited into the Selous Scouts for pseudo operations. Therefore to protect their identity as ZANLA or ZIPRA cadres, the forces would mask them with hoods and keep them out of sight of the locals.

The Fireforce commander would make maximum use of fire from the aircraft into known insurgent positions. He would use the G-Cars for flushing fire so that the K-Car remained on station above the target. In any case, the machine-gun ammunition of the G-Cars was far less expensive and easier to obtain than the 20mm shells of the K-Car. When insurgents were trapped, the sticks would often call for fire from the K-Car or other aircraft after marking the enemy position with a smoke grenade and pulling back.[93]

The sweep lines also used flushing fire or 'Drake' shooting. The troops would fire several rifle shots, normally a 'double-tap', into bushy thickets to drive out anyone hiding there. To promote accuracy and conserve ammunition, the Fireforce troops fired their FN Rifles on semi-automatic rather than automatic fire. Their opponents, by contrast, fired widely and on automatic. Long bursts from an AK rifle lift the barrel towards the sky. Rhodesian fully automatic fire was restricted to the MAG machine gun,

---

[93] Arnold, p. 235.

often laying down sustained fire to cover the outflanking of the position by the remainder of the stick.[94]

Most contacts were with small groups so the Fireforces usually outnumbered their opponents. Later in the war the Fireforces were outnumbered when confronting groups of 100 or more but were never defeated, never driven away. Much of the reason was the presence of air power, particularly the K-Cars and their 20mm cannons. Part of it, however, was the discipline and training of the Fireforce troops and their marksmanship.[95]

Once the contact was over, the Fireforce commander would have the target area thoroughly searched so that all abandoned equipment, ammunition and spent cartridge cases were picked up. This was done for gathering ballistic evidence, intelligence and other purposes and to deny ammunition to any escaping survivors. If there were time, the Fireforce commander would list the identity of the bodies, weapons and equipment. Even if no enemy were encountered, careful sweeping was required so nothing of intelligence value was missed.

The next step was the recovery of all the dead and captured insurgents and their arms and equipment by helicopter or vehicle. Parachutes and the troops on the ground would likewise be recovered. In many cases, the troops would be ferried to the Dakota waiting on a nearby strip or to the vehicles of the 'land-tail'. If necessary, troops would be left to ambush the contact area or to follow up on the tracks of the fleeing survivors. The Fireforce commander, before leaving the area, would brief them on their task, directing them to ambush positions and assigning radio channels for communication with him and the Fireforce base. He would ensure they were adequately equipped for their task and, in particular, that they had the correct maps. If they were needed for fresh sightings the next morning, they could be recovered by helicopter with relative ease. It was not necessary for them to return to their base every time.

Once everyone was back at base, the Fireforce commander would debrief

---

[94] Arnold, p. 235.

[95] Arnold, p. 235.

those involved. He would review the course of events: the initial briefing; the accuracy of the original intelligence; the choice of routes to the target and the formations flown; the calibre of the talk-on and the identification by the OP personnel and their subsequent action; the noise factor; the possible compromise of the OP; actions by local inhabitants; the difficulties presented by the insurgents' choice of base; the efficacy of air weapons; the performance of the stops, the para-drop, the sweeps and action on contact; casualties and their subsequent extrication; reasons for insurgents escaping and their numbers and the efficiency of the recovery and any subsequent action. The Fireforce commander would transmit his comments to the unit which had supplied the men for the OP.[96]

The permanent Fireforces were drawn from the ranks of the white regular soldiers of the Rhodesian Light Infantry, who achieved the highest kill-rate with relatively small loss to themselves, the black professional soldiers of the Rhodesian African Rifles who also achieved enviable results and, in 1978, the national servicemen of the independent companies. There were, of course, occasions when territorials and reservists provided men for the Fireforces. Many impromptu Fireforces were created from troops present at a base. Michael Borlace recalls a contact on 23 March 1977 in which Ian Harvey (later Air Vice-Marshal Harvey of the Zimbabwe Air Force) had cobbled "a couple of scratch sticks together of cooks and bottle-washers" from Rutenga.[97]

The troops assigned to the Fireforces could expect to find themselves called out two or three times a day. Many call-outs produced 'lemons' because the intelligence was faulty or the insurgents had disappeared into the bush or had melded into the local population or because the Fireforce troops did not spend enough time searching the area of a sighting. With deployments in the Rhodesian bush war as long as six to ten weeks, the strain would often tell. Three operational jumps in a single day was something no other paratrooper

---

[96] 'Do's of the Airborne Commander' & 'Don'ts of the Airborne Commander', 'List of Do's and Don'ts of K-Car Commander by Captain E. F. Evans—RAR', and other photostats in author's possession.

[97] Geldenhuys, p. 126.

had ever been expected to do. Indeed paratroops of other nations had endured nothing like it. In 1950–1952, for example, the French colonial paras in Indo-China proudly boasted of their 50-odd combat jumps.[98] This was more than double the 24 operational jumps which the two vaunted French Foreign Legion para battalions made between March 1949 and March 1954.[99] Altogether, the French were to make over 100 combat jumps, the Americans only made one major combat jump in Vietnam. The Americans, of course, were by then making tactical use of helicopters.[100]

---

[98] Leroy Thompson, *Dirty Wars: Elite Forces vs the Guerrillas*, David & Charles, Newton Abbot, 1988, p. 84.

[99] Leroy Thompson, p. 116.

[100] Leroy Thompson, p. 77.

Chapter 14

A Day in the Life of an RAR Soldier

An anonymous recollection, entitled 'A Day in the Life of an RAR Soldier' and published in Michael Quintana's *African Defence Journal*, gives a first-hand glimpse of a Fireforce action from the stick leader's perception. He wrote:

'At 04.00 hours the sentry woke me up from outside my *basha*. I got up and rolled up my sleeping bag and fastened it to my webbing. I then took my towel and washed my face with cold water before taking my rucksack and kit bag to the stores truck for safekeeping. It was still dark but it was one of those nights when the moon decides to set before the sun comes up and as a result it was still hanging up there in the western sky. So by the light of the moon I checked my area and satisfied myself that the CSM [Company Sergeant-Major] would have nothing to discuss with me when I came back—you see he does not normally like to see bits of paper lying around. By the time I finished checking my section area the east was red, the time was 0445 and I took my mug and went to the kitchen. The cook was in a good mood despite the early hour and I got a full mug of tea.

'The whole platoon was there in the kitchen this morning and they were talking in low tones, joking and laughing quietly. We had been briefed the previous evening and everyone knew what he was going to do today but it seemed that no one was worried at all.

'At 0500 hours we were summoned to the Ops tent for more orders (us NCOs that is), and were briefed for ten minutes. Helicopters were allocated to the various sticks and soon after we poured out of the tent to brief our sticks. As the sun peeped over the horizon we were sitting in our helicopters. The pilot in our helicopter switched on his engine and after a whining noise the huge rotors started to turn, as if they really did not intend to, then gathered momentum until they were a blur. All five choppers were now roaring and

Chapter 14

slowly, one by one, lifted off from the side of the bush airstrip. Soon we were up and circling the base camp waiting for the rest of the choppers to lift off. I looked down below me and saw amid the reddish-brown dust the last of the helicopters lifting off.

Before long the choppers were off to the north of our base camp. Up there the wind was cold and crisp and it blew on my face from the open side of the chopper. Down below the trees were green and some turning grey, but they all seemed to be of identical height, so that looking down one was reminded of those advertisements for carpets. I have enjoyed riding in a helicopter ever since I was a recruit and right now I was enjoying myself looking out there below as the world slid past. Then I got to thinking. I thought of the first day that I came to Methuen Barracks, six years previously and of the jumble of years between; it was hard at times. There were moments of happiness and sorrow and I thought of people, faces of soldiers that had come and gone, faces of men who are and were a family that is one of the greatest and happiest of all families, the RAR.

'I was brought back to reality by the banking of the choppers; we were now in an area with a lot of small *gomos* [hills] and we were flying at treetop level along a small river with water and a lot of reeds. There were quite a lot of rocks on the riverbed itself, but the sand showed here and there. The suspected base camp was down near a waterfall next to a big rock and I saw the leading helicopter circling around the rock. All round the area were very thick bushes and tall trees and slightly right and away from the river was a field. Already, one of the choppers had landed there while we were circling.

'The pilot indicated a clearing in the field and gave the sign that he was going to land and went down. As soon as the chopper touched down we spilled out, took up a defensive arc and cocked our weapons. I was ordered via the radio to join the other stick and moved down the river on both sides. I took the left bank and the other stick commander the right and we moved forward. Behind us could be heard the deep bark of the FN and the clatter of the AK. Occasionally a stray bullet went cracking above us. I thought any moment now a bullet would find its way into me, but the sound of the crack indicated that the bullets were well to the left.

A Day in the Life of an RAR Soldier

'Then, without warning, automatic fire broke out about 75 metres in front of us. The bullets hit the rocks in the riverbank and the ricochet made an ugly sound. We opened fire from both sides of the bank—aimed fire was impossible because we could not see anyone, but only hear the firing. A grenade exploded, though I was not sure who threw it—our people or the terrorists. Ahead of us someone shouted an order, and I guessed the direction of the voice. Already we were moving from cover to cover in bounds towards the firing. The fire from the terrorists was not very effective because it was not aimed very well. As we neared the place where the firing came from, it stopped. We carried on firing and this time we were running as fast as we could. Reaching the place we spread out, then, as I was passing a large tree, I saw a man lying face down. I stopped to take a look—he was dead, his AK carbine lying by his side. Here and there in the thick bush were well-concealed hideouts and it seemed they were empty. We went quickly through the area, then fanned out into all-round defence. By that time I was sweating a lot. I reported on my radio and sent a searching party into the camp, then I checked for any casualties in my stick. There were none. The ammunition state was satisfactory.

'When the searching party arrived they reported two dead terrs [terrorists] and about seven packs in the base camp. There were four hides for three men each. I reported this and was told to carry on sweeping until I met a stick that had been deployed 400 metres farther on. There was a stick and I was informed that it was making its way into the area of my contact.

'Then, as we prepared to advance, firing broke out about 300 metres ahead of us and we were told to lay an ambush on the riverbank and we quickly did that and waited. It was getting very hot now as the sun was halfway up, and sweat kept blinding me. I used my face veil to wipe my face.

'Then, as the firing stopped ahead of us, one of my men kicked me and showed the thumbs-down sign and pointed, and sure enough, moving along the riverbed were two terrorists. One had an RPD [machine gun] and, the other an SKS [rifle], and they were walking in the shallow water to lose tracks. We waited until they were parallel to us and let go. They never had a chance. Leaving two men covering me, I took the other man and went to pull the bodies from the water and recover the weapons. The helicopter came in to take away the bodies.

'By that time the day was high and the sun was very hot now. We were told to rest as the trackers were looking for tracks. Other sticks arrived and a follow-up was initiated. After a thorough search of the contact area, we were told to go to the clearing. The helicopters arrived. We ran to them keeping our heads well down because, you see, every soldier who is in love with his head bends down in order to keep it where it belongs.

As the chopper lifted off, I looked down in the contact area, now so peaceful. We climbed high and sped back to base, the wind blew on my face and I thought this was the life—never a dull moment. Then I got to thinking of that cold beer waiting for me and I settled back. Today is good and gone, tomorrow out of sight.'[101]

---

[101] Anon, 'Day in the life of an RAR soldier', *Africa Defence Journal*, Harare, September, 2000, passed to the author by Michael Quintana in September, 2000.

Chapter 15

Fireforce Writ Large: Operation *Dingo*:
Airborne Assault in Mozambique: 23-27 November 1977

Startling in its innovation and daringly suicidal, Operation *Dingo* was not only the Fireforce concept writ large but the prototype for all the major Rhodesian airborne attacks on the external bases of Rhodesian African nationalist insurgents in the neighbouring territories of Mozambique and Zambia until such operations ceased in late 1979. It would produce the biggest SAS-led external battle of the Rhodesian bush war.

Dingo had been first proposed in late November 1976[102] in response to a major build-up of ZANLA forces in central Mozambique. The Rhodesian security forces accumulated growing evidence in late 1976 of two vast camp complexes. The first was at 'New Farm', 17 kilometres north of Chimoio, a small town 90 kilometres directly east of the Rhodesian border city of Umtali and on the main road and the railway to the port of Beira on the Indian Ocean. The second was 200 kilometres from Rhodesia's northeastern border near Tembué, northwest of the town of Tete on the Zambezi River.

ZANLA had learned not to present a concentrated target after the first devastating Rhodesian attack in August 1976 on one of their external bases, Nyadzonya Camp, sited close to the Rhodesian eastern border on a tributary of the Pungwe River in Mozambique. A Selous Scout motorized column had driven into the camp and killed 1,500 inmates. Consequently, New Farm comprised 17 camps scattered over 25 square kilometres of rolling, heavily wooded terrain. The camps combined the farmhouse, buildings and sheds of a previous Portuguese farmer with hundreds of traditional African circular thatched pole and *dagga* (mud-daubed) huts, larger square thatched structures and numerous tents and shelters. The camps were defended by intricate

---

[102] Petter-Bowyer, p. 306

patterns of trenches, dug-in anti-aircraft weapons and an early-warning system of towers for sentries with whistles. New Farm housed ZANLA's operational, administrative and logistical headquarters with offices for Mugabe, Josiah Tongogara, the commander of ZANLA, and his deputy, Rex Nhongo (the *nom de guerre* of the now-retired Lieutenant-General Solomon Mujuru) and their staff. This headquarters controlled ZANLA's activities in Mozambique's central Manica Province, distributing reinforcements and supplies for operations in eastern and southeastern Rhodesia. New Farm was also the main ZANLA training centre, receiving both recruits brought out of Rhodesia and personnel returning from advanced training in Tanzania, China and Ethiopia.

Extrapolating from a photograph of 700 men on the rifle range, the Rhodesians estimated that, in late 1976, New Farm held some 4,000 recruits, trained insurgents, convalescents and others. Tembué was thought to have a couple of thousand more being trained and re-equipped.[103]

Despite these tempting targets, the plan for Operation *Dingo* was almost a cliché when ComOps finally accepted it in mid-November 1977. Despite repeated rejections, it had been persistently updated and resubmitted by its authors: Major Brian Robinson, Officer Commanding, C Squadron, SAS, his close friend and colleague, Group Captain Norman Walsh, Director of Operations of the Rhodesian Air Force, Major Mick Graham (Robinson's second in command), and Captain Scotty McCormack (the SAS intelligence officer).[104] They gained the impression, as Group-Captain Peter Petter-Bowyer puts it, that their proposals "frightened those who listened because they were madly daring and, potentially, incredibly dangerous".[105] Consequently, they could be forgiven if they were somewhat startled when suddenly the Commander of ComOps, Lieutenant-General Peter Walls, not only accepted *Dingo* but also gave it immediate priority. This meant he

---

[103] PPH, Operation Order, Op *Dingo*; Robert MacKenzie, 'Fast Strike on Chimoio', *Soldier of Fortune*, January 1994, p. 41.

[104] The planning team included Captain Grahame Wilson.

[105] Petter-Bowyer, p. 306

Fireforce Writ Large:
Operation *Dingo*: Airborne Assault in Mozambique: 23-27 November 1977

postponed his just-sanctioned Operation *Virile*, an intended demolition of bridges in Mozambique by the Selous Scouts. Walls had no choice in this matter because the Rhodesian Air Force lacked sufficient aircraft to support both operations simultaneously.

What had changed with regard to *Dingo*, and what Robinson and Walsh could not know, was that Ian Smith, the Rhodesian prime minister, needed a quick and heavy blow struck against his main antagonist, Robert Mugabe. Smith had tired of the negotiations on the Anglo-American plan and he chose instead to seek an accommodation with the internally based nationalists, Bishop Abel Muzorewa and the Reverend Ndabaningi Sithole, and a number of important defectors from ZANU and ZAPU. One ZAPU defector was the veteran nationalist and insurgent, James Chikerema, whom Muzorewa immediately made the first vice-president of his political party, the United African National Council (UANC).

Betraying something of the direction about to be taken, Chikerema announced in Salisbury on Monday, 21 November 1977, that he was going to London to tell the British Foreign Minister, David (now Lord) Owen, that the British government was "treacherous", "gutless' and "toothless" and had "no meaningful role in this [Rhodesian settlement] exercise at all because they have no powers to enforce anything they want on this country". In particular Chikerema accused Britain of "treacherous" support for Joshua Nkomo.[106]

With credible nationalist figures like Chikerema on board, and because, for the first time, Smith was prepared to grant unconditional universal suffrage, it seemed that this initiative stood a chance. Such a settlement, Smith hoped, would be internationally recognized and thereby end the UN sanctions. If both internal African support and international recognition were secured, the hand of the Rhodesian government would be strengthened in its fight against the threatened Marxist takeover by Mugabe or Nkomo.

Although Smith wanted to weaken Mugabe for political reasons, he was also reacting to the intensified ZANLA effort to foment revolution across the northeastern, eastern and southeastern areas adjacent to Mozambique.

---

[106] *Keesing's*, 28 April 1978, Vol. XXIV, p. 28942

They had not just penetrated the albeit-mined border but also their FRELIMO hosts, having declared themselves to be at war with Rhodesia, were intermittently harassing Rhodesian security forces' border positions and civilian settlements. The daily news was peppered with reports like that of Saturday, 19 November 1977, when the small village, Vila Salazar, on the southeastern border, was subjected twice to ineffective mortar and small-arms fire. Fire was returned from Rhodesia on one occasion. There was neither damage nor casualties.[107] Zambia, the host of ZIPRA, was not to be left out. Two days later, on Monday, 21 November, security forces at Kanyemba were subjected to an unprovoked hour-long attack by mortars, rifles and heavy machine guns across the Zambezi River from Zambia.[108]

In response, the SAS and Selous Scouts harassed the Mozambican lines of communication in the Gaza, Manica and Tete provinces. The Selous Scout commander, Lieutenant-Colonel Ron Reid-Daly, was inspired to propose Operation *Virile* after destruction of the railway line to Maputo in mid-1977 had forced ZANLA infiltrators to march and porter their supplies over long distances en route to the border. His aim was to terminate ZANLA's transport by road of infiltrating groups from New Farm to Espungabera on the southeastern Rhodesian border by demolishing five major bridges. His proposal, however, was not greeted with much enthusiasm by ComOps, the CIO or the Rhodesian Ministry of External Affairs. Established policy permitted 'hot pursuit' operations but action against Mozambican economic and communication targets like bridges was not. What was feared was that the spectacle of rebel Rhodesia bullying its desperately poor, newly independent neighbour would invite fresh international pressure. Rhodesia, it was argued, had enough on its plate. Reid-Daly was not surprised because previously, in 1975, he had been refused permission to destroy eleven Mozambican bridges. Persisting, he eventually convinced ComOps that the loss of the bridges on the Espungabera road would severely hamper ZANLA particularly as the onset of the heavy summer rains was imminent and alternative routes could

---

[107] *Rhodesia Herald*, 23 November 1977.

[108] *Ibid.*

Fireforce Writ Large:
Operation *Dingo*: Airborne Assault in Mozambique: 23-27 November 1977

be easily ambushed and mined. D-Day for *Virile* was set for Sunday, 20 November 1977.[109]

Ian Smith, however, changed his mind and chose to attack ZANLA's two main bases, New Farm (Chimoio) and Tembué because the alternative, a long-range air strike against the ZANLA training base at Mgagoa, near Iringa in central Tanganyika,[110] posed so many diplomatic problems.

On Saturday, 19 November 1977, Smith sanctioned *Dingo* and Walls suspended Operation *Virile*, halting the Selous Scout column at Hot Springs, south of Umtali. Needless to say, Reid-Daly felt that, if the Selous Scouts could have attacked on schedule, *Virile* would have complemented *Dingo* rather than hindered it.[111]

Dingo remained a considerable gamble because the troops parachuted in would have to be recovered by air and a major loss of aircraft could put hundreds of men in jeopardy. This was made all the more hazardous by a decision of the Mozambican leader, Samora Machel, to afford ZANLA a degree of protection. As a measure of control of his guests and to share with them logistical services, transport and mutual defence, he had stationed elements of the Mozambican Army, *Forças Populares para o Libertação de Moçambique* (FPLM) personnel, at all ZANLA camps, and positioned additional FPLM units close by, some armed with the Russian SAM-7 light anti-aircraft missile. In the event of an attack, the SAM-7 teams would fan out along the roads near camps to intercept the Rhodesian Air Force's irreplaceable aircraft.

While the ZANLA camp at Tembué was some distance from a large FPLM camp, New Farm was better protected as it was close to the relatively developed Umtali–Beira road-rail corridor. Apart from its resident 100-man FPLM garrison, New Farm was supported by an FPLM platoon with mortars and anti-aircraft weapons at Vanduzi, half an hour away by road. The FPLM Brigade Headquarters at Chimoio, an hour away, had 400 FPLM troops, 100

---

[109] Reid-Daly, *Top Secret War*, pp. 283–285.

[110] Cowderoy & Nesbit, pp. 75–76.

[111] Reid-Daly, *Top Secret War*, p. 285.

soldiers of the Tanzanian People's Defence Force (TPDF) and 100 Russian advisers with SAM-7s and other anti-aircraft weapons, mortars, anti-tank guns, armoured cars, T-34/T-54 tanks and transport vehicles. Directly west and close to the Rhodesian border, at Vila de Manica, 90 minutes away from New Farm, was an FPLM battalion headquarters with 725 FPLM and 110 TPDF troops, SAM-7s, anti-aircraft and anti-tank guns, and vehicles. Even closer to the Rhodesian border, at Machipanda, two hours away, was an FPLM company with SAM-7s, anti-aircraft guns and vehicles.[112]

Furthermore, ZANLA must have felt safe from ground attack because both New Farm, 90 kilometres from the Rhodesian border, and Tembué, 200 kilometres, were well out of range of Rhodesian Alouette IIIs. On Operation *Eland*, the attack on Nyadzonya, the Selous Scouts had managed with great daring to move a column of vehicles over a disused border road just north of Vila Manica on Sunday night, 8 August 1976. They had driven through to Vanduzi and then north to catch ZANLA at Nyadzonya unawares just after dawn. New Farm, however, was not in such a remote area or as close to the border. Experience had taught on subsequent operations that, if surprise were essential, a motorized column or even movement on foot was soon discovered. Thus any surprise assault had to be airborne and had to include troops to win the day because there were insufficient numbers of strike aircraft available to deliver a crushing blow. Time and hard usage had reduced the Rhodesian Air Force's front-line strength to nine Hawker Hunter FGA9s, a handful of de Havilland Vampire FB9s and T11s, and four to five English Electric Canberra B2s. These, however, could still wreak telling damage, exploiting the new locally made bombs, before the troops, supported by helicopter gunships, completed the task which included gathering vital information and capturing hard-to-come-by items like the SAM-7 missile.

A major problem, of course, was the recovery of troops. A laden Alouette III could fly to New Farm but could not get back without refuelling and Tembué was three times that distance.[113] The G-Car could fly for some 45

---

[112] PPH Op Order; Cole, p. 171.

[113] Interview, Petter-Bowyer, 24 March 1992.

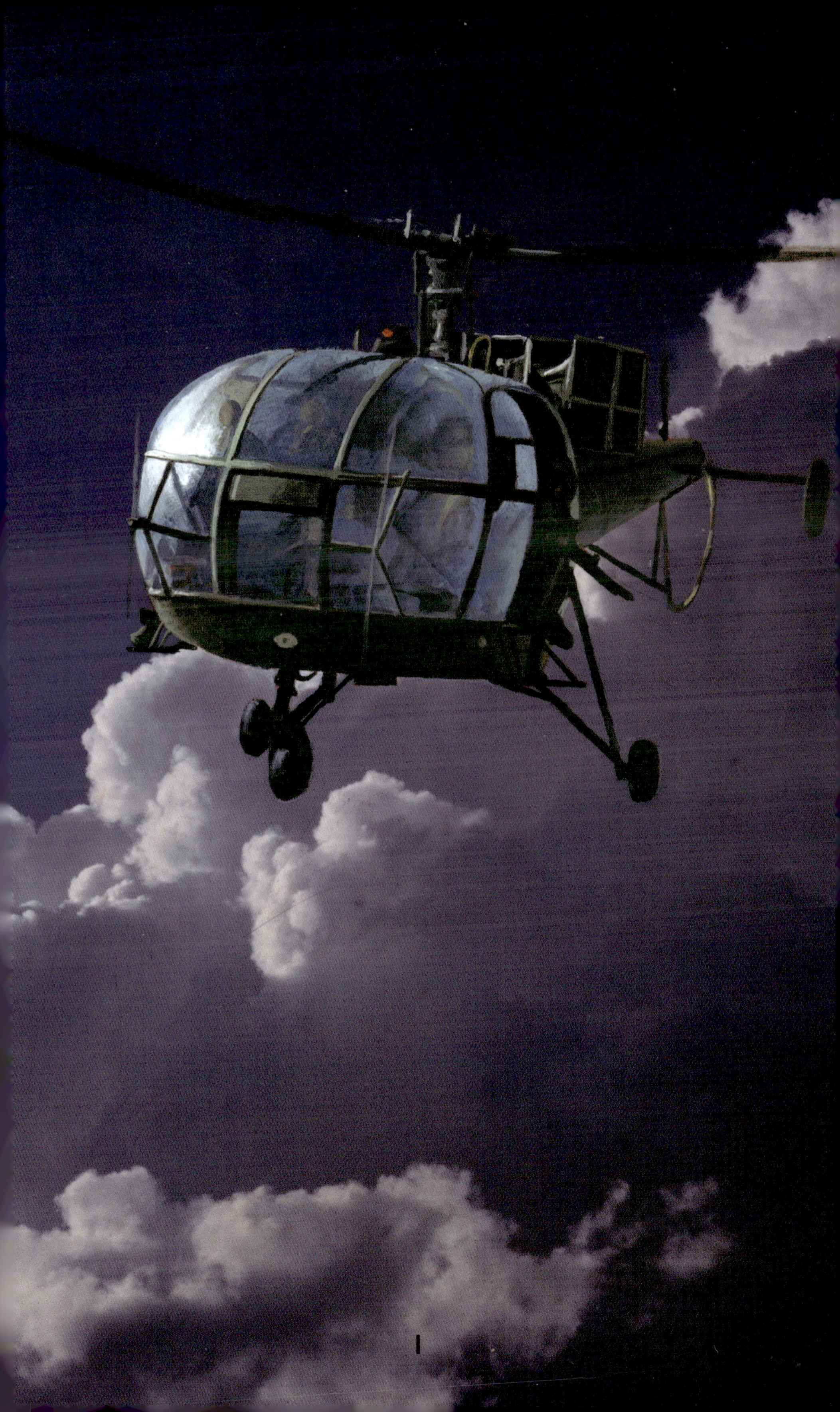

'Battle of Sinoia'
29 April 1966

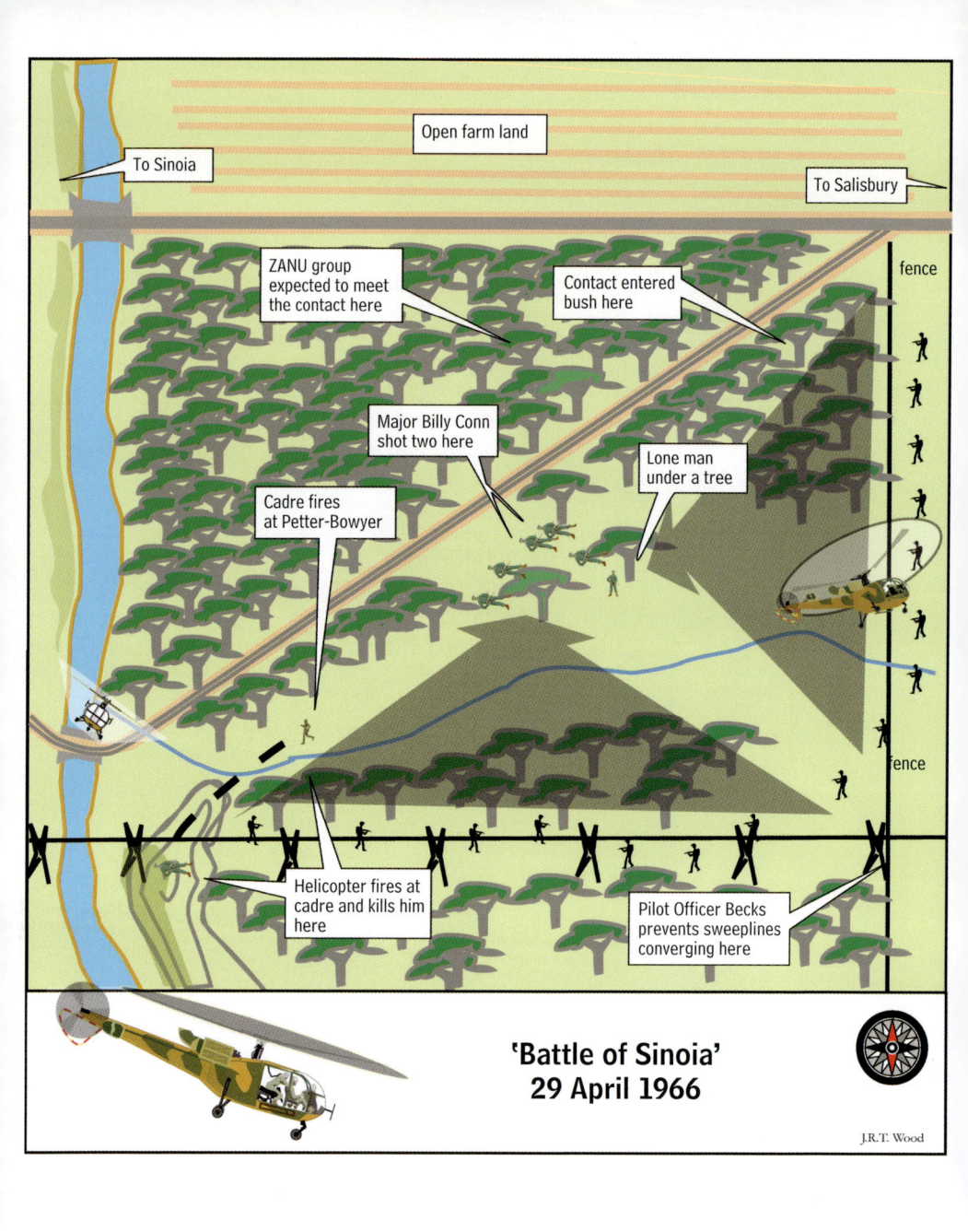

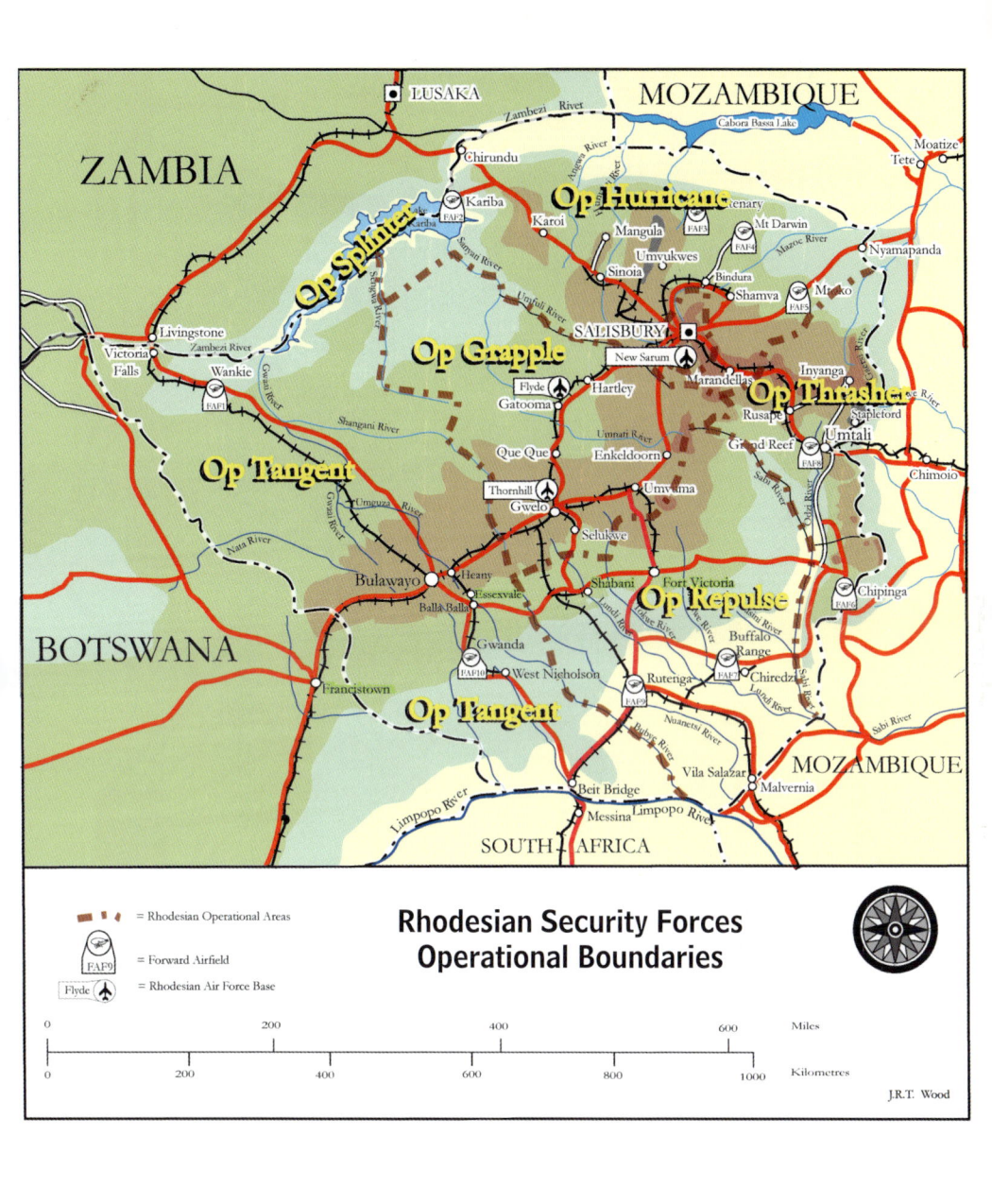

Rhodesian Security Forces Operational Boundaries

ZANLA and ZPRA Operational Boundaries

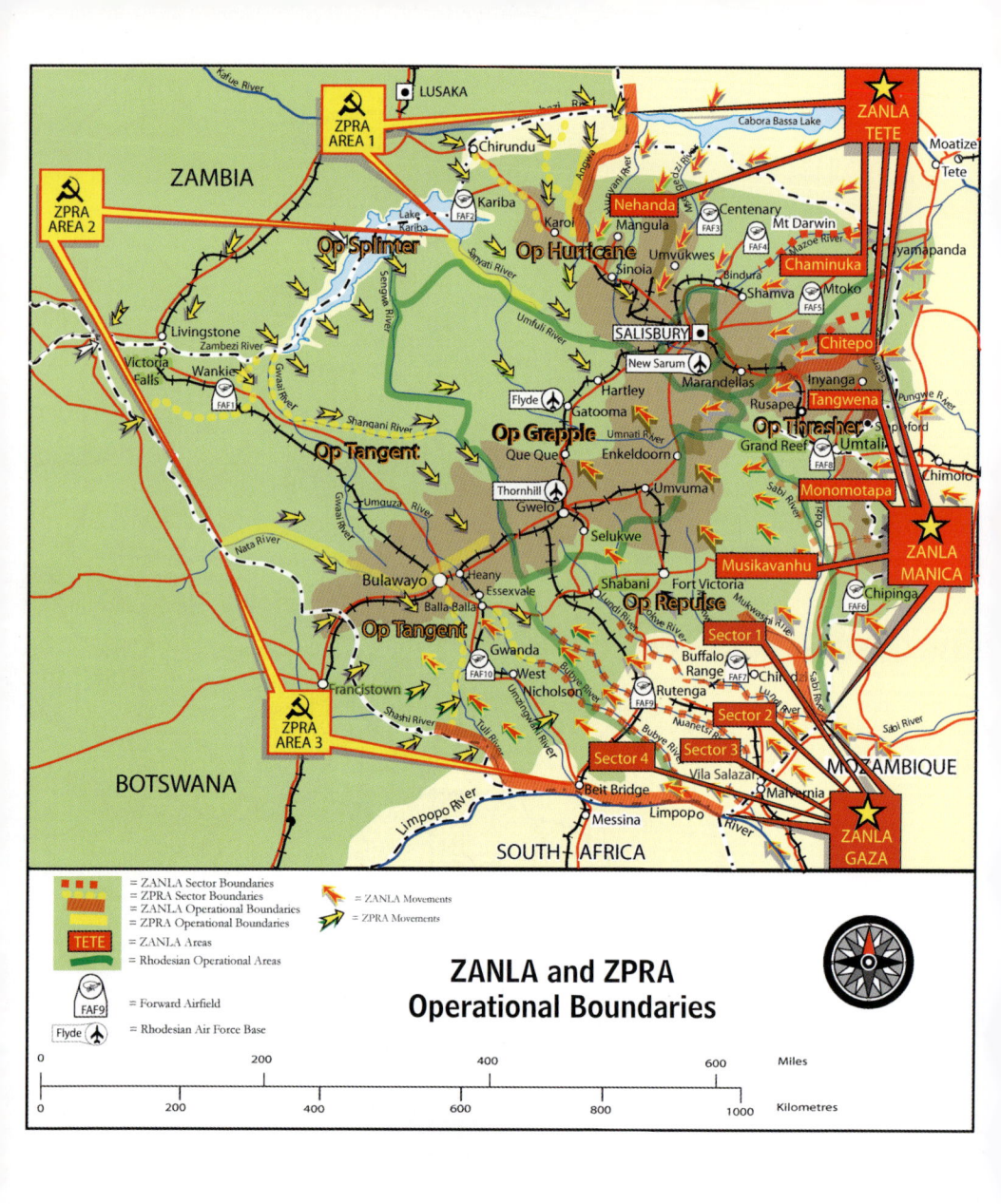

K-Car

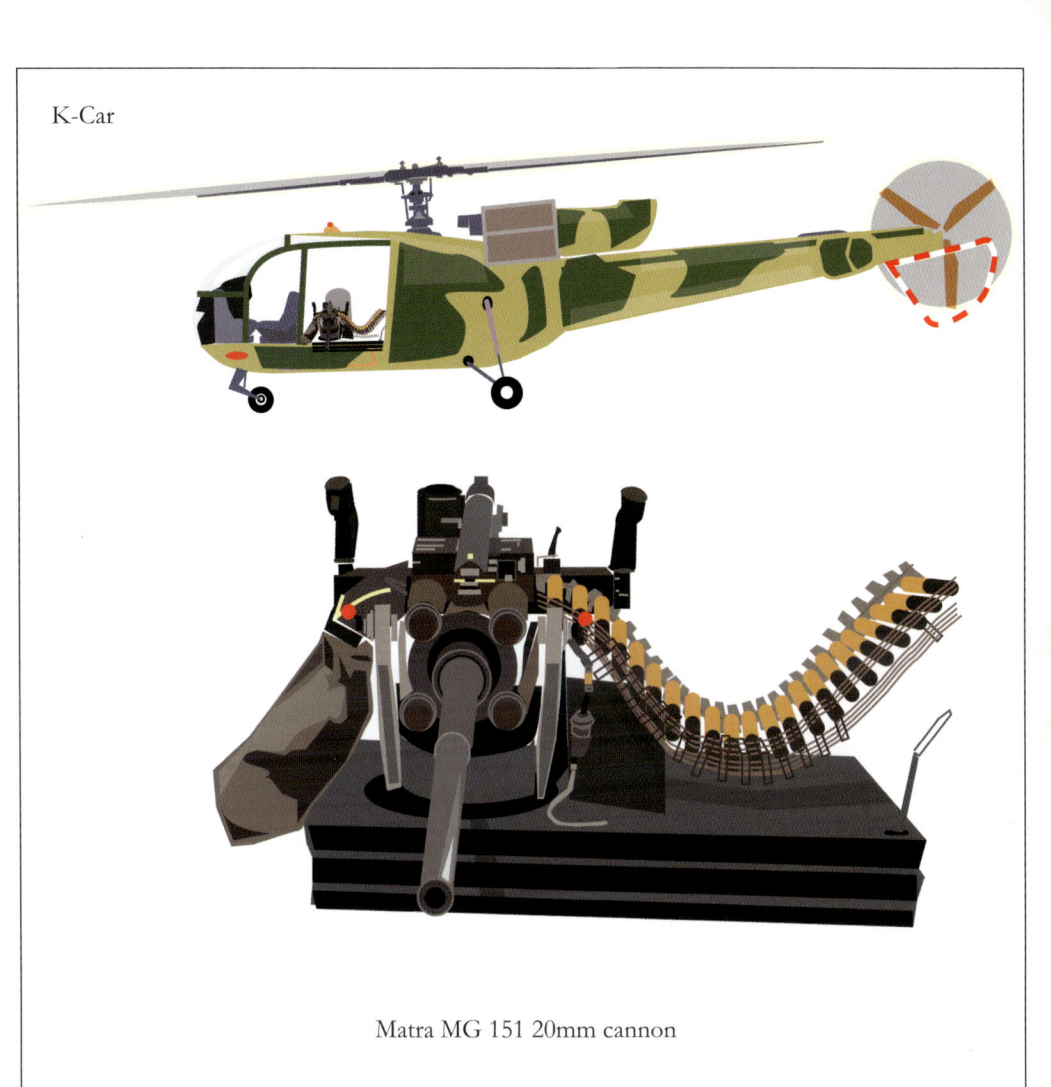

Matra MG 151 20mm cannon

J.R.T. Wood

G-Car

J.R.T Wood

v

A Fireforce Action of the Phase One: 1974-1976

Leading the Fireforce in, the K-Car would fly directly over the target, mark it with white smoke, and then pull up to orbit at 800 feet and to command the air and ground attack. As soon as the enemy positions or the enemy themselves could be seen, the K-Car would open fire with the potent 20mm cannon, while the G-Cars, led by G-1 carrying Stop 1, would orbit the target in a wide left-hand circle, waiting for the K-Car to order them to put their stops down. This was a somewhat cumbersome procedure. The time wasted was used by the enemy to escape and aircrews had to remember to look outside the orbit for signs of fleeing men. Pilots had to remember to widen their orbits constantly. The enemy were able to move at a rate of 500 metres every minute

The Provost, capable of protecting itself with its two Browning .303 guns, was capable of rocket and frantan (napalm) attacks. While waiting its turn it would orbit at 1,500 to 2,000 feet

The tasks of the OP (hidden on the hilltop) were to spot the enemy, take a bearing, call Fireforce and give the exact grid reference and description of the target, a suggested route for 'contour' flying to mask Fireforce from the enemy, numbers of insurgents, what clothes they were wearing, likely escape routes, etc. Once the Fireforce was airborne, the OP would brief the commander again, updating his information so that he could make any necessary adjustments to his plan. As Fireforce approached, the OP would 'talk' K-Car 1 over the target so that it could be marked. Thereafter, the OP would continue to observe and draw the Fireforce commander's attention to enemy movements and the like

To keep the heads of the enemy down, while the stops and the sweep line are put into position, the Trojan puts in a rocket attack

The Matra MG 151 20mm cannon was calibrated to fire at 800 feet from an aircraft travelling at 65 knots

Because each 20mm round cost Rh$35, the gunners restricted themselves to bursts of three shells. The weight of the ammunition carried was also a factor because it affected the endurance of the aircraft. The gunners had trays of 100 or 200 shells

G-Car 3, having put down its stop group, orbits low on a flank to spot escaping enemy, to drive them to ground with its .303 or 7.62 machine gun, and to be available to evacuate casualties or to re-locate stop groups. The K-Car commander would keep at least one G-Car back in case problems developed with the K-Car and he might have to transfer from it

G-Car 1, having dropped its stop group, departs to pick up further sticks from the approaching 'land tail' (i.e. the remainder of the commando, mounted on trucks which would also carry helicopter fuel and ammunition)

G-Cars would make dummy drops to confuse the enemy as to the number of stops being placed in cut-off positions

As soon as they can escape, the insurgents 'bombshell' (running in separate directions), intending to regroup at a prearranged rendezvous. They know that if they stand and fight they will be annihilated. The purpose of the guerrilla is to strike and run, to disrupt and to survive so that he can fulfil his political function of influencing the tribesmen

After dropping off its stop group on an escape route, G-2 flies off to the 'land-tail' to bring in reinforcements. Thereafter the G-Cars would land in a secure place—such as a hilltop—to conserve fuel but still to be on hand to move stops or to remove casualties

A Fireforce Action of the Phase Two: 1977-1979

To keep the heads of the enemy down, while the stops and the sweep line are put into position, the Lynx puts in a rocket attack

The tasks of the OP on the hilltop remained the same. He was to report any sighting and to guide Fireforce onto the target. The Fireforces preferred to fly in behind him if possible in order to see the target from his angle so that no time was wasted

At the command of the Fireforce commander and talked on to the dropping zone by the K-Car or a G-Car pilot, the DC-3 'Paradak' begins its run in at 90 knots, watching the wind drift so that its 16–20 paratroops would land in the landing zone, close together, ready to form the sweep line. The dropping height was between 600 and 300 feet, too low to use the reserve parachute. As the last man left the door, the first man's feet would touch the ground

G-Car 1, having put down its stop group, orbits low on a flank to spot escaping enemy, to drive them to ground with its .303 or 7.62 machine gun, and to be available to evacuate casualties. A further duty of the stand-by G-Car could be to examine the dropping zone, transmit precise QNH altitude reading of the DZ to the Dakota so that it could set its altimeter for a precise above-ground reading. The Dakota would be loitering at an IP (interim point) four minutes' flying time away, ready to react but out of earshot. When the K-Car called for paratroops, the G-Car would talk the Dakota in

G Car 1, having dropped its stop group, departs to pick up further sticks from the approaching 'land tail' (i.e. the remainder of the Commando, mounted on trucks which would also carry helicopter fuel and ammunition)

VII

A Fireforce Action of the Phase Three: Jumbo Fireforce of 1979

Supporting Hunters could be used at the outset to attack the target with rockets, frantan or the devastating blast-and-shrapnel Golf bombs. Talked in by K-Car 1, the Hunters would bomb the smoke of the marking grenade.

Seven minutes out from the target K-Car 1, followed by K-Car 2, would pull away from the formation of helicopters. Once over the target neither K-Car would pull up, as before, but would open fire and then might call in an airstrike to stun the enemy further. K-Car 1 would then climb to direct the ground operation while the four-gun Alpha-fit K-Car 2 roamed over the target area at tree top height, shooting at will

K-Car 2, an Alpha Fit Dalmatian with four .303 machine-guns, acts purely as a gunship

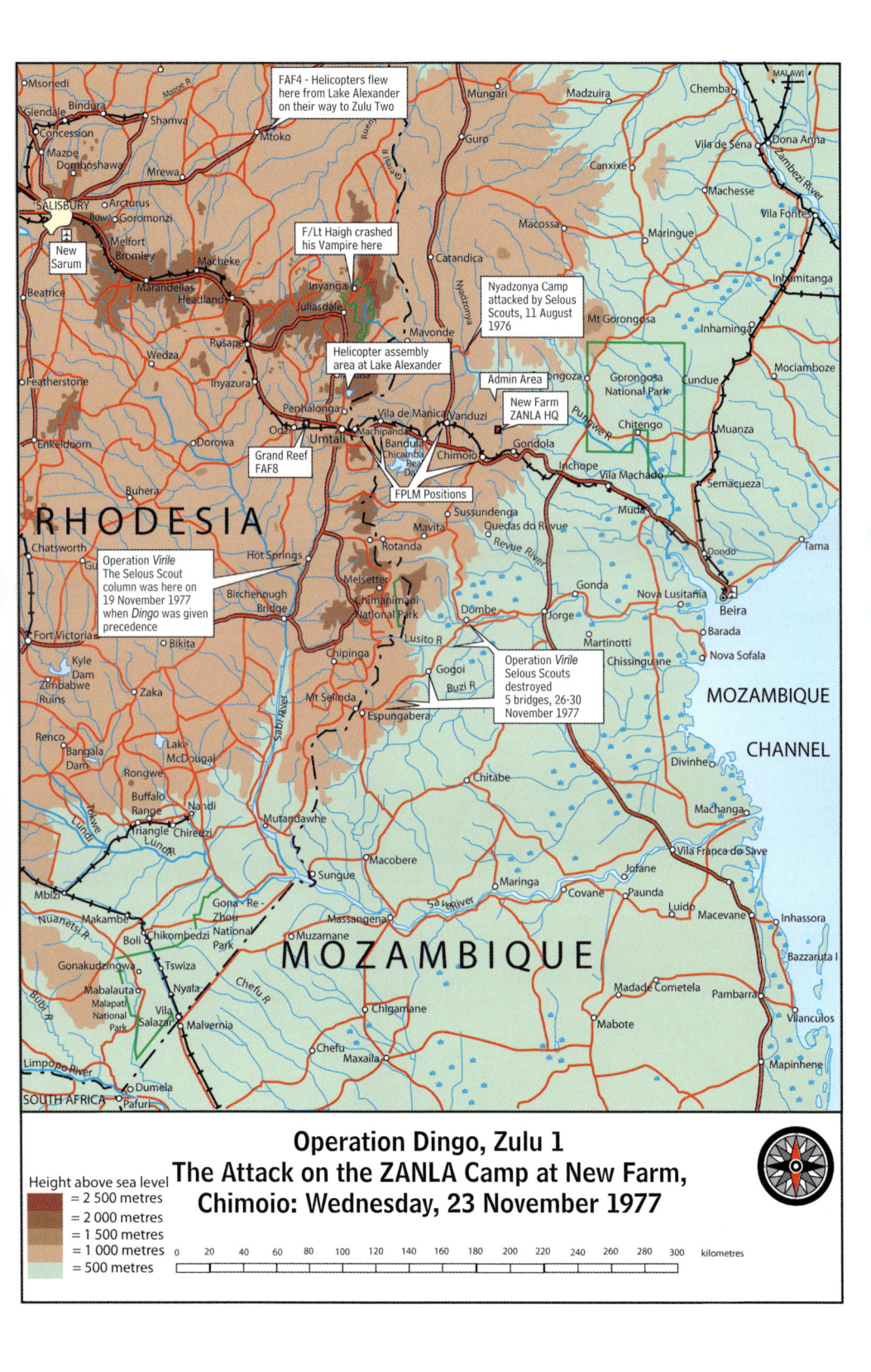
FAF4 - Helicopters flew here from Lake Alexander on their way to Zulu Two
F/Lt Haigh crashed his Vampire here
Nyadzonya Camp attacked by Selous Scouts, 11 August 1976
Helicopter assembly area at Lake Alexander
Admin Area
New Farm ZANLA HQ
Grand Reef FAF8
FPLM Positions
Operation Virile The Selous Scout column was here on 19 November 1977 when Dingo was given precedence
Operation Virile Selous Scouts destroyed 5 bridges, 26-30 November 1977
RHODESIA
MOZAMBIQUE
MOZAMBIQUE CHANNEL
SOUTH AFRICA
MALAWI
SALISBURY
New Sarum
Umtali
Chimoio
Beira
Gorongosa National Park
Zambezi River
Save River
Limpopo River
Sabi River
Height above sea level
= 2 500 metres
= 2 000 metres
= 1 500 metres
= 1 000 metres
= 500 metres
0 20 40 60 80 100 120 140 160 180 200 220 240 260 280 300 kilometres

Operation Dingo, Zulu 1
The Attack on the ZANLA Camp at New Farm, Chimoio: Wednesday, 23 November 1977

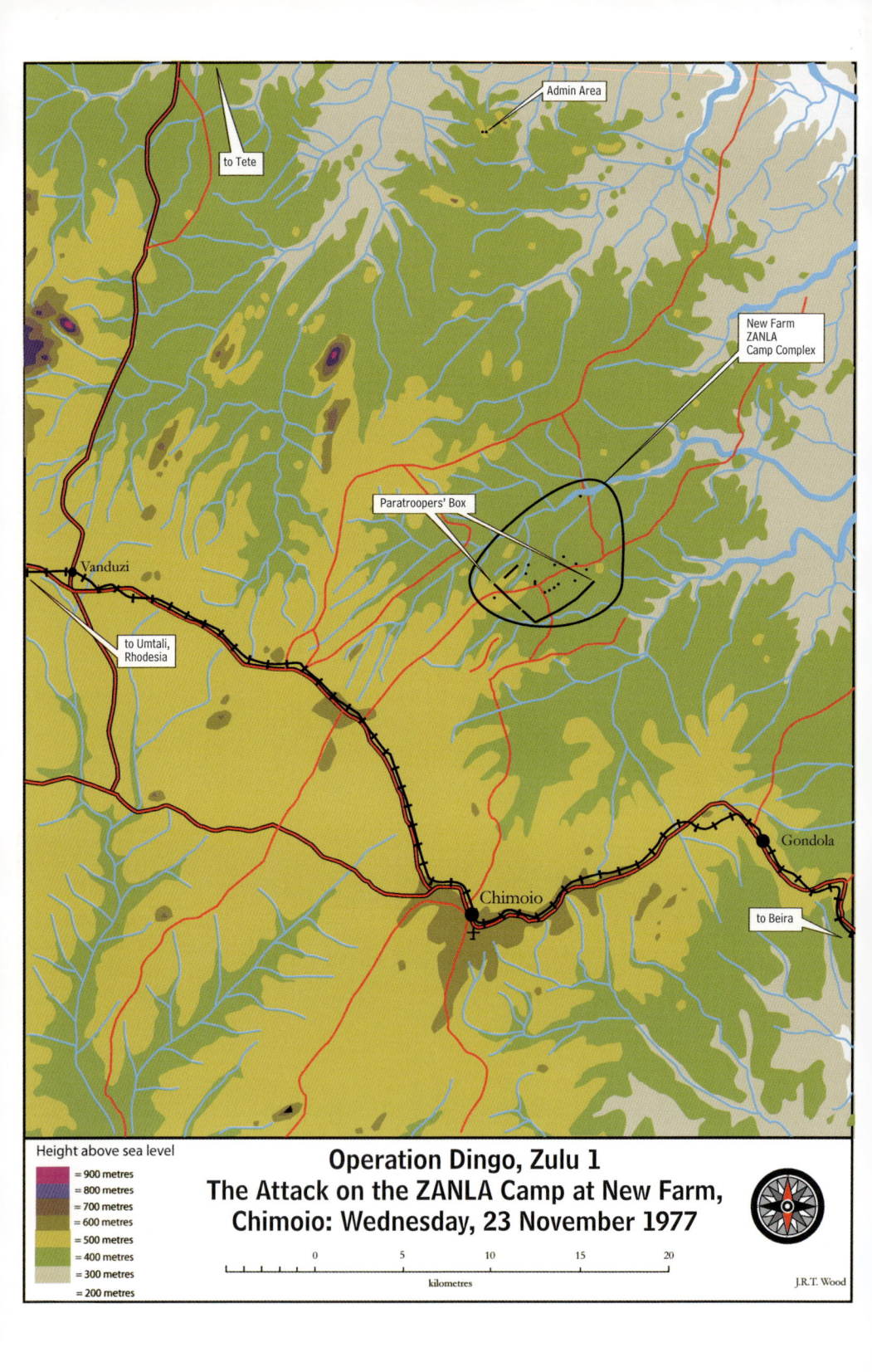

**Operation Dingo, Zulu 1
The Attack on the ZANLA Camp at New Farm,
Chimoio: Wednesday, 23 November 1977**

New Farm
ZANLA Complex of Camps

Rio Mombeze

Recruits' Camp: Complex T
33 barrack huts
43 small huts
3 bell tents
kitchen area
4-6 FPLM, 1,000 recruits & 25 instructors

Old Garage: Complex P
1 large open-sided, metal roof building
29 small huts
Fuel dump
Ammunition Store for Recruits' Camp
Vehicle graveyard
Tool store

Ngangas: Complex Q
88 huts for ngangas & old people
Numbers: unknown

National Stores: Complex R
Old tobacco barn
53 huts
5 bell tents
Main logistics centre
food, ammunition & clothing
4-6 FPLM, 150 ZANLA

Takawira 1: Complex J:
Two camps (Matopos & Takawira)
Matopos contained the Registry
Takawira: 4-6 FPLM plus 500+ semi-trained recruits to be sent on to external training centres in Tanzania, Ethiopia etc.

Pasindina 1: Complex K
19 huts. 4-6 FPLM plus 70- limbless ZANLA, war casualties ex Rhodesia

HQ: Complex H
Most important target
Hierarchy, main office and clerical area.
10 Metal-roofed buildings
41 large thatched buildings
49 small structures
4-6 FPLM plus 200 ZANLA

Thin Camp: Complex S
12 huts housing 'thin' recruits
4-6 FPLM, 150 ZANLA recruits

Engineers Complex
12 buildings - pole and dagga. Engineers for maintenance of HQ

New Garage: Complex A
3 pole and dagga buildings housing long-distance drivers and mechanics
4-6 FPLM, 50 ZANLA

Chitepo College: Complex M:
4-6 FPLM, 250 ZANLA

Nehanda Camp: Complex B:
housing women and juveniles too young for training

Detention Barracks:
20 guards, unknown number of prisoners

Pasindina 2: Complex L: 66 huts (pole and dagga) in rows forming a box
FPLM plus 400 convalescent ZANLA

Chaminuka Camp:
Complex C the security section 4-6 FPLM, 500 ZANLA (ex Beijing) Robert Mugabe stays here on his visits

Parirenyatwa Camp:
Complex M: housing trained and trainee nursing staff
4-6 FPLM 1,200 ZANLA (700 males, 500 females)

0 1 2 3 4 5 6
Kilometres

J.R.T. Wood

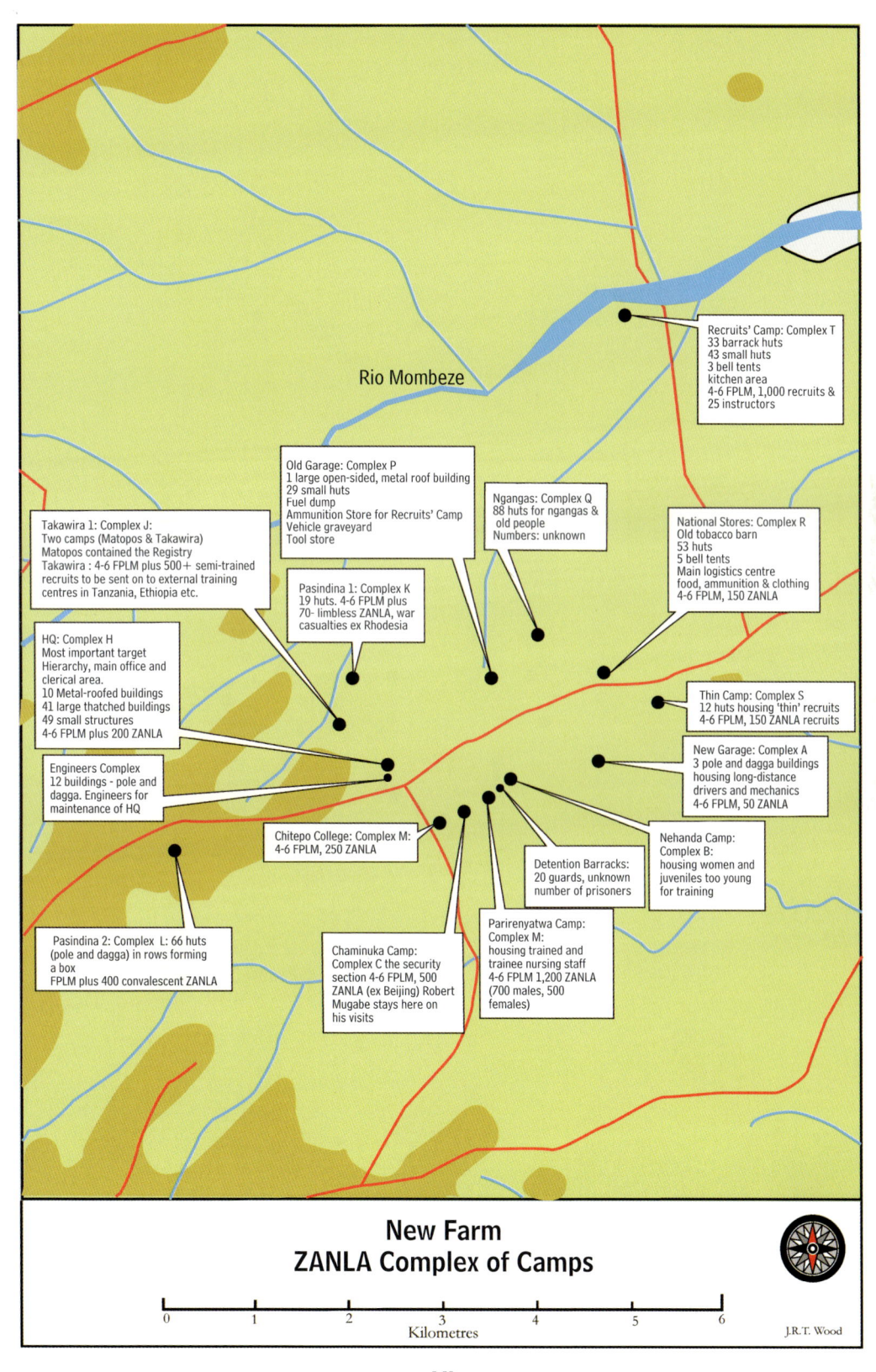

Rio Mombeze

Jack Malloch's DC-8 cargo aircraft flies over the camp at high altitude at 0741, four minutes before H-Hour, at a moment when all ZANLA personnel are standing on the routine early-morning muster parades. The purpose is to deceive them, to lull them into a false sense of security with regard to any noise heard of the approaching attacking jet fighter-bombers

**Operation Dingo, Zulu 1
Deception at Chimoio at H-4 minutes**

0 1 2 3 4 5 6
Kilometres

J.R.T. Wood

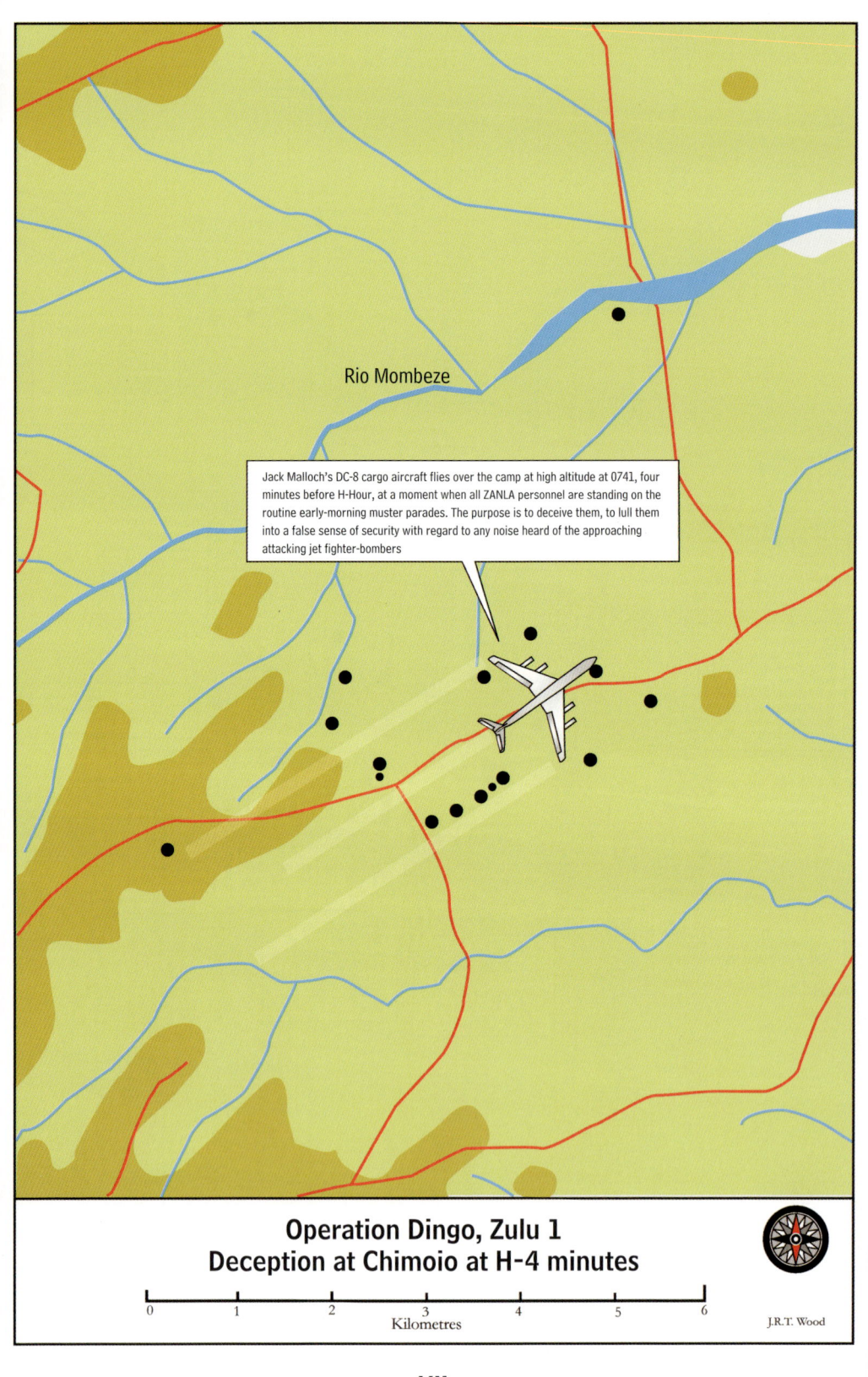

XII

Operation Dingo, Zulu 1
Air strike at New Farm at H-Hour

- 4 x Vampires airstrike
  60lb rockets (32 fired)
  20mm cannon

- Recruits Camp:
  33 barrack huts
  43 small huts
  3 bell tents
  kitchen area
  4-6 FPLM, 1,000 recruits & 25 instructors

Rio Mombeze

- HQ: Complex H
  Most important target
  Hierarchy, main office and clerical area.
  10 metal-roofed buildings,
  41 large thatched buildings
  49 small structures
  4-6 FPLM plus 200 ZANLA

- Red 1 Hunter strafing with four 30mm Aden cannons

- Chitepo College
  4-6 FPLM, 250 ZANLA

- Red 2 Hunter
  2 x 50 gallon frantans (napalm)

- Red 3 Hunter
  2 x 50 gallon frantans (napalm)

- Pasindina 2: Complex L: 66 huts (pole and dagga) in rows forming a box
  4 FPLM plus 400 convalescent ZANLA

Kilometres: 0 1 2 3 4 5 6

J.R.T. Wood

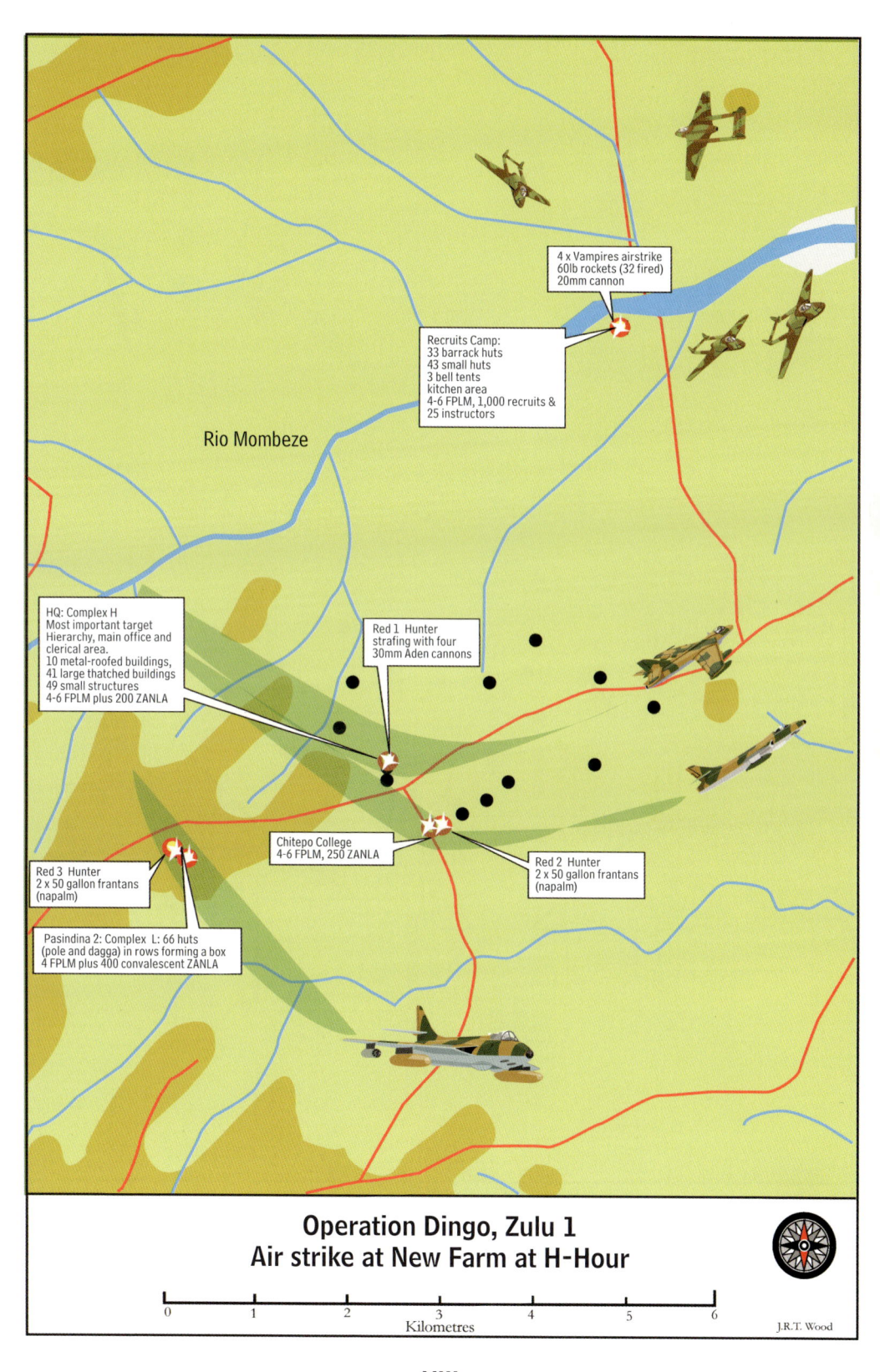

XIII

HQ: Complex H
Most important target
Hierarchy, main office and
clerical area.
10 metal-roofed buildings,
41 large thatched buildings
49 small structures
4-6 FPLM plus 200 ZANLA

Canberra air strike
300 Mk2 'Alpha'
bouncing bombs
(blast & shrapnel)

Canberra air strike
300 Mk2 'Alpha'
bouncing bombs
(blast & shrapnel)

2 x 300 Mk2 Alpha
bouncing bombs
(blast & shrapnel)

Chitepo College: Complex M:
4-6 FPLM, 250 ZANLA

Pasindina 2: Complex L: 66 huts
(pole and dagga) in rows forming a box
4 FPLM plus 400 convalescent ZANLA

Chaminuka Camp:
Complex C
the security section
4-6 FPLM,
500 ZANLA (ex Beijing)
Robert Mugabe stays here
on his visits.

Parirenyatwa Camp:
Complex M:
housing trained and trainee
nursing staff
4-6 FPLM
1,200 ZANLA
(700 males, 500 females)

Rio Mombeze

Operation Dingo, Zulu 1
Air strike at New Farm at H+30 seconds

0 1 2 3 4 5 6
Kilometres

J.R.T. Wood

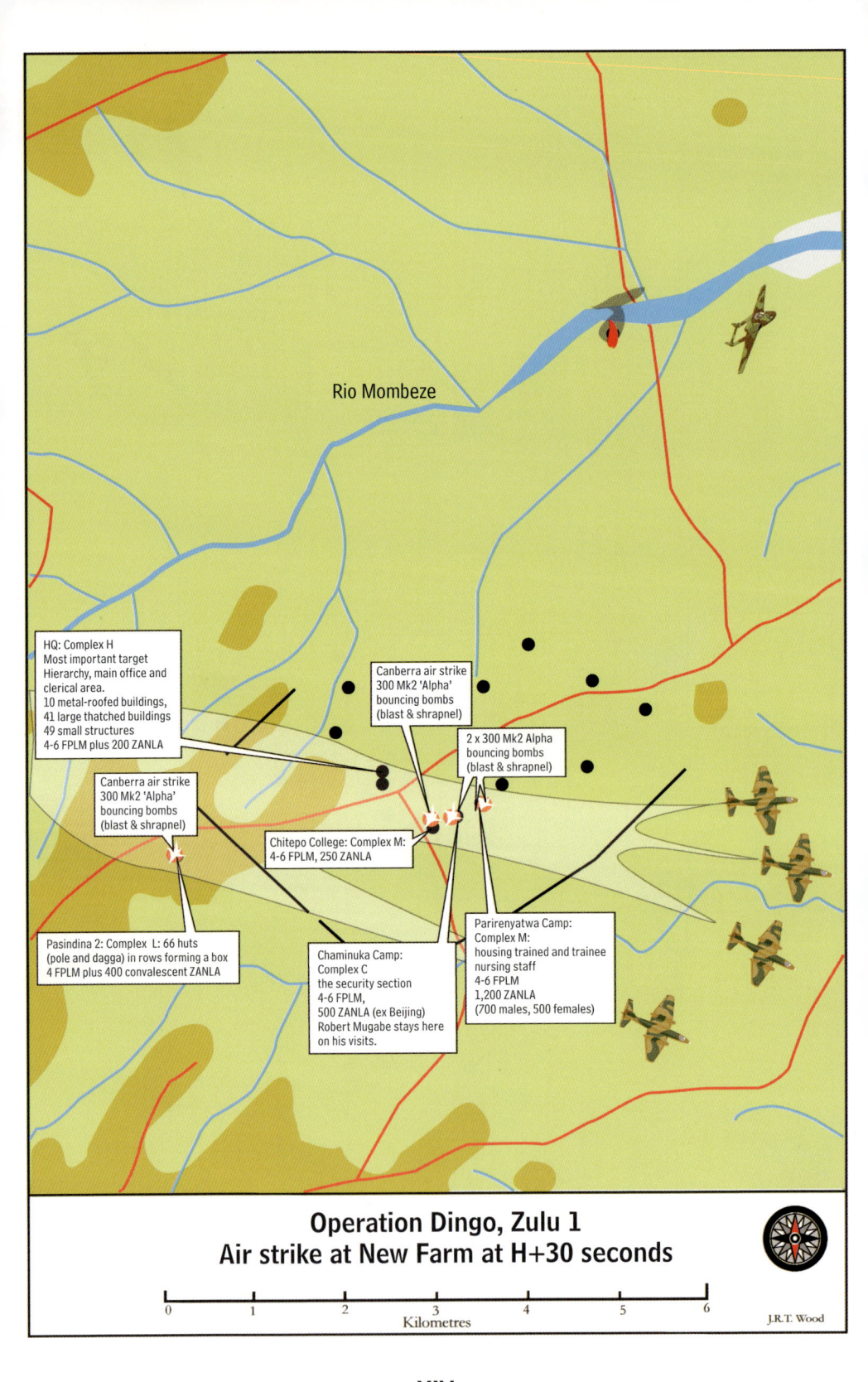

XIV

Four Hunters attack anti-aircraft weapons at positions J & B with 68mm rockets and 30mm cannon at H+2 minutes

Fleeing ZANLA

At H+2 minutes, six Dakotas drop 144 troops (48 RLI & 96 SAS)

Rio Mombeze

Operation Dingo, Zulu 1
Paradrop at New Farm at H+2 minutes

Kilometres

J.R.T. Wood

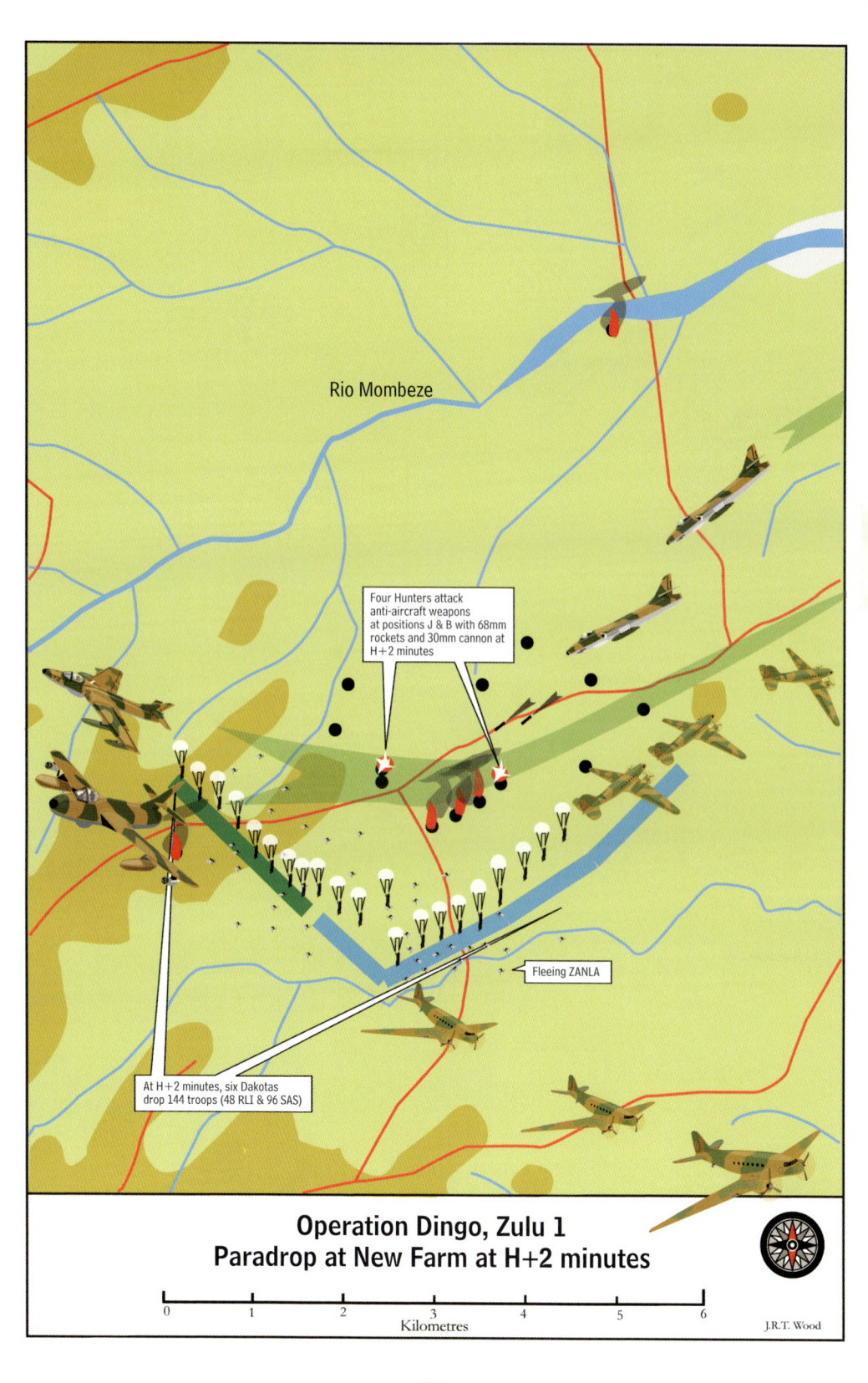

Operation Dingo, Zulu 1
Helicopter action at New Farm at H+5 minutes

Jack Malloch's DC-7 dropped fuel to the Admin Base some 18 kilometres to the north and, commanded by Group Captain Peter Petter-Bower, it provided fuel, ammunition, repairs, first aid etc.

Lynx flying close recce and radio relay

Overall commander Lt-Gen Peter Walls, flying in the command Dak, orbiting north of the target, as ComOps TAC HQ, with secure teleprinter link with ComOps and the Prime Minister's Office in Salisbury

Two K-Cars attack Recruits Camp

Rio Mombeze

Tactical Command
Air Commander Gp Capt Norman Walsh and Ground Forces Commander Major Brian Robinson, flying in the command G-Car (equipped with radios for simultaneous transmission to ground and air)

Ten G-Cars deposit Major Simon Haarhoff and Stop A, 2 Commando, 1 RLI (40 troops - callsigns A-J). Then the G-Cars depart for the Admin Base to refuel and wait for further tasks

A K-Car attacks Old Garage

A K-Car attacks National Stores

Stop 1, Major Jeremy Strong
3 Commando, 1RLI
Troop 11 - Lt Rod Smith
Troop 12 - Lt Mark Adams

Two K-Cars attack the HQ

Two K-Cars attack Chitepo College and Chaminuka, Parirenyatwa and Nehanda camps

Two K-Cars attack Pasindina 2

Fleeing ZANLA

Stop 6, B Troop, SAS
Capt Grahame Wilson

Stop 2, 3 Commando, 1RLI
Troop 13 - Lt John Cronin
Troop 14 - Lt Gordon Thornton

Stop 5, B Troop, SAS
Lt Kenneth Roberts
+ Major Mick Graham

Stop 4, A Troop, SAS
Capt Bob MacKenzie

Stop 3, A Troop, SAS
Capt Colin Willis

Lynx flying wide recce

👤 = 4-man stick

0 1 2 3 4 5 6
Kilometres

J.R.T. Wood

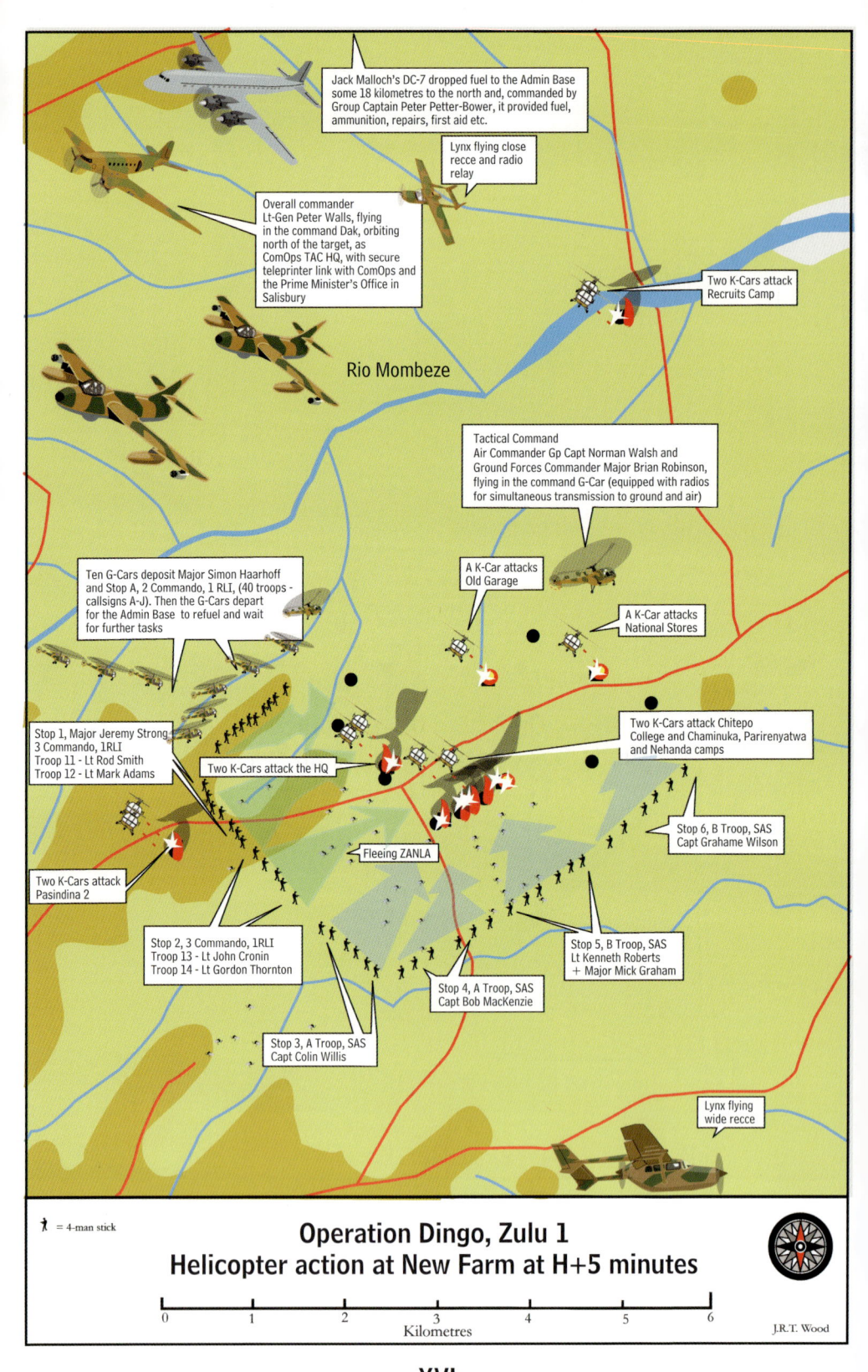

XVI

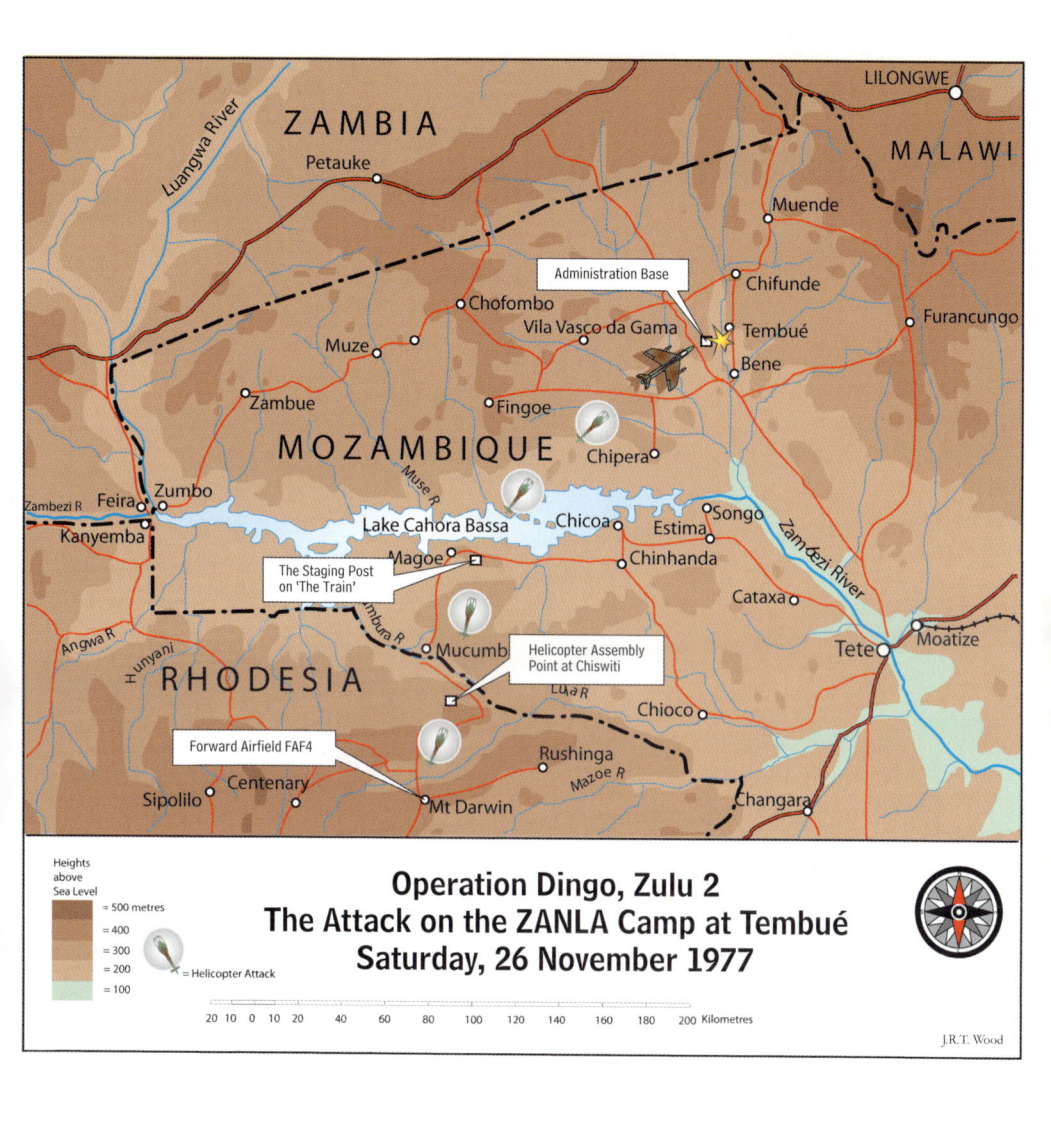

Operation Dingo, Zulu 2
The Attack on the ZANLA Camp at Tembué
Saturday, 26 November 1977

XVII

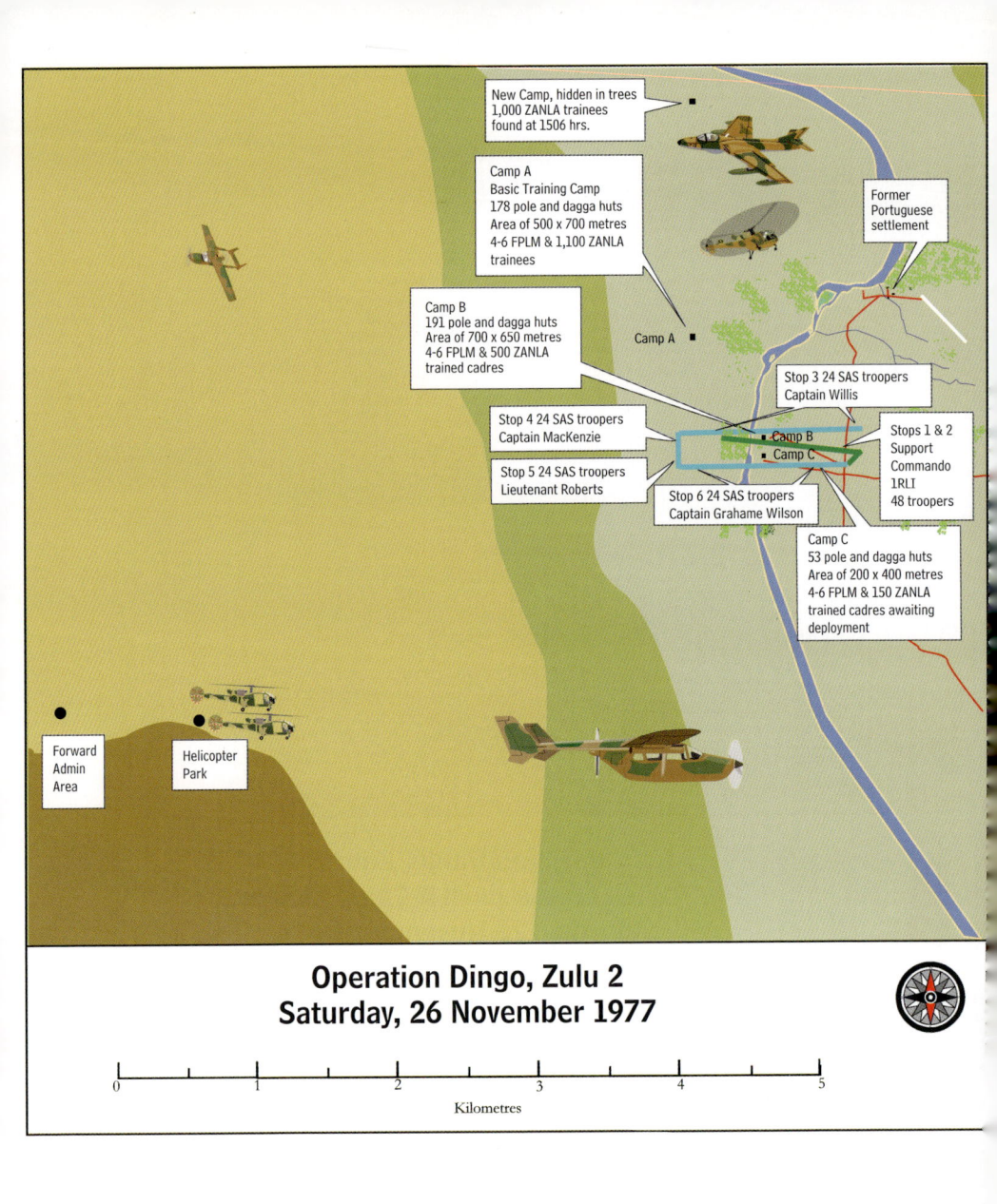

New Camp, hidden in trees 1,000 ZANLA trainees found at 1506 hrs.

Camp A
Basic Training Camp
178 pole and dagga huts
Area of 500 x 700 metres
4-6 FPLM & 1,100 ZANLA trainees

Former Portuguese settlement

Camp B
191 pole and dagga huts
Area of 700 x 650 metres
4-6 FPLM & 500 ZANLA trained cadres

Camp A

Stop 3 24 SAS troopers
Captain Willis

Stop 4 24 SAS troopers
Captain MacKenzie

Camp B
Camp C

Stops 1 & 2
Support Commando
1RLI
48 troopers

Stop 5 24 SAS troopers
Lieutenant Roberts

Stop 6 24 SAS troopers
Captain Grahame Wilson

Camp C
53 pole and dagga huts
Area of 200 x 400 metres
4-6 FPLM & 150 ZANLA trained cadres awaiting deployment

Forward Admin Area

Helicopter Park

Operation Dingo, Zulu 2
Saturday, 26 November 1977

0 1 2 3 4 5
Kilometres

Pookie—mine-detection vehicle

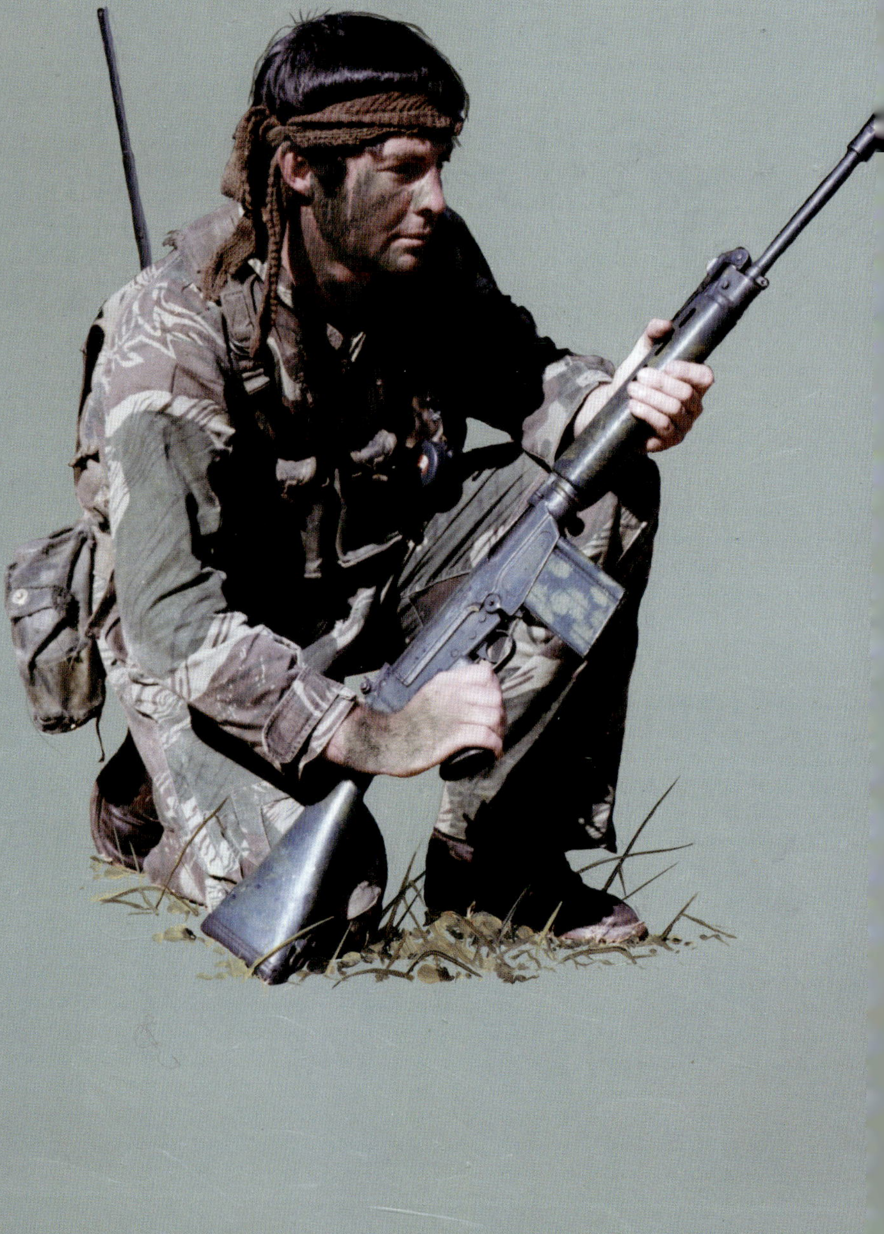

Fireforce Writ Large:
Operation *Dingo*: Airborne Assault in Mozambique: 23-27 November 1977

minutes with 400lbs of fuel on board, a crew of two and four fully equipped troops. The K-Car, with its 20mm cannon and ammunition and a crew of three, had an endurance of an hour and a quarter to an hour and a half when loaded with 600lbs of fuel.

Walsh and Robinson and their team came up with an inspired answer which was adopted in all other Rhodesian external operations thereafter. This was to para-drop fuel drums into an impromptu base called an administration area (admin area)' reasonably close to the target. The Rhodesians, of course, had years of experience of pre-positioning fuel to nullify the Alouette's short endurance.

Their proposal was that, during the initial few minutes of the attack, ten G-Cars would deposit specialists and a stock of ammunition and equipment in an unpopulated area, some 20 kilometres north of New Farm's outermost camp. In the case of Tembué, the proposed admin area was ten kilometres west of the target. Both areas were chosen because there was high ground close by on which to position mortars for their defence. The specialists would include a commander, protection troops, aircraft technicians, medical and SB personnel to interrogate captured ZANLA cadres and speedily pass on any intelligence gathered. The administrative areas would immediately receive drums of fuel delivered by parachute from a DC-7 cargo aircraft. This would allow the Rhodesians to refuel the helicopters and thereby provide continuous air cover over the target and the resupply of ammunition and other requirements for the troops on the ground. Casualties would be flown to the admin area to be stabilized before being airlifted to hospitals in Rhodesia. When the operation was over, the admin area would provide a staging post for helicopter ferrying troops and equipment.

All this would be repeated at Tembué but its remoteness meant that two refuelling staging posts were required. Robinson and Walsh chose a Rhodesian Army camp at Chiswiti just south of the Rhodesian–Mozambican border, designating it the 'Helicopter Assembly Point'. The next one, named the 'Staging Post', was some 50 kilometres north of Chiswiti, sited on 'The Train'—an elongated, flat-topped mountain range so called because it resembles a steam locomotive and a line of carriages. The chosen landing zone was on the 'Guard's Van'. 'The Train' was just south of the Cabora (now Cahora) Bassa Dam on the Zambezi River and east of the small settlement of Magoe. Thereafter, the helicopters would fly 130 kilometres northeastward to the target, attack it and then fly west to the admin area to refuel.

The pre-positioning of fuel, meant, of course, it was possible to use helicopter-borne troops at New Farm, at least. In November 1977, the Rhodesian Air Force had only six DC-3 Dakotas available for para-dropping, giving Robinson a limit of 144 SAS and RLI paratroops. The helicopter-lift added a further 40 RLI troops. Yet this still only gave Robinson a total of 184, albeit battle-hardened, men to tackle the 5,000 or more armed ZANLA cadres at New Farm and the 2,000 at Tembué.

The assault was not the only problem facing Robinson. He had to prevent a breakout of the inhabitants of the camps and ZANLA had already demonstrated in numerous Fireforce contacts a predilection to 'bombshell', to flee in all directions and not simply along obvious escape routes. To negate or contain the 'bombshell', Robinson had designed, and used in Mozambique in 1974, 'boxes' of paratroops to envelop their fleeing enemy.[114] Robinson and his adviser, the Rhodesian Air Force's chief parachute instructor, Flight Lieutenant Frank Hales, therefore planned to use a variation of the 'box' tactic at New Farm and Tembué. The vastness of these camps, 25 square kilometres at New Farm, however, meant that Robinson had only sufficient paratroopers to form two sides of the box and the 40 helicopter-borne RLI troops, the third. The fourth side or 'lid' would have to be 'closed' by the highly effective 20mm cannon fire of the K-Cars. If the box were in place within two minutes of H-Hour, Robinson predicted total surprise, a high kill-rate and a quick subduing of resistance in the camps. A short successful action was particularly required at Chimoio because the troops were needed for the attack on Tembué to sustain the advantage of surprise. Robinson, nevertheless, knew that he ran the risk of a casualty rate of 30 per cent which would have a drastic effect on his plans.[115]

---

[114] MacKenzie, p. 42.

[115] Cole, p. 176.

Fireforce Writ Large:
Operation *Dingo*: Airborne Assault in Mozambique: 23-27 November 1977

With the Geneva Conference with ZANU's Mugabe and ZAPU's Nkomo pending in November 1976, it was inevitable that the early version of this audacious plan should be shelved. Furthermore, the risks were seen as too high for its first audience at SAS headquarters. The RLI were not yet trained to parachute and would only supply the 40 men carried in helicopters, leaving the remaining two sides of the box to be formed by 98 SAS troops. It was also felt there was insufficient air power to guarantee the success of the ground forces. The 16 protection troops allocated to the defence of the admin areas were deemed too few to protect refuelling helicopters. Any loss of helicopters, it was argued, could leave troops stranded in Mozambique and a significant loss of irreplaceable aircraft could cripple the Rhodesian Air Force. The CIO was worried about world opinion and insisted that, whatever the Rhodesians said about the true nature of the two targets, they would be depicted as attacking refugee camps as had happened in the universally condemned Selous Scout raid on Nyadzonya. The 'double-tap' attack on Chimoio and Tembué was dismissed as impractical but it was conceded that the Chimoio plan was worthy of reconsideration.[116]

The SAS–Rhodesian Air Force planners were not deterred, as has been said, and in the year that followed they called attention repeatedly not only to their plan but also to the steady growth of New Farm as ZANLA brought in trained personnel through Beira's port and airport. By November 1977, the regular aerial photography and other intelligence revealed that the population at New Farm had reached 9,000–10,000 while Tembué had 4,000. SAS Captain McCormack, presenting *Dingo* yet again in November 1977, argued that the moment had come to strike because ZANLA would want to deploy as many men as possible into Rhodesia before the coming heavy rains made infiltration more difficult. The Selous Scouts had already convinced Walls of this argument, but this time Ian Smith needed the sort of damage that *Dingo* would wreak on ZANLA.

On receipt of the go-ahead from ComOps, the operational name 'Dingo' was adopted with the attack on Chimoio designated 'Zulu 1' and that on

---

[116] Cole, p. 175.

Tembué, 'Zulu 2'. *Dingo* had a five-fold purpose: of inflicting the maximum casualties possible; gathering intelligence; destroying war matériel; capturing specific items such as the Soviet SAM-7 missile and disrupting the reinforcement and resupply of ZANLA groups inside Rhodesia.

The planning team immediately reviewed their proposals. Using the up-to-date aerial photographs, the team chose the targets for the air strikes. They settled on the precise sites for the helicopter assembly areas, staging posts and admin areas, and the landing zones for the paratroops and helicopter-borne RLI. Planning was aided by the ability of the meteorological service to hack into Intelstat satellite weather transmissions to Europe. The hacking was necessary because her illegal international status excluded Rhodesia from obtaining the information legally. This provided not only better weather prediction than the ground stations in neighbouring African territories could but also a cloud map by 10.00 each day.[117]

The rear base chosen for Zulu 1 was the forward airfield (FAF8) at Grand Reef, 20 kilometres west of Umtali, because it had a landing strip capable of taking a Dakota. The Dakota aircraft would return there, after dropping their troops, to be on hand to fly in the paratroop reserve, extra fuel, ammunition and equipment or to fly casualties back to hospitals in Salisbury. Also operating out of Grand Reef would be the Lynxes, flying in a reconnaissance and support role.

The picnic grounds beside Lake Alexander in the mountains overlooking Mozambique, 20 kilometres north of Umtali, were selected as the helicopter assembly area for Zulu 1. Fuel for the helicopters, a supply point and a medical resuscitation station would be established there.

The rear base for Zulu 2 would be the airstrip at Mount Darwin (FAF4) and the helicopter assembly area, as has been said, at Chiswiti.

New Sarum air base would serve as the base for the Canberra and Vampire strike aircraft when they attacked both targets. The Hunters would fly from their base at Thornhill on the eastern outskirts of the central city of Gwelo and thereafter would re-arm and refuel at New Sarum.

---

[117] Petter-Bowyer, p. 305.

Fireforce Writ Large:
Operation *Dingo*: Airborne Assault in Mozambique: 23-27 November 1977

Everything was ready at New Sarum on Sunday, 20 November. A briefing area to accommodate *Dingo*'s hundreds of personnel was set up between two hangars. Seating was provided by stands (bleachers) brought from the rugby ground, forming three sides of the square. At 15.00, to give them time to absorb the elaborate air-aspects of the plan, Walsh gave the first of three briefings to the commanders of the New Sarum and Thornhill Flying Wings, the squadron and section leaders and K-Car pilots. To assist him, he had maps, air photos and a scale model of New Farm above which were suspended differently coloured circles indicating the flying patterns of the aircraft. Captain Jacques Dubois, second in command of the Mapping and Research Unit of the Rhodesian Intelligence Corps, had supplied a polystyrene and plaster of Paris model which he made all the more realistic by having stretched and glued an air photo over its contours. Furthermore, a captured ZANLA insurgent had confirmed the accuracy of the New Farm model.[118]

Walsh and Robinson used the target model and other aids again when they conducted the full air/ground briefing of *Dingo* commanders at 09.00 on Monday, 21 November. They outlined the command structure. The overall commander was Lieutenant-General Walls. To be on hand to make strategic decisions should FPLM forces attempt to intervene or something untoward happen, he would be aboard the command Dakota, orbiting close to the action. His aircraft was fitted out as an airborne operations room with direct links to ComOps and the Prime Minister's Office via radio and a secure teleprinter.[119]

The direct command was delegated to Norman Walsh, co-ordinating the air effort, and Brian Robinson, directing the troops. Walsh would fly Robinson in the specially modified command helicopter directly above the action.

SAS Major Mick Graham was designated the commander on the ground

---

[118] Interview with Captain Dubois, 2 May 1998: The model was made in late 1976 and had to be enlarged repeatedly as new camps were discovered.

[119] Cole, p. 177.

and second in command. Next in line was Major Jeremy Strong, commander of 3 Commando, 1RLI, whose 48 paratroops constituted Stops 1 and 2. Group Captain Peter Petter-Bowyer was to control the admin area and SAS Captain Peter Jackson, the supply point at Lake Alexander.

The troops remained to be briefed and they began to be withdrawn from the field that day, arriving at New Sarum where they were kept in strict quarantine. On arrival after a long drive from Mabalauta, on the southeastern border, A Troop, SAS, were told no more than to prepare their kit for parachuting. The veteran ex-British soldier, Peter McAleese, thought their target was Malvernia in the southeast.

Such ideas were dispelled at the dramatic third briefing given between the hangars at lunchtime the next day, Tuesday, 22 November.[120]

This happened on an eventful day: two South African tourists were wounded when ambushed in the famed Wankie National Park. Elsewhere, five members of Internal Affairs Department were killed in action, six insurgents and four African men and two African women collaborating with them were killed, seven African civilians were murdered by terrorists and three Red Cross workers were abducted. That evening Vila Salazar was fired on again from Malvernia and there was sporadic fire at civilians and soldiers elsewhere across the Mozambican border.[121]

Robinson, Walsh, McCormack and their team confined this final briefing to Zulu 1, giving no hint that there would be a second target. Again using the model, Robinson gave what McAleese recalls as "the finest ops brief I have ever heard. He was a small, wiry terrier of a man who was the driving force behind the success of the Rhodesian SAS and he really wound us up for the fight that day".[122] The 29 year-old Corporal Anthony Harold Coom of 12 Troop, 3 Commando, 1RLI, recalls, however, that the more the "rather gung-ho" Robinson sounded confident, the more he, Coom, became depressed "at the thought of the odds and the task at hand and the more my stomach

---

[120] Peter McAleese, *No Mean Soldier*, Orion, London, 1993, p. 129.

[121] *Rhodesia Herald*, 23 & 24 November 1977.

[122] McAleese, pp. 129-132.

turned. From the outset you will deduce that this Boys' Own stuff was not really my strong point and in my opinion best left to those who found war appealing".[123]

A main feature of the plan was a novel ruse to mask from the sentries in the watchtowers at New Farm the sound of the approaching armada of 58 aircraft and avoid the camps emptying before a bomb was dropped. It was known from captured ZANLA personnel that there were regular morning muster parades at 07.30.[124] Accordingly, Jack Malloch (the proprietor of the sanctions-breaking airline, Afritair, and a veteran pilot who had flown Spitfire IXs over Italy in 1944 with Ian Smith as his flight commander) was asked to fly his DC-8 cargo jetliner high over New Farm at 07.41, heading northeast. It was hoped that the rumble of his jet engines would alarm the ZANLA personnel until they spotted the DC-8 and concluded that it was a civilian flight out of Maputo, bound for Malawi or beyond. It was expected that any ZANLA who took cover in the nearby trenches would be back in the ranks on parade just as three Hunters and four Vampires delivered the initial air strike at H-Hour (07.45) from the west.

Thirty seconds later, four Canberras would bomb the camps. Four more Hunters would follow to suppress the anti-aircraft fire with rockets and cannon fire to cover the arrival of the six Paradaks at H+2 minutes (07.47). The Dakotas, flying in two sections of three, would drop their 144 paratroops (96 SAS men and 48 of 3 Commando, RLI) to form the southwestern and southeastern sides of the box. A slow drop of a man a second was designed to spread the stop lines sufficiently to cover three kilometres each side.

Three minutes later, at H+5 minutes (07.50), the helicopters would arrive over the target. Ten K-Cars would strafe a variety of camps on the northeastern side, while ten G-Cars offloaded their 40 troops of 2 Commando, 1RLI, behind the northwestern ridge a kilometre from the headquarters camp at New Farm. Such was the ZANLA feeling of security at New Farm that they had failed to occupy the ridge up which the ten 2 Commando sticks,

---

[123] Binda, p. 258.

[124] Cole, p. 177.

led by Major Simon Haaroff, would race to secure the only high ground. With 2 Commando in place, the sweep lines would begin to move inwards, employing fire and movement co-ordinated by Robinson from the command helicopter flown by Walsh. At the same time, the cannon fire of the K-Cars would stem the flood of fleeing ZANLA survivors to the north, turning them onto the 2 Commando stop groups.[125] Above, two Hunters would be providing top cover, while a Lynx flew a wide reconnaissance orbit and another, a close one—as well as acting as a radio relay for the ground troops.

At H+15 (08.00), 20 kilometres to the north of New Farm, ten South African G-Cars (code-named 'Polo') would deposit the admin area personnel, their 81mm mortars, equipment and the reserve ammunition. On hand would be 4,400 20mm cannon shells for the K-Cars and 7,500 .303in rounds for the Browning Mk II machine guns of the G-Cars, demolition explosives and 20,000 7.62mm rifle rounds. One Polo G-Car would immediately mark the dropping zone (DZ) for 80 drums of fuel, deposited by Jack Malloch's second contribution, a Douglas DC-7. All would be ready in short order for the Rhodesian Air Force G-Cars coming in from New Farm to refuel and to stand ready for casevacs and the delivery of resupplies of ammunition and the like. The K-Cars would fly in to replenish their fuel and ammunition, before returning to support the advancing troops and to bottle up ZANLA.

High above, at H+15 minutes, two Vampire T11s would replace the two Hunters flying top cover. In due course, re-armed Hunters would arrive to take their place, some with 68mm armour-piercing rockets to deal with any threat from the FPLM tanks at Chimoio. Three of the Canberras would re-arm with Mk II Alpha bombs while the other would load Golf bombs in case the FPLM indulged in a retaliatory bombardment of Umtali. All Canberras would remain on 'crew-room readiness' for the duration of the operation. When the action was over, the Rhodesian G-Cars would begin to shuttle parachutes, equipment and then men back to the admin area. From there the South African G-Cars would fly them to the vehicles waiting at Lake Alexander. The troops were not told that thereafter the paratroops would be

---

[125] Memorandum, 'Follow-Up to Operation *Dingo*', by Major John R. Cronin, 21 April 1998.

Fireforce Writ Large:
Operation *Dingo*: Airborne Assault in Mozambique: 23-27 November 1977

driven back to New Sarum to prepare for Tembué while the helicopter crews flew to FAF5 at Mtoko en route for the next long haul.

The paratroopers were told they would drop at their familiar height of 400–500 feet to minimize the time in the air under fire. Parachuting into action was second nature to these troops since they were all involved in daily Fireforce actions across Rhodesia. What was different was that this time, instead of dropping to entrap a dozen or so insurgents, they would be jumping into a well-defended, widely dispersed complex containing 9,000–11,000 ZANLA personnel, of whom 4,000–5,000 were expected to be armed. Each Dakota would be carrying one 'stop group' of 24 men, split into six four-man sticks. Each stop group and stick commander would have two VHF A63 radios available to him, carried by himself and a trooper. Some commanders, like Lieutenant John Cronin (late of the US Marine Corps and Vietnam), commanding 13 Troop, 3 Commando, wore both of theirs for increased efficiency.[126] The first radio allowed the stick commander to listen to Robinson and the other stop groups on the battle or command net and to call for air support and the like. The second was for communication on the domestic net of the stop group. This system provided close control because Robinson could listen in to the radio traffic within a stop group and speak directly to individual stick commanders.

The men were ordered not to 'black up' with camouflage cream (a routine practice) and, to avoid being taken for the enemy by their own side, there was a strict instruction that only issue camouflage clothing and kit were to be worn. To prevent friendly-fire mistakes by pilots, and to aid Robinson in knowing where the sticks were under the dense canopy of leaves, the troops had 'Day-Glo' orange patches sewn inside their combat caps and were ordered to wear them inside out.

Without any support weapons, the troops had to rely on their personal weapons and the aircraft to accomplish their task. Each stick carried three FN 7.62mm NATO rifles and an MAG machine gun. Many of the machine gunners, however, would be armed with the lighter Russian RPD or RPK

---

[126] Memorandum by Major John R. Cronin, 23–24 February 1998.

machine guns which fired the 7.62mm intermediate round. Long experience had taught that these gunners would be able to replenish their belts from enemy casualties and stocks. Both the riflemen and the gunners were ordered to load one tracer to five ball rounds to aid target-marking. Many of them armed themselves with 9mm pistols, secured by lanyards, to give themselves a weapon if they were caught up in trees and could not free the rifles or machine guns strapped to their bodies.

In addition to his fighting kit, which included a minimum of four one-litre water bottles, each rifleman would be carrying 260 rounds of rifle ammunition, a 100-round MAG or RPD belt, flares, and up to four grenades (high explosive and incendiary). Two riflemen would have rifle grenades (the 42Z anti-tank and the 'Flying Phosphorus'). The machine gunner would carry ten 50-round belts and two grenades. Captain Robert MacKenzie, the veteran American commander of SAS Stop Group 4, recalled that he had his men carry 600 rifle rounds and the RPD gunners, 1,500.[127] MacKenzie armed himself with an American AR-15 rifle. The men would also be burdened with spare batteries for the radios and other kit. The stick commander, in addition to his FN rifle, grenades, flares, radio, radio codes, maps and compass and protractor, was provided with a gridded air photo to which Robinson would refer him.

Deliberately dispersed by the slow dropping rate to cover the ground, the individual soldier was ordered to get out of his parachute harness quickly on landing, make contact with the nearest man, take cover, wait and shoot. No time would be wasted at first in trying to regroup into formations. The stop group commanders would be dropped in the middle of their zones so that the paratroops would look inwards for his directions. The men on the extreme ends of the DZ were equipped with white phosphorus grenades with which to mark the front line of troops (FLOT) for the aircraft. Robinson ordered that, before advancing, each trooper was to note where he had left his main and reserve parachutes and jumping helmet since these items had to be recovered as they were difficult to replace because of the international

---

[127] MacKenzie, pp. 41–43 & 83–84.

Fireforce Writ Large:
Operation *Dingo*: Airborne Assault in Mozambique: 23-27 November 1977

sanctions. Indeed, the parachutes would be the first loads that the G-Cars would remove from New Farm so that they could be 'backloaded' to New Sarum for repacking for the next attack.

The Zulu 1 briefing completed, a tea break followed before attention turned in detail to Zulu 2, the attack on the Tembué base. Having described the sequence of events, McAleese recalls that Robinson closed by wishing the RLI "good luck". He added as an aside to his SAS men that "Professionals don't need it".[128] Lieutenant Cronin, however, understood that Robinson was wishing them all good luck.[129] The briefing closed with a short speech from General Walls.

The RLI 'land tail' convoy departed immediately on the long 200-kilometre drive east to FAF8, Grand Reef, carrying: 48 reserve paratroops from Major Nigel Henson's Support Commando; 20 Support Commando troops to protect the helicopter assembly area at Lake Alexander and their four 81mm mortars; Henson's second-in-command, Captain Ian Buttenshaw, and 16 men from Support Commando's Mortar Troop and their pair of 81mm mortars bound for the forward administration base; the four-man SB team; the RLI doctor and four medical orderlies; and a quartermaster to set up the supply point at FAF8 Grand Reef. Four Lynxes followed them there.

Already at Grand Reef for the past week after a long drive from the Victoria Falls area were the 40 designated helicopter-borne troops from Major Simon Haaroff's 2 Commando, undergoing intensive training, briefing and preparation for the attack.[130]

Four Vampire FB9s and two T11s of No. 2 Squadron landed at 18.00 at New Sarum where the paratroops had completed their individual unit briefings, revision of drills and assignment of tasks and were preparing their kit for their drop into a 'hot DZ' the next day.

At New Sarum the paratroops were woken at 03.00 on D-Day, Wednesday, 23 November, to give them time to draw their parachutes. Paired off for

---

[128] McAleese, p. 132.

[129] Memorandum by Major John R. Cronin, 23–24 February 1998.

[130] Binda, p. 250.

Chapter 15

mutual support, each man checked his partner's kit and tightened his straps.

Simultaneously, at Grand Reef, the 2 Commando troops donned their kit before boarding their vehicles for the drive to the helicopter assembly point at Lake Alexander.

Seen off by Air Marshal Frank Mussell and led by Squadron Leader Harold Griffiths of No. 7 Squadron, flights of five helicopters began a phased departure from New Sarum at 04.30.[131] In all, flying off were ten K-Cars, ten Rhodesian G-Cars, ten South African Polo G-Cars, and the command Alouette, piloted by Walsh and carrying Robinson.

At 06.00, led by Flight Lieutenant Bob d'Hotman, the six Dakotas rumbled down the long runway, laden with the 97 SAS and 48 RLI paratroopers.

Ahead of the aircraft, the Support Commando protection troops and others rolled 31 drums of fuel into position, ready for the arrival of the helicopters at Lake Alexander at 06.30. The protection troops deployed, their mortars covering the landing, as the helicopters came in on time, refuelled and embarked the 2 Commando troops, Petter-Bowyer and his admin area team and their equipment.

Leaving the ten Polo G-Cars to follow ten minutes later, the 21 helicopters bound for New Farm were back in the air at 07.10. Above them circled the six Dakotas. The Command Dakota, carrying General Walls, headed for its orbiting point 23 kilometres to the north of New Farm. Next the seven Hunters, four Canberras and four Vampires flew past, hugging the ground. As H-Hour approached, the Hunters accelerated ahead of the armada. The weather report of low cloud over New Farm had led to a late change in armament. Instead of carrying Golf bombs which required a high-dive profile, two of the leading Hunters had re-armed with Frantan and Matra 68mm rockets.

Everything was going to plan, except for the weather. Thick clouds also masked the eastern mountains, with a cloud ceiling at 300 feet above ground level some way into Mozambique. Leading the helicopter formation, Squadron Leader Griffiths found his way blocked by cloud and had to find

---

[131] Cole, p. 179.

Fireforce Writ Large:
Operation *Dingo*: Airborne Assault in Mozambique: 23-27 November 1977

another valley to penetrate, throwing out slightly his expected time of arrival at Chimoio. Once out of the mountains, he tucked his armada down onto the treetops to lessen the chance of detection.[132]

Over New Farm, Chimoio, however, the cloud cover was broken enough for the DC-8 ruse to work at 07.41 and thick enough to assist in hiding the attacking aircraft. The DC-8 rumbled overhead with its flaps down to create maximum noise, briefly alarming and dispersing the muster parades below. Perhaps thinking it was no more than a wayward Malawi-bound civilian jet, the parades reformed.

Four minutes later, at H-Hour (07.45), Red Section attacked. The middle Hunter of the formation, Red 1, flown by Squadron Leader Richard Brand, the commander of No. 1 Squadron, fired the opening shots from his four Aden 30mm cannons, strafing the old farmhouse, the nine iron-roofed and 41 thatched buildings and 49 pole and *dagga* huts of the sprawling headquarters.[133] Across the road, Red 2, Air Lieutenant David Bourhill, dropped a pair of frantan bombs onto Chitepo College and its 250 ZANLA students and staff, and climbed away to join Brand. The right-hand Hunter, Red 3, flown by Squadron Leader John Annan, hit New Farm's westernmost camp, Pasindina 2, with two 50-gallon frantan bombs, sending flaming napalm cascading over its 66 grass huts which housed 400 veteran ZANLA convalescents recovering from wounds and illnesses contracted in Rhodesia. Red 3 then raked the huts along the tree line to the north of the target with his 30mm guns. As Red Section turned in again to re-strike, the fierce fires they had kindled drove convection currents into fireballs over the stricken camps.[134]

Simultaneously, five kilometres to the north, the four Vampire FB9s (flown by Squadron Leader Steve Kesby and flight lieutenants Justin Varkevisser, Ken Law and Philip Haigh) fired salvoes of 60lb 'squash head' hollow-charge high-explosive rockets and 20mm cannon shells at the scattering 1,000 recruits and their 25 instructors and six FPLM soldiers mustering in front of

---

[132] Petter-Bowyer, p. 308.

[133] The old farmhouse, nine tin-roofed buildings, 41 thatched buildings and 49 huts.

[134] BECM RAAP, Box 844, Air strike Report, 23 November 1977.

the 33 barrack huts, 43 small huts and three bell tents of the recruits' camp.[135] Kesby recalls the startled flight of the men below as he loosed his rockets.[136]

Thirty seconds later, flying at their bombing speed of 350 knots and height of 300 feet, the Canberras roared over the complex. Overshooting slightly, the leading Canberra spewed her 300 Alpha bombs out from the centre of burning Pasindina 2. The football-sized bombs bounced and exploded throughout the second half of the camp and beyond. The second Canberra smothered the headquarters with its Alpha bombs, killing an estimated 600 ZANLA cadres.[137] Across the road, the two following Canberras sprayed 300 bombs each on the already stricken Chitepo College and its two adjoining neighbours: Chaminuka Camp (where Mugabe stayed during his visits) housing the ZANLA security section and its 500 Peking-trained insurgents; and Parirenyatwa Camp with its 1,200 male and female trainee and trained nursing staff.[138]

In the wake of the Canberras came the returning, diving Red Section Hunters. Coming in from the northwest, Red 1 fired a ripple of 68mm Matra high-explosive rockets at the National Stores, the main logistics centre. Encircled by a bulldozed fire break, this comprised an old tobacco barn, surrounded by 53 huts and five bell tents, housing 150 ZANLA and holding food, clothing and ammunition. A little further on, Red 1 hit the Old Garage with Matra rockets and his 30mm shells. Red 2 followed him strafing both targets. Red 3 hit Pasindina 2 again, strafing the huts along the tree line north of his marking point. All three Hunters then orbited to form the first 'cab-rank' of the day.

The Canberras flew back to New Sarum to re-arm with Alpha bombs but instead of being held there as planned, later returned to orbit New Farm in a cab-rank at 15,000 feet.[139]

---

[135] 33 barrack huts, 43 small huts and three bell tents for 1,000 recruits, 25 instructors and six FPLM.

[136] Beryl Salt, *A Pride of Eagles: The Definitive History of the Rhodesian Air Force: 1920–1980*, Covos Day, Weltevreden Park, 2001, p. 595.

[137] Robert MacKenzie, 'Fast Strike on Chimoio II', *Soldier of Fortune*, February 94, p. 46.

[138] BECM RAAP, Box 844, Air strike Report, 23 November 1977.

[139] Cowderoy & Nesbit, *War in the Air,* pp. 77–78.

Fireforce Writ Large:
Operation *Dingo*: Airborne Assault in Mozambique: 23-27 November 1977

A minute and a half later (at H+2 minutes), flying on right-angle courses to each other, the two columns of three Dakotas each approached their dropping zones.

As they did, four Hunters of Blue and White sections dived over them firing 68mm high-explosive rockets and 30mm cannons at the anti-aircraft gun emplacements, and at the Matopos and Takawira camps behind the headquarters, and Nehanda Camp, close to Chitepo College. Matopos housed the registry and Takawira had 500 semi-trained recruits awaiting transport to external training centres in Tanzania, Ethiopia and elsewhere.

White 1, Vic Wightman, and White 2, Spook Geraty, loosed 40 Matra rockets at the anti-aircraft sites and fired 500 30mm cannon shells, setting the huts at Takawira alight. White 1 was hit above the port intake by a bullet fired from the second gun site.

Blue Leader, Flight Lieutenant J. R. Blythe-Wood, and Blue 2, Air Lieutenant Martin Lowrie, likewise attacked the gun pits and camps.

Blue Leader fired 24 Matra rockets into Gun Pit 2 and then collapsed the tents of Nehanda Camp with shells from his four 30mm cannons. His next target was the complex at National Stores at which he fired 12 68mm rockets and a burst of 30mm shells.

Blue 2 strafed Gun Pit 4 with 30mm cannon shells and then fired his rockets at the mill at National Stores at the command of incoming Group Captain Walsh in the command helicopter.

Following the Hunters were a pair of Vampire T11s, each armed with eight 60lb squash-head rockets.

Although ZANLA gunners fought back, with their anti-aircraft weapons, sending streams of red and green tracer whipping across the sky, the six Dakotas were unscathed as they droned through the smoke and dust at 450 feet above ground, disgorging paratroopers.[140]

The American, SAS Captain Robert MacKenzie, recalled watching the increasing volume of flak rising as his Dakota approached the dropping zone. Peter McAleese saw a Vampire diving in to suppress anti-aircraft fire. He and

---

[140] BECM RAAP, No. 3 Squadron. Rhodesian Air Force, Diary, November 1977 (in private hands).

others noted the thousands of fleeing figures beneath them as they jumped out of the aircraft. Some of the ZANLA were firing their weapons over their shoulders as they ran. McAleese blessed their poor fire discipline.

The six Dakotas dropped in reverse order Stops 1 to 6. Each stop comprised 24 men, grouped in four-man sticks. Dropped furthest to the southwest, Stop 1 was drawn from lieutenants Rod Smith's 11 Troop and Mark Adams's 12 Troop, 3 Commando, and was accompanied by Major Jeremy Strong, their officer commanding. Stop 2 was lieutenants John Cronin's 13 Troop and Gordon Thornton's 14 Troop of 3 Commando. A Troop, SAS, supplied Stop 3 commanded by Captain Colin Willis and Stop 4, led by Captain Robert MacKenzie. Stops 5 and 6 were from B Troop, SAS; Stop 5 commanded by Lieutenant Ken Roberts and Stop 6 by Captain Grahame Wilson, destined to be Rhodesia's most decorated soldier. SAS Major Mick Graham, the ground commander, jumped with Roberts.

Apart from the anti-aircraft gunners, most of the ZANLA personnel scattered. A survivor recalled: 'Within seconds planes were moving about in the air and we were all scared. We couldn't think what to do except to run. I rolled and rolled across the ground and hid under a bush. Then a bomb dropped on the spot where I had just been. I rolled again and fell into a pit and broke my arm. I had to leave my gun. Now people were running in all directions."[141] A female survivor, Olaria Lucia Chikuhuhu, told the British press later that she had muddied her clothes to dull their bright colours and started to walk out of the complex "passing through many sub-bases with a lot of dead bodies of my fellow comrades. I couldn't control my tears. When I looked every direction I saw a Daicotar [Dakota] deploying ground forces". Covering herself with blood, she lay among the bodies feigning death. The Rhodesians kicked her as they examined the corpses but she did not give herself away. Later a grass fire burned towards where she lay but she seems to have managed to get away unseen.[142] Neither Robert Mugabe nor the

---

[141] Cowderoy & Nesbit, *War in the Air,* p. 82.

[142] David Caute, *Under the Skin: The Death of White Rhodesia,* Allen Lane, London, 1982, pp. 140–141.

Fireforce Writ Large:
Operation *Dingo*: Airborne Assault in Mozambique: 23-27 November 1977

ZANLA hierarchy, Josiah Tongogara and Rex Nhongo, were in the camp that day, a fact which Walls regretted when speaking to the press. The wife of Edgar Tekere, Mugabe's mentor (and later his opponent), was there, however, hidden in a latrine.[143]

The dull green parachutes of the RLI and SAS troopers had just opened when they plunged into the trees through which the ZANLA cadres were sprinting. The main line of flight was southwesterly through the line being formed by the RLI Stop 2 and SAS Captain Colin Willis's Stop 3. His parachute entangled in two trees, Willis faced ten ZANLA men sprinting at him. He drew his pistol and knocked one down beneath him. Sergeant Les Clark, coming up in support, shot six more running towards him. Willis swung himself across to one of the trees and climbed down.[144] Captain MacKenzie hit a mopane tree, snagged it, and was brought to a halt six inches above the ground. He hit his quick-release box and took cover behind a tree.[145] McAleese was also caught in a tree and instantly came under fire from a hidden ZANLA. He released the Capewell attachment clips at his shoulders and plunged down onto a large anthill, still wearing his harness. He freed his RPK machine gun and went to work with his partner, Steve Kluzniak, also using an RPK, to eliminate his attacker. The ZANLA rifleman expended his ammunition and then tried to surrender. McAleese showed him no mercy.[146] Further along the line, a stick of four shed their harnesses and opened fire, killing 80 ZANLA.[147]

Charlie Warren, jumping with Major Jeremy Strong and Stop 2, was still in the air when he had a dozen ZANLA cadres running and firing at him and his MAG gunner, Keith White. Distracted, Warren failed to adopt the correct body position and landed hard. Winded, he tugged his rifle free of the parachute's body band and dived into cover. On both sides of him, fire

---

[143] Cole, p. 184.

[144] Cole, p. 182.

[145] MacKenzie, p. 84.

[146] McAleese, p. 134.

[147] Cole, p. 182.

was being exchanged. He fired at a group running 200 metres in front him. Then he and White linked up with Major Strong.

Stop 1, the first down, however, had enjoyed a peaceful landing, as did the eastward Stops 5 and 6. They landed, discarded their parachutes and reformed into their four-man sticks, while watching the arriving K-Cars hammering the camp complexes.[148]

Squadron Leader Griffiths had led in his ten K-Cars on time at 07.50 (H+5) to attempt to 'close the lid' by engaging their pre-selected targets with 20mm cannon fire. Two K-Cars attacked the headquarters complex. Two more fired on the complex containing Chitepo College, Chaminuka and Parirenyatwa camps, and the detention barracks. Farther north, a K-Car shot at Old Garage Camp, a large open-sided metal-roofed building and 29 huts. Old Garage served as a fuel dump, a vehicle graveyard, an ammunition store for the Recruits' Camp and a tool store. Just to the east, a K-Car hammered National Stores with bursts of 20mm shells.

While the paratroopers found their feet and shook out into extended order with ten metres between each man, ZANLA troops continued to fight back. At 07.52 K-Car K3 drew heavy small-arms fire west of Pasindina 2, the convalescent camp, 300 metres to the rear of 3 Commando's Stops 1 and 2. Two minutes later the southeastern flank, manned by the SAS Stops 4, 5 and 6, faced an attempted break-out of hundreds of ZANLA cadres.

Three kilometres to the north of the National Stores, a pair of K-Cars attacked the Recruits' Camp, while two K-Cars strafed the burning remains of Pasindina 2, to ensure that there would be no threat to the thin Rhodesian line from the rear.

At 07.56 ten G-Cars, carrying Stop A, Major Haaroff and his 40 troopers of 2 Commando, pulled up from treetop level and climbed to orientate themselves before landing on a grassy strip behind the northwestern 30-foot-high ridge. In the brief moment of the orbit the troops could not only smell the frantan but also saw the chaotic flight of people running through the smoke and the flashes of exploding ordnance. On the way in, Jimmy

---

[148] Binda, p. 252.

Fireforce Writ Large:
Operation *Dingo*: Airborne Assault in Mozambique: 23-27 November 1977

Swan and the men of his stick had seen the last of the paratroops jumping to the east of them.[149]

Among the 2 Commando troopers taking up all-round defence of their G-Cars was the commanding officer of the RLI, Lieutenant-Colonel Peter Rich, acting as a rifleman and Haaroff's radio operator in order not to miss the show.[150] Rich thus joined his son, Lieutenant Michael Rich, a troop commander in 2 Commando, on the battlefield.[151] Peter Rich later commented on the singular experience of a Rhodesian father and son taking cover close to each other under fire on an external operation. "As an old shottist," he said, he had time to regret that his son, Michael "tended to snatch the trigger!"[152] This was not the first battlefield that 51-year-old Peter Rich had been on, having fought in the Korean War as a platoon commander in the Norfolk Regiment and in Malaya with 22 SAS. Michael Rich recalls it as "Quite a unique experience to be in the same assault line as your Dad! I recall that there were only two heads sticking up above the grass—his to see if I was okay and mine to see if he was okay! He also kept issuing me instructions/requests out of the corner of his mouth like 'Get me a Bakelite AK bayonet' as he couldn't be seen, as the CO, to be grabbing souvenirs!"[153]

The G-Cars lifted off and Stop A sprinted to the crest of the ridge. There they waited, facing the dense bush of the valley, waiting for the order to advance.[154]

The G-Car flown by Flight Lieutenant Bill Sykes, leading the South African Polo helicopters, had broken away from the helicopter stream to deliver Wing Commander Peter Petter-Bowyer, the RLI doctor and RLI Captain Buttenshaw and their teams to the admin area 20 kilometres from New Farm's outer camp. Circling above, having flown ahead of the helicopters, was the

---

[149] Binda, p. 252.

[150] Memorandum by Major John R. Cronin, 23–24 February 1998.

[151] Interview: Lieutenant-Colonel Brian Robinson, 8 May 1998.

[152] Binda, p. 246.

[153] Email from Mike Rich, 25 May 2005.

[154] Binda, p. 252.

Chapter 15

DC-7 flown by Jack Malloch with Squadron Leader George Alexander, the commander of No. 3 Squadron, as his co-pilot. Seeming to be a suitably clear area on the aerial photograph, the first surprise for Petter-Bowyer was the unsuitable nature of his new base with its shoulder-high grass interspersed with clumps of bushes. The second surprise was the sight of the DC-7 lining up on its first dropping run, two minutes early. This posed a danger of the load dropping among the Polo helicopters unloading tools, spares, medical equipment, mortars and stocks of ammunition. Petter-Bowyer talked the DC-7 around for its second run, dropping pallets of fuel drums. He recalls Alexander's agitation as his drums landed near the helicopters, hazarding a parachute being caught by the rotating helicopter blades. Buttenshaw also found his area of responsibility nightmarish, impossible to defend because of its size and the densely treed landscape. He posted sentries, chose a position for his mortars and their stock of 100 bombs and deployed his fire controller on the prominent hill, overlooking the base. Then, leaving one team to man the mortars, he sent the other to assist the pilots and technicians in gathering up parachutes, rolling scattered drums into refuelling positions for the incoming helicopters from the target area and trimming the bush around the points. All this would occupy everyone for the first two hours.[155] Then there would be stricken helicopters to repair.[156]

The air strikes at New Farm had shattered buildings and littered the ground with hundreds of dead, wounded or stunned ZANLA personnel. Later the mass of lifeless bodies on the parade ground reminded John Cronin of rows of mown wheat.[157]

Yet such was the sustained fire from the ZANLA positions that, aside from the six Dakotas, every aircraft flying over the target after the initial air strike was hit.[158]

Particularly heavy fire from Old Garage and the Ngangas Camp (88

---

[155] Petter-Bowyer, pp. 308–310; Binda, p. 244.

[156] Salt, p. 598.

[157] Memorandum 'Follow-up to Operation *Dingo*, Major John R. Cronin, 21 April 1998.

[158] Cole, p. 183.

Fireforce Writ Large:
Operation *Dingo*: Airborne Assault in Mozambique: 23-27 November 1977

thatched pole and *dagga* huts) prompted Walsh to call in Red 2 to attack Old Garage, the neighbouring National Stores and their adjoining complexes. Red 2 obliged, hammering both targets with 30mm cannon shells. In all, the three Hunters of Red Section had fired a thousand cannon shells.[159]

Blue 2 then strafed the mill at Old Stores with 45 Matra rockets and fired a salvo of 140 30mm cannon rounds into the Ngangas Camp.

At 08.00, the aircraft spotted a large gathering of ZANLA cadres west of the convalescent camp, Pasindina 2. Simultaneously, an anti-aircraft gun south of Chitepo College, the home of the political commissars, fired at a K-Car and a Lynx. The Lynx limped back to Grand Reef with fuel weeping through a bullet hole while Walsh called in Red 3.[160] Red 3 neutralized the gun and then rocketed and strafed a position 200 metres south of Chaminuka and Parirenyatwa camps and the headquarters, where the hard core of ZANLA were making a stand. Behind the sweep line, a pair of K-Cars renewed the attack on Pasindina 2.

Having allowed the stop groups time to organize themselves, Major Brian Robinson made sure that he could see the whereabouts of all of them from the orbiting command helicopter. At 08.10, he ordered them to advance. He then oversaw their careful use of fire and movement, with the four-man sticks covering each other. The task of co-ordinating the sweep lines with 37 call signs taught him to wear leather gloves on future operations to avoid the blisters which he soon suffered from his thumb constantly depressing the pressel switch on his radio.

A minute later, at 08.11, a pair of K-Cars, Griffiths's K1 and K1 Alpha, left to refuel and re-arm at the admin area.

Two minutes later, commenting on heavy firing coming from the Recruits' Camp's rifle range, K-Car K4 called for a Vampire strike. As he did, for the moment, the firing lessened.

The 40 RLI men of Stop A pushed through the bushy undergrowth of the tree line below their ridge and halted at its edge. Almost immediately they

---

[159] BECM RAAP, Box 844, Air strike Report, 23 November 1977.

[160] Cowderoy & Nesbit, p. 82.

faced a charge by crouching, running, wildly firing ZANLA cadres. Stop A's experienced riflemen responded with economical and accurate 'double-taps'. The MAG gunners fired short bursts. This response broke the charge. Jimmy Swan counted 22 ZANLA dead, including light-skinned bodies which he presumed were Cuban instructors. The weapons of the fallen were piled up and booby-trapped with a grenade. The sweep line advanced and soon drew fire, including stick grenades, as they crossed a clearing. Covered by a K-Car, the troops skirmished forward to the next tree line. The fight around Swan resulted in a further 17 ZANLA dead. The ZANLA response, mortar fire from Takawira Camp, drove Stop A into cover. They returned fire and called for an air strike.[161]

Advancing northeast, the RLI Stops 1 and 2 immediately drew fire from the bush in front of them. Soon, however, they were shooting at running figures and 'double-tapping' likely cover. They aimed low to secure hits and gave little quarter.

The SB wanted prisoners, but, with no reserves to guard them, the troops left taking prisoners to the mopping-up phase. MacKenzie secured a prisoner, used him to indicate strong points and then left him handcuffed to a bush for later collection. Much to MacKenzie's annoyance, an RLI MAG-gunner dispatched the prisoner. Tony Coom, however, remembers orders to kill a mutilated and mortally wounded cadre, rather than detain him as a prisoner.[162] John Connelly, an ex-Royal Engineer turned RLI machine gunner, obeyed. Yet the troops were not totally merciless, letting through two women running with a baby. [163]

The SAS Stops 3 and 4 of Willis and MacKenzie faced greater difficulties in the brush-filled gullies to their front. Nevertheless, moving fast, their tracers picking out defenders for supporting fire, the SAS advanced to 150 metres short of the first trenches in front of the interlinking camps of Chitepo College, Chaminuka, Parirenyatwa and Nehanda.

---

[161] Binda, p. 254.

[162] Binda, p. 260

[163] Memorandum 'Follow-up to Operation *Dingo*, Major John R. Cronin, 21 April 1998.

Fireforce Writ Large:
Operation *Dingo*: Airborne Assault in Mozambique: 23-27 November 1977

At 08.26, however, a 12.7mm machine-gun bullet holed the main rotor of the command helicopter. Walsh steered the crippled aircraft northward towards the admin area while Robinson tried to get a helicopter to pick up his deputy, Major Mick Graham, to take over command. As Graham could not be extricated for the moment from the fighting in the trees, Robinson was forced to order the troops to hold their positions and await his return. Walsh charged Alpha 4, the orbiting Lynx, with tactical control of Chimoio's airspace in his absence. Alpha 4 was promptly also hit by concentrated small-arms fire but continued to orbit.[164]

As he flew away, Walsh reported to the command Dakota, saying that the huts of New Garage were burning, two-thirds of the tents of Nehanda Camp had collapsed but the K-Cars were drawing heavy anti-aircraft fire from there. Chaminuka Camp appeared untouched with its anti-aircraft weapons still in action. The main building and the accommodation of the HQ were damaged and there were numerous fires north of the road. There was no damage south of the road. Numerous huts were on fire in the Matopos and Takawira camps. Pasindina 2, although half alight, was still the source of heavy anti-aircraft fire. Huts were burning in Chitepo College but its anti-aircraft guns kept firing. National Stores was alight and, although there had been a large explosion there, heavy anti-aircraft fire persisted from there. The Recruits' Camp was burning and half the huts had been destroyed.[165]

A lesson had been learned for future operations. Walsh and Robinson would fly in the command Dakota, sitting facing each other for ease of discussion and using its superior communications equipment to conduct the operation through a Lynx flying over the battle. The Lynx, flying above the range of small arms, would carry Robinson's second-in-command to provide co-ordination between Robinson and the ground commanders. Both the Dakota and Lynx had incomparable endurance compared with the helicopter.[166]

At the admin area technicians set about transferring the radios and other

---

[164] BECM RAAP, Box 844, Air strike Report, 23 November 1977

[165] BECM RAAP, Box 844, Air strike Report, 23 November 1977.

[166] Conversation with Lieutenant-Colonel Brian Robinson, 5 September 1997; Cole, p. 189.

equipment from Walsh's helicopter to a G-Car. There were other helicopters requiring repairs. Geoff Dartnall's K-Car required new tail-rotor blades and a patch in one of his main rotor blades. He did not find the bullet in his self-sealing fuel tank until the next day. He was given the tail rotors from another aircraft and returned to the action. A third helicopter had taken a hit in the engine. A G-Car took off for Grand Reef to collect a new engine, main blades and a tail rotor and by the end of the day all aircraft were fit to fly.[167]

At 08.30 K-Car K6 arrived at the admin area to refuel and re-arm. Along the stalled sweep lines, the exchange of fire continued. Drawing intensive fire from a heavy-calibre weapon firing from Chaminuka Camp, SAS Captain Willis of Stop 3 threw smoke and called for assistance. Reinforced at 08.36 by K-Car K2A rejoining the fight, K2 responded to Willis and called for an air strike by the Vampires of Voodoo Section.

As he did, Venom Section re-struck the Recruits' Camp. Venom 2, Vampire FB9 No. 1386, flown by Flight Lieutenant Philip Haigh (once of the Royal Air Force), was severely damaged by a ricochet or fire from the ground.[168] (Steve Kesby records Haigh being hit in the initial attack but the signals log has it happening during the re-strike.) Kesby flew in formation with Haigh, radioing ahead to warn New Sarum to expect an emergency landing but lost him in the cloud. With his engine failing, Haigh attempted to save the stricken aircraft by gliding into a field over the border in the Inyanga district. Despite achieving a perfect belly-landing, it ended in disaster when the aircraft struck a ditch and disintegrated, killing him.[169] Few belly-landings in the Vampire were successful because she was built partly of wood, a legacy of De Havilland's success in building the 'wooden wonder', the Mosquito.

At 08.44 the two Vampire T11s of Voodoo Section came to Willis's aid, silencing the anti-aircraft gun in Chaminuka Camp. A minute later, however, when they re-struck it they drew heavy fire from the edge of a maize field from a multi-barrelled gun.

---

[167] Salt, pp. 596–597.

[168] BECM RAAP, Box 844, Air strike Report, 23 November 1977.

[169] Salt, pp. 596–597.

Fireforce Writ Large:
Operation *Dingo*: Airborne Assault in Mozambique: 23-27 November 1977

One of the T11s, summoned by Haaroff of Stop A, then rocketed Takawira. Stop A were lucky because they escaped unscathed when a pair of the Vampire's 60lb rockets were fired in their direction by mistake. Jimmy Swan recalled graphically the stick commanders calling in vain for the pilot to pull out while their men hugged the earth. Back on their feet they moved towards the burning huts of the Takawira 1.[170]

At 08.45, called in by a K-Car, a Hunter attacked Chitepo College from south to north, firing 27 Matra rockets and 405 rounds of 30mm.

Although the ZANLA gun crews stood their ground and fought back, the waiting Rhodesian troops watched with frustration as the vast mass of the inhabitants of New Farm melted away northward due to the failure of the K-Cars to contain them. There were never sufficient K-Cars on station due to their constant need to fly away to refuel and re-arm. Even so, the strung-out line of Rhodesians began to worry that should the ZANLA muster sufficient men for a concerted breakout or a counter-attack it would be impossible to defeat it. MacKenzie, for one, thought that a ZANLA group of 30 would easily break through the thinly held line. What was clear was that the enemy did not know how few troops were confronting them.[171]

At 08.47 K-Car 2A was ordered to assist Stop 2 because the camp complexes around Chitepo College and Nehanda Camp were reacting.

At 08.52 an air strike from a Hunter hit the multi-barrelled gun. Four minutes later Willis was ordered to pinpoint the source of the anti-aircraft fire for an additional strike by Red 3 because Chaminuka Camp was still emitting heavy fire from the area to the left of the last Hunter strike. K-Car 2A was still drawing a voluminous response from the Parirenyatwa, Chaminuka and Nehanda camps. Called in to re-strike the target, Red 3 planned his run in from west to east from the ridge south of Chitepo College to the Parirenyatwa complex. Stop 2's men were still drawing heavy fire from the river line. Furthermore, it appeared that a large-calibre anti-aircraft gun was back in action at the college.

---

[170] Cowderoy & Nesbit, *War in the Air*, p. 80.

[171] MacKenzie, p. 45.

At 09.09 Red 3 attacked Chitepo College with his 68mm Matra rockets and a minute later came to the assistance of Stop 2. At 09.19 he made his planned strafing run from east to west on the Nehanda, Chaminuka and Parirenyatwa camps and Chitepo College. His 30mm shells and 68mm rockets struck all four targets and silenced the gun at Chitepo College.

By then the conditions had become dangerous for air operations because of the thick pall of smoke trapped below the lowering clouds. [172] Nevertheless, the fight went on with K-Car 6, re-armed and refuelled, attracting rifle fire from the National Stores. His 20mm cannon had a stoppage.

At last, at 09.30, Walsh and Robinson returned to command the attack aboard the replacement G-Car, albeit from a higher orbit. [173] K-Car 6 withdrew to clear his jammed weapon. The incoming replacement Hunter, White Leader, silenced the gun in Gun Pit 1.

Robinson ordered the resumption of the advance of the troops who immediately encountered resistance in the area between the National Stores and Thin Camp. Haaroff ordered Stop A forward and then halted them just inside a tree line. Almost immediately, his 40 men were firing bursts at a short range into a mass of cadres, trying to run through their sweep line. The charge was repulsed, leaving 33 cadres dead in thickets and the broken ground. Stop A, as before, piled up the captured weapons and booby-trapped them.

Haaroff resumed the advance towards the camp. His men moved forward, firing into likely cover and giving all the bodies littering the ground a coup de grâce to avoid being attacked from behind.[174]

At 09.33 Lynx A4 was relieved by Lynx D4 and flew away to re-arm and refuel at Grand Reef, Umtali. This changeover coincided with two Vampires of Voodoo Section, strafing with their 20mm cannons the northern sector of the Recruits' Camp complex, attacking an active multi-barrelled anti-aircraft

---

[172] BECM RAAP, Box 844, Air strike Report, 23 November 1977.

[173] McAleese records this as 12 noon but the delay was certainly nothing like that. Robert MacKenzie's recalled time is more likely to be accurate, McAleese, p. 135; MacKenzie, p. 45.

[174] Binda, p. 256.

Fireforce Writ Large:
Operation *Dingo*: Airborne Assault in Mozambique: 23-27 November 1977

gun and suppressing rifle fire coming from the old rifle range.[175]

At 09.45, as Stop 2 was still under fire, Walsh sent a K-Car to assist him. As he did, the command Dakota reported to ComOps that the resistance from large calibre anti-aircraft had been silenced. Even so, all K-Cars had been hit and small-arms fire was still emanating from complexes at Chitepo College and the Parirenyatwa, Chaminuka and Nehanda camps and from the National Stores and Thin Camp.

The additional Canberra was ordered to neutralize Chitepo College and Parirenyatwa, Chaminuka and Nehanda camps before they were swept.[176] The cab-ranking Vampires, Venom 1 and 4, led the way with a 20mm strafing run through Chitepo College, Chaminuka and Parirenyatwa camps. They were followed by Canberra, Green 3, dousing the camps with 300 Mk II Alpha bombs. The bombing was accurate but Green 3's reward was to be hit twice by bullets and shrapnel.[177]

Two minutes later, because the majority of the aircraft was being hit, the command Dakota proposed a Canberra Alpha bomb strike on the HQ complex and Parirenyatwa Camp. Stops 1, 2 and 3 were ordered to throw smoke to mark the targets in front of them for a strike by the two Hunters of White Section parallel to the markers. Fired on by a heavy machine gun in Gun Pit 2, White 2 struck it at 09.55 and then he and White 1 strafed Matopos and Takawira camps with Matra rockets and 30mm cannon shells, leaving numerous buildings ablaze. One Hunter sustained a bullet hit in its starboard gun pack.[178]

At 10.04 White Section attacked the targets again to discourage any further fire as Stops 1, 2 and 3 prepared to resume their advance while Stops A, 4, 5 and 6 covered the ground in front of them.

The sweep recommenced at 10.05. K-Car A1 provided top cover for Stop 2 until replaced two minutes later by K-Car 1A.

---

[175] BECM RAAP, Box 844, Air strike Report, 23 November 1977.

[176] BECM RAAP, Box 844, ComOps TAC(HQ) to ComOps, 23 November 1977.

[177] BECM RAAP, Box 844, Air strike Report, 23 November 1977.

[178] BECM RAAP, Box 844, Air strike Report, 23 November 1977.

At 10.09 a K-Car was fired at from east of the main hill.

A minute later, the orbiting aircraft were told that Haigh's crashed Vampire had been found by a helicopter. [179]

At 10.18 Robinson demanded a strength return from Stops 1, 2 and 3 and was told all men were present.

There remained a prospect of outside interference as, at 10.20, the Rhodesian intercept service, 8 Signals Squadron, heard an FPLM radio operator announcing the despatch of an anti-aircraft unit to reinforce the embattled ZANLA and a call for infantry from Vila Manica and Catandica to the west. Nevertheless, Lynx E4 reported at 10.22 that he had seen no movement on the roads and railways in the wider area.

At 10.25 Blue Section's Hunters withdrew to refuel at New Sarum.

At 10.27 20 men were ordered to enter the Chitepo College complex. Aerial surveillance by the K-Cars was to continue on the Matopos, Takawira and Pasindina areas.

While the arrival of the Canberra was awaited, Walsh ordered Venom Section to put in as many strikes as possible on Chitepo College and Parirenyatwa Camp.

At 10.32 the Lynx warned the command Dakota that two Land Rovers were approaching on the road towards the area.

At 10.40 Stops 1, 2 and 3 halted their advance to allow the Hunters, Blue 1 and Blue 2, to mark Chitepo College and Parirenyatwa Camp for the strike by the Canberra Green 3. Blue Section strafed an area 400 metres south of Chitepo College and the Nehanda and Chaminuka camps, drawing fire. A bullet struck Blue 1's starboard windscreen.

In the dust, smoke and haze, Blue 1's mark was not seen and at 10.48 the Canberra's bombs landed 200 metres north of the target. [180] The troops radioed that there was fire from the ground whenever an aircraft appeared and not only was Blue 1 hit but also five K-Cars. [181]

---

[179] BECM RAAP, Box 844, ComOps FAF8 to ComOps, 23 November 1977.

[180] BECM RAAP, Box 844, Air strike Report, 23 November 1977.

[181] BECM RAAP, Box 844, Air strike Report, 23 November 1977.

Robinson ordered Stops 1, 2 and 3 to resume their sweep.

At 10.52, the pilots in the area were told that it was confirmed that Haigh had crashed.

Two minutes later, Griffiths, flying K-Car 1, was ordered to withdraw for an in-flight briefing.

At 10.55, Blue 1 cleared the area and en route three minutes later suggested an additional air effort.

The incoming Red Section, expected over the target in 15 minutes, was warned at 11.00 there was still a fair amount of opposition. Stop 2 confirmed this was so at 11.07 because they were drawing fairly heavy fire from the camp area

Robinson asked General Walls at 11.10 for guidance as he wanted the sweep to continue but, if it bogged down, he wanted permission to withdraw it. Walls replied that the sweep should continue but should not get bogged down. Robinson responded at 11.15 by ordering the men on the eastern flank, Stops 4, 5 and 6, to prepare to advance northward. As he did, Red Leader and Red 2, Bourhill, attacked targets with 24 Matra rockets and 520 30mm shells from an easterly direction. In doing so, a bullet hit the rear fuselage of Red 1's Hunter No. 8116, damaging it superficially.[182]

Two minutes later, Stops 4, 5 and 6 started their sweep.

At 11.20 Willis of Stop 3 reported he was just south of Parirenyatwa and Chitepo camps and that firing from there was enduring. In response, at 11.32, K-Car 3 called on Red Section to strike towards Chitepo College. Stop 3 immediately flanked a recoilless rifle, attacked and killed the eight-man crew.

Canberra Green 4 reported at 11.41 he was five minutes out.

At 11.56 Robinson ordered all the stops to commence sweeping inwards. The SAS Stops 3 and 4 had reached the edge of the trees and faced a long zigzag trench line a 100 metres away. Covered by MAG/RPD bursts, the SAS troopers stormed the trenches, seizing several 100 metres of them but finding only a few insurgents cowering in them. MacKenzie ordered his men

---

[182] BECM RAAP, Box 844, Air strike Report, 23 November 1977.

to reorganize and replenish their magazines and machine-gun belts.

During this action Stops 1 and 2 moved into MacKenzie's line of fire. John Cronin's RLI 13 Troop had to shelter for ten minutes behind a low wall, a remnant of the Portuguese occupation.[183] SAS bullets, however, wounded Mark Adams's 12 Troop flank man, the only casualty that Tony Coom's stick suffered under his command. Radio contact was made and the firing switched away.

Shortly thereafter, Adams's men came under fire from a dug-in Soviet DShK 12.7mm heavy machine gun.[184]

In the confusion, summoned by Stop 2 for support, K-Car A4 mistook the stick next to Coom in Stop 1 for the enemy and fired. The shrapnel peppered Johnny Norman. Terry Hammond and Paul Furstenburg who escaped with relatively minor wounds. John Connelly was not so lucky.[185] Two G-Cars were ordered to stand by for a casevac.

At 12.00 a Hunter dived in to suppress fire in front of the troops and at 12.07 a G-Car attempted the casevac. Although Stop 1 silenced the heavy machine gun, the arriving G-Car drew fire and was waved off. The wounded had to wait while Stop 1 attacked and cleared the vicinity. That done, Tony Coom radioed the G-Car to remove the wounded.[186]

As K-Car 20mm ammunition was running low, Petter-Bowyer's admin area, at 12.12, asked Grand Reef for more.

At 12.19, Robinson ordered MacKenzie's Stop 4 to move to the Matopos, Takawira and Pasindina camps. Leaving two sticks in a defensive position, MacKenzie and 16 men advanced in extended line through the trees towards what he called the 'Intelligence Centre' (presumably the 'registry' at Matopos Camp, behind the ZANLA headquarters). In a clearing, en

---

[183] Memorandum 'Follow-up to Operation *Dingo*, Major John R. Cronin, 21 April 1998.

[184] Binda, p. 260. The DShK was the standard Warsaw Pact heavy machine gun used in a dual role as an effective infantry and anti-aircraft weapon. It had a cyclic rate of 575 rounds per minute and a range of 2,000 metres.

[185] Chris Cocks, *Fireforce: One Man's War in The Rhodesian Light Infantry*, 30° South Publishers, Johannesburg, 2006, pp. 144–146.

[186] Binda, p. 260.

Fireforce Writ Large:
Operation *Dingo*: Airborne Assault in Mozambique: 23-27 November 1977

route, he encountered a ZANLA crew of four firing their DShK 12.7mm machine gun at the orbiting aircraft from the top of a 30-foot-high tower. After creeping forward unnoticed to the edge of the trees, the SAS shot the gun crew and their protection party at the base of the tower.

Moving on, MacKenzie's sticks encountered another anti-aircraft position sporting an unmanned Chinese twin-barrelled 37mm gun. Perhaps because the ZANLA gunners did not know how to operate it, it had not yet been cleaned of its original grease. If they had used it, the Rhodesian Air Force could well have suffered worse damage than it did. As it was too heavy to be flown out, MacKenzie would later blow it apart with plastic explosive.

MacKenzie resumed his advance through the trees, flushing out and killing some 20 cadres hiding beneath fallen tree trunks and in holes in a dry riverbed. After 150 metres, his men crossed the trenches of the Intelligence Centre, a small empty camp of 18 pole and *dagga* huts, serving as offices, classrooms and storerooms. His men searched the huts, finding trunks of documents which MacKenzie and one of his officers browsed through before arranging their dispatch by air to Rhodesia. Among the documents was a typed ZANLA report on the Selous Scout raid on their Nyadzonya camp which gave the lie to the claims that it had been a refugee camp.[187] McAleese was amazed at just how much was recorded on every ZANLA member.[188] Apart from documents, Corporal Bates Mare discovered a dark room and dozens of modern 35mm Leica, Pentax and Nikon cameras, and two film cameras. The troopers shared them out among themselves. Once MacKenzie had completed his assessment of the papers, the SAS fired the huts and moved back to the rest of his men near the headquarters.[189]

Stop 1 overran the troublesome, dug-in heavy machine gun at 12.19, finding it to be a wheeled 12.7mm machine gun with a great deal of ammunition on hand. Told to mark where it was and to move on, the troops resumed their advance. They encountered only dead bodies. Then in sight of the main

---

[187] Reid-Daly, *Top Secret War*, pp. 283–285.

[188] McAleese, p. 136.

[189] MacKenzie, p. 46.

camp, they were again fired at by their own side, this time by the advancing troops of A Stop. Major Strong radioed Haaroff and the firing ceased. He had Stop 1 re-sweep the area and recover the 12.7mm. As they did, Peter Donnelly was wounded by enemy fire when clearing a reedbed.[190]

Also at 12.19 SAS Stop 5 was ordered to move through Chitepo College and Parirenyatwa and Chaminuka camps and to halt at the edge of the ploughed fields beyond.

A minute later, K-Car 5 was instructed to support Wilson's 24 men of Stop 6 advancing northward towards the camp complex at National Stores.

Robinson's next order was the clearing and search of the camps by the sweep lines.

When complying, MacKenzie was shown an open-air classroom under the trees, which had been devastated by Alpha bombs from a Canberra. Among the blown-over blackboards, 60 ZANLA students lay dead, their bloodied notebooks, filled with quotes from Chairman Mao, strewn around them. In the shattered, burning headquarters, MacKenzie found a briefcase stuffed full of documents. Before he could examine it, he was ordered by Robinson to take two sticks to the ZANLA motor-repair facility at Old Garage, a kilometre away across the open ground of the centre of New Farm.[191]

By 12.30 RLI Stops A, 1, 2 and 3 were searching Pasindina 1, Matopos and Takawira camps, and the HQ complex. In the course of this, Tony Coom's MAG gunner, clearing a brick ablution building, encountered a locked door and fired through it. His bursts tore into an unseen press of women and children who had taken refuge behind it. It was an experience which was to haunt him for the rest of his life.

Stop 2 had approached the pig pens in front of the main complex, finding bodies strewn across the ground. The men skirmished forward and began clearing the buildings with grenades. A storeroom yielded nine insurgents who were foolish enough to make a break for it while being interrogated by a stick leader. The escape was quickly terminated by fire from 3 Commando.

---

[190] Binda, p. 262.

[191] Including McAleese, Steve Kluzniak, Rob Rodell, Chunky Chesterman, Dick Borman.

Fireforce Writ Large:
Operation *Dingo*: Airborne Assault in Mozambique: 23-27 November 1977

In the HQ, the troops found a quantity of documents which were reserved for inspection by the SB. In a barn next door, they found a quartermaster's store packed with exotic foodstuffs such as Swedish sardines, Israeli tinned orange juice which they consumed despite SB warnings that they might be poisoned. There were also sacks of maize meal, sugar, rice and cashew nuts as well as uniforms and other military kit.

At Takawira, Stop A had the unpleasant and dangerous task of clearing bunkers with 1kg bunker bombs. Stop A would eventually account for some 120 deaths. As they searched the camp, the troops saw ZANLA cadres on the western ridge. They ignored them until a more aggressive group fired two RPG-7 rockets at them. Stop A's riposte killed 14 insurgents before moving on to search the Matopos Camp. Stop A had scored 167 confirmed kills.[192]

The search by SAS Stops 4, 5 and 6 of Parirenyatwa, Chaminuka, Nehanda camps and the National Stores also uncovered food stocks. Andy Johnson of the SAS was foolish enough to drink from a can of poisoned condensed milk and had to be flown out by a G-Car for treatment. He recovered. McAleese concluded that he was the victim of the SB's tactic of poisoning clothing and food left in strategic places where ZANLA insurgents might appropriate them. Coom confirms that SB personnel warned him and his men against eating anything. Furthermore, a SB member stopped one of Cronin's men from taking looted aspirin for a headache, warning they might be poisoned. Thereafter captured stock was left alone.[193]

Robinson issued a situation report. He noted that there had been no heavy anti-aircraft fire since 09.30. Gun Pit 4's weapon was deserted. Green Leader's third attack on the Nehanda, Chaminuka and Chitepo College complexes was on target, setting fire to huts in all three areas. He did not estimate enemy casualties but recorded the Rhodesian wounded as the three RLI soldiers hit by K-Car fire.[194] Within two minutes, at 12.32, however, Captain

---

[192] Chris Cocks, *Fireforce: One Man's War in the Rhodesian Light Infantry*, 30° South Publishers, Johannesburg, 2006, pp. 144–146.

[193] Memorandum, 'Follow-up to Operation *Dingo*', by Major John R. Cronin, 21 April 1998.

[194] BECM RAAP, Box 844, FAF8 to ComOps, 23 November 1977.

Willis of Stop 3 requested an immediate casevac for a serious casualty.

At 12.38 Walsh ordered the pair of Vampires of Voodoo Section to strike the area near the dams.

The orbiting Canberra Green 4 left to refuel at 12.45. Below him the Stops 1 to 6 were searching Pasindina 1, Matopos and Takawira camps, the HQ complex, Chitepo College and Parirenyatwa, Chaminuka and Nehanda camps.[195]

At 12.48 the Vampires of Voodoo Section were called in to attack the area around New Garage.

At New Sarum, in preparation for the post-Zulu 1 period, orders were issued at 12.50 for two Canberras to be armed with 500lb bombs with each load having two with instantaneous fuses and four with delayed fuses timed to explode over 72 hours. Their purpose was to kill or at least terrify the surviving ZANLA cadres when they returned to their camps.[196]

At 12.51 Walsh ordered White Section to strike the Pasindina 1 Camp in support of Haaroff's Stop A.

At 12.54 Lieutenant Roberts of Stop 5 called for a casevac in addition to the casualty suffered by Captain Colin Willis's Stop 3. The sweep of camp complexes was completed and had killed fifty.

At 12.55, talked in by a K-Car, White Section fired 500 30mm rounds at a group of ZANLA cadres gathered at the river junction northeast of the Recruits' Camp. The scattered insurgents were also attacked in four other areas.[197]

Stop A called at 13.07 for an air strike on an area between Pasindina 1 and Matopos and Takawira camps. White Section responded immediately.

The air above the burning camps was still hazardous. At 13.14 Flight Lieutenant Mark McLean, a reserve pilot flying a K-Car, suffered a superficial wound when a bullet, fired vertically, holed the floor, grazed his forehead and shattered his flying helmet.

---

[195] BECM RAAP, Box 844, ComOps TAC HQ to ComOps, 23 November 1977.

[196] BECM RAAP, Box 844, ComOps TAC (HQ) to Air HQ, 23 November 1977.

[197] BECM RAAP, Box 844, Air strike Report, 23 November 1977.

Fireforce Writ Large:
Operation *Dingo*: Airborne Assault in Mozambique: 23-27 November 1977

A minute later there was another call for an air strike to stem a breakout from the National Stores camp complex.

The danger also still lurked in the camps. At 13.20 Stop 1 called for a further casevac by 13.35. In response, G-Car Pink 5 first collected a stretcher case from Stop 3 at 13.30 before removing a 'sitting casualty' from Stop 1.

At least there was still no sign of a Mozambican reaction force. Lynx F4 reported at 13.31 that nothing was moving on any of the roads in the urban or rural areas.

At 13.35, at the behest of a K-Car, White Section again attacked the group of escapees at the river junction.[198]

Robinson suggested to Walls that his forces remain in the target area until 16.00 and then recover to the admin area and withdraw to Rhodesia on the next day. General Walls agreed to reassess the position at 15.30.

At 13.40 Blue Section took over flying top cover from White Section.

As part of the mopping-up, Robinson at 13.50 ordered the SB personnel to be flown to the HQ complex in a G-Car, escorted by a K-Car. To deal with a pocket of resistance, two Vampires, Voodoo 1 and 2, attacked Pasindina 1 Camp, firing seven rockets and their 20mm cannons. They struck it twice as well as the nearby HQ.[199]

Seven minutes later an urgent call for a casevac came from Sergeant Phil Cripps of Stop 5. Walsh ordered the K-Car and G-Car, which were in the process of delivering the SB members to the HQ, to effect the casevac. What had happened was a woman cadre had fired at Stop 5 from the camp at New Garage and the bullet had hit SAS Trooper Frans Nel between the eyes. His stick commander, Corporal Trevor Kershaw, responded by having his men turn their combat caps inside out to hide the Day-Glo patches which were betraying them when taking cover. Robinson assured Roberts that the casevac of Nel and two other wounded men would be uplifted as soon as possible.

There was still resistance from the bush west of Pasindina 1 so at 14.00

---

[198] BECM RAAP, Box 844, Air strike Report, 23 November 1977.

[199] BECM RAAP, Box 844, Air strike Report, 23 November 1977.

Robinson ordered Stop A: "Pull back and a Hunter strike will be put in. You are then to have another go." Fifteen minutes later, Stop A marked the target with white phosphorus and Blue 1 and 2 aimed six Matra rockets and 600 rounds of 30mm at it. In all, Blue Section expended 36 Matra rockets and 850 30mm cannon shells on this sortie.[200]

At that moment, the Lynx F4 reported again that, on his wide recce, he still had seen no movement in the town or on the roads.

The clearing of camps continued with the aid of the SB team. Stop 2 was at the HQ complex. Stop 3 was searching Chitepo College and the Chaminuka and Parirenyatwa camps, and found numerous documents.

Walsh cancelled the Vampire cab-rank at 14.21 because of the thickening weather.

The casevac, however, had still not taken place because Roberts reported that his Stop 5 was still embroiled in a heavy contact at New Garage and it was not safe for the aircraft to land.

At 14.28, Robinson informed MacKenzie of Stop 4 he would obtain a demolition kit from the admin area for the destruction of a new 23mm anti-aircraft gun. Stop 2 had found so many documents that Robinson radioed that the SB would have to be selective and take out only what they needed by helicopter.[201]

Ten minutes later, however, sporadic contacts were continuing in and around most of the camps. All call signs had reached their objectives and the SB personnel were at the HQ. Because a considerable quantity of documents had been found at Chitepo College,[202] Walsh ordered Lynx A4 to fly in an additional SB team from Grand Reef.

At 14.45, presuming the troops would be withdrawn by dusk, the planners proposed that, directed by pre-set radio activated flares, the two Canberras already armed with eight 500lb bombs with delayed fuses and four with

---

[200] BECM RAAP, Box 844, Air strike Report, 23 November 1977.

[201] BECM RAAP, Box 844, New Sarum Ops to ComOps, 23 November 1977.

[202] BECM RAAP, Box 844, ComOps TAC HQ to ComOps, 23 November 1977.

instantaneous ones would bomb New Farm that night.[203]

By 14.50, documents found at the HQ and Chitepo College had been selected and a G-Car ordered to collect them. Robinson also requested further demolition equipment for the ammunition dump and water for the troops. Another development was that a captured cadre would indicate an arms cache.

Five minutes later, Walsh ordered another attempt to remove Stop 5's casualties.

At 15.00 Stop 2 radioed that they had seized a 14.5mm machine gun and asked if it could be flown out. Walsh replied it would be, if possible.

By then the clearing of the HQ, Chitepo College, Parirenyatwa and Chaminuka camps and National Stores was completed. Stop A, however, was bogged down in Matopos, Takawira and Pasindina 1 camps. A new 23mm anti-aircraft gun was being destroyed.

Reviewing his immediate plans, Robinson proposed to Walls that troops should remain in the target area until 16.00 and then spend the night in the admin area before being flown back to Rhodesia the next day. All helicopters would withdraw to the Lake Alexander assembly area for the night.[204]

At 15.07 Lynx A4 reported that there was still no sign of movement on the roads and in the towns.

K-Car 6 reported at 15.12 that his accompanying G-Car had collected Stop 5's casualties. In the interim, however, Nel had died. He and Philip Haigh were the only Rhodesians to be killed that day. Nel's body and the two wounded were flown to the medical team at the admin area where the two wounded were stabilized for their onward journey.[205]

At 15.20 Walls agreed the troops should stay until 16.00, provided they could be withdrawn to the admin area by last light. He warned, however, that the weather was causing a problem for helicopters attempting to land at the Lake Alexander assembly area.

---

[203] BECM RAAP, Box 844, Air HQ to New Sarum, 23 November 1977.

[204] BECM RAAP, Box 844, ComOps TAC HQ to ComOps, 23 November 1977.

[205] Cocks, p. 145.

At 15.27 the K-Car, flying top cover, warned Stop A that there was a gun pit, housing large calibre anti-aircraft weapon, some 150 metres in front of them but there was no sign of movement in it.

At 15.45, Captain Wilson of Stop 6 complained he had not yet received the demolition kit he needed. White Section radioed they were leaving because of their low fuel state even though their replacements had not arrived.

Ten minutes later, the SB team was ordered to move to Chaminuka Camp where there were tons of documents needing their attention.

At 16.00, the command Dakota flew back to Grand Reef to refuel. It was airborne again at 17.10 and returning to the operational area.

Walsh ordered Petter-Bowyer to be flown southward to the target area to assess the effects of his new weaponry. The carnage wrought by them, shook Petter-Bowyer.[206]

At 17.20, after Haaroff had asked if the RLI Stops A, 1 and 2 were to be uplifted for the night, a G-Car began to shuttle Stop A to the admin area with Lynx E4 supervising the movement.

Ten minutes later, Robinson decided that all other stops would remain at New Farm. This would mean there would be some 60 men to be flown out from the admin area that night. He planned to fly the troops from New Farm at 05.45 to the admin area and to start the shuttle home from there at first light. All these movements would be preceded by air strikes. He ordered Captain Wilson's Stop 6 and Lieutenant Roberts's Stop 5 to spend the night at New Garage. Captain MacKenzie's Stop 4 was to stay at Chaminuka Camp while Stops 1, 2, and 3 moved to recover the parachutes from the dropping zone before camping south of the Engineers' Camp and northwest of the road. Finally he recorded the results as 500 insurgents killed and 20 captured at the cost of SAS Trooper Frans Nel killed and 13 wounded. The SAS wounded were: Lieutenant Watt, Corporal Greyling, Trooper Cranswick (lung blast in intensive care), Corporal Ratte and Trooper Ramsay. The RLI wounded were Warrant Officer Ken Reed, Colour Sergeant John Norman and troopers Paul Furstenburg, John Connelly, M. Grobbler, Bruce Kidd,

---

[206] Petter-Bowyer, p. 312.

Fireforce Writ Large:
Operation *Dingo*: Airborne Assault in Mozambique: 23-27 November 1977

Terry Hammond and Peter Donnelly.[207]

By 17.45 Stops 1, 2 and 3 were recovering parachutes and basing up southwest of Matopos and Takawira camps and the HQ complex. Stop 4 was at Chaminuka Camp and Stops 5 and 6 at New Garage. MacKenzie moved his men into an entrenched area in the trees and set up all-round defence. He established his headquarters in a bomb crater. At dusk an SAS corporal tied the green and white Rhodesian national flag to a tree.

Five helicopters were held for the night at the admin area, while the rest flew men and equipment back to Lake Alexander. The adventures of the day, however, were not entirely over. Two bullets hit the G-Car carrying Jimmy Swan's stick, forcing the pilot to land on a small island in the Chicamba Real Dam, close to the Rhodesian border. The crew and the four soldiers, low in ammunition, had a nervous wait in the growing darkness until a helicopter arrived with spares. The repaired G-Car flew to Lake Alexander to refuel and then on to New Sarum, Salisbury, to be inspected in preparation for Zulu 2. It had been a long, exhausting day. The helicopter commander, Squadron Leader Harold Griffiths, for example, had flown for nine hours and 35 minutes.[208]

The planned bombing of New Farm was postponed but the night there was hardly peaceful. After darkness fell, ZANLA stragglers, thinking the Rhodesians had gone, returned home calling out "Comrade, comrade". The stop groups called back "Comrade" and then fired on them as they approached.[209] In one fight in the dark, three ZANLA cadres were killed when a small group blundered into the SAS. In all, some 60 cadres were killed in the night.

At 05.30 on Thursday, 24 November two Hunters, one armed with frantan bombs and one with Matra rockets, arrived to provide top cover for the clearance patrols in the still-burning camps of New Farm. Accompanying them were two photo-reconnaissance Canberras.

---

[207] BECM RAAP, Box 844, ComOps TAC HQ to ComOps, 23 November 1977.

[208] Flying Log of H. G. Griffiths, Vol. 4.

[209] McAleese, p. 137.

There were still grisly surprises. At 05.40 MacKenzie's Stop 4 found a further 70 dead bodies.

Although it was reported at 05.42 that New Farm was all quiet, except for the Recruits' Camp, three minutes later, Lynx E4 directed Red Section's Hunters, flown by Wightman, Geraty and Annan, onto a suspected insurgent hideout on which they dropped four frantan bombs before bombing Nehanda Camp.[210] As they did, a Canberra dropped a load of Alpha bombs along the densely bushed river line, drawing a small-arms-fire riposte.

MacKenzie requested the services of an SB team at the HQ complex. He was searching it, thinking that he might have found the ZANLA paymaster's briefcase the previous day. The briefcase, however, turned out to be full of documents and a new Rolex watch. At his men's suggestion, MacKenzie pocketed the watch and later sold it for more than his monthly pay. During the search of the main farmhouse, his troops discovered the bodies of four prisoners who had been executed by ZANLA before the start of the attack. Their hands were tied behind their backs and they had been shot in the back of the head.[211]

Aware of the hundreds of escapees in the surrounding bush and the threat of a response from the FPLM units in the area, Walsh, at 05.50, ordered K-Car K4 to search the areas to the southeast, southwest and south of New Farm.

At 06.00, as a pair of Hunters arrived to take over the cab-rank, Stops 1 to 6 spread out along the dropping zone, collecting parachutes and jump helmets.

Five minutes later, General Walls demanded the plan for the day. Walsh and Robinson replied that the helicopters would fly to the admin area to await developments at New Farm where the troops were recovering parachutes. The SB team would join MacKenzie at the HQ complex.

At 06.30 Walsh's first order of the day was an air strike on the Recruits' Camp.

At 06.50 the cab-rank changed with Vampires replacing the Hunters.[212] The cab-rank was planned to last five hours.

---

[210] BECM RAAP, Box 844, air strike, 24 November 1977.

[211] McAleese, p. 137.

[212] BECM RAAP, Box 844, ComOps TAC HQ to ComOps, 24 November 1977.

Fireforce Writ Large:
Operation *Dingo*: Airborne Assault in Mozambique: 23-27 November 1977

At 07.01 Walsh had Lynx E4 conduct a reconnaissance along the road south of target to Chimoio and beyond. He worried that the clouds closing in would hamper his air operations.

Robinson issued a succession of orders. At 07.15 he instructed Stops 2 to 6 to continue to recover parachutes. He sent Stop 1 to clear the westernmost camp, Pasindina 2, which had not been searched on the previous day, and thereafter to move southward down the road as the aircraft were still attracting rifle fire from the complexes.

Wilson of Stop 6 signalled at 07.30 that his men had collected their parachutes and were ready for their removal by G-Car.

The command Dakota telexed Walls's initial assessment to ComOps which stated that "at worst, [the] job was worthwhile, at best [it] may have been bloody excellent." Walls felt that the claim of 560 kills was an underestimate as the deaths in Pasindina 2 and Recruits' Camp and some other areas had not been counted. He welcomed that there had been no mention of the attack on New Farm on the news broadcasts. Finally, he warned that the weather was not proving helpful for top cover and helicopter movement.[213]

MacKenzie had finished the search of the HQ and asked Robinson at 07.40 if there was anything to be done at Old Garage. Five minutes later, Stops 2, 3, 5 and 6 announced their parachutes were ready for collection. Robinson agreed that MacKenzie's Stop 4 should search Old Garage. As they headed off, they could hear explosions as other call signs destroyed supplies, ammunition and weapons. There were bursts of small-arms fire as pockets of ZANLA cadres were encountered. In one exchange of rifle grenades, 3 Commando's CSM, WOII Ken Reed, was wounded in the face.[214] One stop group captured an African woman and was told to hold her until the SB could interrogate her. If this were not possible, she was to be released.

MacKenzie had found an empty gun pit and at 08.10 requested demolition kits to destroy the fuel dumps and vehicles at Old Garage. The kits had to be flown in from Lake Alexander.

---

[213] BECM RAAP, Box 844, ComOps TAC HQ to ComOps, 24 November 1977.

[214] Memorandum, 'Follow-up to Operation *Dingo*', by Major John R. Cronin, 21 April 1998.

Chapter 15

The operations within Rhodesia intruded with 3 Brigade, Umtali, asking for the use of a Lynx to deal with a sighting of 20 insurgents. Walls released troops from the reserve and helicopters to deal with them.

The search of Pasindina 2 yielded only one body but a number of documents.

At 08.37 Stop 1 reported their search of the wooden buildings of Pasindina 2, the convalescent camp, had yielded a body and a quantity of documents. They did not mention the two prized folding-butt FN rifles found by Tony Coom. Lieutenant Mark Adams appropriated one and Coom retained the other and would use it for the rest of his service in 3 Commando.

At 08.45, Stop 4 was informed that the incoming helicopters would arrive in 15 minutes but the demolition kit was not on board. Lieutenant Roberts reported at 08.50 that his Stop 5 had captured two young cadres, one who spoke fluent English. Wilson had his six sticks of Stop 6 ready for uplift but he admitted they had only recovered eight parachutes from the trees.

Robinson reported to the command Dakota at 09.00 that Stop 1 had cleared Pasindina 2, the convalescent camp, capturing one and killing one. They had found documents, maps and more. Stop 2 was recovering parachutes. Stop 3 had used explosive charges to destroy a 75mm recoilless rifle shell, a Mercedes 2.5-tonne ambulance, a Peugeot 504 sedan and two Gestetner roneo machines. Using white phosphorus, they had set fire to a small quantity of medical supplies. They smashed three typewriters with an axe and bent the barrels and smashed the stocks of 25 SKS rifles.[215] Stop 4 had found overhead and underground fuel dumps at Old Garage and had sufficient demolition kits to blow them up together with the workshop and vehicles there. Stop 5 was recovering parachutes and had made captures. Robinson added that he would send Wilson's Stop 6 to clear the Recruits' Camp. He expected to have all the troops flown out of New Farm by 12.00.[216] He ordered Wilson to be ready to be flown to the Recruits' Camp.

All resistance, however, had not been quenched. At 09.05 Stop 4 had found

---

[215] BECM RAAP, Box 844, Op Dingo, Destruction Return, 21 December 1977.

[216] BECM RAAP, Box 844, ComOps TAC HQ to ComOps, 24 November 1977.

more vehicles at Old Garage and a last pocket of 40 ZANLA cadres hiding in a nearby *donga* (gully). After an initial exchange of fire, the cadres broke cover and were shot down.[217] Among the dead was the man in charge of New Farm's transport section, Lazarus Mandeya.[218]

Elsewhere two anti-tank landmines were buried in the approach roads from Chimoio to delay any reaction force, and anti-personnel mines buried at random and booby-traps set to deter re-occupation. The troops set fire to the remaining huts, a dangerous practice as ammunition hidden in the thatch began to explode. Their search uncovered a further 12.7mm machine gun at 09.50. Robinson ordered its destruction. Another 12.7mm gun was found by Stop 4 and recovered at 09.55.

At 10.00, the RLI Stops 1 and 2 announced they were ready for uplift. Walsh responded by ordering at 10.35 eight G-Cars to transport Wilson's Stop 6 to the Recruits' Camp. Three K-Cars were to escort them to the Recruits' Camp. Two G-Cars were sent to collect parachutes. The remainder of the stops would be flown out as soon as possible direct to the admin area and onward to Lake Alexander. The shuttle continued for the rest of the day.

By 14.00 the helicopter shuttle had extracted Stops 1 and 2 from New Farm. Tony Coom's stick had an interesting ride back to Lake Alexander as his Alouette ran low on fuel and the pilot was forced to land it on the summit of a mountain on the border to secure fuel from a cache of drums hidden there. Charles Warren describes an argument he had with his South African G-Car pilot which needed the intercession of Major Strong. Awaiting him and his fellow troops were a posse of military police to search them for loot. There were, however, too few MPs and too many arriving helicopters for all the loot to be found. Once assembled at Lake Alexander, the 3 Commando troops were transported to Grand Reef, where Dakotas awaited their arrival to fly them to New Sarum. Waiting at Grand Reef to congratulate them were

---

[217] McAleese, pp. 138-139.

[218] Edgar '2Boy' Zivanai Tekere, *Tekere: A Lifetime of Struggle*, SAPES Books, Harare, 2007, p. 86.

generals Peter Walls and John Hickman, the commander of the Rhodesian Army.[219]

Before then, at 10.45, MacKenzie's Stop 4 completed the demolition of Old Garage's well-equipped workshop and office in the old metal-roofed farm building, petrol and diesel tanks, the new twin 37mm AA gun, a bus, a ten-tonne truck, a Commer pick-up truck, five motorcars, including a large new BMW, a Land Rover and two diesel engines. They bent the barrels and broke the stocks of 45 various small arms.[220] MacKenzie kept for his own use a white Peugeot light truck which had been serviced at a service station in Salisbury only three weeks previously before being stolen and brought over the border. He had used it to collect what heavy machine guns could be recovered from the anti-aircraft positions and flown out. While engaged in this, eventually acquiring 13 DshK 12.7mm guns, MacKenzie heard on the command channel two cab-ranking Hunters conclude that his white truck was carrying a group of escaping ZANLA. His transmission of "Stop, stop!" drew a response from General Walls in the command Dakota, ordering off the Hunters.[221]

At 10.55 Wilson's Stop 6 was flown to the Recruits' Camp expecting resistance but by 11.03 was searching it. At that moment, the SB team was flown out from Stop 4.

Pasindina 2 had been swept and, at New Garage, Roberts of Stop 5 reported two kills and the use of a white phosphorus grenade to set fire to 75 spare tyres, complete sets of vehicle spares and tools, and a small quantity of maize.[222] His men then used explosive charges to destroy eight barrels of oil, a new generator plant, a new compressed-air plant, a new John Deere tractor, an ambulance and a 4.5-tonne truck. They bent the barrels and smashed the butts of 30 SKS rifles.[223]

---

[219] Binda, pp. 262 & 264.

[220] BECM RAAP, Box 844, Op *Dingo*, Destruction Return, 21 December 1977.

[221] MacKenzie, p. 46.

[222] BECM RAAP, Box 844, ComOps TAC HQ to ComOps, 24 November 1977.

[223] BECM RAAP, Box 844, Op *Dingo*, Destruction Return, 21 December 1977.

Fireforce Writ Large:
Operation *Dingo*: Airborne Assault in Mozambique: 23-27 November 1977

In the Recruits' Camp, Stop 6 burnt 40 tonnes of clothing, 40 bags of maize and ten tonnes of medical supplies. They used explosive charges to destroy a grinding mill, 5,500 12.7mm and 14.5mm rounds, seven 12.7mm barrels and a complete 82mm mortar. They punctured ten to 12 tonnes of tinned food and bent the barrels and broke the stocks of 200 SKS rifles.[224] At 11.40 an extra G-Car was sent to the Recruits' Camp to uplift documents.

All targets were cleared and demolition tasks completed by 12.00. Wilson estimated the Recruits' Camp had housed 700 people. He had found 31 dead there and vast blood trails. Time precluded a further search and, at 12.25, Wilson signalled Stop 6 was ready for uplift from the Recruits' Camp.[225]

Roberts of Stop 5 radioed at 13.00 that his 20 men and their 20 parachutes were ready to be flown out.

MacKenzie's men prepared for the night's bombing of New Farm by setting up RAMS beacons. The RAMS (radio-activated marker system) was a Rhodesian invention and comprised two flares set at prescribed distances from a target which were ignited by a radio signal from an approaching Canberra to enable it to bomb accurately at night.[226]

MacKenzie then announced Stop 4 had collected 24 canopies and was ready for departure. Willis of Stop 3 reported likewise that he had 13 parachutes and was ready to go. All resistance, however, was not over because a Dakota dropping pamphlets drew fire.

At 16.00, as the airlift was underway, Ian Smith made his move because Zulu 1 had struck the blow he intended. At Government House in Bulawayo he declared that, because the latest Anglo-American initiative had failed to achieve a settlement between himself and his opponents, including the 'external' nationalists (Mugabe and Nkomo), he would settle with the 'internal' nationalists led by Bishop Muzorewa. The basis of the constitution would be full adult suffrage and he promised the existing mainly white electorate the chance to approve it in a referendum before a general election

---

[224] BECM RAAP, Box 844, Op *Dingo*, Destruction Return, 21 December 1977.

[225] BECM RAAP, Box 844, ComOps TAC HQ to ComOps, 24 November 1977.

[226] Petter-Bowyer, p. 276.

brought in a majority-rule government in 1978. In the event, the process took longer and the election was only held in April 1979.[227]

The SAS were flown out of Mozambique in relays and by 17.40 the airlift was over. The helicopter crews stopped at FAF8 Grand Reef for the night to rest and recuperate before flying the next day to Mtoko for the next phase, Zulu 2. The exhausted aircrews were rewarded by a three-course meal which included strawberries and cream.[228] The SAS were flown back to New Sarum to be treated to steak and eggs at the air force mess.

Finally, New Farm, Chimoio, was bombed that night by a Canberra using the RAMS to assist it in aiming its six delay-fused 500lb bombs.[229]

Zulu 1, with its wealth of intelligence gained and its harassing value through its high kill, was the most successful of the Rhodesian camp attacks. The cost was the lives of Philip Haigh and Trooper Frans Nel and the wounding of 13 soldiers.[230] In the coming two years, similar attacks would be mounted in the Chimoio area and elsewhere, but never again would the Rhodesians trap such a concentration of their enemy.

While the troops recovered their breath, Smith's declaration drew an immediate response from Nkomo who declared that the war would continue and that Smith was merely buying time by gathering his 'stooges' around him. The Mozambican government ignored Smith's commitment and instead expressed its outrage at the attack on New Farm to Rhodesia's only ally, South Africa. In response, the South African diplomats muttered threateningly to the Rhodesians about withdrawing their helicopters. Previously in 1976, after the furore over the Nyadzonya raid, they had withdrawn their helicopter pilots serving in Rhodesia. The Rhodesian diplomatic representative in Pretoria, Air Vice-Marshal Harold Hawkins, replied that the strike had been

---

[227] Smith Papers (SP), Cory Library, Rhodes University SP/4/006(M), C 419, J. F. Gaylard to H. Hawkins, 24 November 1977, telex; *Keesing's*, Vol. XXIV, p. 28942; Colin Legum, *Africa Contemporary Record, Annual Survey and Documents, 1977–1978,* Africana Publishing Company, London, 1979, p. B1026.

[228] BECM RAAP, Box 844, ComOps to Air HQ, 24 November 1977.

[229] BECM RAAP, Box 844, Air HQ to New Sarum, 24 November 1977.

[230] Cocks, pp. 144–146.

Fireforce Writ Large:
Operation *Dingo*: Airborne Assault in Mozambique: 23-27 November 1977

a pre-emptive one on 3,000–4,000 ZANLA cadres fresh from training in Tanzania and poised to enter Rhodesia. He made a parallel to the South African raids into Angola. Nevertheless, the South African Secretary for Foreign Affairs, Brand Fourie, warned that the Rhodesians would again be accused of using military action to wreck a political initiative, this time the Anglo-American proposals.[231]

Operation *Dingo*, of course, was only halfway over. As planned, the next day, Friday, 25 November, the helicopters flew northeast to the forward airfield at Mtoko (FAF5). From there, on Saturday, 26 November, they would fly to Tembué, refuelling at Mount Darwin (FAF4), the helicopter assembly area at Chiswiti near the Rhodesian border, and the staging point being set up ahead of them on the Train, just south of the southern shore of the Cabora Bassa dam. From the target the helicopters would fly on to the admin area to be set up ten kilometres west of Tembué.

At New Sarum the SAS and RLI paratroops and the aircrews showered, dressed in clean clothes, cleaned their weapons and drew new maps and air photos. The Director Ops then conducted the final air briefing attended by the officers commanding New Sarum and Thornhill, the squadron commanders, section leaders and the K-Car pilots. The main briefing followed at 09.00 in the SAS model room at Cranborne using another polystyrene and plaster of Paris model of the target produced by Captain Dubois of the RIC.

Premised on the difficulties that could arise through the loss of aircraft and the consequent stranding of troops 200 kilometres inside Mozambique, the briefing on Zulu 2 began by stating that, as at New Farm, Chimoio, there was an insignificant FPLM presence in the ZANLA three-camp complex at Tembué. There were, nonetheless, FPLM forces in the area. The garrison of Tembué town was a 30-minute drive away to the north and comprised a 150-man FPLM company headquarters, supported by anti-aircraft guns and mortars. Bene, the small town 20 minutes away to the south, had a platoon base manned by ten FPLM men armed with rifles. Three hours

---
[231] SP/4/006(M), C 429, H. Hawkins to J. F. Gaylard, 24 November 1977, telex.

away to the west was a battalion headquarters at Fingoe with 450 men, anti-aircraft guns, mortars and vehicles. Three hours to the east at Furancungo, near the Malawian border, was another FPLM company headquarters with 150 men, anti-aircraft guns and mortars. To the southwest, six hours away down the main road, at the provincial capital of Tete, was the FPLM brigade headquarters with 600 men, anti-aircraft guns, SAM-7 Strela rockets, mortars and vehicles. Lastly, at the far-off port of Nacala on the Indian Ocean was air support.

The Tembué base was the ZANLA command headquarters for Tete Province and their general and specialist-skills training centre. It was believed to contain 650 trained cadres and 1,000 recruits, living in three camps, flanking the southward-flowing Luia River, a tributary of the Capoche River which joins the Zambezi River east of the Cabora Bassa dam. The first of the camps, Camp A, was a basic training centre covering an area of 700 by 500 metres. It consisted of 178 pole and *dagga* thatched huts, and had a population of 1,000 including some women and four to six FPLM personnel. Camp B had 191 huts in an area 700 by 650 metres. It housed 500 trained personnel who were learning advanced specialist skills. It also had a detachment of four to six FPLM soldiers as did Camp C. Camp C had 53 huts in an area 200 by 400 metres, housing some 150 fully trained ZANLA cadres awaiting deployment.

Subject to serviceability, the Rhodesian Air Force would deploy seven Hunters, five Vampires, the command Dakota and six Dakotas carrying paratroopers, Jack Malloch's DC-7, four Lynxes, four Canberras and 31 helicopters, namely the command G-Car, eight K-Cars, 12 G-Cars and ten South African Polo G-Cars.

All three camps would be attacked by Hunters, Vampires and Canberras at H-Hour (08.00) on Saturday, 26 November. The dropping of 96 SAS and 48 Support Commando, 1RLI, paratroopers would follow immediately, boxing in camps C and B.[232]

The airstrip at Chiswiti in northeastern Rhodesia would serve as the

---

[232] BECM RAAP, Box 844, Operation Order Zulu 2; McAleese, pp. 137–140.

Fireforce Writ Large:
Operation *Dingo*: Airborne Assault in Mozambique: 23-27 November 1977

helicopter assembly area, guarded by 20 RLI troopers armed with four 81mm mortars. An RLI doctor and three medical orderlies would be there to deal with any incoming casualties. Special Branch would be waiting there for prisoners, two of whom would be flown to the forward admin area. More SB officers would be available if Walsh and Robinson required them. Army Headquarters would provide an administration unit to operate at Chiswiti by 08.00 on 26 November and, on the advice of the RLI quartermaster and the Officer Commanding, 3 Air Supply Platoon, administration points would be established and staffed at Mount Darwin, Chiswiti and the forward admin area.

From Chiswiti an air force controller, Squadron Leader Rex Taylor, and a 16-man RLI protection force with 60mm mortars, would be flown on November by G-Cars to set up a helicopter refuelling and staging post on the mountain called the Train, east of the village of Magoe just south of the Cabora Bassa dam.

Pink Section's 12 G-Cars, carrying Petter-Bowyer, two SB operators, a two-man medical team, and an air force armourer, would fly via the Train to the forward admin area, some eleven kilometres southwest of the Tembué complex. They would be joined there by 16 RLI troopers, their two 81mm mortars and the fuel drums and equipment parachuted from Jack Malloch's DC-7. The forward admin area would comprise two sub-areas, one as a helicopter park and the other for refuelling and re-arming.

The parachute reserve of 48 RLI paratroopers would be stationed at the airfield at Mount Darwin because it was the nearest one with a 940-metre-long runway capable of handling Dakota aircraft. It would also hold 150 drums of fuel in reserve. An air force controller there would co-ordinate the movement of aircraft flying in troops and equipment from Lake Alexander in the wake of Zulu 1. Thereafter aircraft movements and matters would be co-ordinated by the air force officers at Chiswiti, the Train and the forward admin area.

The aim of Zulu 2 was threefold: the killing and capturing of the maximum number of terrorists; the gathering of intelligence and the destruction of ZANLA's war matériel.

The standard action for the paratroopers on landing was to shed parachutes and harnesses and to join any other troopers in the immediate vicinity, take cover, wait and shoot. Time was not to be wasted in trying to find the individual's stick. The men on the extremity of the drop would be ready to indicate the location of their groups with phosphorus grenades. Each trooper would note the position where he left his jump helmet, parachute and reserve parachute to enable him to recover them. The Support Commando, 1RLI, Stop 1, dropped eastward of camps B and C, would immediately despatch a four-man stick a kilometre farther east to set up an early-warning position on the north–south road and to lay a landmine with a centre blast in the road to prevent any interference by vehicles. The ambush would remain in position throughout the later withdrawal phase of the operation.

After the initial air strikes, the sweep lines would advance toward and through their targets under the direction of Major Robinson in the command helicopter. Any demand for close air support during the sweep would require the indication of the target by a thrown phosphorus grenade. Once the camps had been swept, they would be thoroughly searched and the SB flown in to assist. After the search, the sticks would recover their parachutes and equipment for collection by G-Cars. Thereafter the withdrawal of men would begin by helicopter.

In preparation on Friday, 25 May, the SAS and RLI paratroopers would assemble at New Sarum while the RLI 'land tail' vehicles would transport northward from Salisbury the 48-man paratroop reserve, the protection troops for Chiswiti and the Train, the air force controllers, medical, Special Branch, quartermaster teams and 240 drums of fuel. Having dropped off the paratroop reserve at Mount Darwin where the airstrip was capable of taking Dakota aircraft, the convoy would continue to Chiswiti to set up camp and facilities for helicopters and troops. At 18.00 the seven Hunters would arrive at New Sarum along with their supporting services. The squadron leader of No. 1 Squadron would be responsible for the move. Simultaneously, the helicopters and Lynxes would land at Mount Darwin (FAF4). The Hunter, Vampire, Canberra and the DC-7 aircraft would operate from New Sarum. The Dakotas would depart from New Sarum in the initial wave.

Fireforce Writ Large:
Operation *Dingo*: Airborne Assault in Mozambique: 23-27 November 1977

At 05.10 on Saturday, 26 November, ten G-Cars would fly out of Mount Darwin, bound for the Train after refuelling on the way at Chiswiti. At 06.00 they would deliver to the Train: nine drums of fuel, 16 RLI troopers, Squadron Leader Rex Taylor and his assistant air traffic controller, an air force armourer, two SB officers and two medics.

At 05.55 eight K-Cars, each loaded with 440 20mm cannon shells, and command G-Car would depart Mount Darwin and arrive at the Train at 06.35 to refuel.

At 06.25 the six Dakotas would take off from New Sarum laden with 144 paratroopers.

At 07.00 the DC-7 would follow, carrying 16 RLI troopers and 80 drums of fuel. It intended to drop 20 drums at the Train and 60 at the forward admin area along with 2,500 20mm shells for the K-Cars. Later the DC-7 would return with a further 20 drums of fuel for the admin area.

At 07.05 the K-Cars and the command G-Car would lift off the Train, aiming to reach Tembué at 08.05. They would be followed from the Train at 07.15 by 12 G-Cars bound for the admin area, with an expected time of arrival of 08.15.

At 08.00, H-Hour, a Hunter would open the attack by raking Camp B with 30mm cannon fire followed by a second Hunter bombing it with a pair of frantan bombs and strafing it with its cannons. Two other Hunters would likewise bomb and strafe Camp C. Another pair of Hunters would do likewise to Camp A, accompanied by four Vampire FB9s firing eight 60lb rockets each and strafing with their 20mm cannons. As they did, the seventh Hunter would circle above, ready to supplement their efforts. Then 30 seconds later the four Canberras would douse Camp B with 1,200 Alpha Mk II bouncing bombs.

Covered by these attacks, the Dakotas at H+2, 08.02, would drop their paratroopers in a box formation, sealing off camps B and C. The air attack would be renewed at H+5, 08.05, by three pairs of K-Cars strafing camps A, B and C. A further K-Car would fire on the treed west bank of the Luia River, west of Camp C. Another K-Car would do likewise to the bank west of Camp B. The command helicopter would take control of the battle with the assistance of the command Dakota, orbiting nearby. Above the battle, a Lynx would provide close-in reconnaissance, while another flew wide, watching for FPLM reaction to the attack on Tembué.

Five kilometres west-southwest of Tembué, at 08.15 (H+15) the DC-7 would drop 60 drums of fuel into the forward admin area along with 16 RLI troopers. Just before then the G-Cars would arrive with ammunition, Peter Petter-Bowyer, the commander, the two SB men, the doctor, the medic and the air force armourer. Otherwise, the G-Cars would be flying empty to conserve fuel as the 176-kilometre-leg was at the maximum of their normal range. The G-Cars would then wait a kilometre away to be on hand for casevac, troop re-deployments and later for the withdrawal of troops and equipment.

After the initial air strike, Hunter aircraft would provide top cover during the sweep of the camps by the paratroops. During the withdrawal phase, Vampires would replace the Hunters but two Hunters would re-arm with air-to-air weapons and remain on standby at New Sarum to intercept any reaction by Mozambican MiG-21 aircraft. The Canberras would re-arm with Alpha bombs with the exception of one which would load 1,000lb bombs. After dropping the paratroops, the six Dakotas would land at FAF4 Mount Darwin to stand by to fly in reserve troops if necessary and fuel, ammunition and casevac. The Lynx aircraft would fly out of Mount Darwin to provide continuous reconnaissance.

The briefing prescribed the air force call signs as: Red, White and Blue for the Hunters; Venom for the Vampires; Silver for the Dakotas; Alpha 3 for the DC-7, Alpha 4 for the Lynxes; Green for the Canberras; Pink for the G-Cars; Yellow for the South African Polo G-Cars; 11 Alpha, 22 Alpha and so on for K-Cars. The overall command of Zulu 2 would be from the command Dakota, call sign 'Cyclone 3' or '0' while the direct command of air and ground operations would be the responsibility of Group Captain Walsh and Major Robinson, flying again in the command helicopter, call sign 'Delta 0'. When the command helicopter had to refuel, Major Graham, call sign 9 Alpha would take over flying in Squadron Leader Griffiths's K-Car, Alpha 7. Stop 1 and 2 would be provided by Support Commando, 1RLI, while the

Fireforce Writ Large:
Operation *Dingo*: Airborne Assault in Mozambique: 23-27 November 1977

SAS deployed Captain Colin Willis's Stop 3, Captain MacKenzie's Stop 4, Lieutenant Roberts's Stop 5 and Captain Wilson's Stop 6.

A detailed recovery plan was provided along with movement tables. The initial plan included the supply of ammunition, fuel and helicopter spares to Chiswiti via Mount Darwin. The signals diagram allocated call signs and stressed that, because this was the first time that the VHF A76 radios would be used externally, every effort had to be made to recover them. As before a secure teleprinter would be available in the command Dakota. The last aircraft to withdraw would be the K-Cars flying directly to Chiswiti from Tembué. Before then the G-Cars of the Rhodesian Pink and the Polo Yellow Sections would have flown out the paratroops, the protection troops, prisoners and equipment including parachutes. The helicopters would accomplish this, flying in relays.[233]

Zulu 2 was underway when, at 05.10, on Saturday, 26 November, Yellow Section's ten Polo G-Cars lifted off from Mount Darwin bound for Chiswiti to refuel before flying onto the Train. They were followed into the air at 05.55 by the eight K-Cars, each armed with 440 20mm cannon shells, and the command helicopter flown by Walsh and carrying Robinson. Yellow Section landed on the Train at 06.00 and disembarked Squadron Leader Rex Taylor and his assistant, an air force armourer, two SB members, two medics, 16 RLI troopers and nine drums of fuel. What had not been done was a planned prior examination of the dropping zone which did not assist the task of the team. The K-Car fleet, followed by the Pink Section G-Cars, arrived 35 minutes later to refuel.

At 06.25 the six Dakotas took off from New Sarum laden with 144 paratroops.

At 07.00 the DC-7 followed, carrying the 16 2 Commando, 1RLI, protection troops, 2,500 20mm rounds and 80 fuel drums—20 for the Train and 60 for the admin area. Five minutes later, the K-Cars and the command helicopter flew northeastward towards the target at Tembué. They aimed to arrive at 08.05. Ten minutes later, at 07.15, Pink Section's 12 G-Cars left for

---

[233] PPH, Untitled briefing papers.

the forward admin area with an arrival time 08.15. Aboard were Peter Petter-Bowyer and his team.

At 07.20 New Sarum reported the Hunters of Red, White and Blue sections and the Canberras of Green Section and the Vampires of Venom Section were airborne. Below and ahead of them at 07.30 Walsh reported weather clear. At 07.50 Venom reported they would be two minutes late. Just before 08.00 the G-Cars, having made good time, landed at the forward admin area, this time finding it suitable for its purpose. Standing on the roof of a G-Car, Petter-Bowyer called in the para-drop by Jack Malloch and Squadron Leader George Alexander, flying the DC-7. Again the drop had problems. Dropping the 16 troops and their heavy containers, too low, under the safe height of 300 feet above the ground, resulted in injuries and damaged weapons. Next the 40 drums, 5,000 rounds of ammunition were scattered over a wide area, 1,800 square metres, and one parachute candled.[234] Among the troops was Corporal Jimmy Swan, who was fortunate to land on a soft piece of ground which spared him and his 60mm mortar any damage. He recalls cutting one trooper out of the tree on which his parachute had snagged, the medics patching up the injured and preparing them for later evacuation.[235] The technicians immediately set to work positioning the drums in clumps to facilitate multiple refuelling. Later they would have to change a stricken-helicopter engine with one flown in from New Sarum via the Train. A difficulty experienced was that the army radios proved inadequate and a public address system was needed in the sprawling camp.[236]

As Petter-Bowyer talked in the DC-7, at 08.00, H-Hour, the attack was opened by simultaneous air strikes by Hunters on camps A, B and C.

Blue Section, Flight Lieutenant Blythe-Wood and Air Lieutenant Lowrie, strafed Camp A with 43 Matra 68mm rockets and 800 30mm shells. They reported that 80 per cent of the target was destroyed and that people were seen running to the river line.

---

[234] BECM RAAP, Box 844, Op *Dingo*, radio message, 26 November 1977.

[235] Binda, p. 270.

[236] Petter-Bowyer, p. 310.

Fireforce Writ Large:
Operation *Dingo*: Airborne Assault in Mozambique: 23-27 November 1977

Squadron Leader Richard Brand's Red Section opened the attack on Camp B with a 30mm cannon barrage followed by two 50-gallon frantan bombs which Red 2 reported hit the target.

White Section, Geraty and Wightman, dived down releasing four canister-loads of flechettes over Camp C and strafing it with 750 cannon shells. The whistling, jostling flight of 18,000 six-inch steel darts was reminiscent of the barrage of medieval arrows which darkened the sky over the battlefield at Crécy in 1346 a.d. At Crécy 7,000 English archers loosed 100,000 arrows a minute and, again at Agincourt in 1415 a.d., the storm of arrows mowed down the packed ranks of French cavalry. At Tembué, however, the target, the parade ground at Camp C, was empty. The expectation of striking the muster parade had led their inventor, Petter-Bowyer, to press for the use of flechettes. Unbeknown to the Rhodesians, however, the muster parade had been held at 04.30, whereafter the ZANLA cadres had broken into small groups as they did every day.[237] In any case, Camp B, not C, was the principal camp. Furthermore, 1,000 trained men had moved to a new camp three kilometres to the north and 300 to Bene to the south on the previous day. That left 3,500 personnel in camps A, B and C. The debrief of Zulu 2 would regret that a pressure weapon, such as the 450kg Golf bomb, had not been used.[238] Walsh had chosen not to use the flechettes at New Farm because the inevitable international outcry after the expected inspection by international agencies such as the UN High Commission for Refugees. He did not expect such inspections at the remote Tembué camp. Flown in later in the day to inspect the strike, Petter-Bowyer found the parade ground was littered with pink plastic tailfins and steel shafts buried deep into the earth. A lone tree was festooned with the darts from the top to its base.

As the four low-flying Canberras approached, Red Section silenced the anti-aircraft weapons at Camp B with a salvo of 24 Matra rockets and 400 30mm shells, which also set the sleeping quarters alight.[239]

---

[237] PPH, Ops 001, debrief Op *Dingo* Phase 2 (Z2), 28 November 1977.

[238] PPH, Ops 001, debrief Op *Dingo* Phase 2 (Z2), 28 November 1977.

[239] BECM RAAP, Box 844, Op *Dingo*, radio message, 26 November 1977.

The Canberras dropped 1,200 Alpha bombs on Camp B but their direction was faulty and the strike left much of the camp unscathed with many bombs exploding harmlessly in the surrounding bush. Of 70 huts, only a dozen were struck. Moreover, the air bursts left the anti-aircraft and mortar positions unscathed as they had solid roofs protecting them. Consequently, the Hunters faced heavy machine-gun fire from Camp B as they returned to attack their targets again. It was felt that frantan bombs might have been more effective against these positions.[240]

The last initial air attack was on Camp A, where five Vampires blasted it with 60lb squash-head rockets and 20mm cannon shells.

As at New Farm two days previously, most of the inhabitants of the camps, aside from the anti-aircraft gunners, scattered. ZANLA cadres were seen fleeing to the cover of the nearby riverbed as, at 08.04, Squadron Leader Griffiths, the K-Car leader, ordered the Hunters to break off because his K-Cars were overhead the camps. Blue Section responded, proposing to strafe the river line west of Camp A where so many of its inmates had run. The K-Car attack on the tin-roofed garage and its vehicles ignited the fuel stored there.

The K-Cars over camps B and C were immediately under fire from a 12.7mm machine gun firing from east to west. The Dakotas droned across the area, spewing long lines of paratroopers, attempting to form a tight box around it. Feeling they were dropped too close to their target, the paratroopers descended among hundreds of fleeing ZANLA cadres.

Despite the intense fire from the ZANLA gunners which hit some of the aircraft, fortune favoured the Rhodesians because the damage was not serious and they did not suffer a single fatality that day. The most fortunate of them was an SAS sergeant whose life was saved when his tangled, unopened canopy snagged a tree, braking his fall. Dropping from 450 feet, there had been no time to deploy his reserve parachute.[241]

Major Brian Robinson, flown by Norman Walsh in the command

---

[240] BECM RAAP, Box 844, Op *Dingo*, telex, 27 November 1977.

[241] Cole, p. 188.

1 Commando, 1RLI paras en route to the DZ.

Above left: Major André Dennison, OC A Company, 2RAR. Ex British SAS, he was a dynamic Fireforce commander and much loved by his troops. He was killed by friendly fire at the end of the war. *Photo RAR Regimental Association (UK)*

Above right: Support Commando, 1RLI paras kit up. *Photo Harry Whitehead*

Above: An air force dispatcher checks over 2 Commando, 1RLI paras prior to boarding.

Centre: RLI stick leaders brief their troops prior to a Fireforce call-out. *Photo Tom Argyle*

Left: Soviet-supplied ZIPRA heavy ordnance. The threat of a conventional ZIPRA invasion from Zambia was ever-present; however, the Zambezi River presented a formidable obstacle. *Photo RAR Regimental Association (UK)*

Top: An Alouette G-Car, with an RLI stick on board, taxiies out of the revetments at Grand Reef. The MAG gunner is sitting half out the door. *Photo Tom Argyle*

Above: A Lynx takes off at Grand Reef. *Photo Tom Argyle*

An Alouette G-Car, with its load of RLI troopers, gets ready to move out. *Photo Tom Argyle*

Above left: Lieutenant-Colonel Peter Rich, CO 1RLI 1975–1978, fought with 2 Commando on Operation *Dingo* as a rifleman, uniquely, at the side of his son, Lieutenant Mike Rich. *Photo RLI Cheetah magazine*

Above right: 2 Commando, 1RLI troops watch a Paradak taking off for a Fireforce operation. *Photo Jeremy Hall*

2 Commando, 1RLI paras kitting up. *Photo Max T*

Some very young 2 Commando, 1RLI paras deplane, while the Paradak stands by at an airfield, awaiting further instructions from the Fireforce commander. Rather than orbiting endlessly to await the drop order, quite often a Fireforce commander would permit the Dakota to land at a nearby strip, if available. *Photo Max T*

Above: The Paradak stands by. *Photo Max T*

Right: A 2 Commando, 1RLI MAG gunner scans the approaching LZ from the door of a G-Car. *Photo Max T*

Above left: Major Brian Robinson, OC C Squadron, SAS, brilliant co-architect of Operation *Dingo* and commander of the ground forces.

Above centre: Group Captain Norman Walsh commanded the air effort on Operation *Dingo*. With Robinson, he masterminded the operation and must take the credit for the precision and professionalism of the air operation. *Photo Beryl Salt / A Pride of Eagles*

Above right: Flight Lieutenant Frank Hales, OC PTS, was involved in the logistical planning of Operation *Dingo*. *Photo Craig Fourie collection*

The helicopter assembly area for Operation *Dingo* at Lake Alexander, north of Umtali. The vehicle in the foreground is a Unimog 2.5. *Photo Tom Argyle*

Top: Alouettes assembled at Lake Alexander for Operation *Dingo*. *Photo Beryl Salt / A Pride of Eagles*

Above: Approaching Lake Alexander. *Photo Peter Petter-Bowyer / Winds of Destruction*

Right: Operation *Dingo*. To avoid enemy radar, the Paradaks flew at treetop level on their way to Chimoio. *Photo Pete McDonald*

Top: A Lynx scurries just above the treetops to a target during Operation *Dingo*.
Photo Beryl Salt / A Pride of Eagles

Above: Operation *Dingo*. Helicopters above old Portuguese farmlands.
Photo Peter Petter-Bowyer / Winds of Destruction

Top left: Operation *Dingo*, Zulu 1. Northernmost corner of the Admin Base, as seen from a K-Car. *Photo Peter Petter-Bowyer / Winds of Destruction*

Top right: Operation *Dingo*, Zulu 1. Captain Ian Buttenshaw, 1RLI, commanded the mortar detachment. *Photo RLI Cheetah magazine*

Above: An Alouette G-Car in action. *Photo Dennis Croukamp*

Air Lieutenant Phil Haigh (*left*), killed in action on Operation *Dingo* when his Vampire FB9 was shot down. Next to him is K-Car pilot Francois du Toit, who was later killed in action when his helicopter was shot down by FRELIMO. *Photo Peter Petter-Bowyer / Winds of Destruction*

Above: Operation *Dingo*, Zulu 1. Helicopters struggled to find parking places to refuel at the Admin Base. *Photo Peter Petter-Bowyer / Winds of Destruction*

Right: A FRELIMO BTR-152 destroyed at Chimoio by Corporal Fraser Brown of 2 Commando, 1RLI.

Above left: Corporal Jimmy Swan, a 2 Commando, 1RLI stick leader at Chimoio. *Photo Jimmy Swan*

Above centre: Lieutenant John Cronin, an American, OC 13 Troop, 3 Commando, 1RLI at Chimoio. *Photo Tom Argyle*

Above right: Corporal Tony Coom, a 3 Commando, 1RLI stick leader at Chimoio. *Photo Tom Argyle*

Above left: Major Jerry Strong, OC 3 Commando, 1RLI, commanded Stop 1 at Chimoio. *Photo Jerry Strong*

Above right: Three SAS stalwarts. *From left*: Captain Colin Willis, Lieutenant Peter Cole and Captain Bob Mackenzie. Willis commanded Stop 3 at Chimoio and the American MacKenzie Stop 4. *Photo Craig Fourie collection*

Above left: Operation *Dingo*, Zulu 2. A Dakota flies low level over Cabora Bassa Dam to the target at Tembué in the Tete Province of Mozambique. *Photo Beryl Salt / A Pride of Eagles*

Above right: Operation *Dingo*, Zulu 2. Alouettes over Cabora Bassa. Forty helicopters crossed this stretch of water at least four times. *Photo Beryl Salt / A Pride of Eagles*

Centre: Operation *Dingo*, Zulu 2. An Alouette pilot identifies the island on Cabora Bassa where he can refuel. *Photo Beryl Salt / A Pride of Eagles*

Left: A Dakota parachutes resupplies of fuel and ammunition into Tembué. *Photo Beryl Salt / A Pride of Eagles*

Left: The forward admin base on Operation *Dingo*, Zulu 2 was ten minutes' flying time from Tembué and 225 kilometres inside Mozambique. Helicopters can be seen on the left. *Photo Beryl Salt / A Pride of Eagles*

Below: Operation *Dingo*, Zulu 2. The reserve force of helicopters at Chiswiti assembly area just inside Rhodesia. *Photo Peter Petter-Bowyer / Winds of Destruction*

Bottom: A G-Car awaits a paradrop of troops and resupplies at the admin base near Tembué. *Photo Peter Petter-Bowyer / Winds of Destruction*

Above: This scene was repeated 360° around at the admin base near Tembué. Petter-Bowyer's ops bivouac can be seen on the right behind the tree. *Photo Peter Petter-Bowyer / Winds of Destruction*

Left: Petter-Bowyer's one man 'ops centre' at the admin base—makeshift but effective. *Photo Peter Petter-Bowyer / Winds of Destruction*

An Agusta Bell 205A ('Huey'), named a Cheetah by the Rhodesians. Eleven of these second-hand helicopters were smuggled in from Israel to form No. 8 Squadron, which only commenced operations in 1979—such was the poor mechanical condition of the helicopters. *Photo Tom Argyle*

Above: The troop-carrying capacity of the Cheetah was double that of the Alouette, which considerably changed the complexion of Fireforce. *Photo Jon Caffin*

Right: Cheetah pilot. *Photo Jon Caffin*

A good-quality photo of a Lynx.

The Selous Scout Operation *Virile* was put on hold while *Dingo* was in progress. The aims of *Virile* were to destroy bridges and lines of rail in the Espungabera/Gogoi area 150 kilometres south of Chimoio. The Selous Scout 'flying column' concept surpassed all expectations during their raid on Nyadzona Camp in August 1976, where an estimated 2,000 ZANLA cadres were slaughtered. In these two photos, the mayhem and devastation caused by the rampaging Scouts during Operation *Virile*, assisted by elements of 2 Commando, 1RLI, can clearly be seen, along with sundry captured Mozambican civilian buses and trucks. *Photos Dennis Croukamp*

Above: Cheetahs at an airstrip in the Zambezi Valley prepare to take on RLI troops for a cross-border raid into Zambia against a ZIPRA camp, 1979. *Photo Max T*

Right: Cheetahs en route to a Fireforce call-out. The pilot sports a 3 Commando para badge on his helmet. *Photo Peter Petter-Bowyer / Winds of Destruction*

Major Nigel Henson, OC Support Commando, 1RLI 1977–1979, greeted here by his spaniel on his return from a Fireforce engagement. *Photo Nigel Henson*

Top: Some of Henson's troops. *Photo Nigel Henson*

Above left: A Cheetah flares. *Photo Craig Fourie collection*

Above right: Operation *Oppress*, 1979. Support Commando, 1RLI troops advance towards ZANLA's Petulia base in Mozambique's Gaza Province. *Photo Ross Parker*

Left: RAR troops deplane from Cheetahs after a successful operation. *Photo Beryl Salt / A Pride of Eagles*

Centre: An unusual photo. Alouettes lined up on a bush track in the Zambezi Valley, ready for take-off into Zambia. *Photo Beryl Salt / A Pride of Eagles*

Below: SAS troops rest up during an operation in Mozambique. *Photo Craig Fourie collection*

Top: Relieved and weary, these two SAS soldiers are uplifted by Alouette from an external operation. *Photo Johan Joubert*

Above left: An SAS RPD machine gunner in fine spirits. *Photo Johan Joubert*

Above right: An RLI MAG gunner in a reflective mood. *Photo RLI Cheetah magazine*

Fireforce Writ Large:
Operation *Dingo*: Airborne Assault in Mozambique: 23-27 November 1977

helicopter, took charge of the attack. He radioed Stops 1–6 who reported they were on the ground, sorting themselves out and getting into line, ready to move forward. The resident FPLM personnel at their base two kilometres to the north at the former Portuguese settlement did not intervene. Indeed, they were seen standing on roofs, watching the action.[242]

At 08.10 a pair of Vampires of Venom Section arrived to take over the cab-rank duties. As they did, K-Car 2 called for a strike by Blue Section on the area of the garage as he was being fired on from there. Robinson ordered the troops to prepare to throw smoke to mark their positions to aid the strike. He would repeat this order a couple of times as the aircraft attacked.

At 08.23 Walsh ordered K-Cars K1 and K2 to form a stop line south of Camp C as Captain Wilson's Stop 6 had been dropped too far to the west. At 08.27 Robinson ordered Wilson to move east and cross the river, spread out and then advance north towards Camp C. Robinson added a warning a minute later that there were trenches in Stop 6's way, filled with ZANLA insurgents. He also had Lieutenant Ken Roberts's Stop 5 move eastward to the river line to prevent escape down it.

At 08.30 Lynx A4 had good news to impart. On his wide reconnaissance, he had seen no movement on the road to the north or in Tembué town. There seemed also no likelihood of vehicles approaching the forward admin area from the south because the road appeared cut.

Robinson guided the sweep lines converging on camps B and C, using fire and movement. Willis of Stop 3 interrupted Robinson's flow of orders at 08.42 to say that he was leaving behind a casualty from the jump for collection by G-Car and a man to guard him. Stop 2 also requested the replacement of two damaged radios.

Outside interference still seemed unlikely at 08.47 because Lynx F4 reported there was nothing approaching on the southern route. Lieutenant-General Walls in the command Dakota wondered if he could have an estimate of the ZANLA casualties but Robinson replied, "Not yet."

Robinson and Walsh, of course, had more than enough other matters to

---

[242] Cole, p. 188.

worry about as they directed their troops and aircraft. The circling K-Cars were reporting the whereabouts of trenches and bunkers and pockets of resistance. At the same time, the Stop 3's casualty had to be removed; his companion, lacking a nearby landing zone, moved him to the nearby road.

At 08.55, out of ammunition, a K-Car called in a Hunter attack on some 20 ZANLA cadres west of the river. Flight Lieutenant Abram obliged by raking the area with 120 30mm shells on a southerly heading and returned to fire 18 68mm rockets on a westerly one.

The returning, re-armed K-Cars kept up the attack and, at 09.02, Robinson directed a Hunter strike ahead of Stop 6, who were then advancing from the south on Camp C.[243] He ordered Stop 1 to sweep the area of the strike but they were too far from it.

The advance continued, closing in on camps B and C. The ZANLA response was sufficiently muted for G-Car Pink 4 to deliver the two replacement radios to Stop 1 and to collect Stop 3's casualty.

ComOps informed Army HQ and Air HQ at 09.17 that it was "Too early to assess numbers but prospects good for bad day for floppies [insurgents]. Some heavy guns but appears those remaining now not manned. K-Cars have slain at least a few score by the sound of it but this unconfirmed. Appears only one jump casualties [sic]. Construction group to NE took gap, no sign of interference at this stage".[244]

At 09.24 the command Helicopter had to depart to refuel. Robinson ordered Stops 4 and 5 to remain at the river to intercept anyone running from the two camps as the other sweep lines moved in to search them. Calling an air strike on Camp B, Walsh's parting orders were to demand more re-armed and refuelled K-Cars with one to watch Camp A for any return of its inhabitants.

At 09.25 Red Section's Hunters and the Vampires of Venom Section struck Camp B with Red 1 and 2 attacking two anti-aircraft guns. Light resistance was encountered and a Vampire drop-tank was hit. The leading

---

[243] BECM RAAP, Box 844, Op *Dingo*, radio message, 26 November 1977.

[244] BECM RAAP, Box 844, Op *Dingo*, radio message, 26 November 1977.

Fireforce Writ Large:
Operation *Dingo*: Airborne Assault in Mozambique: 23-27 November 1977

Vampire aborted due to radio failure. Pilots reported seeing few people and experiencing little resistance to the air attack.[245]

Two minutes later, more K-Cars were returning from the refuelling and Major Mick Graham, acting for Robinson and flying in a Lynx, sent K-Car K2A to Camp A to "keep the show going". He took over the co-ordination of the converging sweep lines.

Lynx A4 informed Graham at 09.34 that a civilian truck was approaching some distance away and promised to monitor its progress.

At 09.40 a K-Car reported having a potential prisoner with his hand up in an open area. Graham then had to warn Stop 2 to be wary because Stop 4 to the west of them was firing on insurgents. At 09.46 he informed K-Car 2A he needed to block the flight of insurgents between Stops 1 and 2. K-Car K3 moved across. Two minutes later, Graham asked K-Car K3 to support Wilson's Stop 6 as they began to search Camp C. At that moment, Lynx A4 departed to refuel and was replaced by Lynx D4. At 09.54, D4 spotted a group of cadres north of Camp A and drew heavy fire from a nearby road. The presence of that group would only be explained in mid-afternoon.

At 10.03 the command Dakota reported to ComOps that Stops 1 and 2 were "clearing towards B and C. Will clear through to river line. Numerous trenches and bunkers in B and C which could contain CTs [Communist Terrorists]. Stop 3 has moved south towards north end of B. Stop 6 will move to road running through C and hold. Stops 1, 2 and 3 are engaging CTs who are attempting to break from the area. Stops 4 and 5 are holding on west bank of river engaging CTs as they flee".[246]

At 10.07 Graham was told there were many pits in Camp B full of insurgents. One insurgent had been killed in Camp C and an African woman captured. He was also informed that the SB team would be flown to Camp C once it was secured.

At 10.08 Graham reported to Robinson that call sign 6 was searching Camp C while Stops 1 and 2 advanced on Camp B from the north and

---

[245] BECM RAAP, Box 844, Op *Dingo*, radio message, 26 November 1977.

[246] BECM RAAP, Box 844, Op *Dingo*, radio message, 26 November 1977.

south respectively. Stop 5 was in a blocking position to the west. Finally, he said, K-Car K2A had been shot at between camps A and B in the area of the rifle range where Lynx F4 had spotted a small camp equipped with an underground bunker.

At 10.15 Stop 1 was exchanging fire with the cadres in the trenches on the southern edge of Camp B.

At 10.16, taking back command from Graham, Robinson asked Stops 1 and 2 for their locstats and was told that Stop 2 was in the middle of Camp B. Stop 1 was 300–400 metres to the south and firing on numerous cadres. Stop 1 intended to advance towards Stop 2. Stop 2 would avoid Stop 1's line of fire by moving northwest of the camp.

At 10.19 Camp C was secure and the SB team was flown in to examine it. Stops 1 and 2 were still searching Camp B with Stop 1 still having contacts. Moreover, there was resistance from the small camp near the rifle range between A and B.[247]

At 10.22 K-Car K3 reported to Robinson that he had fired into the bunker in the latter camp but was too deep for his 20mm cannon to destroy it and that it would have to be attacked later. He had destroyed other bunkers and all response had ceased. At that Major Mick Graham's aircraft left to refuel.

To avoid the casualties incurred at New Farm, Robinson warned Stop 2 that Stop 1 was moving north in an extended line towards Camp B.

Two minutes later he ordered Stop 5 to move to a landing zone in the riverbed to await uplift to Camp A. He asked Wilson whether Camp C had been cleared and Wilson confirmed it was ready for examination by the SB.

At 10.28 K-Car K3 informed Walsh that the camp near the range seemed to have a large weapons cache and he suggested two sticks be flown in to investigate.

At 10.32 Robinson asked for a K-Car to support Stop 1's northward sweep.

Two minutes later, two Hunters, flying top cover, called in by K-Car K2, fired 18 Matra rockets and 120 30mm cannon shells at a 20-strong insurgent

---

[247] BECM RAAP, Box 844, Op *Dingo*, radio message, 26 November 1977.

group in the eastern area of Camp B.[248]

At 11.11 Walsh called for an additional K-Car from the forward admin area and Robinson ordered Stop 4 to be flown to a blocking position east of Camp A.

By 11.15 Stop 1 reported that they had secured Camp B and had killed 25 cadres in their attack on it and Stop 2, forty-five. They had found a few dead bodies in Camp B itself but, of course, the initial Alpha bomb had overshot most of it.

Instead of going to Camp A, Stop 5 had been flown to the newly discovered small camp and, by 11.18, had thrown a bunker bomb into the well-constructed bunker and would clear it when the smoke cleared.

At 11.20 Robinson summed up for Walls, reporting that Camp C appeared to be an FPLM camp. Stops 1 and 2 were starting a detailed search of Camp B. Stop 5 were examining the small camp and its arms cache at the rifle range. They had captured two insurgents who would be flown to the forward admin area for interrogation. Stop 4 would be moved to clear Camp A with the assistance of a Stop 5 stick once the range area was cleared. Stop 1 and 2 had killed 70 and Stop 6, 23 insurgents.[249]

Stop 6 added at 11.23 that Camp C seemed to be a receiving and controlling centre. They had one prisoner and one trooper with a minor jump injury. The SB team wanted to move onto Camp B. Stop 1 was searching Camp B's west side and warned it would take 15 minutes. Robinson responded by ordering Stop 3 to move south from their blocking position.

At 11.28 Robinson turned his attention to Camp A where MacKenzie's Stop 4 had arrived. He ordered MacKenzie to begin the sweep and promised to reinforce him if he had trouble.

At 11.30 Wilson reported that Stop 6 had completed a further search of Camp C and only had huts to burn. The SB personnel were still with him because Camp B was not yet clear. Robinson promptly asked Stop 2 if they required the SB and ordered them not to burn the complex until the SB had

---

[248] BECM RAAP, Box 844, Op *Dingo*, radio message, 26 November 1977.

[249] BECM RAAP, Box 844, Op *Dingo*, radio message, 26 November 1977.

completed their task. Firing south of Camp C led him to ask Wilson if he had men there engaging three insurgents. No reply was recorded. Instead Stop 1 replied, saying the huts of Camp B contained only clothing which the SB need not examine. Stop 1 proposed therefore to remove any documents.

At that moment, MacKenzie reported that one of his men of Stop 4 had missed the lift by helicopter to Camp A. The log does not record where the missing man was or what happened to him.

The welcome news at 11.42 was that Lynx E4 had checked all surrounding roads and had seen nothing moving on them.

At 11.43 Stop 5 discovered an arms cache in the small camp. It contained mortar bombs, weapons and more and was being examined in detail.

Zulu 2 was entering its final phase: at 11.45, Robinson ordered Wilson to leave a protection party with the SB team and have Stop 6 collect parachutes. Then, because Stop 1 was finding interesting documents, Robinson ordered the SB team and its protection party to move to Camp B. As Robinson did that Stop 1 reported finding weapons.

As the command helicopter had to refuel at 11.50, Robinson decided to transfer to a K-Car at the forward admin area. Before he did this, Stop 1 informed him that, because the documents indicated there was a magazine in the area of camps B and C, captured insurgents were to be brought there to indicate its whereabouts.

Stop 1 was still having contacts with the enemy at 11.55 and asked for support from a K-Car, a replacement FN rifle and water. Walsh ordered K-Car K3A to supply the top cover.

While Robinson was transferring to a K-Car, he was told at 11.58 that G-Car Pink 2 was arriving with Stop 1's water, the spare rifle, demolition explosives and the prisoners to indicate the whereabouts of Camp B's magazine.

At 12.03, in Walsh's absence, K-Car K3A warned the command Dakota that he would have to leave shortly because he had only 15 minutes of fuel left.

Stop 5 reported they had emptied the bunker of a 75mm recoilless rifle, an 82mm mortar, grenades and much ammo and asked for a demolition kit.

The sitrep at 12.10 recorded the results of the air strikes which had set fire to five long buildings and surrounding huts at Camp B, and destroyed two 12.7mm machine-gun positions. The complex of huts north of Camp C was burning. There had been no firing from Tembué village at reconnaissance aircraft. No vehicles had been seen moving from there. One civilian truck had been seen going to Bene and six people climbed out of it. No other vehicles were seen on the Bene road. Two large ten-tonne trucks were seen heading west some 30 kilometres northwest of Tembué. Bene airfield was deemed unserviceable due to overgrown grass but Tembué airfield was serviceable.[250]

At 12.14 Stop 1 asked the command Dakota to arrange for additional water and 7.62mm ammunition.

At 12.15 Robinson was back in the area and reported that the search of Camp C was completed. Stops 1 and 2 were searching Camp B and had recovered numerous interesting documents and weapons. They found the radio hut but no radio. They were still having intermittent contacts. Stop 5 had emptied the bunker near the range and would destroy its weapons and ammunition. MacKenzie's Stop 4 was in action in Camp A.

A rock rolling down the side of a *donga* alerted MacKenzie to six ZANLA cadres hiding in a cave. Before they could fire their SKS rifles, MacKenzie killed them all with rapid bursts from his 5.5mm AR-15 rifle. Shortly afterwards MacKenzie, Sergeant Les Clark and Trooper Gerry McGowan, an RPD gunner, flushed a large group out from another *donga*, killing 86 of them.[251]

More mundane tasks were occupying the others. Stop 6 was collecting their parachutes. Robinson, at 12.17, ordered that any incoming helicopters should bring water for his thirsty troops.

At 12.18 Stop 4 was still in action. Stop 1 reported they had killed a total of 70 in Camp B. The immediate roads remained free of any traffic, Squadron Leader Griffiths reported at 12.23.

The action was not over. Stop 1 alerted Robinson at 12.25 to a heavy

---

[250] BECM RAAP, Box 844, Op *Dingo*, Sitrep, A4/F4/9A, 26 November 1977.

[251] BECM RAAP, Box 844, Op *Dingo*, radio message, 26 November 1977; Cole, p. 188.

weapon firing to the north of them. Robinson asked MacKenzie if he required covering fire. MacKenzie replied he needed K-Car support.

At 12.30 Stop 3 explained to Robinson that the firing heard in his area was at ZANLA cadres who had run into his stop line.

Robinson asked MacKenzie if he still required a K-Car because the weather was becoming stormy. MacKenzie replied, "Not required this time."

At 12.38 the incoming Red Section were ten minutes out from the target.

At 12.41 Stop 1 informed Robinson that the main portion of Camp B was cleared. Robinson accordingly ordered Willis's Stop 3 to sweep the area southward to Camp B. He told Stop 1 to wait for Stop 3 to reach Camp B and then clear the area back to the dropping zone before collecting parachutes. Stop 1 replied that they had just found an 82mm mortar tube and would load it on a helicopter if possible.

At 12.45 Robinson briefed Major Mick Graham who was flying in to relieve him. He explained that Stop 4 was searching Camp A from south to north. Stop 5 was clearing the camp near the range. Stops 1 and 2 had searched Camp B. Stop 3 was moving down to join 1 and 2. Stop 6 was collecting parachutes.

At 12.50 Red Section replaced the top cover.

Stop 4 was still searching Camp A. Stops 1 and 2 had cleared Camp B and Stop 3 was moving to join them before recovering parachutes which Stop 6 was already doing. Stop 5 had cleared the range camp. Weather was closing in from the north and it was raining.[252]

At 12.51 Lynx E4 warned that the weather to the north and northeast did not look good.

At 13.07 Stop 6 confirmed the total of their kills as twenty-three.

By 13.15, however, MacKenzie's Stop 4 was in trouble because the southern portion of Camp A had been re-occupied by ZANLA and he required assistance to drive them out. The rain, however, made it difficult for the K-Cars to support him. He asked Lynx A4 to check the southern end of the camp. At 13.22, as he began to advance southward, MacKenzie informed

---

[252] BECM RAAP, Box 844, Op *Dingo*, radio message, 26 November 1977.

Fireforce Writ Large:
Operation *Dingo*: Airborne Assault in Mozambique: 23-27 November 1977

Graham he had found 100 SKS and 20 British SLR rifles.

At 13.23 Graham asked Roberts of Stop 5 for a sitrep and was told that he was waiting for demolition explosives to destroy the weapons and ammunition he had found. Graham replied that Stop 1 had the necessary explosives and they would be sent to Roberts as soon as possible.

Two minutes later, MacKenzie reported that his Stop 4 had found the camp office and he needed the SB team to examine it.

At Camp B, Stop 3 warned Stop 1 that he would shortly blow up the mortar ammunition found there.

Red Section withdrew at 13.30.

G-Car Yellow 12 delivered the ammunition and water requested by Stop 1 and was asked to fly the SB team from Stop 1 to Stop 4 at Camp A and demolition explosives from Stop 1 to Stop 5. Graham ordered Stop 2 to collect parachutes and plans began to be laid for G-Cars to fly in to remove them. G-Car Pink 4, not Yellow 12, at 13.52, flew the SB team to MacKenzie at Camp A.

Robinson returned at 13.54 and was told by Graham that Stops 1, 2 and 3 were in Camp B and would meet the G-Cars in the landing zone to load the parachutes.

At that moment, Stop 5 started his demolition, using explosive charges to blow up eight boxes of 82mm mortar rounds, eight boxes of RGD and two of concussion grenades, 15 boxes of 7.62mm intermediate bullets, eight 75mm recoilless rounds, two TMH mines, four boxes of TNT, four boxes of 7.62mm long ammunition, and 15 SKS rifles.

Stop 4 had cleared Camp A and the SB team were checking the HQ block and warned that they would need at least an hour to do so.

MacKenzie blew up 140 SKS rifles, 20 British SLR rifles, a 12.7mm heavy machine gun, 30 rifle grenades, 10,000 7.62mm intermediate rounds, 15 slabs of TNT, one 3.5-inch rocket launcher, an 82mm mortar, a 4.5 truck, 1,000 sets of denims and ten tonnes of maize.[253] That left the weapons and ammunition found at camps B and C to be destroyed.

---

[253] BECM RAAP, Box 844, Op *Dingo*, Destruction Return, 21 December 1977.

The rain prompted the cancellation of the top cover at 14.00. The aircraft remained on standby at New Sarum. Robinson informed Walls that six G-Cars were needed to fly out Stops 1, 2, 3, 5 and 6. He added that he knew that Stop 1 had killed 40 ZANLA cadres, Stop 6, 23, and the K-Cars, fifteen.

K-Car 1A proposed at 14.05 to fly out three of the 12.7mm machine guns found at Camp B, if they were dismantled. Stop 1 responded by ordering Stop 2 to dismantle them. The interesting aspect of these weapons was that they were found mounted on mounds and not dug-in positions as normal. Both guns were loaded and cocked but their crews had fled. The third gun was on open ground, lying on its side.

At 14.08 Stop 3 asked Robinson the fate of the remaining arms and ammunition and was told to destroy all of them bar the 12.7mm machine guns. Willis responded by blowing up three 75mm recoilless rifles and 25 of their 75mm shells, two 82mm mortars, 15 TMH and a box of anti-tank landmines, five boxes of TNT, two boxes of grenades, a 3.5-inch rocket launcher and six SKS rifles.

The SB team had finished at Camp A and MacKenzie radioed for a G-Car to remove them, documents and two prisoners, who later turned out to be Rhodesian Internal Affairs district assistants abducted on 21 November and driven to Tembué where they were imprisoned. MacKenzie added that his men had killed 150 cadres in Camp A.

The withdrawal began in earnest. At 14.20 six G-Cars flew the 24 men of Stop 1 to the landing zone to gather the parachutes. G-Car Pink 4 flew to Camp A to collect the documents et al. Next, Robinson, who had just estimated the total kill at 300–350, was told by the command Dakota that Stop 2 would be the first unit to be flown out. Stop 2 had just seen two red trucks driving on a nearby road but was told to ignore them. Stop 3 still needed another half an hour to complete the demolition of Camp B's armoury. This was done by 14.48 and Willis signalled they were ready for uplift. They were flown to join Stop 3 collecting parachutes along the landing zone.

By 14.49 MacKenzie had discovered why the camps had been somewhat empty. He radioed Robinson, telling him that a captured cadre had explained that 1,000 cadres had left during the previous night for another camp to the north and 500 had gone to Bene to the south. Walsh despatched a Lynx to search for the northern camp.

Otherwise, MacKenzie reported his men were still searching the area and encountering insurgents. He required the assistance of a K-Car and a further 45–60 minutes to complete his task.

At 15.00 Stop 6 had reported they had gathered all the parachutes they could. Stop 3 signalled they would be ready for uplift shortly. Stop 5 had finished his demolition and was collecting parachutes. Stop 4 was still clearing Camp A with the supporting K-Car drawing fire. At 15.04 Stop 1 was notified that G-Cars would collect them in two minutes. Stop 6 was to be flown out in ten minutes.

At 15.06 Walsh reported to the command Dakota that the new camp mentioned by MacKenzie's captured man had been found one and a half kilometres north of Camp A. Permission was given at 15.10 for it to be bombed. By 15.27 it was known to comprise newly constructed huts under trees and a parade ground. Lynx C4 was ordered to mark it for an air strike by Hunters followed by Canberras, bombing with Alpha bombs.[254]

Preparations for the airlift continued with Stop 6, at 15.14, the first to be ready. At 15.30 Stops 1, 2 and 6 were likewise ready for uplift with their parachutes. Stops 3 and 5 were collecting their parachutes but Stop 4 was still combing through Camp A.

Reporting to Walls, whose command Dakota was shortly due to return to Mount Darwin to refuel, Robinson warned it might not be possible to remove all the stop groups by nightfall. He added that some 350 ZANLA cadres had been killed and numerous caches of heavy weapons, small arms and ammunition had been located and destroyed.[255]

At 15.38 Walsh had to fly Robinson back to the forward admin area to refuel again. As they flew the exchanges with Walls continued. The plan evolved to fly out Stops 1, 2 and 6 plus all the parachutes and jump helmets and to leave Stop 4 at Camp A and Stops 3 and 5 at Camp B overnight. The

---

[254] BECM RAAP, Box 844, Op *Dingo*, radio message, 26 November 1977.

[255] BECM RAAP, Box 844, Op *Dingo*, radio message, 26 November 1977.

Chapter 15

few hours of daylight left and the stormy weather meant that Walls decided the command Dakota would not return. Instead, he would monitor progress from Mount Darwin.

The penultimate blow of the day was struck at 16.35. Blue Section's Hunters, flown by Blythe-Wood and Lowrie, fired 64 Matra rockets into the newly discovered camp to mark it for the four low-flying Canberras of Green Section. Green Section's Alpha bombs were on target, setting half the huts on fire. Returning, Blue Section strafed it with 700 30mm shells.[256] Both sections flew back to New Sarum where the Canberra aircrews were stood down at 18.20.[257]

Stop 1 was flown to guard the forward admin area for the night while Stop 3 at Camp C, Stop 4 at Camp A and Stop 5 at Camp B prepared their night-ambush positions.

The day's drama, however, was not over. The helicopter fleet carrying Stops 2 and 6 faced a line of storms which meant they did not all reach Mount Darwin as planned. One Alouette ran out of fuel short of the Train and had to land on an island in Cabora Bassa dam to await delivery of four drums of fuel by parachute from Malloch's DC-7. After refuelling, the helicopter was escorted over the Rhodesian border by other helicopters. The growing darkness, the rain and the turbulence led to the dispersal of the helicopters. The first wave, en route to Mount Darwin, made an unplanned stop at the Centenary country club. The second wave, including Walsh and Robinson in the command helicopter and Stops 2 and 6, landed at Chiswiti. It was the end of another long day.[258] Squadron Leader Griffiths, for example, had flown K-Car K1 for eight hours and 35 minutes.[259]

The FPLM, however, had the chance to strike the final blow of the day. At 18.05 the BSAP post at Kanyemba reported that a DC-4 aircraft had been hit by a missile while flying north over the Zambian–Mozambican border

---

[256] BECM RAAP, Box 844, Op *Dingo*, radio message, 26 November 1977.

[257] BECM RAAP, Box 844, Op *Dingo*, radio message, 26 November 1977.

[258] Cole, p. 188.

[259] Flying Log of H.G. Griffiths, Vol. 4.

Fireforce Writ Large:
Operation *Dingo*: Airborne Assault in Mozambique: 23-27 November 1977

between Feira and Zumbo at the Zambezi–Luangwa river confluence. The DC-4 was one of Rhodesia's sanctions-breaking aircraft, an Air Trans Africa DC-4, owned by Jack Malloch and carrying ten tonnes of fresh prime beef for export. The aircraft turned south and crash-landed just over the southern bank of the Zambezi River close to the Rhodesian border. The event was confirmed by the FPLM report from Zumbo at 07.40 which admitted responsibility for firing the missile and related that the aircraft had been found and its crew, two white men, Captain Mouzon and First Lieutenant Nibel, had been captured.[260]

The last order of the day granted the RLI troops of Stop 2 a day off duty to refit before they returned to the operational areas.[261] This was extended to all the troops on the next day.[262]

The aircraft of the Rhodesian Air Force were airborne by 05.15 on Sunday, 27 November, heading back to assist the troops left at Tembué. Stops 3, 4 and 5 had endured an eventful night, listening to vehicles moving and bursts of heavy machine-gun fire to the north. Robert's Stop 5's sentries had been active shooting at stragglers. MacKenzie retook Camp A at first light, killing more ZANLA cadres and rescuing one of their prisoners, an African Selous Scout.[263]

At 06.25 all G-Cars were regrouping at Chiswiti, ready to depart to bring back Stops 1, 3, 4, and 5 as soon as possible.[264] The first four were expected at Tembué at 09.00 along with Hunters and Vampires. It was estimated that 40 helicopter lifts would be required using the available 22 G-Cars.

The area was still not entirely peaceful because, at 07.11, a 14.5mm machine gun and a multi-barrelled weapon fired at Lynx E4 as it flew over the road south of Camp B.[265]

---

[260] BECM RAAP, Box 844, Op *Dingo*, radio message, 26 November 1977, B2, 27 November 1977.

[261] BECM RAAP, Box 844, Op *Dingo*, telex, 26 November 1977.

[262] BECM RAAP, Box 844, Op *Dingo*, telex, 27 November 1977.

[263] Cole, p. 187; BECM RAAP, Box 844, Op *Dingo*, radio message, 27 November 1977.

[264] BECM RAAP, Box 844, Op *Dingo*, radio message, 27 November 1977.

[265] BECM RAAP, Box 844, Op *Dingo*, radio message, 27 November 1977.

At 08.20 SAS Major Mick Graham informed all stops that the command Dakota and Robinson were en route and would take over command. Five minutes later, Graham warned the command Dakota and the helicopters to be wary of flying over known anti-aircraft positions west of Bene.

The Hunter cab-rank formed at 09.00 above camps A, B and C to cover first the flight of four G-Cars, A Section, expected at 09.45. The first helicopter flight, A Section, was ordered to pick up 24 parachutes and eight men from Stop 5. B Section was to fly out 12 men from Stop 1.

At 09.32 K-Cars K2 and K2A arrived over the camps, covering the arrival of the G-Cars.

The lack of a threat to the withdrawal of troops led to the reduction of the standby force of four Canberras at New Sarum by one having six 1,000lb bombs removed, leaving two armed with 300 Alpha bombs each and one with six 500lb bombs.[266]

At the camps the four-G-Car sections were arriving at the stops and the forward admin area to collect men and parachutes. By 10.52 all the men of Stop 3 were en route home and only MacKenzie's Stop 4 and the forward admin area personnel remained to be collected by the second wave before 12.30.[267] What MacKenzie had not done was to recover Stop 4's parachutes, 20 of which were draped in the trees.

At 11.07 one of the Vampires at New Sarum was diverted to support the Selous Scouts' Operation *Virile* which was about to commence. The rest were stood down.[268]

At 12.18 Stop 4 had been lifted out and the remaining task of the G-Cars was to remove from the forward admin area 20 men, including prisoners and the personnel who had manned the radio relay.

At 13.10 the last six G-Cars took off from the forward admin area, ending Zulu 2.

---

[266] BECM RAAP, Box 844, Op *Dingo*, telex, 27 November 1977.

[267] BECM RAAP, Box 844, Op *Dingo*, telex, 27 November 1977.

[268] BECM RAAP, Box 844, Op *Dingo*, telex, 27 November 1977.

Fireforce Writ Large:
Operation *Dingo*: Airborne Assault in Mozambique: 23-27 November 1977

★★★★★

There was, however, no respite for ZANLA or the FPLM because, at last light, Operation *Virile* was underway with Selous Scout Major Albert Sachse's vehicles driving over the Mozambican border on a little-used track just east of Espungabera, heading for the main road to the small town of Dombe. The first bridge was blown to isolate Espungabera before the column headed northeast to Dombe, led by the unique Pookie landmine-detection vehicle. When the Pookie broke down on the rugged road, it was replaced in the lead by an innocent-looking 'Q' armoured bus with a concealed armament of a Soviet-made 12.7mm and two American .5in Browning heavy machine guns and carrying 'passengers' armed with RPD machine guns. A narrow shave in an FPLM ambush, however, led to the bus being replaced at the head of the column by two less vulnerable armoured cars, sporting 20mm Hispano cannons. In addition, the road was cleared ahead by two Hunters strafing vehicles. The Hunters attacked Dombe to discourage FPLM interference while the Scouts demolished the high-level four-spanned bridge over the Mabvudzi River. The column turned back to blow the six-spanned bridge over the Lusito River, at 09.00 on Monday, 28 November. The next attack, on a sawmill, however, contrived to annoy the South Africans because, during it, the Selous Scouts directed a Hunter attack onto what they mistook for a gun emplacement. What was destroyed was the main radio relay station for the Cabora Bassa–to–Transvaal power line. On Tuesday, 29 November, the Scouts blew up two more bridges and abandoned heavy road-making machinery. At dusk they returned to the Espungabera area and crossed back into Rhodesia at 10.00 on Wednesday morning, 30 November, leaving Espungabera cut off from the northeast by fast-flowing rivers. Ambush parties thereafter harassed the portering of supplies between the destroyed bridges, calling down Hunter strikes on FPLM vehicles bringing supplies to the river crossings. What surprised the ambush was the unpopularity of the governing FRELIMO among the local Mozambicans they met. This encouraged the Rhodesian government to support the resistance movement which came to be known as RENAMO.[269]

On Monday, 28 November, nothing was said publicly about *Virile* but it was announced in a brief communiqué that in the past five days Rhodesian forces had attacked camps near Chimoio and Tembué, killing more than 1,200 ZANLA.[270] The unofficial estimate was that ZANLA had suffered some 5,000 casualties. It was calculated that ZANLA had suffered a loss of 20 per cent of its strength in the two raids.[271]

If the Rhodesians were hoping to remain tight-lipped, they were forced to respond as the British press had much to say. Derek Ingram of the Gemini News Service had been in Chimoio town on the morning of 23 November and had heard the explosions and seen the smoke rising on the northern horizon. He was only able to visit the camp after the last troops left but would report seeing the bodies of nearly 100 young teenagers being buried. Ian Christie, another British journalist, joined him, counting the remains of 20 young teenage girls in one grave. Christie noted that the 70 other corpses strewn about were mostly female and many of them children. At the Parirenyatwa Camp hospital which had burned down, eight men lay under a tree, all shot through the back of the head, Christie wrote. A napalm attack had burnt children between eight and 14 years old at Chindunduma Primary School. Later there were photographs published of mass graves with bodies piled in layers.[272]

To counter this depiction of *Dingo* as a massacre of the unarmed and the innocent, ComOps spokesmen, including General Walls, admitted that there had been unarmed ZANLA personnel killed, but they maintained that most of those killed had been armed. They spoke in praise of a courageous group who, armed with folding-butt FN rifles, had resisted fiercely when cornered. The point at issue, the Rhodesians insisted, was that the camps were full of future infiltrators and that the camps could not just be allowed to exist.

---

[269] Reid-Daly, *Top Secret War*, pp. 285–296.

[270] Legum, p. B342.

[271] McAleese, p. 142; PPH, Ops 001, debrief Op *Dingo* Phase 2 (Z2), 28 November 1977.

[272] Caute, pp. 140–141.

Fireforce Writ Large:
Operation *Dingo*: Airborne Assault in Mozambique: 23-27 November 1977

General Walls warned that his forces would continue to operate externally. He added that, if women inhabited the camps, they could be killed.[273]

The Rhodesians were surprised when Britain's Foreign Secretary, Dr David Owen, while deploring *Dingo* as a "savage and pretty brutal attack" and condemning it for endangering the peace of the whole of southern Africa, stated that it might have shown Mugabe and Nkomo and their Patriotic Front "that the Rhodesian Defence Force is not on its back".[274]

In the aftermath of *Dingo* and *Virile*, a revolt within ZANU/ZANLA over the conduct of the war led to the arrest and incarceration of Cleotus Chigowe after he had abducted Mugabe's close colleagues, Edgar Tekere and Dr Herbert Ushewokunze.[275]

While it took some time for ZANLA's fortunes to revive, by March 1978, Ian Smith would achieve a settlement with the internal nationalists which held the potential of defeating Mugabe and Nkomo. He was well on the road to that settlement before *Dingo* was complete, because on Friday, 25 November, the Reverend Ndabaningi Sithole (who had founded ZANU in 1963 only to be ousted by Mugabe in 1974) welcomed Smith's invitation to talk. Senator Chief Jeremiah Chirau, president of Zimbabwe United People's Organization, did likewise on Sunday, 27 November.[276] The key player, however, was Bishop Muzorewa. Although he praised Smith's commitment to majority rule on Saturday, 26 November, within three days he was responding to the outrage of his constituents and refusing to negotiate with Smith because of the killing of his kinsmen at Chimoio and Tembué. It took a few weeks before Muzorewa was prepared to negotiate.[277]

With luck on the Rhodesian side, Operation *Dingo* had been a stunning technical and political success. It had harassed ZANLA in its safe havens, killed or wounded 20 per cent of its strength, and set back the reinforcement

---

[273] Cole, pp. 188–189.

[274] Flower, pp. 191–193; *Keesing's*, 28 April 1978, Vol. XXIV, p. 28948.

[275] Cole, p. 189; Tekere, p. 98.

[276] Legum, p. B1026.

[277] Legum, p. B1026; Flower, pp. 191–193; *Keesing's*, 28 April 1978, Vol. XXIV, p. 28948.

effort by months. The Rhodesian intelligence services gleaned much from the vast quantity of documents recovered. Lessons had been learned that improvisation could counter the short range of the Alouette III and other disadvantages. The experiment of using a command helicopter taught that a more capable aircraft was needed. More flexible tactics on the ground with regard to the sweep lines were acknowledged as necessary. The new A76 radios were praised but were found to be likely to fail if wet.[278] Difficult-to-obtain weapons had been captured but it was apparent that, if heavy weapons, like the 37mm anti-aircraft gun, were to be recovered, larger and more powerful helicopters were required.[279] A year later, the Rhodesian Air Force acquired Agusta-Bell 206s with greater range and lifting capacity.

Many more airborne and other raids followed. If the enemy became wary, and success on a *Dingo* scale was never repeated, Rhodesia's external operations convinced her neighbours that the war had to end. The raids forced Mugabe and Nkomo to the conference table in 1979 and had them accept the compromise devised by Lord Carrington and the British Foreign Office at Lancaster House, London, that December. The ironic outcome was the accession to power of Robert Mugabe in subsequent elections—the least desired outcome.

---

[278] PPH, Ops 001, debrief Op Dingo Phase 2 (Z2), 28 November 1977.

[279] PPH, Ops 001, debrief Op Dingo Phase 2 (Z2), 28 November 1977.

Chapter 16

Fireforce in Action at the Height of the War

The records of Support Commando, 1RLI (commanded by Major Nigel Henson) in the crucial months of February to May 1979 give a taste of Fireforce action at the height of the war, at the moment when the new constitution of Zimbabwe–Rhodesia was brought in, conceding majority rule for the first time.

In the general election in late April, Bishop Muzorewa and his United African National Council gained the majority of the seats in the new Legislative Assembly with the overwhelming support of the electorate who had defied the terrorizing efforts by Mugabe's ZANLA, and Nkomo's ZIPRA to deter them from voting. Muzorewa's popularity would quickly fade because the governments of the west, and, in particular, the new British Conservative government of Margaret Thatcher, refused to recognize the legality of his election.

The forces ranged against Muzorewa—ZANLA and ZIPRA—took a terrible pounding from the onslaught of the Rhodesian security forces both internally in Rhodesia and externally in their host countries of Mozambique, Zambia and, on one occasion, deep in central Angola. Support Commando was in the thick of the fighting as one of five Fireforces. The pilots of the Fireforces had the additional burden of constantly being drawn away to support a programme of continual air and ground external attacks by the Rhodesian SAS, the RLI and Selous Scouts. In April, Support Commando itself would raid Mozambique.

In February 1979, Support Commando was supplying troops for two Fireforces, Delta and Echo. At 13.45 on 22 February, on a bright, hot afternoon, elements of Support Command, 1RLI, acting as Fireforce Delta and commanded by Lieutenant Vernon A. Prinsloo, contacted 12 green-clad

Chapter 16

ZANLA cadres at UL 128518 (a grid reference[280]) in the mopane forest and thorn bush of Sengwe TTL in the extreme south of Rhodesia, close to the South African and Mozambican borders. Fireforce Delta had been brought in to reinforce a call sign of the mounted infantry regiment, the Grey's Scouts, who had been following the spoor of a group of ZANLA. The Greys had killed an insurgent and called for Fireforce Delta to seal off the escape routes with stop groups and sweep the area.

Fireforce Delta (comprising a K-Car, three G-Cars and a Lynx) had been pre-positioned nearby but in the five minutes it took to reach the target, the ZANLA were fleeing southeast. The Fireforce flew over the southern area and a keen-eyed trooper in a G-Car spotted the insurgents some three kilometres from the contact area. The K-Car attacked the group while Stop 1 was dropped on a river line a kilometre west of the target. Stop 2 was dropped about a kilometre south of Stop 1 on a track. Both stops swept eastward parallel to each other. Stop 3 was dropped in a small kraal 800 metres to the west of the target. By this time the insurgents had bombshelled, fleeing in all directions. One insurgent put up his hands and surrendered to the K-Car. Stop 3 took him and a wounded man into custody and immediately thereafter killed a third. The K-Car's 20mm cannon knocked down three insurgents in a gully 100 metres away to the west and sent Stop 2 to investigate. The K-Car scored its fourth kill another 100 metres on and dispatched Stop 1 to clear the area. The Lynx pilot then spotted two ZANLA running west behind Stop 1 who turned about and searched west along the other side of the river line. The Lynx put in two Frantan attacks onto these two insurgents, apparently without success, but Stop 1 killed an insurgent on arrival, re-swept the area and shot and killed two more.

Lieutenant Prinsloo recorded in his report that nine ZANLA cadres were killed, two were captured and one escaped. He noted the poor state of the

---

[280] The drawing of grid lines on ordnance survey maps was a product of the First World War to enable the speedy pinpointing of positions for artillery and other purposes. The grids are labelled with the letters of the alphabet. The map-reader finds the lateral and vertical lines and then calculates the position sought in tenths of the relevant square, taking the horizontal measurement first. References are given in four or six figures.

ZANLA weaponry, with its woodwork old and rotting. His 12 men had recovered four SKS self-loading rifles, six AK and one AKM assault rifles, six stick grenades, 12 30-round AK magazines, one 40-round AK magazine, three percussion grenades, 2,000 rounds of 7.62 intermediate rounds, five RPG-7 rockets and four RPG-7 boosters and an 82mm mortar secondary charge. His troops had fired 250 rounds of 7.62mm ball and had thrown a white phosphorus grenade. The K-Car had fired 100 20mm shells and the Lynx had dropped two frantan bombs and fired 120 rounds of .303in ball from its front guns. A mini-flare projector had been lost along with three FN magazines. Prinsloo noted that interrogation had revealed that the insurgents had not known that the Fireforce was in the area despite its earlier move to a position close by to await the call-out.[281]

Two days later, at 10.30 on the rainy morning of 24 February, Support Commando's other Fireforce, Echo, commanded by Major Nigel Henson, contacted an unknown number of ZANLA cadres at US 222435 in the Chiweshe Tribal Trust Land, north of Salisbury and southwest of the white farming area of Centenary. Henson was faced with many problems. He had only a K-Car, a G-Car and a Lynx; the target area was large (five kilometres by three) and covered in thick bush. Visibility from the air was poor and heavy rain swept in at ten-minute intervals throughout the day. Henson had responded to a confirmation received at 10.15 from the SB that 95 insurgents were in the area but he was not given a precise location. Henson had been forewarned and, having only one troop-carrying helicopter, had pre-positioned the 64 men of his second-wave sticks, comprising six RLI and ten PATU sticks, with fuel about five minutes from the contact area.

No movement was seen from the aircraft when they arrived over the suspected area. Henson deployed Stops 1–7 in a curving line from south to north along the banks of the Ruya River. Stops 3–5 started sweeping northward and contacted an insurgent across a small tributary of the Ruya. The result was the wounding of Trooper Cummings so Henson requested air strikes by the Lynx with frantan and a Mini-Golf bomb. He reinforced Stops

---

[281] PPH, RLIP, contact report by Lieutenant V.A. Prinsloo, 22 February 1979.

3, and 5 with Stops 6 and 7 but the ZANLA cadres replied with mortar fire. Henson moved Stops 8–11 to the west and had them sweep northeastward. Stops 3–7 killed an insurgent armed with a 60mm mortar on the hill in front of them and then resumed their sweep. On the second central hill, Stop 8 reported ZANLA ahead. The Lynx and the K-Car attacked but an immediate sweep found nothing. Henson ordered a further sweep of the area, and this time Stops 3–7 came under intense fire from the summit. Further air strikes were put in and the sweep line found three ZANLA bodies on the northern flank of the hill.

In his report, having recorded the killing of four ZANLA cadres, the escape of 15, and the wounding of Trooper Cummings, Henson stressed the difficulties of operating in heavy rain which had masked the escapes. The size of the area of operations had also militated against a bigger kill. An AKM assault rifle, a PPSH submachine gun, a 60mm mortar, grenades, ammunition and documents were recovered and handed to the SB at Mount Darwin. Henson confessed that the idea of tackling 95 ZANLA insurgents with a K-Car and a G-Car was daunting because the lack of G-Cars had drastically limited his ability to move his troops. Those killed, Henson wrote, had been more inept with their attempted escape than he had yet experienced.[282]

Intelligence gathered by 1 (Independent) Company led the JOC to devise an all-arms attack on five ZANLA camps sited in the grassland, scattered trees and thorny undergrowth of the Mtetengwe Tribal Trust Land, north of Beitbridge in the south of Rhodesia. The plan was that a Canberra would bomb the first and second camps (at SL 978892 and SL 971887) at first light on 6 March. Simultaneously, artillery would shell the third and fourth camps (at SL 955853 and SL 956841) while Fireforce Delta attacked the fifth camp (at TL 016872).

The plan went somewhat awry. The artillery bogged down on a muddy road and could not get into position. The Canberra had communications problems and had to abort.

---

[282] PPH, RLIP, contact report by Major N. D. Henson, 24 February 1979.

Fireforce Delta, comprising Lieutenant Vernon Prinsloo's Support Commando men, a K-Car, three G-Cars, a Lynx and a PRAW aircraft, had pre-positioned nearby, decided to continue with its task. Stops 1 and 2 were dropped on a 'cut line' (a bush-cleared fire break) to the east of the camp. Stop 3 was placed on a ridge in the south near the river, which ran directly north to the camp and beyond. When the K-Car flew over the camp, Prinsloo could see the sleeping places and the blankets but no movement. Stops 1 and 2 moved directly west along the cut line to the river and then along its banks southward towards the camp. On reaching the proximity of the camp area at 06.30, they shot and killed three ZANLA cadres in the undergrowth. The thorns were so thick that the troops spent much of their time on their hands and knees. An insurgent killed himself by blowing his head off with a grenade. Seeing movement in the undergrowth, the troops fired and killed ten African women. Prinsloo had Stops 4 and 5 dropped in the east on a tributary of the main river to work down it towards the camp. Stops 1, 2, 4 and 5 then swept the swamp just to the north, working up the main river towards Stop 3. In the thick thorn bush, six more African women were killed in dense thorn bush. The sweep returned towards the camp and captured two females. The bodies of a female and an insurgent were recovered. The thorns were so thick that the bodies of the other three insurgents and the African women could not be recovered and were left behind. The captured females informed the security forces that the camp had held seven insurgents and eleven women. In the aftermath, the troops were sent on foot to check the other four camps, finding them unoccupied.

Lieutenant Prinsloo recorded the score as four ZANLA cadres and eight civilians killed. His twelve RLI troopers and eight riflemen from 1 (Indep) had recovered one AK and one SKS rifle, seven AK magazines and 500 rounds of 7.62mm ammunition, one offensive and two stick grenades. The K-Car had fired 15 20mm shells and the troops 500 rounds and had also thrown one high-explosive and four white phosphorus grenades. The only loss was an empty MAG belt.[283]

---

[283] PPH, RLIP, contact report by Lieutenant V. A. Prinsloo, 6 March 1979.

Chapter 16

At 11.00 on the next day, 7 March, Prinsloo and his Fireforce Delta were back in action. They had responded to a sighting by call sign 33B, Selous Scouts manning an OP, of eight insurgents at OG 624854 in the Godhlwayo Tribal Trust Land, south of Bulawayo, in the *Tangent* operational area. Call sign 33B bungled the talk-on and time was wasted. Then the K-Car spotted and killed an insurgent in the camp at QG 624855. Prinsloo ordered Stops 1 and 2 to be dropped to sweep the area of the camp. During the sweep, an orbiting G-Car noticed two insurgents about two kilometres northwest. The K-Car flew over, shot both of them and diverted Stops 1 and 2 to search this area while Stops 3 and 4 were dropped to the east to sweep the original camp. When Stops 1 and 2 failed to find one of the two men the K-Car had shot, it was concluded that he had escaped wounded. After searching the area, all stops were recovered. The Fireforce returned to base.

An hour later, call sign 33B, called Fireforce Delta back to a position five kilometres northeast of the contact area because they could see that three insurgents had regrouped on a hill. Fireforce arrived and one insurgent broke cover as Stop 1 was put on the ground. The K-Car opened fire and killed him. Stop 2 joined Stop 1 and swept the northern flank of the hill while Stop 3 searched the kraal to the south of the hill. Stops 1 and 2 flushed two insurgents off the hill who fled northeast only to be killed by Stops 3 and 4. One SKS and three AK rifles, five stick grenades, an armour-piercing rifle grenade and 400 rounds of AK ammunition were recovered and handed to SB at Gwanda. Recording the score of five ZANLA killed and three escaped, with one of the escapees being wounded, Prinsloo felt that, if the first talk-on had been accurate, all eight insurgents could have been killed.[284]

On 9 March 1979, the Fireforce manned by 1 Commando 1RLI and commanded by Major Frederick Watts, contacted 23 ZANLA and killed 21 of them.[285]

At 16.00 that day Major Henson's Support Commando's Fireforce Echo (a K-Car, three G-Cars and a Lynx) contacted an unknown number of

---

[284] PPH, RLIP, contact report by Lieutenant V. A. Prinsloo, 7 March 1979.

[285] PPH, RLIP, Honours & Awards, Continued.

ZANLA at US 8085, in the Masoso Tribal Trust Land in the Zambezi Valley on the northern border with Mozambique. The country was flat, covered with thick jesse thorn bush interspersed with patches of maize lands and a northward-flowing river.

Fireforce Echo had been diverted from another call-out but the talk-on by an OP, call sign 12C, was inaccurate and confused, and wasted 20 minutes while the aircraft milled about. Henson was particularly annoyed when 12C refused to fire his target marker to indicate the target in the Mvuradona Valley. The orbiting K-Car only found anything when its aircrew spotted two insurgents fleetingly. The K-Car fired its 20mm cannon at a point where an east–west track crossed the riverbed. The Lynx followed with frantan. Henson had Stop 1 put down on the track where it skirted a field of maize to the west of the river. Stop 2 was dropped on a maize land close to the riverbed and just north of the sighting. Stop 3 was put down on a third maize field in the south. The first in action was Stop 2 who shot and killed an insurgent shortly after landing. They swept forward to the site of the air strike where blood spoor and an AK were found. Stop 1 killed an insurgent on the eastern edge of their maize land. Stop 3, working up the riverbed, soon encountered an insurgent and killed him. The light had faded so ambushes were set up on the riverbed. A sweep at first light yielded no signs of further insurgents. Henson blamed the talk-on, the thick bush and the poor light for what he considered a poor score of three ZANLA and one wounded escaped. The troops recovered an RPD light machine gun, a PPSH submachine gun, two AK rifles, grenades, ammunition and documents which were handed to SB at Mount Darwin.[286]

On 12 March, Second Lieutenant Simon John Carpenter distinguished himself in a contact with insurgents while commanding a sweep line of ten men from Support Commando's Fireforce Delta. When five insurgents in a concealed position held up the sweep line, Carpenter coolly outflanked the position, with the result that his section killed all five.[287] A month later, in

---

[286] PPH, RLIP, contact report by Major N. D. Henson, 9 March 1979.

[287] PPH, RLIP, A/33 Honours & Awards.

April 1979, Carpenter was to account personally for two insurgents who were concealed in a well-sited defensive position which completely dominated his own position.[288]

At 16.00 on 12 March, Major Nigel Henson's Fireforce Echo contacted an unknown number of ZANLA at VQ 384518 in the Makoni Tribal Trust Land, east of Rusape, in the *Thrasher* operational area. This took place in an area of open fields divided by thickly bushed river lines, flowing north to southwest, and a range of heavily wooded rocky hills, running northwest to southeast. The river divided the hills. The OP was on the summit of the northwestern hill overlooking the valley.

Because the target had seemed so important, Fireforce Echo, comprising a K-Car, three G-Cars, a Dakota and a Lynx, had been summoned from Mount Darwin, getting airborne at 13.00. Arriving at Rusape, Fireforce Echo was told at the briefing in the Selous Scout fort that there were three targets, in the form of huts, within the square kilometre. The first hut was at the foot of the OP's hill, the second across the river line directly east between two hills and the third also across the river but at the foot of the southeastern hill.

Once over the target, Henson had Stop 1 put down to the west of the first hut, Stop 2 was put on the river to the north and Stop 3 just south of the third hut. Then, before any action could be taken on the ground, the orbiting K-Car spotted an insurgent sitting in a zinc bath in a maize field just northwest of the second hut. Attending the man were two African women who abandoned their role as bath attendants and fled. The bather, however, now under 20mm fire from the K-Car, reached out for an AK-47 and fired back. The naked African stood his ground while the K-Car circled, firing. Then he ran out of ammunition and began to run. The K-Car gunner knocked him down, killing him.[289] The K-Car crew then spotted two insurgents in the riverbed just beyond at the confluence of a small tributary and fired at a further insurgent who was captured by Stop 1. Henson ordered

---

[288] PPH, RLIP, A/33 Honours.

[289] PPH, RLIP, contact report by Major N. D. Henson, 9 March 1979.

the Dakota to drop his paratroopers. Para sticks were dropped to the west of the first hut and Eagle 1 and 2 (para sticks) were placed in the north, either side of the confluence of the river and a tributary. They began a sweep down the river and killed two insurgents in the river line near the confluence. At that moment, a G-Car, moving away to refuel, saw 12 insurgents running in a ravine two kilometres to the southwest. Eagle 4 was brought in down the ravine in the southeast and began to sweep northwest. Henson knew the direction the insurgents were fleeing but was unable to cut them off because his aircraft were running out of fuel. The K-Car headed off to a nearby location where fuel supposedly had been pre-positioned but found nothing. Henson was furious because the SB personnel at the Selous Scout fort at Rusape had assured him that this had been done. The K-Car had to return to Rusape to refuel while the G-Cars found some diesel carried by a PATU stick and refuelled with the help of watering cans. The jet fuel for the G-Cars did not arrive until 20 minutes before last light. Thus, no fire from the air could be brought to bear on the fleeing men and the stops could not be re-positioned. All that Henson could do, shortly before last light, was to have Stop 2 and Eagle 4 uplifted and placed in ambush. Sweeps the next day yielded nothing. Henson recorded the score as three ZANLA killed and one captured. Two SKS and two AK rifles and miscellaneous documents were recovered.[290]

Twenty-four hours later, on 13 March, Henson's Fireforce Echo (comprising a K-Car, two G-Cars, a Dakota and a Lynx) was back in action, called out to a sighting of ten to 15 ZANLA cadres in a camp at US 849839 in the Masoso Tribal Trust Land in the northeast close to the Mozambican border. Fireforce Echo took off from Mtoko at 15.40 and at 16.15 reached the target area among low, sparsely vegetated hills intersected by thickly bushed river lines running north. The initial talk-on at 16.15 was poor and finally the K-Car spotted some insurgents one kilometre to the east and opened fire. Henson had Stop 1 dropped in the north where the two river lines converged and Stop 2 was placed in the east of one of the southern hills. The para sticks were dropped

---

[290] PPH, RLIP, contact report by Major N. D. Henson, 12 March 1979.

in the south. Eagles 1 and 2 swept north along the westerly river. Eagles 3 and 4 joined Stop 2 and swept the southern hill from the east. Eagles 5 and 6 went north and then moved east along the northern flank of the next range of hills. There they joined Eagles 1 and 2 on their sweep northward along the western river. The K-Car killed an insurgent on the southern side of the second range of hills and killed another in the river ahead of the sweep line led by Eagle 1. Stop 1 killed one at the confluence of the river.

Eagles 1 and 2, led by Temporary Corporal Neil Kevin Maclaughlin, had killed two insurgents in the river line before they reached the second range of hills. Success was attributed to Maclaughlin's clever use of minor tactics. Maclaughlin, ignoring his own vulnerability to enemy fire, moved down in the open ground of the riverbed to control the sweep effectively. After Eagles 5 and 6 joined him, Maclaughlin's sweep line came under fire from a third group of four insurgents, hidden in thick cover on the riverbank near a hut just to the east. The sweep line returned fire, killing two of the enemy. Undeterred, the ZANLA kept up their fusillade, bringing down Trooper M. J. Jefferies. Corporal Maclaughlin ran forward through the hostile barrage to assist Jefferies. Maclaughlin administered first aid and then, while the aircraft and the sweep line fired to distract the enemy, carried Jefferies to safety. The K-Car ordered a G-Car to casevac Jefferies, delaying the advance.

When Maclaughlin led his men forward again, they shot and killed an insurgent within the first few metres. Stop 2 and Eagles 3 and 4 killed three insurgents in the easterly river line as they reached it. They killed a further insurgent on the western flank of the southern hill. They then swept the second range.

Action continued during the night. Ambushing the area between the two ranges of hills, Stop 1 opened fire on locals coming in to remove three undiscovered but wounded insurgents. One local was killed, adding to the existing tally of 12 ZANLA dead. The three wounded ZANLA escaped into the night. Three SKS, two FN and six AK rifles, one DP machine gun and documents were recovered and handed to the SB at Mount Darwin. Henson concluded that, if he had not had to stop the advance to casevac Jefferies, a complete kill could have been achieved. The discovery of ZANLA armed with FN rifles worried him because of the danger which their powerful rounds posed to his troops and aircraft. He recommended the decorating of Corporal Maclaughlin.[291] Consequently, Maclaughlin was awarded the Bronze Cross of Rhodesia on 8 June.[292]

At 09.30 on 19 March, Support Commando's Fireforce, commanded by Lieutenant Prinsloo, contacted ten insurgents at US 858688, again in the Masoso Tribal Trust Land, after being called out by Selous Scouts on an OP to a sighting in an area that had a river flowing eastward across its northern sector. A tributary joined it from the southeast. To the east of the tributary was a long hill running southeast to northwest. To its south was a large hill running east–west, on the southern flank of which there were three clusters of huts. On the northern flank, there was a small village in the east and a line of kraals beyond that. The bush of the area was thick and was dense at the river. The Selous Scout OP was on a hill three and a half kilometres to the east.

Prinsloo ordered Stops 1 and 2 to be placed in the west at the foot of the first hill. The paratroops were dropped with Eagle 2 across the river, Eagle 3 to the west on the southern flank of the hill and Eagle 1 just south of the river in the west. Stops 1 and 2 swept up the eastern stream of the tributary and then worked back down it towards the river where Eagle 2 joined them. They moved back towards the main hill at the foot of which was the insurgent base camp behind a rocky outcrop. Halfway to the hill, they killed three ZANLA cadres. They moved on to the base camp where they met Eagle 3 who had come in from the west along the hill. Eagle 3 continued along the hill and killed an insurgent in front of the small village of huts before moving north. Stops 1 and 2 and Eagle 2 moved north. Eagle 1, in the west, moved south and immediately killed an insurgent. Shortly afterwards they killed another and then another further on, before sweeping back to the north. In all seven insurgents were killed and three escaped. Seven SKS rifles and a nearly new

---

[291] PPH, RLIP, contact report by Major N. D. Henson, 13 March 1979; Honours & Awards, Continued.

[292] PPH, RLIP, Honours, *op. cit.*

AK were recovered along with webbing, grenades, magazines, ammunition and documents, all of which were handed to the SB at Rushinga. The Selous Scout OP remained to observe the area. Prinsloo was complimented for a well-controlled action.[293]

Support Commando seems to have been stood down for a rest but was back in action on 1 April, when Corporal Christopher William Rogers and his section were pinned down by accurate fire from four insurgents at close range. The insurgents succeeded in wounding Rogers and another RLI soldier. Ignoring his wounds, Rogers continued to exchange fire with the insurgents. The exchange was extremely heavy at times but Rogers managed to kill two of his enemy. He neutralized the insurgent position, enabling other troops to close with and eliminate the entire insurgent group. Rogers was awarded a Military Forces Commendation (Operational) for his deeds.[294]

The first majority-rule election was approaching and it was known that ZANLA and ZIPRA would attempt to ensure that the Africans did not vote by sending into Rhodesia a substantial number of their more experienced men to deter them. Measures were taken to counter them. Later in April 1979, there would be a mass mobilization of all territorials and police reservists. Before then, the Fireforces went to work. Support Commando, for example, was deployed on Monday, 2 April. A small sub-unit was detached to provide protection for some of the more vulnerable polling stations and the remainder of the commando was divided into two Fireforces, one stationed at Grand Reef airfield, near Umtali, and the other at Inyanga, farther to the north on the Mozambican border.[295]

By 13.00, that day, 2 April, Henson and 36 Support Commando men (flying in a K-Car, three G-Cars, a Lynx and a Dakota) were in action in what would be a four-and-a-half-hour-long contact with an unknown number of ZANLA cadres. The ZANLA group had been spotted by an OP, manned by

---

[293] PPH, RLIP, contact report by Lieutenant V. A. Prinsloo, 19 March 1979.

[294] PPH, RLIP, Honours, *op. cit.*

[295] Frank Terrell, 'RLI Support Commando/Group: Support Commando, Rhodesian Light Infantry—Mozambique 1979', *The Elite*, Orbis Publishing, London, 1987, Vol. 10, Issue 113, pp 2241–2247.

Fireforce in Action at the Height of the War

Peter Curley of the Selous Scouts, at VR 923043, just northeast of the Inyanga Downs and close to the Gairezi River on the eastern border with Mozambique. The area comprised hills incised with thickly bushed river lines.

Although he had not had a clear sighting, Curley thought he could see a weapon in the doorway. Henson knew that Fireforce would not have been summoned without the Selous Scout being confident that there were ZANLA present, so he put his stops down. He placed Stop 1 in the south on the western flank of a long range running northward. Stop 3 was landed in the middle and Stop 2 in the north. The para sticks were dropped to form a sweep line to search three river lines, flowing eastward towards a river at the foot of the eastern range. The southern end of the sweep encountered 13 insurgents and killed them before discovering their camp on the side of a spur. Most were shot dead in the main river valley. Henson noted that the ZANLA had adopted the tactic of running, hiding and then throwing grenades. In support of the troops, the K-Car fired 18 20mm shells and the Lynx dropped three frantan bombs. Henson praised his troops for their good soldiering, saying "the troopies were complete stars". These 'stars' nevertheless managed to lose two empty MAG belts, two sleeping bags and two pangas and sheaths.[296]

After being called to a sighting by an OP team, Henson's Fireforce (36 men, a K-Car, three G-Cars, a Lynx and a Dakota) at 09.30 on the next day, 3 April, contacted an unknown number of insurgents at VR 168038 on the Wensleydale Estate, a white-owned farm, north of Headlands. The contact lasted one hour on a thickly bushed rocky ridge. To the north of the east–west ridge was a westward-flowing river. Between the river and the ridge was heavy bush. Henson strung out his troops in a sweep line from the river to the south of the ridge. The K-Car killed an insurgent who was hidden in the bush and the sweep line killed another nearby. Just before then, two insurgents had been captured. One AKM and two SKS rifles were recovered.[297]

---

[296] PPH, RLIP, contact report by Major N. D. Henson, 2 April 1979.

[297] PPH, RLIP, contact report by Major N. D. Henson, 3 April 1979.

Success came again that Tuesday for Henson. At 15.00 his Fireforce (still 36 men and a K-Car, three G-Cars, a Lynx and a Dakota), contacted ten ZANLA cadres at VR 058055 on the Rathcline Estate, northwest of Inyanga village. Again, an OP team had summoned Henson. This contact lasted one and a half hours in thick bush in front of a hill which ran southwest to northeast. The Inyangombe River, flowing north, curved round to the east behind the hill. The K-Car killed three insurgents while the troops killed four, two in the bush, one on the hill and one over the hill by the river. Henson summed up: "An excellent action by an extremely well-trained and steely-eyed commando." Four AK and three SKS rifles were recovered and handed to the SB at Inyati Mine.[298]

Success continued the next morning, on 4 April, but at the cost of the life of Lance-Corporal Martin Overbeek. Henson and 56 Support Commando troopers were called to a sighting by a Selous Scout OP, manned by Sergeant 'Jenks' Jenkinson, of approximately 50 ZANLA cadres in a base camp at VR 345051, again on the Rathcline Estate. At 10.30 contact was made and would continue for eight hours in terrain which Henson described as "unreal". He was confronted by a square-shaped mountain, crowned by a series of summits and stretching four kilometres in one direction and two in the other. The size and importance of the target led Henson to call in an initial strike with 300 Alpha bombs by a Canberra bomber. This was precisely on target and the Fireforce's K-Car, three G-Cars, Lynx and Dakota, arrived exactly on time.

On the summit of the northern hill, a stick, led by Temporary Corporal Peter Malcolm Binion, approached a clump of rocks and was surprised by point-blank rifle fire from two ZANLA insurgents hidden there. Lance-Corporal Martin Overbeek was killed instantly. Corporal Binion immediately returned the fire. Then, while the remainder of his stick put down covering fire, Binion dashed forward in full view of the two ZANLA men to a position from where he was able to kill them. Shortly afterwards, Binion received a minor shrapnel wound from an exploding RPG rocket,

---

[298] PPH, RLIP, contact report by Major N. D. Henson, 3 April 1979.

fired at short range by a third insurgent. Ignoring his wound, Binion closed with and killed this man. A further insurgent was killed close by.

Later the sweep killed two ZANLA cadres on the western end of that hill, two on the eastern flank of the second northern hill, one on the west of its southern flank. Two more insurgents were killed near the stream that flowed to the southeast across the feature. The K-Car killed one at the southern base of the easternmost summit. In all 12 insurgents, dressed in the green uniforms of Mozambique's FPLM, were killed and one wounded escaped. Ten AKM and two SKS rifles and an RPG-7 were recovered.

Calling the terrain the most difficult he had ever experienced, Henson had high praise for his troops. He recommended the decoration of Corporal Binion[299] who would be awarded the Bronze Cross of Rhodesia. Binion had been a stick leader for two years and had been involved in numerous successful actions.[300]

On the way back to base, the K-Car began to vibrate and the pilot, Luigi Mantovani, landed it. When the blades came to rest, it was clear they were so badly damaged by ZANLA bullets that flying was out of the question.

---

[299] PPH, RLIP, contact report by Major N. D. Henson, 9 March 1979.

[300] Binion's citation reads: 'Corporal Peter Malcolm Binion has been a patrol commander with Support Commando, 1st Battalion, The Rhodesian Light Infantry, for a period of two years. During this period, he has been involved in many contacts with the enemy and has personally accounted for numerous terrorists.
'On 4th April 1979, Corporal Binion was the Second-In-Command of a patrol which was sweeping towards some terrorists. As the patrol approached a clump of rocks, the patrol commander was killed instantly at point blank range by fire from two terrorists who were concealed in the rocks. Corporal Binion immediately put down covering fire himself and under covering fire from the remainder of the patrol, he manoeuvred himself into a position where he was able to kill the two terrorists at considerable danger to himself. Shortly afterwards, the patrol came under rocket fire at short range from another terrorist who was using an RPG rocket launcher. Corporal Binion received a minor shrapnel wound. Despite this, he was able to close with and kill this terrorist.
'On 7th April 1979 Corporal Binion was again involved in a contact in which six terrorists were killed. He personally accounted for four of these terrorists.
'Throughout these and other engagements, Corporal Binion has shown remarkable courage and tenacity. His desire to close with and kill the enemy is uppermost in his mind. His standard of professional soldiering, and dedication to duty are of the highest order.'
PPH, RLIP, Honours.

Mantovani radioed for new blades. The request was relayed to No. 7 Squadron at New Sarum, outside Salisbury. New blades were promptly placed aboard a Dakota and flown to Grand Reef. A G-Car brought the blades to the stranded K-Car where Mantovani, the technician and Henson replaced the damaged blades. The afternoon light was fading when the K-Car lifted off for base. Helicopter blades have to be calibrated and the technician had been unable to do this in the field. The consequent level of vibrations from the unbalanced blades worried Mantovani enough for him to keep landing after short intervals.[301]

Other forces were scoring similar successes. For example, on 5 April, a Fireforce from 1 Commando, 1RLI, commanded by Major Frederick Watts, contacted two groups of insurgents totalling 27 men and killed 21 of them. In the next eleven days, until 16 April, Watts, his men and the aircraft of his Fireforce would eliminate 106 ZANLA insurgents.[302]

Corporal Binion again scored at 15.00 on 7 April, when Henson's Support Commando men contacted seven insurgents, dressed in green FPLM uniforms and kit, at VR 175003 in the extreme south of the Weya Tribal Trust Land, just north of the white farming area of Headlands. One insurgent escaped and six were killed with Binion accounting for four of them on a low ridge just northeast of a high rounded hill.[303] The K-Car killed the fifth insurgent on the ridge and the sixth at its western end. Rifles, grenades and ammunition were picked up and handed to the SB at Inyanga.[304]

On 11 April, Support and 3 commandos and a detachment from the Rhodesian African Rifles were sent into Mozambique to attack a complex of five staging camps, which were believed to hold up to 250 ZANLA. The operation was aborted when the helicopters and Dakotas were circling the camps because ZANLA cadres had already left. Support Commando returned to Grand Reef where it was reinforced by its Inyanga detachment.[305]

---

[301] PPH, RLIP, contact report by Major N. D. Henson, 9 March 1979.

[302] PPH, RLIP, Honours.

[303] PPH, RLIP, Honours.

[304] PPH, RLIP, contact report by Major N. D. Henson, 7 April 1979.

[305] Terrell, p. 2243.

That day, Rhodesia mobilized its territorials and reservists to protect the election. They would be stood down on 24 April.[306]

At 10.15 on the next morning, 12 April, Henson and 28 of his men, supported by a K-Car, three G-Cars, a Lynx and a Dakota, made contact with an unknown number of ZANLA at UP 673648, in the Sabi Tribal Trust Land east of Buhera, after a sighting by an OP team. The contact lasted four hours. For once, the terrain was favourable and was divided by converging river lines, flowing west to east towards the Sabi River. The K-Car killed one insurgent in the northwest at the confluence of the central river and the Sabi. A G-Car killed insurgents in a village in the southwest. Stop 2 was dropped astride the river in the west and killed an insurgent after advancing a few metres and Eagle 1 was placed on the most southerly tributary above the confluence and killed an insurgent again after advancing a few metres. An insurgent was captured near the northern tributary. Just north of the confluence, the sweep line killed the remainder of the insurgents. The final score was 15 insurgents killed and one captured, all dressed in FPLM kit. Rifles, machine guns, grenades, magazines and ammunition were picked up and handed to the SB at Dorowa. Henson concluded that the contact was "like eating green mealies [maize]".[307]

Four days later, on 16 April, Henson, a K-Car, two G-Cars, a Dakota, a Lynx and 29 of his men were summoned to a sighting by an OP team of an unknown number of ZANLA at VR 586237 in the Zimbiti Tribal Trust Land, northeast of Inyanga. The sighting had been on the northern flank of a twin-peaked mountain. A stream flowed down from the saddle between the peaks. On the saddle was the OP. Henson put his helicopter-borne troops down on the eastern flank and dropped his para sticks to the north. He formed a sweep line on the eastern end of the northern flank. When the sweep reached the stream at 14.00, it encountered 15 ZANLA cadres, clad in FPLM uniforms, and killed ten of them while five made their escape. Rifles, grenades and ammunition were picked up and were handed

---

[306] Caute, pp. 324–325.

[307] PPH, RLIP, contact report by Major N. D. Henson, 12 April 1979.

to the SB at Inyanga. Henson was particularly pleased by the performance of his troops during the six hours of the operation.[308]

At 12.00 on 17 April (the day that the four days of voting by all inhabitants over the age of 18 began), Henson and 27 of his men, supported by a K-Car, two G-Cars, a Lynx and a Dakota, again made contact with the enemy. This time it was with seven ZANLA, at VQ 030056 in the south of the Chiduku Tribal Trust Land, west of Umtali. The contact lasted four and a half hours among three and a half kilometres of kraal lines with brick buildings, rubber hedges and thousands of mango trees stretching along an east–west road, parallel to a westward-flowing river. The K-Car killed insurgents on the road just short of a stream, which flowed south to the river. The sweep line killed insurgents at a house by the stream and in the houses either side of the road. Trooper M. C. Moore was shot and killed in front of a pair of houses across the river in the southeast. In all, nine green-and-blue-clad insurgents were killed and two escaped. Ten rifles, grenades and ammunition were picked up and were handed to the SB at Inyazura. Henson recorded that the contact had taken place in a very difficult area "virtually FIBUA [fighting in built-up areas]".[309]

On 19 April, Fireforce Bravo, commanded by Lieutenant Prinsloo, responded to a sighting by call sign 13G, a Selous Scout OP team, of ten ZANLA cadres in a village at VQ 004089, close to the last contact in the Chiduku. This result was a contact with 13 insurgents, starting at 10.00 and lasting four hours in a series of kraal complexes along a river. When the Fireforce was overhead, the K-Car threw out a smoke marker. Call sign 13G indicated the target with smoke and a number of people were seen to run from the kraal. The K-Car fired on them and stops were landed. Stop 2 was placed in the south on the river. The paratroopers were then dropped in the west and a sweep line went up the river in a northerly direction and swept east through the kraals. After killing the majority of the insurgents, Eagle 4 was approaching yet another kraal cautiously when Trooper R. F. Poole was

---

[308] PPH, RLIP, contact report by Major N. D. Henson, 16 April 1979.

[309] PPH, RLIP, contact report by Major N. D. Henson, 17 April 1979.

shot through the chest. Corporal Binion, the MAG gunner, ran to help but Trooper Poole was mortally wounded and died a little while later. The K-Car then killed the insurgent responsible as he fled from the hut. A feature of the contact was that the insurgents were wearing civilian clothes over their denims and tried to conceal their weapons under their clothes. Some left their weapons in the kraals and ran. Four AK rifles were handed to the SB who also removed four more from burning buildings. Prinsloo commented that there were obvious dangers in approaching insurgents who were holed up in kraals. The final tally was ten ZANLA cadres killed, two captured and one escaped.[310] The death of three members of the Mortar Troop of Support Commando reduced it to 13 men. To recover their morale the members were sent on four days' leave in Salisbury.[311]

A military spokesman said on 21 April that during the elections 230 guerrillas had been killed for the loss of 12 regular soldiers and security-force auxiliaries. There had been a total of 13 attacks on polling stations, most of them at night and all, according to officials, "ineffectual".[312] The result of the elections was announced on 24 April, with Muzorewa's UANC winning 67.27 per cent of the votes and securing 51 seats of the 80 seats in the new Legislative Assembly of Zimbabwe–Rhodesia. The poll had been over 60 per cent and ZANLA and ZIPRA were stunned by the Africans' defiance of their orders not to vote. As the ZANLA and ZIPRA insurgents went to ground and their leaders left the country for orders, the Rhodesian security forces kept up the pressure.

To harass ZANLA on its own ground, ComOps proposed to send Support Commando on Sunday, 29 April, 50 kilometres over the southern border into Gaza Province of Mozambique. Called Operation *Oppress*, the intention was to attack a logistics and transit base at Chicualacuala called Petulia. The mission was to destroy the base and kill or capture any ZANLA personnel present. The base comprised three camps, containing a resident section of

---

[310] PPH, RLIP, contact report by Lieutenant V. A Prinsloo, 19 April 1979.

[311] Terrell, p. 2243.

[312] *Keesing's Contemporary Archives*, 10 August 1979, Vol. XXVI, p. 29757

22 ZANLA cadres. Intercepted radio messages indicated that fresh ZANLA men were being brought in. The operation was to comprise an air strike followed by a ground attack by Support Commando. The Rhodesian Air Force was to supply two Hunters, three Canberras, seven G-Cars, three K-Cars, two AB205A Cheetahs, two Lynxes, and three Dakotas (including a command Dakota equipped with radios and secure teleprinters to control the operation from the air).[313]

At Grand Reef on 28 April, Support Commando, reinforced by the return from leave of the Mortar Troop, was issued extra light machine guns and RPG-7 rocket launchers and drew as much ammunition and grenades as the men could carry. Each rifleman took ten 20-round magazines two 50-round cloth bandoliers, numerous grenades, extra machine-gun belts for the gunners and spare RPG-7 rockets. In the evening, the commando was flown to Buffalo Range to be briefed by intelligence officers on the importance of the staging post, which had been monitored by security forces but had hitherto been deliberately left alone. As an influx of ZANLA cadres into Rhodesia was expected, it was deemed an appropriate moment to bomb and attack the base. Support Commando was expected to encounter at least two members of the ZANLA hierarchy, who would be dressed in camouflage uniforms with hammer-and-sickle insignia on the collars. Eastern Bloc military advisers were also believed to be in the area and in the vicinity. High-ranking officers were not to be killed but captured if possible. Combined Operations wanted at very least one ZANLA guerrilla for interrogation. The operation was being used to test an experimental landmine of which a stop group would lay a number in the approach road to delay a reaction by Mozambique's FPLM. In the event, it became clear that the survival of Support Commando's men had depended on the mines functioning.[314]

On 29 April, the Hunters, flown by Squadron Leader Vic Wightman and Flight Lieutenant Tony Oakley, attacked the target with Golf bombs, 30mm cannon shells and 68mm rockets. Three Canberras, piloted by Squadron

---

[313] BECM, RAAP/MI/106/37, 'Confirmation Orders: Op *Oppress*', Salisbury, 26 April 1979.

[314] Terrell, p. 2243.

Leader Chris Dixon and Flight lieutenants Greg Todd and Glen Pretorius, followed them immediately, dropping 300 Mk II Alpha bombs each.[315] The 50 men of Support Commando, flying in the eight G-Cars and two AB205A Cheetahs, came in with the escort of two K-Cars and two Lynxes, landing on the fringes of the camps in the brown fog of dust and smoke of the air strikes. Sergeant Frank Terrell, a former British marine commando serving in Support Commando, recalls the sound of continuous explosions of burning ammunition, the methodical reply of an anti-aircraft gun to the repeated attacks of the Hunters. Eventually a Hunter silenced it. The RLI troops began their advance and first encountered a ZANLA kitchen littered with dead. They shot dazed ZANLA cadres while carefully avoiding unexploded red-painted round Alpha bombs. The camp was burning so fiercely that the troops could not at first penetrate its lines of bunkers, weapon pits and tents. The camp was littered with equipment. Red Army helmets lay among abandoned or destroyed anti-aircraft guns. The undamaged guns were dismantled by the RLI troopers when clearing the trenches and bunkers. The huge haul of rifles and equipment was collected but no further ZANLA cadres were encountered. It was clear, from the dropped weapons, that they had fled before the ground attack.

Once the area was secure the Cheetahs flew in to be loaded with AK and SKS rifles, grenades and one 12.7mm and three 14.5mm heavy machine guns. Uniforms, packs, web-equipment, propaganda leaflets and enormous quantities of tinned food were burned. Major Henson then had the troops search the surrounding bush. The search yielded six empty pistol holsters and a leather briefcase, which contained papers bearing names and weapon numbers, messages, letters and photographs of uniformed ZANLA cadres in the company of East German or Soviet military instructors. A follow-up was instituted and Terrell believes that the troops were closing on six high-ranking ZANLA officers but ran out of time to overhaul them. The day was drawing to a close, and the remaining light was needed to airlift the attacking force out. The command Dakota, carrying Lieutenant-Colonel

---

[315] Geldenhuys, p. 283.

Chapter 16

Brian Robinson and Group Captain, later Air Vice-Marshal, Hugh Slatter called off the pursuit.

During the airlift, the FPLM sent in a counter-attacking force in a convoy of trucks which was brought to a halt by striking the landmines laid by the stop group.

Although Support Commando had not secured a prisoner, Operation *Oppress* was pronounced a success because 28 ZANLA insurgents had been killed without any RLI casualties. As had happened so often before in the Rhodesian war, a large number of ZANLA cadres had vacated the camp on the previous night, 28 April, but Support Commando was to eliminate many of the escapees within days. On 14 May, it killed or captured 21 ZANLA infiltrators from a large group which had recently crossed from Mozambique and which included several high-ranking officials. A follow-up on the border on 16 May resulted in a running, day-long fight with the survivors of the group. Two of the dead were wearing Ethiopian camouflage uniforms with hammer-and-sickle insignia on the collar.[316]

In a seven-week period in April/May 1979, Support Commando, 1RLI, under the command of Major Nigel Henson, together with its supporting aircraft, accounted for 165 insurgents in Fireforce operations and, on Operation *Oppress*, and had seized large amounts of heavy weapons. Henson's skill, aggression and other qualities as a leader earned him a recommendation for the award of the Officer of the Order of the Legion of Merit (Military Division, Combatant).[317] *The Sunday Mail* reported on 20 May that worn-out, dispirited insurgents were surrendering. "Their morale is shattered," remarked a senior police officer who added that hundreds more were longing to give up but feared execution by the fanatical cadres "trained in communist Ethiopia by Cubans".[318]

The data collected and collated by Rhodesian military intelligence confirmed that ZANLA's morale, in particular, was shattered by the defection

---

[316] Terrell, pp. 2243–2247.

[317] PPH, RLIP, A/33 Honours, *op. cit.*

[318] Caute, pp. 361–362.

of the rural Africans to Muzorewa and by the devastating onslaught by the Fireforces since February 1979. To exploit this, what Muzorewa needed was international recognition, but the British Conservatives went back on their promises to him. Not wishing to defy the British Commonwealth, the United Nations and the Non-Aligned Movement, Margaret Thatcher's government persuaded Muzorewa to accept the settlement negotiated at Lancaster House which brought Robert Mugabe to power, ending the grim toll of war, to which the helicopter and Fireforce had contributed so much.

Selected Bibliography

Anon., 'The Armament Story', The Zimbabwe Medal Society Journal, No. 61, March 2008.

Barker, Jim, *Paradise Plundered: The Story of a Zimbabwean Farm*, Jim Barker, Harare, 2007.

Binda, Alexandre, *The Saints: The Rhodesian Light Infantry*, 30° South Publishers, Johannesburg, 2007.

Binda, Alexandre, *Masodja: The History of The Rhodesian African Rifles and its Forerunner, The Rhodesia Native Regiment*, 30° South Publishers, Johannesburg, 2007.

Brent, W. A., *Rhodesian Air Force: A Brief History 1947–1980*, Freeworld Publications, Kwambonambi, 1987.

Brent, W. A. *Rhodesian Air Force: The Sanctions Busters*, Freeworld Publications, Nelspruit, 2001.

Burke, G. K., 'Insurgency in Rhodesia—the Implications', RUSI and Brassey's Defence Yearbook 1978–79, London, 1980.

Caute, David, *Under the Skin: The Death of White Rhodesia*, Allen Lane, London, 1982.

Cilliers, J. K., *Counter-Insurgency in Rhodesia*, Croom Helm, London, 1985.

Cocks, Chris, *Fireforce: One Man's War in The Rhodesian Light Infantry*, Galago, Alberton, 1988.

Cocks, Chris, *Fireforce: One Man's War in the Rhodesian Light Infantry*, 30° South Publishers, Johannesburg, 2006.

Cole, Barbara, *The Elite: The Story of The Rhodesian Special Air Service*, Three Knights Publishing, Amanzimtoti, 1984.

Cronin, John R., 'Follow-up to Operation *Dingo*', memorandum, 21 April 1998.

Selected bibliography

Cronin, John R. &. Mackenzie, Robert C., 'Counter-Insurgency in Southern Africa', a paper delivered to the Center for Strategic and International Studies, Washington DC, 1986.

Cowderoy, Dudley & Nesbit, Roy, *War in the Air: Rhodesian Air Force 1935–1980*, Galago, Alberton, 1987.

Flower, Ken, *Serving Secretly, Rhodesia's CIO Chief on Record*, Alberton, Galago, 1987.

Geldenhuys, Prop, *Rhodesian Air Force Operations*, Just Done Productions, Durban, 2007.

Godwin, Peter & Hancock, Ian, *'Rhodesians Never Die': The Impact of War and Political Change on White Rhodesia, c. 1970-1980*, Oxford University Press, Oxford, 1993.

Gunston, Bill & Batchelor, John, *Phoebus History of the World Wars, Special, Helicopters 1900–1960*, Phoebus Publishing, London, 1977.

Gunston, Bill (ed), *The Encyclopaedia of World Air Power*, Hamlyn-Aerospace, London, 1981.

Hamence, Michael & Brent, Winston, *Canberra in Southern Africa Service*, Freeworld Publications, Nelspruit, 1998.

Hoffman, B., Taw, J. M., Arnold, D., *Lessons for Contemporary Counterinsurgencies: The Rhodesian Experience*, RAND Corporation, Santa Monica, 1991.

Legum, Colin, *Africa Contemporary Record, Annual Survey and Documents, 1977–1978*, Africana Publishing Company, London, 1979.

Lovett, John, *Contact: Rhodesia at War*, Galaxie Press, Salisbury, 1977.

MacKenzie, Robert, 'Fast Strike on Chimoio', *Soldier of Fortune*, January 1994.

MacKenzie, Robert, 'Fast Strike on Chimoio II', *Soldier of Fortune*, February 1994.

Martin, David & Johnson, Phyllis, *The Struggle for Zimbabwe: The Chimurenga War*, Zimbabwe Publishing House, Harare, 1981.

McAleese, Peter, *No Mean Soldier*, Orion, London, 1993.

Melson, Charles D., 'Killing Machine' draft, 2003.

Moorcraft, Paul L. & McLaughlin, Peter, *Chimurenga! The War in Rhodesia*

1965–1980, Sygma/Collins, Marshalltown, 1982.

Moorcraft, Paul, & McLaughlin, Peter, *The Rhodesian War: A Military History*, Pen & Sword, Barnsley, 2008.

Parker, Jim, *Assignment Selous Scouts: Inside story of a Rhodesian SB Officer*, Galago, Alberton, 2006.

Petter-Bowyer, P. J. H., *Winds of Destruction: The autobiography of a Rhodesian combat pilot*, 30° South Publishers, Johannesburg, 2005.

Reid-Daly, Lt-Col Ron, *Top Secret War*, Alberton, Galago, 1982.

Reid-Daly, Lt-Col Ron, 'War in Rhodesia', in Al J. Venter (ed), *Challenge: Southern Africa within the African Revolutionary Context*, Gibraltar, Ashanti, 1989.

Salt, Beryl, *A Pride of Eagles: The Definitive History of the Rhodesian Air Force: 1920–1980*, Covos Day, Weltevreden Park, 2001.

Stiff, Peter, *Selous Scouts: A Pictorial Account*, Galago Publishing, Alberton, 1984.

Tekere, Edgar '2Boy' Zivanai, *Tekere: A Lifetime of Struggle*, SAPES Books, Harare, 2007.

Terrell, Frank, 'RLI Support Commando/Group: Support Commando, Rhodesian Light Infantry—Mozambique 1979', *The Elite*, Orbis Publishing, London, 1987, Vol. 10, Issue 113.

Thompson, Leroy, *Dirty Wars: Elite Forces vs the Guerrillas*, David & Charles, Newton Abbot, 1988.

Wood, J. R. T., 'Fireforce: Helicopter Operations, 1962–80', in Tim Newark (ed), *Military Illustrated*, London, Vol. 72, 1994, pp. 21–24.

Wood, J. R. T., 'Fireforce', chapter 12 of Al J. Venter, *The Chopper Boys: Helicopter Warfare in Africa*, Southern Book Publishers, Halfway House, 1994.

Wood, J. R. T., 'Cave Clearing in the Rhodesian Bush War 1961–1980', in *The Lion & Tusk: The Magazine of The Rhodesian Army Association*, Vol. 9. No. 2, March 2003.

Wood, J. R. T., 'Countering the Chimurenga: The Rhodesian Counterinsurgency Campaign 1962–1980', in Daniel Marston & Carter Malkasian (eds), *Counterinsurgency in Modern Warfare*, Osprey Publishing,

Oxford & New York, 2008.

Wood, J. R. T., 'Counter-Punching on the Mudzi: D Company, 1st Rhodesian African Rifles, on Operation *Mardon*, 1 November 1976', in *Small Wars and Insurgencies*, Frank Cass, London, Vol. 9, No. 2 (Autumn 1998), pp. 64–82.

Wood, J. R. T., 'Pookie: A History of the World's first successful Landmine Detector Carrier', in Jon Guttman (ed), *Military History*, Leesburg Virginia, 1998.

Wood, J. R.T., 'The "Pookie, landmine detecting vehicle" Mine Detector', in *Marine Corps Gazette*, Vol. 81, No. 1, January 1997, Marine Corps Association, Quantico, Virginia.

Wood, J. R. T., *A Matter of Weeks rather than Months: The Impasse between Harold Wilson and Ian Smith: Sanctions, Aborted Settlements and War: 1965–1969*, Trafford, Victoria, 2008.

Wood, J.R.T., *So Far and No Further! Rhodesia's bid for independence during the retreat from Empire: 1959–1965*, 30° South Publishers, Johannesburg, 2003.

Wood, J. R. T., *The War Diaries of André Dennison*, Ashanti Publishing, Gibraltar, 1989.

Wood, J. R. T., *The Welensky Papers: A History of the Federation of Rhodesia and Nyasaland*, Graham Publishing, Durban, 1983.

Index

1961 Constitution, 23.
1969 Constitution, 35.
1978 March settlement, 44.
1979 Constitution, 44, 203.
1979 election, 46.
1979 general election, 214.
1980 election, 47, 49.
20mm Hispano cannon, Operation Dingo, 154, 155, 163, 179, 184, Operation Virile, 199.
20mm Matra MG 151 cannon, 31, 57, 63, 64, 65, 81, 84, 88, 91-94, 101, 103, 115, 116, 129, 130, 141, 146, 154, Fireforce, 204, 209, Operation Dingo, 136, 188.
23mm anti-aircraft gun, 164, Operation Dingo, 165.
25-pounder gun/howitzer, 28.
30mm Aden cannon, Operation Dingo, 141-143, 149, 153-155, 157, 162, 164, 179, 182, 183, 186, 188, 196, Operation Oppress, 222.
35mm Leica, Pentax and Nikon cameras, Operation Dingo, 159.
37mm anti-aircraft gun, 202, Operation Dingo, 159, 172.
4.5-tonne truck, Operation Dingo, 172.
42Z rifle grenade, 62.
5.5in medium gun, 84.
60lb squash-head hollow-charge high-explosive rocket, 143, Operation Dingo, 141, 153, 184.
60mm mortar, contact, 206, Operation Dingo, 177, 182.
68mm Matra aircraft rocket, 73, Operation Dingo, 136, 140, 142, 143, 149, 154, 157, 164, 167, 182, 183, 186, 196, Operation Oppress, 222.
75mm recoilless rifle, 170, Operation Dingo, 190, 194.
81mm mortar, Operation Dingo, 136, 139, 177.
82mm mortar, Fireforce, 205, Operation Dingo, 173, 190, 192, 193.

A63 radios, 137, A63/A76 VHF radios, 100.
A76 radios, 202, Operation Dingo, 181.
Adams, Lieutenant Mark, OC 12 Troop, 3 Commando, 1RLI, Operation Dingo, 144, 158, 170.
Aden, 33, insurgency, 29, 30.
admin area, 171, Operation Dingo, 129-132, 134, 136, 140, 147, 149, 151, 158, 163-168, 177.
administrative bases, 85.
African agitation, 23.
African National Congress (of South Africa), 53, mistakes, 36.
African nationalists, 23, 24, 37, 43, 44, 77, Pearce Commission, 35.
Agincourt, 1415 a.d., 183.
Agusta-Bell 205A Cheetah helicopter, 52, 59, 83, 94, 202, ability and capacity, 85, 87, Operation Oppress, 222, 223.
Air Trans Africa, 54, shooting down of DC-4, 197.
Air Unit, 26.
aircraft pens, 99.
aircraft protection, wire netting, 99.
Airey, Air Sub-Lieutenant Richard, killed in Canberra explosion, 67.
air-training unit, 26.
AK-47 Russian assault rifle, 20, 115, 120, 121, 205, 207-212, 214, 216, 221, 223, bayonet, 147.
AKM Russian assault rifle, 205, 206, 215, 217.

Index

Alexander, Squadron Leader George, OC No. 3 Squadron, Operation Dingo, 148, 182.
Algeria, 55, 90.
Allum, P. K., Commissioner of Police, assisted Carrington, 48.
Alouette I, SE3120, Sud Aviation helicopter, 56.
Alouette II, Sud Aviation/Aerospatial helicopter, 55, 56.
Alouette III, Sud Aviation/Aerospatial helicopter, 19, 20, 21, 30, 31, 55, 56, 59, 61, 91, ability and capacity, 57, 66, 75, 81, 83-87, 103, 128, 129, 202, crash, 82, hot extraction, 84, losses, 58 Operation Dingo, 128, refuelling, 86, Sinoia, 76-78, Fireforce, 204-208, 210-212, 214- 216, 219, 220, grenade accident, 62, Operation Dingo, 135, 136, 139, 140, 146, 147, 158, 161, 163, 165, 167, 171, 176-182, 185, 186, 190, 193-198, Operation Oppress, 222, 223.
G-Car, command 133, Operation Dingo, 140, 143, 149, 151, 176, 179, 180, 181, 185, 186, 190, 196.
G-Car troop-carrier, 19, 58, 63-65, 84, 88, 89, 91, 93, 94, 100, 102, 106, 109, 111, 115, 129, 211, 218, twin Brownings, 62.
K-Car gunship, 57, 58, 63-66, 84, 88, 91-94, 100, 101, 103, 104, 107, 109-113, 115, 116, 128, 130, 151, Dalmation, 65, Fireforce, 204-212, 214-220, Operation Dingo, 129, 133, 135, 136, 140, 146, 149-151, 153-158, 160-163, 165, 166, 168, 171, 175, 176, 179-181, 184-190, 192, 194-196, 198, Operation Oppress, 222, 223, shot down Botswana Islander, 81.
Z-Car South African troop-carrier, 58.
Altena Farm, 37.
ammunition, failure to set up local production, 67.
ANFO, explosive, ammonium nitrate and diesel, 67, 69, 70.
Anglo-American settlement initiative, 125, 173, 175.

Angola, 47, 203, South African raid, 40, 175.
Annan, Squadron Leader John Douglas, Fireforce, 92, Operation Dingo, 141, 168.
AR-15 rifle, 138, Operation Dingo, 191.
Arab states, 37.
Armed Struggle, 22.
Artouste gas turbine, 56, Mk II, 55.
assassination, 36, 43.
Astazou, gas turbine, 56, 57.
Audaxes, Hawker, army co-operation aircraft, 26.
auxiliary forces, 45, 46, 47.

ballistic evidence, 116.
Banda, Dr Hastings Kamuzu, President of Malawi, 22, 30.
Barfoot, Frank Eric, Commissioner of Police, Sinoia incident, 36, 77.
Barnes, Flight Lieutenant John, K-Car pilot, 88.
Battle of Chinoyi (*see also* Sinoia), 36.
Becker radio direction finder, 83, 97.
Becks, Pilot Officer David, Sinoia, 78.
Beech 95 C-55 Baron, 52.
Beira, 75, 123, 127, 131.
Beirut, 59.
Beitbridge, 206.
Belgium, Rolls-Royce jet engines, 50, withdrawal from Congo, 30.
Bellringer, Finch, helicopter technician, 19, 20.
Belvedere Airport, Salisbury, 26.
Bene, 175, 183, 191, 195, 198.
Benecke, Flight Lieutenant Kevin 'Cocky', 70, 98.
Bentley, Air Vice-Marshal Alfred Muloch, commander of RRAF, 31.
Binga, 82.
Binion, Temporary Corporal Peter Malcolm, Support Commando, 1RLI, awarded BCR, 217, Fireforce, 216, 218, 220.
Binns, Detective Inspector 'Dusty', Sinoia, 77, 78, 79.

Blythe-Wood, Flight Lieutenant John, Operation Dingo, 196.
BMW, Operation Dingo, 172.
Bobogrande Kraal, Chiweshe, 91.
Boeing, gas turbines, 56.
Bolton, Air Lieutenant Ray, survived helicopter collision, 107.
bombshell, 111, 130.
Borlace, Air Lieutenant Michael, 66, 101, contact, 117.
Botswana, 40, 43.
Botswana Defence Force, Islander shot down, 81.
Bourhill, Air Lieutenant David, Operation Dingo, 141, 157.
Bradshaw, Group-Captain R. A., 62.
Brand, Squadron Leader Richard, OC No. 1 Squadron, Operation Dingo, 141, 183.
Britain, 22, 26, 48, 50, 125, 201, arms embargo, 32, retreat from Empire, 29, Rhodesia's external relations, 32.
British Army, 29.
British Conservative Government, failed to recognize Muzorewa, 203.
British Empire, 26, 29.
British Foreign and Commonwealth Office, Lancaster House Conference, 202.
British Government, 23, 26, 32, criticized by Chikerema, 125, Lancaster House Conference, 48.
British Labour Government, 44.
British Middle East Command, Rhodesian reinforcement, 29.
British South Africa Company, 25.
British South Africa Police, BSAP, 23, 25, 76, B-Cars, 58, border control, 37, helicopter support, 88, independent action, 44, JOC, 34, OCC, 76, OPs, 105, radios, 78, role in defence, 26, shooting down of DC-4, 196, Sinoia, 77, voice procedure, 31.
Police Anti-Terrorist Unit, PATU, 25, 205, buffalo beans, 86.
Police Reserve, 25, 30, 86, Sinoia incident, 36, 77.
Police Reserve Air Wing, PRAW, 25, 207.
Special Branch, SB, 25, 34, 39, 76, 80, 96, 97, 100, 221, Fireforce, 205, 206, 208, 209, 211, 212, 214, 216, 218-220, frustrated assassination of Mugabe, 43 military planning cycle, 36, Operation Dingo, 129, 139, 150, 161, 163, 164, 166, 168, 169, 172, 177-181, 187-190, 193, 194, planning cycle, 42, road-runners, 96.
Support Unit, 25, Sinoia, 77.
Britten-Norman BN-A Islander, 52, Defender, shot down, 81.
Broadbent, Flight Lieutenant Russell, 52.
Browning machine gun.
.303in Mk II, 51, 52, 62-64, 136, Dalmation, 64.
.5in, 63, 64, Operation Virile, 199.
BSAP, *see* British South Africa Police.
buffalo beans, 86.
Buhera, 219.
Bulawayo, 208.
bunker bomb, Operation Dingo, 161, 189.
Burma Valley, 74.
Buttenshaw, Captain Ian, 2IC Support Commando, 1RLI, Operation Dingo, 139, 147.

Cabora Bassa Dam, 130, 175-177, 196.
Cabora Bassa–Transvaal power line, Operation Virile, 199.
Canadair Argonaut transport aircraft, 31.
Canberra, English Electric, B12 light bomber, 52, B2 light bomber, 29, 31, 32, 52, 128, Fireforce, 41, 106, 206, 216, Nyasaland Emergency, 30, Operation Alcora, 53 Operation Dingo, 132, 135, 136, 140, 142, 155-157, 160, 162, 164, 167, 168, 173, 174, 176, 178-180, 182-184, 195, 196, 198, Operation Oppress, 222, photographed Dar es Salaam, 53, starter, 50, weapons, 67-69.
Cannon, Chief Superintendent John, DFC, MiC BSAP Sinoia, 76, 78, 79.
Capoche River, 176.
Carmichael, George, helicopter technician,

Index

79.
Carpenter, Second Lieutenant Simon John, Support Commando, 1RLI, 209.
Carrington, Peter Alexander Rupert, 6th Baron Carrington, British Foreign Secretary, 48, Lancaster House Conference, 202.
Catandica, 156.
Centenary, 37, 38, 54, 83, 205.
Centenary Country Club, Operation Dingo, 196.
Central Intelligence Organization, CIO, 25, 38, 48, 80, Director, 34, 44, exploited schisms, 36, OCC, 76, Operation Dingo, 131, Operation Virile, 126, RNM, 45, secret police, 48.
Council for Scientific and Industrial Research (CSIR), 64, mine-protected vehicles, 38.
Cessna 185, 51, 97, 421A, 52.
Chaminuka Camp, New Farm, Chimoio, 142, 146, 149-156, 160-162, 164-167.
Charter, 1889, 25.
Charumuka, Nathan, ZANU cadre, killed, 79.
Chatambudza, Christopher, ZANU cadre, killed, 79.
Chicamba Real Dam, 167.
Chicualacuala, 221.
Chiduku Tribal Trust Land, 220.
Chigowe, Cleotus, abducted Tekere and Ushewokunze, 201.
Chigwada, Brown, ZANU cadre, 76.
Chikerema, James Dambaza, 125, criticized Britain, 125, Interim Government, 125.
Chikuhuhu, Olaria Lucia, survivor of Operation Dingo, 144.
Chimbodza, Simon, ZANU cadre, killed, 79.
Chimoio, 41, 83, 123, 127, 130, 131, 136, 141, 151, 169, 171, 174, 175, 200, 201.
Chimurenga, 22, 23, 75.
China, insurgent training, 124.
Chindunduma Primary School, New Farm, Chimoio, 200.

Chipinga, 23.
Chirau, Chief Jeremiah, member of Interim Government, 44, internal settlement, 201.
Chirundu, 75, 79.
Chiswiti, Operation Dingo, 129, 132, 175-179, 181, 196, 197.
Chitepo College, New Farm, Chimoio, 141-143, 146, 149-151, 153-157, 160-162, 164, 165.
Chitepo, Herbert Wilshire Hamandini, ZANU external leader, Sinoia, 75, strategy, 38.
Chiweshe Tribal Trust Land, 91, 205.
Christie, Ian, British journalist, 200.
CIO, *see* Central Intelligence Organization.
Clark, Sergeant Les, A Troop, SAS, Operation Dingo, 145, 191.
Clostermann, Pierre, Free French air ace, 51.
Cochrane & Son, 68.
Collett, Lieutenant Dale, Selous Scout Regiment, 90, pseudo warfare, 91.
Collimateur lightweight reflector gunsight, 61, 63.
Combined Operations (ComOps), 34, 80, formation, 44, Operation Dingo, 124, 131, 133, 155, 169, 186, 187, 200, Operation Oppress, 221, 222, Operation Virile, 126, strategy, 45.
Commer pick-up truck, Operation Dingo, 172.
Commonwealth defence, 29, 31, Rhodesian SAS, 30.
Commonwealth Monitoring Force, 48.
Commonwealth, Lancaster House, 225.
Comoro Islands, 59.
Congo River, Operation Alcora, 53.
Congo, Democratic Republic of, 30, 32, mutinies, 30.
Conn, Major P. A. 'Billy', 2IC 1RLI, Sinoia incident, 79.
Connelly, Trooper John, 12 Troop, 3 Commando, 1RLI, Operation Dingo,

150, 158, 160, wounded, 166.
Conservative Government, 35.
Cook, Flight Lieutenant Victor Bernard, 19-22, 66, artillery spotting, 84, awarded SCR, 21, contact, 88, 89, dummy drops, 88.
Coom, Corporal Anthony Harold, 12 Troop, 3 Commando, 1RLI, Operation Dingo, 134, 150, 158, 160, 161, 170, 171.
counter-insurgency campaign, 35, 49.
Counter-Insurgency Civil Committee, 34.
Counter-Insurgency Committee, 34.
counter-intelligence, 43.
Cranborne Air Base, 26.
Cranswick, Trooper, C Squadron, SAS, wounded, Operation Dingo, 166.
Crécy, 1346 a.d., 183.
Cronin, Lieutenant (later Major) John Rolfe, OC 13 Troop, 3 Commando, 1RLI, Operation Dingo, 137, 139, 144, 148, 158, 161.
cross-border raids, 40.
CSIR, *see* Council for Scientific and Industrial Research.
Cuba, insurgent training, 224, intervention in Angola, 47.
Cummings, Trooper, Support Commando, 1RLI, wounded, 205, 206.
Curley, Sergeant Peter, Selous Scout Regiment, 215.
Cutmore, Sergeant Brian, killed in helicopter collision, 107.
Cyprus, 29.

d'Hotman, Flight Lieutenant Bob, No. 3 Squadron, Operation Dingo, 140.
Dakota, Douglas C-47, 27, 29, 30, 52, 85, 94, 96, 113, 116, 218, aborted external operation, 218 Fireforce, 41, 210, 211, 214-216, 219, 220, Operation Dingo, 130, 132, 135, 137, 140, 143, 144, 148, 151, 155, 156, 166, 169, 171, 173, 176-181, 184, 187, 190, 191, 194-196, 198, Operation Oppress, 222, 223, paradropping, 87, 93, 104, 113.
command Dakota, Operation Dingo, 133, 140, 151, 155, 170, 172, 176, 180, 181, 185, 195, Operation Oppress, 222.
Dalmatian Project, 64.
Dar es Salaam, photographed, 53.
Dartnall, Master Sergeant Geoffrey, helicopter technician, Operation Dingo, 151.
Day-Glo, 102, 104, 108, 137, 163.
DC-4, Douglas, shot down, 197.
DC-7, Douglas, Operation Dingo, 129, 136, 148, 176, 177-181, 182, 196.
DC-8, Douglas, Operation Dingo, 83, 135, 141.
de Havilland Aircraft Company Flying School (*see also* Gipsy Moth, Mosquito, Tiger Moth, Spitfire and Vampire), 26.
Denga, Abel, ZANU Crocodile Gang and Armaggedon Group, 75.
Dennison, Major André, OC A Company, 2RAR, 95, 114.
district assistants, 37, Operation Dingo, 194.
Dixon, Squadron Leader Christopher J. T., OC 3 Squadron, Rhodesian Air Force, Operation Oppress, 223.
dogs, tracking, 87.
Dombe, Operation Virile, 199.
Donnelly, Trooper Peter, 12 Troop, 3 Commando, 1RLI, Operation Dingo, wounded, 160, 167.
Dorowa, 219.
DP *Degtyarev* Soviet 7.62mm light machine gun, 212.
DShK 12.7mm Soviet heavy machine gun, 88, Operation Dingo, 66, 151, 158, 159, 171-173, 184, 191, 193, 194, Operation Oppress, 223, Operation Virile, 199.
du Plessis, Deon, journalist, 19.
Dubois, Captain Jacques, 2IC Mapping and Research Unit, RIC, Operation Dingo, 133, 175.
Dupont, Clifford Walter, 1st President of Rhodesia, T-28 aircraft, 32.

Durban, Operation Sand, 52.
Dyer, Squadron Leader Ron, Senior Officer Air Armaments, 68.

Eastern Bloc, 23, aided insurgents, 43, Operation Oppress, 222.
Empire Training Scheme, 26, 29.
Espungabera, 126, Operation Virile, 199.
Ethiopia, 143, insurgent training, 124, 224.
Ethiopian uniforms, 224.

F1 Soviet grenade, 75.
FAF (forward airfield), commander, 103.
   1 Wankie, 54.
   2 Kariba, 54.
   3 Centenary, 54, 92.
   4 Mount Darwin, 54, 92, 210, Fireforce, 206, Operation Dingo, 132, 175, 177-181, 195, 196.
   5 Mtoko, 54, 137, Operation Dingo, 174, 175.
   6 Chipinga, 54.
   7 Buffalo Range, 54.
   8 Grand Reef, 54, 88, 218, Fireforce, 214, Operation Dingo, 132, 139, 140, 149, 151, 154, 158, 164, 171, 174, Operation Oppress, 222.
   9 Rutenga, 54.
Farndell, Major Pieter, 2IC Support Commando, 1RLI, 66.
Federal Army, 25, 28, 30, Malaya, 29, paratroops, 30.
Federal Government, 31.
Federal Intelligence and Security Bureau, 25.
Federal troops, 22, Nyasaland Emergency, 30.
Federation of Rhodesia and Nyasaland, 22, 23, 25, 28-30, break-up, 31.
Field, Winston Joseph, Rhodesian Prime Minister, 23, 25, created OCC, 76.
Fireforce, 21, 31, 39, 41, 44-47, 53, 54, 55, 59, 64, 65, 66, 75, 83, 84, 87, 88, 90-93, 95, 97-99, 102, 105-107, 109, 110, 113, 115-117, 119, 123, 130, 137, 203, 205, 208, 214-216, 218, 224, base, 96, commander, 83, 93, 94, 99, 100-104, 106-117, Jumbo, 94, K-Car pilot, 106, land-tail, 85, 96, 104, 106, 108, 109, 116, Operation Dingo, 139, left orbit, 78, Operation Dingo, 123, Phase One, 93, Phase Three, 94, Phase Two, 93, Plan Alpha, 94, results, 95, 225, support weapons, 70, tactics, 96, trackers, 108.
Fireforce, Alpha, 64, Bravo, 220, Delta, 64, 95, 180, 203, 204, 206-209, Echo, 203, 205, 208-211.
flak jacket, 91.
flechettes, 74, Operation Dingo, 183.
Flettner F1 282 Kolibri helicopter, 55.
Flower, Ken, Director, CIO, assisted Carrington, 48, OCC, 76, served Mugabe, 48.
FN, *Fabrique Nationale*, FAL 7.62mm NATO rifle, 20, 36, 101, 102, 108, 115, 120, 137, 138, 190, 212, folding butt, 170, 200.
Focke-Wulf 190, 63.
Fort Victoria, 66, 76.
forward admin area, Operation Dingo, 175, 177, 179-182, 185, 189, 190, 195, 196, 198.
Fourie, Brand, South African Seretary for Foreign Affairs, Operation Dingo, 175.
FPLM, *Forças Populares para o Libertação de Moçambique*, 133, Battalion HQ, Vila de Manica, 128, Brigade HQ Chimoio, 127, New Farm, Chimoio, 127, Operation Dingo, 141, 156, 168, 175, 176, 180, 185, 189, 196, Operation Oppress, 222, 224, Operation Virile, 199, presence in ZANLA camps, 127, tanks, 136, uniforms, 217-219.
France, 51, 55, Lynx, 51, pilot training, 31, retreat from Empire, 29.
frantan, napalm, 51, 52, 72, 90, 205, Fireforce, 204, 205, 209, 215, Operation Dingo, 140, 141, 146, 167, 168, 179, 183, 184.
Freeman, Detective Inspector Bill, Sinoia,

79.
FRELIMO, *Frente de Libertaçao de Moçambique*, 24, 37, 45, 47, declared war on Rhodesia, 126, incursion, 46, Operation Virile, 199, signals intercepted, 42, supported ZANU, 48.
French colonial paras, 118.
French Foreign Legion para battalions, 118.
Furstenburg, Trooper Paul, 11 Troop, 3 Commando, 1RLI, Operation Dingo, wounded, 166.
Fylde Air Base, 53.
Fynn, Air Lieutenant Kerry, killed in helicopter collision, 107.

Gadzema, Viljoen murders, 76.
Gairezi River, 215.
Garden, Flight Sergeant Peter J., killed in Alouette crash, 82.
Gauntlet, Gloster, fighter aircraft, 26.
Gaza, 40, 48, 221.
general election, 1962, 23.
Genet, SIAI Marchetti SF260 basic trainer aircraft, 52.
Geneva Conference, 43, 131.
Geraty, Flight Lieutenant 'Spook', 70, Operation Dingo, 143, 168, 183.
Ghana, 23.
Gipsy Moth, de Havilland, 26.
GM2 reflector gunsight, 61.
Goatley, Air Lieutenant Charles, 81.
Goddard, Air Sub-Lieutenant Keith, killed in Canberra explosion, 67.
Godhlwayo Tribal Trust Land, 208.
Golf 450kg percussion bomb, 69, 140, Operation Dingo, 136, 183, Operation Oppress, 222.
Government House, Bulawayo, 173.
Governor-General's Saluting Troop, 28.
Graham, Major Mick, 2IC C Squadron, SAS, Operation Dingo, 124, 133, 144, 151, 187, 188, 192, 193, 198.
Grey's Scout Regiment, mounted infantry, 42, 204.

Greyling, Corporal, C Squadron, SAS, wounded, Operation Dingo, 166.
Griffiths, Squadron Leader Harold, OC No. 7 Squadron, Operation Dingo, 140, 146, 149, 157, 167, 180, 184, 191, 196.
Grobbler, Trooper M., 3 Commando, 1RLI, Operation Dingo, wounded, 166.
Guard Force, 42, 46.
Gunpit 4, 143, 161.
Guzuzu, David, ZANU cadre, killed, 79.
Gwanda, 208.
Gwelo, 27, 29, 32, 82, 132.

Haaroff, Major Simon, OC 2 Commando, 1RLI, Operation Dingo, 136, 139, 146, 147, 153, 154, 160, 162, 166.
Haigh, Flight Lieutenant Philip, killed, Operation Dingo, 141, 151, 156, 157, 165, 174.
Hales, Flight Lieutenant Frank, OC Parachute Training School, Rhodesian Air Force, box tactic, 130.
Hammond (*also* Cooper-Hammond), Trooper Terry, 12 Troop, 3 Commando, 1RLI, Operation Dingo, 158, wounded, 167.
Hardy, Lieutenant Mike, Selous Scout Regiment, 91.
Hart, Hawker, bomber aircraft, 26.
Hartley, 53, 76.
Harvey, Air Vice-Marshal Ian Mowbray, 117.
Havnar, Captain Douglas, OC Support Company, 10RR, killed in helicopter collision, 107.
Hawkesworth, Gerald, abductee, 90.
Hawker, *see* Hart & Hunter.
Hawkins, Air Vice-Marshal Harold, Chief of Air Staff, later Rhodesian Accredited Representative to South Africa, 82, Operation Dingo, 174.
Headlands, 215, 218.
Heath, Sir Edward Richard George, British Prime Minister, 35.
helicopter assembly point, Operation

Index

Dingo, 132, Chiswiti, 129, Lake Alexander, 132, 134, 136, 139, 140, 165, 167, 169, 171, 177.

helicopter-borne troops, 21, 55, 87, 90, 91, 93, 101, 105, 107, 108, 113, 130, 132, 139, 219.

Henderson, Ian, Kenyan pseudo-warfare expert, 39.

Henson, Major Nigel, OC Support Commando, 1RLI, 66, 95, 103, 203, 206, awarded OLM, 224, contact, 95, Fireforce, 205, 208, 209-212, 214-220, Operation Dingo, 139, Operation Oppress, 223, repaired K-Car, 218, tactical rules, 112.

H-Hour, Operation Dingo, 130, 135, 140, 141, 176, 179, 182.

Hickman, Lieutenant-General John Selwyn Varcoe, Rhodesian Army Commander, 39, 44, Operation Dingo, 172.

Himalayas, 56.

HMS *Fearless*, talks, 35.

HMS *Tiger*, talks, 35.

Hofmeyr, Flight Lieutenant Murray, 77, 78.

Home-Smith Agreement, 37.

Hopkins, Captain John, RAR, 114.

hot pursuit, 40, 126.

Hot Springs, Operation Virile, 127.

HQ complex, New Farm, Chimoio, 141, 151, 155, 160-164, 167, 168.

Huggins, Godfrey Martin, Lord Malvern, Rhodesian and Federal Prime Minister, 27, 28.

Hunter, Hawker, FGA Mk IX fighter, 29, 32, 84, 94, 128, Fireforce, 41, 106, Operation Dingo, 83, 132, 135, 136, 140-143, 149, 153-158, 164, 167, 168, 172, 176, 178-180, 182, 184, 186, 188, 195, 196, 197, 198, Operation Oppress, 222, 223, Operation Virile, 199, starter, 50, weapons, 69, 72, 73.

Hunyani Farm, 76.

Hunyani River, 77, 78.

Icarus parachute flare, 104.

Indo-China, 55, 118.

Ingram, Derek, Gemini News Service, Operation Dingo, 200.

Inkomo, 65.

Intelligence Centre, New Farm, Chimoio, 158, 159.

Intelstat satellite weather transmissions, Operation Dingo, 132.

Interim Government, 44.

Internal Affairs, Department of, 37, 134, administrators, 38.

Inyanga, 214, 220, barracks, 88, district, Haigh crash, 151, Downs, 215, village, 88, 216.

Inyanga North Tribal Trust, 88.

Inyangombe River, 216.

Inyazura, 220.

Iran, 37.

Iraq, 38.

Jackson, Captain Peter, C Squadron SAS, Operation Dingo, 134.

Jarvie, Sergeant Henry, helicopter technician, 92.

Jefferies, Trooper M. J., Support Commando, 1RLI, wounded, 212.

Jenkinson, Sergeant 'Jenks', Selous Scout Regiment, 216.

John Deere tractor, Operation Dingo, 172.

Johnson, Trooper Andy, C Squadron, SAS, Operation Dingo, 161.

Joint Operations Centre, JOC, 34, 36, 80, 95, 96, 107, 114, 206, Operation Hurricane, 38.

Joint Planning Staff, 34.

joint-service counter-insurgency actions, 36.

Kaman helicopter, 56.

Kandeya Tribal Trust Land, 91.

Kandoreka, Reverend, 96.

Kanyemba, shelled by Zambia, 126, shooting down of DC-4, 196.

Kariba, 36, 54, hydro-electric dam, 76.

Kaslik, a Maronite suburb of Beirut, 59.
Katanga crisis, 30.
Katoog, 64.
Kenya, 26, 55, flood relief, 29.
Kershaw, Corporal Trevor, B Troop, C Squadron, SAS, Operation Dingo, 163.
Kesby, Squadron Leader Steve, Operation Dingo, 141, 151.
Kidd, Trooper Bruce, 12 Troop, 3 Commando, 1RLI, Operation Dingo, wounded, 166.
King's African Rifles (KAR), 28.
Kissinger, Henry, US Secretary of State, pressed Smith, 40, 43, 44, 53.
Kluzniak, Trooper Steve, A Troop, C Squadron, SAS, Operation Dingo, 145.
Knight, Dr Brian, Rhodesian Air Force Medical Officer, 98.
Korea, 55.
Korean War, 147.
Kuwait, 59, crisis, 29.

Lancaster House Conference, 47, 202, ceasefire, 48.
land, 23, 40.
Land Rover, Operation Dingo, 156, 172.
landmines, 38, 41, 106, 222, 224, border barrier, 126, Operation Dingo, 171, 194.
Law, Flight Lieutenant Kenneth Charles, Operation Dingo, 141.
Lebanon, 60.
Lee-Enfield .303 rifle, 78.
Leopard Rock Hotel, 84.
Livingstone, 82.
Llewellin Barracks, 33, Depot, RRR, 28.
Lowrie, Air Lieutenant Martin, Operation Dingo, 143, 182, 196.
Luger 9mm pistol, 75.
Luia River, 176, Operation Dingo, 179.
Lunt, Squadron Leader Edward, 65, 66.
Lusaka, 46, 80.
Lusito River, Operation Virile, 199.
Lynx, Reims-Cessna FTB 337G aircraft, 21, 52, 94, 97, 104, 106, 164, contact, 88, Fireforce, 41, 170, 204, 205, 207, 208, 209, 210, 211, 214-216, 219, 220, Operation Dingo, 132, 136, 139, 149, 151, 154, 156, 163-166, 168, 169, 176, 178, 180, 185, 187, 188, 190, 192, 195, 197, Operation Oppress, 222, 223, purchase, 51, weapons, 67, 70, 73, 104.

Mabalauta, 134.
Mabvudzi River, Operation Virile, 199.
Machel, Samora, President of Mozambique, 47, harboured ZANU/ZANLA, 127, wooed by South Africa, 48.
Machipanda, 84, 128.
MacKenzie, Captain Robert C., OC A Troop, C Squadron, SAS, Operation Dingo, 138, 143, 144, 145, 150, 153, 157-160, 164, 166-169, 172, 173, 181, 189-195, 197, 198.
Maclaughlin, Temporary Corporal Neil Kevin, Support Commando, 1RLI, awarded BCR, 213, Fireforce, 212.
Macmillan, Harold, British Prime Minister, 22.
MAG *Fabrique Nationale Mitrailleuse d'Appui General* 7.62mm machine gun, 36, 61, 62, 77, 78, 89, 97, 102, 108, 114, 115, 137, 138, 145, 150, 157.
Magoe, 130, 177.
Major Haddad's Christian militia, 60.
majority rule, 23, 32, 40, 43, 53, 174, 201, 203, accepted by Smith, 44.
Makoni Tribal Trust Land, 210.
Malawi, 22, 83, 85, 135, 141, 176.
Malaya, insurgency, 29, 33, 34, 38, 55, 95, 147.
Malianga, Washington, ZANU spokesman, 80.
Malloch, John 'Jack' M., owner of Air Trans Africa, 54, loss of DC-4, 197, Operation Dingo, 135, 136, 148, 176, 177, 182, 196.
Malvernia, 134.
Manica, 40.
Mantovani, Air Lieutenant Luigi, K-Car pilot, 217.

Index

Manyerenyere, Gordon, ZANU cadre, killed, 79.
Mao Ze Dong, Chairman, quotes, Operation Dingo, 160.
Maoist concept of revolution, 35.
Maputo, 126, 135.
Mare, Corporal Bates, A Troop, C Squadron, SAS, Operation Dingo, 159.
Marymount Mission, 62.
Masoso Tribal Trust Land, 209, 211, 213.
MAT-49 French 9mm submachine gun, 75.
Matabeleland, 95, South African Fireforce, 54, ZANLA offensive, 46.
Matopos Camp, New Farm, Chimoio, 143, 151, 155, 156, 158, 160-162, 165, 167.
McAleese, Corporal Peter, A Troop, C Squadron, SAS, Operation Dingo, 134, 139, 143, 145, 159, 161.
McCormack, Captain Scott, Intelligence Officer, C Squadron, SAS, 124, Operation Dingo, 131, 134.
McGowan, Trooper Gerry, A Troop, SAS, Operation Dingo, 191.
McGregor, Flight Lieutenant Rob, K-Car pilot, 92.
McQuaid, Air Lieutenant Bill, G-Car pilot, 88.
Messerschmitt 109, 63.
Methuen Barracks, RAR Depot, 120.
Mgagoa, Tanganyika, ZANLA training base, 127.
military intelligence, 37, 224.
Military Intelligence Directorate (MID), 39, 46, external operations, 43.
mined barrier, 39.
mine-protected vehicles, 38.
Mini-Golf/Juliet percussion bomb, 70, 106, Fireforce, 205.
Mirage III jet fighter, 52.
Mk I 20lb bomb, 67.
Mk II Alpha bouncing bomb, 67, 69, 70, 72, 136, 155, Fireforce, 216, Operation Dingo, 142, 155, 160, 168, 184, 189, 195, 196, Operation Oppress, 223.

Moore, 'Messus', Support Commando, 1RLI, 103.
Moore, Quartermaster John, 1RLI, 79.
Moore, Trooper M. C., Support Commando, 1RLI, killed, 220.
mortar, 99, 206, attack on Vila Salazar, 126, helicopter-borne, 8, Operation Dingo, 150, 184, 190, 193.
Mosquito, de Havilland, 152.
Mount Blanc, 56.
Mount Darwin, 54, 90, 91, 92, 175, 209, 212.
Mountbatten, Louis Francis Albert Victor Nicholas, 1st Earl Mountbatten of Burma, Chief of Imperial General Staff, 30.
Mouzon, Captain, DC-4 shot down, 197.
Mozambican Government, Operation Dingo, 174.
Mozambique, 24, 37, 43, 46-48, 66, 83-85, 88, 123, 125, 130-132, 140, 174, 175, 203, 209, 215, 217, 218, 222, 224, Gaza Province, 40, 48, 126, 221, Manica Province, 40, 48, 124, 126, Nyadzonya Camp, 53, Sofala Province, 48, Tete Province, 37, 41, 48, 90, 126.
Mtetengwe Tribal Trust Land, 206.
Mtoko, 54, 88, 211.
Mudukuti, ZANU cadre, 76.
Mugabe, Robert Gabriel, ZANU President, later President of Zimbabwe, 19, 24, 35, 48, 142, 201, accession to power, 225, assassination attempt, 43, criticized by Owen, 201, Geneva Conference, 43, 131, Interim Government, 125, 173, 201, Lancaster House Conference, 202, New Farm accommodation, 124, Operation Dingo, 125, 144, ousted Sithole, 44, rejected 1979 election, 203, resumption of war, 47, served by Flower, 48, won 1980 election, 47, 48.
Munton-Jackson, Air Lieutenant Guy, killed in Alouette crash, 82.
Mussell, Air Marshal Frank, Operation Dingo, 140.

Muzorewa, Bishop Abel, Prime Minister of Zimbabwe–Rhodesia, 47, 53, 95, 96, 203, 1979 Constitution, 203, auxiliaries, 45, elected, 46, external operations, 47, Interim Government, 44, 125, 173, internal settlement, 201, lack of strategy, 47, popular support, 225, won 1979 election, 221.

Mvuradona Valley, 209.

Nacala, 176.
National Democratic Party, 23.
National JOC, 44.
National Stores, New Farm, Chimoio, 142, 143, 146, 149, 151, 154, 155, 160, 161, 163, 165.
Nehanda Camp, New Farm, Chimoio, 143, 150, 151, 153-156, 161, 162, 168.
Nel, Trooper Frans, B Troop, C Squadron, SAS, killed, Operation Dingo, 163, 165, 166, 174.
New Farm, Chimoio, ZANLA base, 41, 123, 124, 126-131, 133, 135, 136, 139-142, 147, 148, 153, 160, 165-171, 173-175, 183, 184, 188.
population growth, 131.
New Garage, New Farm, Chimoio, 162-164, 167.
New Sarum Air Force Base, 32, 54, 82, 218, air gunners, 62, Operation Dingo, 132-134, 137, 139, 140, 142, 151, 156, 162, 167, 171, 174, 175, 178-182, 194, 196, 198, Operation Virile, 198.
Ngangas Camp, New Farm, Chimoio, 148, 149.
Nhongo, Rex, Lieutenant-General Solomon Mujuru, Deputy Commander of ZANLA, New Farm accommodation, 124, Operation Dingo, 145.
Nibel, First Lieutenant, DC-4 shot down, 197.
Nkomo, Joshua Mqabuko Nyongolo, ZAPU President, 23, 24, 47, 48, 203, alleged support from Britain, 125, criticized by Owen, 201, criticized

Smith, 174, excluded by Smith, 44, Geneva Conference, 43, 131, Interim Government, 125, 173, 201, Lancaster House Conference, 202.
Non-Aligned Movement, Lancaster House, 225.
Norfolk Regiment, 147.
Norman, Colour Sergeant John, 3 Commando, 1RLI, wounded, Operation Dingo, 158, 166.
North American T-28 Trojan, 32, 51, T-6 Harvard, 27.
Northern Rhodesia (*see also* Zambia), 22, 30.
Northern Rhodesia Regiment, 28.
Northern Rhodesian Government, 28.
Northern Rhodesian Legislative Council, 28.
Nyadzonya, ZANLA camp, 53, 123, 128, 131, 159, 174.
Nyasaland (*see also* Malawi), 22, 28.
Nyasaland Emergency, 30.

Oakley, Flight Lieutenant Tony, Operation Oppress, 222.
Oberholzer, Petrus, murdered by ZANU, 75.
oil embargo, 75.
oil pipeline, 75.
Old Garage, New Farm, Chimoio, 142, 146, 148, 160, 169, 170, 171, 172.
Oman, Rolls-Royce jet engines, 50.
OP (observation post), 66, 83, 93, 94, 95, 97-99, 104-106, 109, 110, 117, 208-210, 213, 214, 216, 219, 220, Fireforce, 215.
Operation Alcora, 53.
Operation Dabchick, 83.
Operation Dingo, 41, 44, 66, 83, 123, 125, 127, 131, 133, 175, 200-202, plan, 124, Zulu 1, 131, 132, 134, 139, 162, 173, 174, 177, Zulu 2, 85, 132, 139, 167, 174, 175, 177, 180, 181, 190, 198, debrief, 183.
Operation Eland, 128.
Operation Hurricane, 38, pseudo warfare, 91.

Index

Operation Mascot, 86.
Operation Nickel, 53.
Operation Oppress, 221, 224.
Operation Repulse, 101.
Operation Tangent, 208.
Operation Thrasher, 210.
Operation Tripper, 37.
Operation Virile, 125, 126, 127, 198, 199, 200, 201.
Operations Co-Ordinating Committee (OCC), 34, 36, 44, Sinoia, 77.
Organization of African Unity (OAU), 75.
Overbeek, Lance-Corporal Martin, Support Commando, killed, 216.
Owen, David Anthony Llewellyn, Baron Owen, British Foreign Secretary, criticized by Chikerema, 125, criticized Mugabe, 201.

Pafuri, 40.
parachutes, 85, 104, 105, 114, 136, 138, 139, 145, 146, 148, 166-170, 173, 178, 181, 190-195, 198.
paratroopers, 30, 41, 54, 87, 90, 93-96, 101, 105, 106, 108, 110, 113, 114, 118, 130, 132, 134-137, 139, 140, 143, 146, 147, 175-181, 184, 211, 213, 220, box, 130.
Parirenyatwa Camp, New Farm, Chimoio, 142, 146, 149, 150, 153-157, 160-162, 164, 165, 200.
Pasindina 1 Camp, New Farm, Chimoio, 160, 162-165.
Pasindina 2 Camp, New Farm, Chimoio, 141, 142, 146, 149, 151, 156, 158, 169, 170, 172.
Paxton, Flight Lieutenant Richard, 66.
Pearce Commission, 35.
Pegasus harness, 57, 84.
Pembroke, Percival, light transport aircraft, 29.
Perhat, Rory, helicopter technician, 89.
Permanent Staff Corps, 26, 27.
Percival Aircraft Company, *see* Pembroke & Provost.

Peter, ZANU cadre, killed, 79.
Petter-Bowyer, Group Captain Peter John Hornby, 83, 98, awarded MFC, 80, 37mm rocket, 73, aerial reconnaissance, 90, 91, arming the Alouette, 61, Dalmation project, 64, flechette, 73, 183, frantan, 72, Golf bomb, 69, helicopter refuellling, 86, landed in Zambia, 82, map-reading, 80, Mini-Golf bomb, 70, Mk II Alpha bomb, 68, Operation Dingo, 124, 134, 140, 147, 158, 166, 177, 180, 182, Sinoia, 76, 78, smoke generator, 102, target marking, 104, tracking, 87.
Petulia, ZANLA base, Gaza Province, Mozambique, 221.
Peugeot light truck, Operation Dingo, 172.
Pioneer Column, 25.
Police Act, 25, 77.
Polo, A Flight (South African), 7 Squadron, Rhodesian Air Force, Operation Dingo, 136, 140, 147, 176, 180, 181.
Pookie, landmine-detecting vehicle, 41, 228, Operation Virile, 199.
Poole, Trooper R. F., Support Commando, 1RLI, killed, 220.
Portugal, 53, military coup, 40.
Portuguese Air Force, 31.
Portuguese Army, tracking, 37.
Portuguese forces, 90.
Portuguese Government, 35.
PPSH Soviet submachine gun, 206, Fireforce, 209.
Pretorius, Flight Lieutenant Glen, Operation Oppress, 223.
Price, Major Don H., OC 1 (Indep) RAR, 64.
Prinsloo, Lieutenant Vernon A., Support Commando, 1RLI, Fireforce, 203, 204, 207, 208, 213, 220.
protected villages, 34, 38, 42.
Provost, Percival, T52 piston-engined basic trainer, 28, 29, 32, 50-52, 90, 97, Browning Mk II .303in, 63, Nyasaland Emergency, 30, replacement, 31, 51,

starter, 50, weapons, 73.
pseudo-gangs, 39.
psychological warfare, 38.
Psychological Warfare Unit, 42.
Puma, Aérospatiale helicopter, 54, 63.
Pungwe River, 123.

Q armoured bus, Operation Virile, 199.
Queen Victoria, 25.
Quintana, Michael, publisher, 119.

racial parity, 35.
railways, 24, 45, 156, sabotage, 35.
RAMS (radio-activated marker system), Operation Dingo, 173, 174.
Ramsay, Trooper, C Squadron, SAS, wounded, Operation Dingo, 166.
RAR, *see* Rhodesian African Rifles.
Rathcline Estate, 216.
Ratte, Corporal Willem, C Squadron, SAS, wounded, Operation Dingo, 166.
Recruits' Camp, New Farm, Chimoio, 142, 146, 149, 151, 154, 162, 168, 169, 170, 171, 172, 173.
Red Cross, 134.
Red Mine, Hunyani Farm, 76.
Reed, WOII Ken, 3 Commando, 1RLI, wounded, Operation Dingo, 166, 169.
Reid-Daly, Lieutenant-Colonel Ronald Francis, CO Selous Scout Regiment, Operation Virile, 126, 127.
RENAMO (*see also Resistência Nacional Moçambicana*, RNM/MNR), 200.
Resistência Nacional Moçambicana, RNM/MNR (*see also* RENAMO), 45, 47.
RGD5 Soviet grenade, 75.
Rhodes, Cecil John, mining magnate, Cape Prime Minister, 25.
Rhodesia, 19, 21, 24-27, 35, 38, 40, 46-48, 54, 58-60, 65, 80, 82-86, 90, 123, 124, 126, 129, 131, 132, 137, 139, 141, 144, 159, 163, 165, 170, 174, 176, 197, 199, 202-204, 206, 213, 217, 222, climate, 31, 55, denied supplies by Vorster, 53, external operations, 126, first

president, 32, incursions, 35, Intelstat, 132, northeastern border, 37, republic, 50, sanctions evasion, 51, shortage of manpower, 75, South African helicopters, 53, total mobilization, 219.
Rhodesia Defence Regiment, 46.
Rhodesia Regiment (RR)/Royal Rhodesia Regiment (RRR), 26-28, 10 Battalion, Support Company, 107, 3rd and 7th Battalions, 33, contact, 88, 89.
Rhodesian African Rifles (RAR), 27, 28, 33, 96, 114, 117, 119, 120, aborted external operation, 218, contact, 91, discharged rifle grenade, 62, Fireforce, 41, proposed ten battalions, 37, Suez, 29.
1 (Independent) Company, 95, contact, 64, Fireforce, 207, intelligence gathering, 206.
Second Battalion, 2RAR, 95, 114.
Rhodesian Air Force, *see* Royal Rhodesian Air Force.
Rhodesian Air Training Group, 26.
Rhodesian Armoured Car Regiment, 28.
Rhodesian Army, 19, 25, 26, 62, 84, 97, 172, adopted MAG, 36, Chiswiti Camp, 129, expansion, 37, HQ, Operation Dingo, 186, JOC, 34, OCC, 76, OPs, 105, order of battle, 33 voice procedure, 31.
3 Air Supply Platoon, Operation Dingo, 177.
3 Brigade, 170.
Tracker Combat School, Kariba, 36.
Rhodesian Corps of Engineers, 28, 33.
Rhodesian Corps of Signals, 28, 33, 8 Signals Squadron, 42, Operation Dingo, 156.
Rhodesian Department of Defence, 37.
Rhodesian Field Artillery Regiment, 28, 33, 84, Fireforce, 206.
Rhodesian Front, 23.
Rhodesian Government, 34, 53, 199, anti-Communist stance, 37, curbed camp attacks, 40, majority rule, 32.
Rhodesian Intelligence Corps (RIC), 42, 43, 98, 100, Operation Dingo, 133, 175.

Index

Rhodesian Legislative Assembly, 203.
Rhodesian Light Infantry (RLI), 21, 30, 33, 66, 95, 96, 114, 117, contact, 90, 91, Fireforce, 41, formation of, 30, MAG gunner, Operation Dingo, 150, 160, Operation Dingo, 41, 130-132, 139, 140, 145, 147, 149, 160, 161, 166, 175, 177, 178, 179, 180, 181, 197, Operation Oppress, 223, 224, Sinoia, 79.
  1 Commando, 218, Fireforce, 208, results, 95.
  2 Commando, Operation Dingo, 135, 139, 140, 146, 147, 181, results, 95, Stop A, 165, Operation Dingo, 146, 147, 149, 153-155, 161, 162, 164, 166.
  3 Commando, 64, 170 aborted external operation, 218, contact, 64, Operation Dingo, 135, 160, 171, results, 95. 11 & 12 Troops, Stop 1, Operation Dingo, 134, 144, 146, 155-160, 163, 166, 167, 169-171. 13 & 14 Troops, Stop 2, Operation Dingo, 134, 137, 144-146, 150, 153-155, 156-158, 160, 164-167, 169-171.
  Support Commando/Group, 66, 95, 103, 109, 114, 203, 209, 214, 224, aborted external operation, 218, contact, 92, Fireforce, 205, 207, 208, 213, 214, 216, 218, results, 224, Mortar Troop, 221, Operation Oppress, 222, Operation Dingo, 139, 140, 176, 178, 180, Stop 1, 178, 180, 185-198, Stop 2, 157, 185, 187-189, 191-197, Operation Oppress, 221, 223, results, 95.
Rhodesian Ministry of External Affairs, Operation Virile, 126.
Rhodesian mobilization, 1979, 214.
Rhodesian Security Council, 34.
Rhodesian security forces, 36, 37, 54, 203, 221, 1979 election, 46, ceasefire, 48, coup, 48, harassed by FRELIMO, 126, Operation Dingo, 123, reputation, 49.
Rhodesian Service Corps, 33.
Rhodesian Treasury, 37.
Rich, Lieutenant Michael, 2 Commando, 1RLI, Operation Dingo, 147.

Rich, Lieutenant-Colonel (later Brigadier) Peter, CO 1RLI, Operation Dingo, 147.
road runner, bugged transistor radio, 96.
Roberts, Lieutenant Kenneth, OC B Troop, C Squadron, SAS, Operation Dingo, 144, 162-164, 166, 170, 172, 173, 181, 185, 193, 197.
Robinson, Major (later Lieutenant-Colonel) Brian Garry, OC C Squadron, SAS, Operation Dingo, 124, 125, 129, 130, 133, 134, 136-140, 149, 151, 154, 156-158, 160, 161, 163-166, 168, 169, 170, 171, 177, 178, 180, 181, 184-196, 198, Operation Oppress, 224.
Rogers, Corporal Christopher William, Support Commando, 1RLI, awarded MFC, 214.
Rogers, Squadron Leader John, OC No. 7 Squadron, 61.
Rolls-Royce, Avon Series 207 jet engine, 50.
Royal Air Force, 27, 29, 151.
  No. 233 Squadron, 26.
  No. 237 (Rhodesia) Squadron, 27.
  No. 266 (Rhodesia) Squadron, 27.
  No. 44 (Rhodesia) Squadron, 27.
Royal Navy, 26.
Royal Rhodesian Air Force (RRAF)/ Rhodesian Air Force (RhAF), 25, 28, 31, 32, 54, 61, 63, 97 arming helicopters, 61, counter-insurgency, 29, DC-7, 54, Federal break-up, 31, Fireforce, 105, front-line strength, 128, helicopters, 62, 87, Agusta-Bell 205A Cheetah, 202, JOC, 34, map-reading, 80, Munton-Jackson crash, 82 OCC, 76, Operation Dingo, 124, 131, 159, 176, 197, Operation Oppress, 222, Operation Virile, 125, Parachute Training School, 30, 130, pilot training, 33, pilots, 60, purchased Lynx, 51, radios, 78, sanctions evasion, 50, seconded South African pilots, 53, Sinoia, 79, threat from SAM-7, 127, weapons, 72.
  Air HQ, Operation Dingo, 186.

Armament Section, 69.
Drawing Office, 68.
General Service Unit/Rhodesian Air Force Regiment, 31, 54.
No. 1 Squadron, 26, 27, 29, 32, 94, Operation Dingo, 141-143, 149, 153-157, 162, 163, 164, 166, 168, 178, 180, 182-186, 192, 193, 196.
No. 2 Squadron, 29, 32, Operation Dingo, 139, 155.
No. 3 Squadron, 29, 32, Dakota strength, 130, Islanders, 52, Nyasaland Emergency, 30, Operation Dingo, 148, paradropping, 30.
No. 4 Squadron, 29, 32, 90, 98, counter-insurgency, 50.
No. 5 Squadron, 32, 68, Nyasaland Emergency, 30, Operation Dingo, 151, 152, 154-157, 162, 163, 182, 185, 186, 196.
No. 6 Squadron, 29, 31, Genets, 52, reformed, 50.
No. 7 Squadron, 31, 32, 60, 61, 218, air gunnery, 62, Alpha Flight, 53, 59, night flying, 82, Operation Dingo, 140.
No. 8 Squadron, AB205A helicopters, 52.
Volunteer Reserve, 30, 54.
RPD, *Ruchnoy Pulemyot Degtyarev* Soviet light machine gun, 121, Fireforce, 209, Operation Dingo, 137, 138, 157, 191, Operation Virile, 199.
RPG, rocket-propelled grenade, 41, 66, 161, 205, 216, 217, 222.
RPK, *Ruchnoy Pulemyot Kalashnikov* Soviet light machine gun, Operation Dingo, 138, 145.
RT60B radio rescue beacons, 65.
Rusape, 210, 211.
Rushinga, 92, 114, 214.
Rutenga, 21, 54, 88, 117.
Ruya River, 90, 205.

Sabi River, 219.
Sabi Tribal Trust Land, 219.
Sabi-Lundi junction, 40.
Sachse, Major Albert, Selous Scout Regiment, Operation Virile, 199.
Salisbury, 27, 32, 53, 76, 77, 79, 82, 88, 125, 132, 167, 172, 178, 205, 218, 221.
SAM-7, STRELA, Soviet anti-aircraft rocket, 65, 68, capture of, 128, 132, Operation Dingo, 127, 176.
sanctions, 35, 43, 50, 54, 58, 59, 61, 104, 125, 135, 139, 197, evasion of, 37.
SAS model room, Cranborne, Operation Dingo, 175.
SAS, Special Air Service.
22 Regiment, 147, results, 95.
C (Rhodesia) Squadron, 40, 90, 101, 130, Chipinga arson, 23, external operations, 39, 126, 203, formation, 30, Malayan campaign, 29, Operation Dabchick, 83, Operation Dingo, 41, 123, 124, 131, 133-135, 138-140, 143-145, 150, 151, 157-159, 161, 163, 166, 167, 174-178, 181, 184, 198, tree-jumping, 33. A Troop, Stop 3, Operation Dingo, 144, 145, 150, 151, 155-157, 160, 162-164, 167, 169, 170, 173, 181, 185-187, 189, 192-198, Stop 4, Operation Dingo, 138, 144, 146, 150, 155, 157, 158, 161, 164, 166-173, 181, 185, 186, 187, 189-193, 195-198. B Troop, Stop 5, Operation Dingo, 146, 155, 157, 160-162, 164-167, 169, 170, 172, 173, 181, 185, 186, 188, 189, 192-194, 195, 196, 197, Stop 6, Operation Dingo, 144, 146, 155, 157, 160, 161, 166, 167, 169-173, 181, 185-187, 189-192, 194-196.
Savory, Major Allan, politician and ecologist, 39.
School of Infantry, 101.
Security Forces Auxiliaries, SFAs, casualties, 221.
Selous Scout Regiment, 90, 95, 98, 110, attack on Nyadzonya, 40, external operations, 126, 203, intelligence, 42, Nyadzonya raid, 53, 123, 128, 131, 159, OPs, 105, 208, 213, 214, 215, 216,

Index

220, Operation Dingo, 197, Operation Virile, 125, 127, 131, 198, 199, pseudo operations, 39, 91, 97, 115, Rusape Fort, 210, 211.
Selukwe, 107.
Sengwe Tribal Trust Land, 204, flechette, 73.
Shaw, 'Beaver', helicopter technician, shot down Botswana Islander, 81.
Shenjere, Ephraim, ZANU cadre, killed, 79.
Sikorsky R-6A helicopter, 55.
Silver Cross of Rhodesia (SCR), 21.
Sinoia, 61, 76, 79, battle of, 75-77, 80, Old Location African Township, 77.
Sipolilo, 83.
Sithole, Reverend Ndabaningi, ZANU president, 24, auxiliaries, 45, Interim Government, 125, internal settlement, 201, ousted by Mugabe, 44.
SKS 7.62mm Soviet self-loading rifle, 75, 121, 207, Fireforce, 205, 208, 211-213, 215-217, Operation Dingo, 170, 172, 173, 191, 193, 194, Operation Oppress, 223.
Slatter, Air Vice-Marshal Hugh Clarke Scudamore, Operation Oppress, 224.
SLR, Self-Loading Rifle British 7.62mm rifle, Operation Dingo, 193.
Smith, Ian Douglas, Rhodesian Prime Minister, 22, 23, 27, 43, 54, 174, accepted majority rule, 125, declared republic, 35, UDI, 32, 50, 58, Interim Government, 173, 201, internal settlement, 44, Operation Dingo, 125, 127, 131 pressed by Vorster, 40, 43, 53, 67, by Vorster and Kissinger, 40, 43, RAF service, 135, Security Council, 33.
Smith, Lieutenant Rod, OC 11 Troop, 3 Commando, 1RLI, Operation Dingo, 144.
smoke generator, 94, 104.
smoke grenade, 93, 101, 105, 115.
Smuts, Field Marshal Jan Christiaan, South African Prime Minister, 27.

SNEB 37mm aircraft rocket, 51, 73, 104, 110, Long Tom, 73.
Société Turboméca, 55, 56.
South Africa, 23, 25, 27, 38, 43, 47, 48, 58, 64, 76, ammunition supplies, 67, deployed police, 36, Operation Dingo, 174, Operation Sand, 52, pilot training, 31.
South African Air Force (SAAF), 27, 31, 95, Canberra B12, 52, helicopters, 53, 58, withdrawal of, 53, pilots, 60, Puma helicopter, 63, trained Rhodesian pilots, 52.
South African Army, Parachute Battalion, 54, 95.
South African Government, 35, wooed Machel, 48.
South African Police, Field Force, 37, 53, helicopters, 58.
South African tourists, 134.
South Vietnam, 32, 68.
Southern Rhodesia (*see also* Rhodesia), 22, 26, 27, 30, 31, right of defence, 28.
Southern Rhodesian Air Force (SRAF) (*see also* Royal Rhodesian Air Force), 26-28.
Southern Rhodesian Government, 22, 27.
Southern Rhodesian Legislative Assembly, 26.
Soviet instructors, 35.
Soviet Union, 23, 47.
Soviet/Cuban intrusion, 40.
Special Air Service, *see* SAS.
Special Urban Emergency Units (SWAT teams), 87.
Spider 24-barrel 12-gauge shotgun, 41.
Spitfire IXs, 135.
Staghound Mk II armoured car, 28.
staging post, Operation Dingo, 129.
state of emergency, 22.
Sterling submachine gun, 78.
stick, Rhodesian Army four-man half-section, 20, 36, 97, 100, 102, 103, 107-109, 111-114, 116, 119-121, 137, 138, 145, 147, 150, 153, 158, 160, 163, 167, 171, 178, 189, 205, 207, 208, 211, 216, 217.

Strong, Major Jeremy Treadwell, OC 3 Commando, 1RLI, Operation Dingo, 134, 144, 145, 160, 171.
Sud-Aviation, French aircraft manufacturer, 56.
Suez Canal Zone, 29.
Sunday Mail, 224.
Supermarine Spitfire Mark XXII, 27.
Swan, Corporal James, 7 Troop, 2 Commando, 1RLI, Operation Dingo, 147, 150, 153, 167, 182.
Swart, Lieutenant 'Blackie', RAR, 114.
Swedish sardines, 161.
Sykes, Flight Lieutenant Richard W. J., Operation Dingo, 147.
Szydlowski, Joseph, founder of *Société Turboméca*, 55.

T-34/T-54 tanks, 128.
Takawira Camp, New Farm, Chimoio, 143, 150, 151, 153, 155, 156, 158, 160-162, 165, 167.
Tanganyika, 23.
Tanzania, 143, insurgent training, 124, 175.
Tanzanian People's Defence Force (TPDF), 128.
Taylor, Squadron Leader Rex, Operation Dingo, 177, 179.
Tekere, Edgar Zivanai, 201, Operation Dingo, 145.
Tembué town, 185, 191.
Tembué, ZANLA base, 41, 85, 123, 124, 127-132, 137, 139, 175, 176, 177, 179, 180, 181, 183, 191, 194, 197, 200, 201, population growth, 131.
Camp A, 176, 179, 182-184, 186-197, 198.
Camp B, 176, 179, 182-184, 186-198.
Camp C, 176, 179, 182-193, 196, flechettes, 183.
Camps C and B, 176.
Templer, Field Marshal Sir Gerald, Governor and C-in-C Malaya, 34.
Terrell, Sergeant Frank, Support Commando, 1RLI, Operation Oppress, 223.
Territorial Army, 30.
Tete Province, 37, 176.
Tete town, 123, 176.
Thatcher, Margaret, British Prime Minister, 46, failed to recognize Muzorewa, 203, Lancaster House, 225.
Thin Camp, New Farm, Chimoio, 154, 155.
Thompson, Bob, helicopter technician, 65.
Thornhill Air Force Base, 29, 32, 54, 82, armourers, 73, Operation Dingo, 132, 133, 175.
Thornton, Lieutenant Gordon Stanley, OC 14 Troop, 3 Commando, 1RLI, Operation Dingo, 144.
Tiger Moth, de Havilland training aircraft, 26.
TNT, 73, 75.
Todd, Flight Lieutenant Greg, Operation Oppress, 223.
Tongogara, Josiah, ZANLA commander, New Farm accommodation, 124, Operation Dingo, 145.
Train, Operation Dingo, 129, 175, 177, 178, 179, 181, 182, 196.
Tresha, Master, ZANU Crocodile Gang and Armaggedon Group, 75.
Trojan, Aermacchi AL60-B2L light aircraft, 51, 97, Fireforce, 83, 90, 106, weapons, 73.
Turner, Corporal Anthony, killed in helicopter collision, 107.

Umtali, 75, 88, 123, 127, 132, 154, 170, 214, 220, shelled, 136.
Umtali–Beira corridor, 127.
United African National Council (UANC), 125, 1979 election, 203, 221.
United Nations, Lancaster House, 225.
United States of America, 37.
Upton, Mike, helicopter technician, 88, 101.

Index

US Air Force, jungle clearing, 68.
US Army and Navy, 32.
US Consul-General, Salisbury, 32.
US Government, Carter Administration, 44.
US Marine Corps, 36, 137.
US State Department, arms embargo, 32.
Uzi submachine gun, 20.

Vampire, de Havilland, FB52 fighter bomber, 52, FB9 fighter bomber, 28, 30, 31, 32, 52, 128, Operation Dingo, 132, 135, 139-141, 143, 149, 151, 155, 156, 164, 168, 176, 178-180, 182-186, 197, Operation Virile, 198, T11 jet trainer, 28, 31, 32, 52, 128, Operation Dingo, 136, 139, 143, 151-154, 162, 163.
Vanduzi, 127, Operation Eland, 128.
Varkevisser, Flight Lieutenant Justin, Operation Dingo, 141.
Vertol H-21 twin-rotor helicopter, 55.
Vervier, Ernest, designer of MAG, 36.
Very flare pistol, 104.
Victoria Falls, 53, 82, 139.
Vietnam, 59, 118, 137.
Vila de Manica, 156, Operation Eland, 128.
Vila Salazar, shelled, 126, 134.
Viljoen, Johannes and Johanna, murdered, 76.
Vorster, Balthazar Johannes, South African Prime Minister, pressed Smith, 43, 44, 53, 67, withdrawal of helicopters and police, 40.
Vumba, 84.

Walls, Lieutenant-General George Peter, Commander Combined Operations, 34, 44, 80, 165, 169, Malaya, 29, Operation Dingo, 124, 133, 139, 140, 145, 157, 163, 165, 168, 170, 172, 185, 189, 194, 195, 200, Operation Virile, 131, suspended, 127, political solution required, 44.
Walsh, Air Marshal Norman, Operation Dingo, 66, 124, 125, 129, 133, 134, 136, 140, 143, 149, 151, 154-156, 162-166, 168, 169, 171, 177, 180-186, 188-190, 195, 196.
Wankie, 54, 95, airfield, 53.
Wankie National Park, 134.
Ward, Air Lieutenant Clive, 88.
Warren, Lance-Corporal Charles, 13 Troop, 3 Commando, 1RLI, Operation Dingo, 145, 171.
Watt, Lieutenant Darryl, C Squadron, SAS, wounded, Operation Dingo, 166.
Watts, Major Frederick Robert, OC 1 Commando, 1RLI, Fireforce, 208, 218.
Welensky, Sir Roy, Federal Prime Minister, 28, Commonwealth defence, 30, expansion of RAR, 37.
Wensleydale Estate, 215.
Weya Tribal Trust Land, 218.
white electorate, 23, 173.
white emigration, 45.
white farmers, 40.
white phosphorus grenades, 102, Fireforce, 207, Operation Dingo, 138, 172.
White, Trooper, Keith, 3 Commando, 1RLI, Operation Dingo, 145.
Whitehead, Sir Edgar Cuthbert Fremantle, Southern Rhodesian Prime Minister, 23.
Wightman, Squadron Leader Charles Lorimer 'Vic', Operation Dingo, 143, 168, 183, Operation Oppress, 222.
Williams, George 'Soapy', US Assistant Secretary of State for Africa, US arms embargo, 32.
Willis, Captain Colin, A Troop, C Squadron, SAS, Operation Dingo, 144, 145, 150-153, 157, 162, 173, 181, 185, 192, 194.
Wilson, Captain Grahame Alexander, OC B Troop, C Squadron, SAS, 170, Operation Dingo, 144, 160, 166, 169, 172, 173, 181, 185, 187-190.
Wilson, James Harold, British Prime Minister, 35.
Wrigley, Flight Lieutenant George, 92.

Youth League, 22.

Zaire, 30.
Zambezi River, 24, 37, 40, 45, 75, 82, 123, 126, 130, 176, 197.
Zambezi Valley, 90, 209.
Zambezi–Luangwa River confluence, shooting down of DC-4, 197.
Zambia (*see also* Northern Rhodesia), 22, 24, 43, 46, 47, 75, 82, 85, 123, 203, Federal break-up, 31, incursions, 40, incursions into Rhodesia, 35, shelled Kanyemba, 126, ZIPRA base, 40.
ZANLA (Zimbabwe African National Liberation Army), 19, 38, 39, 44, 45, 47, 48, 64, 65, 88, 89, 96, 97, 115, 123, 127, 128, 142, 143, 175, 177, 201, 203, 210, 217, 218, 1979 election, 46, 214, Armaggedon Group, 77, 78, assembly points, 48, attack on Altena Farm, 37, attacked by Rhodesian forces, 40, bombshell, 130, captures, 129, casualties, 48, Chitepo College, 141, contact, 92, 204, 205-209, 211-217, 219, 220, contact men, 91, defeats, 36, defied, 221, feared Alpha bombs, 69, first incursion, 36, flechette strike, 74, Headquarters, New Farm, Chimoio, 158, incursions, 35, 37, 40, 126, intimidation, 40, landmine offensive, 41, Maroro Camp, 86, MNR, 46, morale, 224, Mozambican staging camps, 218, Mucheneze Camp, 83, New Farm, Chimoio, 124, Nyadzonya camp, 53, Nyadzonya report, 159, offensive, 125, Operation Dingo, 123, 127, 133, 135-137, 144-146, 148, 149, 150, 153, 156, 159-162, 167, 169, 171, 172, 175, 183-186, 191, 192, 194, 195, 197, 200, 201, Operation Oppress, 221-224, Operation Virile, 199, paymaster, 168, reinforcement and supply, 132, rejected 1979 Constitution, 203, strength at New Farm, 130, Tembué base, 127, 176, trained personnel, 131.
ZANU (Zimbabwe African National Union), 24-35, 131, 201, Crocodile Gang, 75, defectors, 125, Geneva Conference, 43, incursion, 75, informers, 36, Marxism, 37, negotiations, 40, ousted Sithole, 44, Patriotic Front, 44, Sinoia, 76, 79, strategy, 38, supported by FRELIMO, 48.
ZAPU (Zimbabwe African People's Union), 23-25, 35, 47, defectors, 125, Freedom Farm, 82, Geneva Conference, 43, 131, informers, 36, Marxism, 37, negotiations, 40, Patriotic Front, 44.
Zimbabwe, 59.
Zimbabwe Air Force, 59, 117.
Zimbabwe–Rhodesia Legislative Assembly, UANC win, 221.
Zimbiti Tribal Trust Land, 219.
zinc bath, 210.
ZIPRA (Zimbabwe People's Revolutionary Army), 36, 39, 45, 47, 96, 115, 126, 203, 1979 Constitution, 203, 1979 election, 46, 214, assembly points, 48, attacked by SAS, 40, casualties, 49, conventional warfare, 45, defeats, 36, defied, 221, feared Alpha bombs, 69, Francistown base, 81, incursion, 40, recruiting, 40, sabotage, 35, threat from, 47.
ZP-U 14.5mm Soviet heavy machine gun, Operation Dingo, 165, 197.
Zwimba Tribal Trust Land, 76.